BIBLE SUMMARY FOR ADULTS AND STUDENTS

MICHAEL KOTCH

ISBN 978-1-0980-5315-4 (paperback)
ISBN 978-1-0980-5316-1 (digital)

Christian Faith Publishing, Inc.
832 Park Avenue
Meadville, PA 16335
www.christianfaithpublishing.com

Scripture quotations for all books, except the book of Revelation, are from the ESV Bible (The Holy Bible, English Standard Version), copyright 2001, by Crossway, a publishing ministry of Good News Publishers.

Scripture quotations from the book of Revelation are from the New American Bible (St. Joseph Medium-Size Edition), copyright 2011, by Catholic Book Publishing Corp., NJ

Printed in the United States of America

No prophecy of scripture comes from someone's own interpretation.
For no prophecy was ever produced by the will of man, but men
spoke from God as they were carried along by the Holy Spirit.
—2 Peter 1:20–21

CONTENTS

PREFACE

The intention of this Bible summary is to reveal to its reader all the major events and teachings of the Bible, presented in a chronological order that ties everything together in a coherent manner. Every book in the Bible has been summarized and included in this Bible summary to some extent. Although this Bible summary attempts to give its reader a clear understanding of the entirety of the Bible, it is not the Bible but a summary of the Bible. The English Standard Version (ESV) Bible that much of this Bible summary comes from is 1,042 pages long. There is so much more in the Bible that was not able to be included in this Bible summary. The Bible is the actual Word of God. This is a summary of the Word of God, intended to give you an excellent overview of the Bible, but it is not a replacement for reading the entire actual Bible for yourself. If you read the Bible and live out what it says in your life, you will be transformed.

ACKNOWLEDGMENT

I would like to give a special thanks to Father Kevin Bobbin. Without his help and guidance, *Bible Summary for Adults and Students* would not be possible.

CHAPTER 1

INTRODUCTION AND OVERVIEW OF THE BIBLE

BRIEF SUMMARY OF THE BIBLE, GOD'S PLANS FOR US, AND WHY JESUS IS THE MOST IMPORTANT PERSON IN THE BIBLE

God is our father. One of the ways he chooses to talk with us, his children, is to send an extensive series of personal messages to us from him. This is the Bible. In the Bible, God explains who he is, who we are as his children, how he wants us to live our lives, and the things he will do for us. In this first chapter, I will give you an overview of what the Bible is about and why we need to read it.

God created human beings because he wanted a family to love and be with him. He created the first man and woman to begin this family, who was Adam and Eve. God created man and woman as sinless. God used to appear to this first man and woman (Adam and Eve) and speak with them regularly. He put them in charge over all the plants and animals that he created, and he allowed Adam to name all the animals. Adam and Eve were without sin, and they had a close relationship with God (Genesis chapters 1 and 2).

God wants all human beings to go to heaven and be with him when they die. However, heaven is a sinless place. Heaven is where God lives, and sin is not allowed there. If a person committed a sin, he or she is not allowed into God's presence in his home, heaven.

11

God gave man and woman free will (they can choose if they wanted to follow God's commands or not). God did not want them to be like robots or slaves who could not choose what they wanted to do. He wanted man and woman to love him because they chose to, not because they had to because they were programmed to and had no other option.

When God spoke with Adam and Eve in the Garden of Eden, one of the things that he told them was that they were not allowed to eat fruit from the Tree of the Knowledge of Good and Evil. He warned them that if they ate from the tree, they would surely die (Genesis 2:16–17). One day the devil appeared disguised as a serpent and told Adam and Eve that they would not die if they ate from the tree. He told them that God was lying to them and that God was actually afraid if they ate from the tree, they would become all power-ful just like he was. Adam and Eve had a choice to make: follow what God told them, or follow what the devil told them. They chose to fol-low what the devil told them. They went against God's word to them, and they ate from the tree (Genesis 3:1–19). This was a sin, and they broke their fellowship with God. They now had sin on them. Because of this, now when they died, they would not be allowed into heaven, because heaven does not allow sin to enter into it.

Sin is like a virus that infected their souls and was passed on to the souls of all their children, including us. For example, Adam and Eve's first children were Cain and Abel. Cain became angry at God over a small matter, and he killed his brother, Abel, in his sinful anger (Genesis 4:1–17). Sin was already horribly affecting mankind right from the start with Adam and Eve and their children, Cain and Abel. There was no hope for mankind to be right with God and get to heaven and be with him without God's help.

God loves people, and he wanted all of us to love and follow him while we are on earth and to be with him in heaven as his chil-dren after we die. God also wanted us to know him, know about him, and live our lives the way he wanted us to. Therefore, God gave us the first part of his plan to help us. It taught us right from wrong, and it partially taught us about him, what he wants from us, and how he wants us to live. He gave us the law (books of Exodus, Leviticus,

Numbers, and Deuteronomy in the Bible). The Old Testament in the Bible is filled with laws, or rules, from God that let the people know how God wanted them to live. They taught us right from wrong. If the people followed them perfectly, they would not commit any sins and they would get to heaven. Among the examples of these laws are the Ten Commandments (Genesis 20:1–21). Before God gave us the law, people did not know right from wrong. The world was very sinful and evil, and it needed to be shown by God that much of the things that people were doing were very wrong. Their hearts needed to change from loving what was evil to loving what was good. The first step in this was they had to be informed about what God said was good and bad.

There were many laws and rules in the Old Testament of the Bible (the Old Testament is before Jesus came; The New Testament starts when Jesus came to Earth and it is all about him). Mankind tried to follow God's laws for us, but people were weak and they kept messing up and breaking the rules (they kept sinning).

The Old Testament is the story of God letting the people of Israel know right from wrong through his laws and rules and the people of Israel trying to follow God's laws and rules. People were (and still are) of a sin nature as a result of Adam and Eve's sinning against God. In the Old Testament the people would routinely be in a lot of distress as a result of the sins they committed. They would cry out to God for help and he would save them. They would be good for a while, but would start to turn away from God and sin again. Their sins would get worse and worse until eventually, they would experience the disastrous consequences of their sins. They would cry out to God, and he would save them again; then they would start to sin, their sinning would get progressively worse, etc. This pattern happened over and over again throughout the Old Testament. The first part of God's plan to both save and transform people taught them right from wrong by God giving them the law. If the people followed God's laws and rules perfectly, they would not sin. The problem was, the people were too weak and sinful to follow them perfectly, and they (we) sinned over and over again.

The people all sinned and needed more than the law to save them. God's law cannot save anyone once they have sinned. The law can warn people against sinning to let the people know it was wrong and to not do it, but once a person sinned, the law could not save them from that sin. If anything, it condemned them. It told them what God's rule was, and if the person broke it, he could not say, "I did not know I was sinning," because God informed them it was a sin in the law.

Both God and man were in a bind, and the fate of mankind depended on how God dealt with this bind. God is a completely holy and sinless God. He will not allow sin to be in his presence, in his home. When a person sins, the person has that sin on them. We all sinned. We all sinned many times in our lives and have countless sins on us by the time that we die. If God just forgave us for our sins, he would not be holy. He would say, "I know that all of you committed countless sins in your lives. That's okay, I will let it pass. You can enter heaven, all of you, with all of your sins on you."

God would be surrounded by an infinity of sin in his presence, in his home. God is completely holy, and that cannot happen. Here is the bind. God could condemn the sin, as he should because he is all holy. Now none of us get into heaven because we are all covered in sin. The only other eternal place for beings to go besides heaven is hell. God created us because he wanted children and to have a family with them. If God straight out condemned us for our sins, we completely failed God's plan for his family and all his children (us) are in hell. That is not good at all either. So the bind for God is this: How does the sinning of the people get the judgment that a holy God requires, yet save his children who did the sinning from the wrath of his judgment, clean them from their sins, and have them enter heaven as completely sinless to be children in God's family? Mankind's fate hung in the balance depending on what God would do with this problem. This is where Jesus comes in.

God implemented the second part of his plan to save and redeem us from our sins so that we can have a relationship with him while we are on earth, and go to heaven and be with him when we die. God the father, God the Son (Jesus), and God the Holy

Spirit decided that Jesus, who was God in heaven, would come to earth and also be a human like all of us. While on earth, Jesus led a completely sinless life in deed, word, and thought. He was and will always remain the only person to never sin in any way throughout their life. He was in complete obedience to the will of God the Father—obedience to the point of accepting his Father's will that he should die as a sacrifice for the sins of all mankind. Only a perfect, sinless sacrifice would be acceptable to God the Father to pay for the sin of the entire world, and Jesus was that by leading a life of perfect, sinless obedience to God the Father. He was the perfect, sinless obedience to God the Father that the rest of mankind was too weak to be. All the sins that people committed in our lifetimes (including us) were taken off of us and placed on Jesus. Jesus was then punished to death with all our sins placed on him. He was punished in our place, with our sins on him. Because of him doing this, whoever accepts and follows Jesus as their God can now be forgiven of their sins by God, because Jesus paid for all of them, and God the Father accepted his death as a sacrifice and payment for all our sins. Jesus, flawless in following the will of God the Father for his entire life, was punished for our sake. None of us were strong enough to avoid sinning for our entire lives, so he did it for us. By following him, we are now able to be forgiven of our sins by God. By accepting Jesus and what he did for us, and following him as our God, this now enables us to go to heaven when we die.

If we do not accept Jesus and what he did for us, out of our free will to choose this, our sins cannot be forgiven. If we follow Jesus as our God (along with God the Father and God the Holy Spirit), our sins can be forgiven by God. If we reject following Jesus, no forgiveness of our sins is possible. His act of dying on the cross for us, punished with our sins taken off of us and placed onto him, is the only method accepted by God the Father to pay for our sins. We rejected the plan God made for us to be forgiven of our sins. We are then declared guilty of our sins by God when we die. We now cannot be with God and get into heaven because sin is not allowed there. Instead, we go to a place where people go who reject Jesus and what he did for us: hell.

The Old Testament shows why we need a savior (we are too weak to follow God's laws that were designed to prevent us from sinning). The New Testament is about the Savior (Jesus). Completely obedient to the will of God the Father, Jesus led a sinless life and took all our sins on him and got put to death with our sins on him. Now we can be forgiven of sin by God, so we can be friends with him while we are on earth and go to heaven when we die. God fixed the bind that he and we were in: What does an all holy God do with the people who all committed countless sins against him, who yet want to be part of God's family, which God wants too?

In addition to informing people about the fall of man, God's salvation plan to redeem man, and how to enter into this salvation plan, the Bible has a second major purpose. It informs us about how we are supposed to live our lives while on earth. Both the Old and New Testaments are full of information about how God wants us to live our lives. Information is given to us about this in two major ways. The first is by God directly telling us how we are to live our lives. He speaks to the people directly and through prophets all throughout the Bible about this. Additionally, the Bible is a collection about the lives of numerous people involved in God's grand plan for mankind. By reading about the circumstances these people were in, and the blessings and consequences they received based on their actions in these circumstances, we learn so much from them that we can apply to our own lives.

The Bible mainly focuses on events that took place in the country of Israel. God said that he made all the countries of the world, yet he wanted a country that would be his own special one. He chose Israel to be this country just because he wanted to, not because they were better than anyone else. He also chose Israel as his own personal country because of a promise he made to Abraham, who was willing to make a very big sacrifice to God because God asked him to (Genesis 22:1–19). We will read about this series of events soon. The Bible states that God used Israel as an example for all the world to follow based on what God did with the Israelite people.

CHAPTER 2

THE BEGINNING OF THE OLD TESTAMENT: CREATION

The Bible is divided into two sections. The first section is the Old Testament. This is before Jesus was born. The New Testament begins with the birth of Jesus, proceeds through his life, death, resurrection, and the apostles spreading the Gospel after Jesus returned to heaven. We will now start at the beginning of the Bible. This is the book of Genesis, the first book in the Bible in the Old Testament.

THE OLD TESTAMENT
THE BOOK OF GENESIS
BEFORE THE FLOOD

The Bible starts with the Old Testament, which takes place before Jesus came to earth to save us from being lost due to our sins. The first book of the Bible is the book of Genesis. In the beginning, there was God and the angels that lived with him in heaven. However, he did not make the universe in which we live in yet. At one point, he decided he wanted to make our universe and make us to live in it on earth. He made the universe in six God-days. We do not know how long a God-day is.

On the first day, the universe did not exist yet and everything outside of heaven was dark. Then God said, "Let there be light" (Genesis 1:3). God's light then filled everything. On the second day, God made a separation between heaven and the universe. Then, God made the earth, and he separated the oceans from the dry land. On the third day, God made all the plants, trees, flowers, fruits, and vegetables on the earth. On the fourth day, God made the sun to light the day and the moon and the stars to light the night. Before the sun, moon, and stars, it was light from God that lit up everything. On the fifth day, God made all the birds in the sky and all the fish and sea creatures. On the sixth day, God made all the rest of the animals on the earth (Genesis 1:1–25).

Additionally, on the sixth day, God made man in his own image. The first man that God made was named Adam. He made him out of the dust from the ground, and he breathed the breath of life into his nostrils, and he became alive. God planted a garden named Eden, and this was where he placed Adam. Adam worked in the garden of Eden and kept it. God decided that it was not good for Adam to be alone, so he made a helper fit for him. God caused Adam to fall into a deep sleep. While he was sleeping, God took one of Adam's ribs and closed up the spot where he took it from with flesh. God made a woman from the rib that he took from Adam, and he brought the woman to him. Adam was pleased with the woman and said,

> This at last is bone of my bones and flesh of
> my flesh; she shall be called Woman because she
> was taken out of man. (Genesis 2:23)

> And the man and his wife were both naked
> and were not ashamed. (Genesis 2:25)

The first woman that God made was named Eve. God told them to be fruitful and multiply and fill the earth. He gave them dominion over every living animal on earth. After God made man and woman, his work of creating everything in the universe and on earth was finished, so God rested on the seventh day, blessed it, and made it holy. (Genesis chapters 1 and 2).

ADAM AND EVE'S SIN AGAINST GOD (THE FALL)

God placed Adam and Eve as rulers over all the animals on earth. God allowed Adam to name all the animals that existed. God would walk and talk with Adam and Eve in the Garden of Eden. There were all kinds of plants, fruit, and vegetables in the Garden of Eden for Adam and Eve to eat. In the Middle of the Garden of Eden was a tree called the Tree of Knowledge of Good and Evil. God said to Adam and Eve,

> You may surely eat of every tree of the garden, but of the tree of the knowledge of good and evil you shall not eat, for in the day that you eat it, you shall surely die. (Genesis 2:16–17)

One day the devil, who is an enemy of God, came to Eve as a serpent. In case there is any doubt that the serpent in the garden of Eden in Genesis is actually the devil, the Bible later clears this up:

> And the great dragon was thrown down, *that ancient serpent, who is called the devil and Satan, the deceiver of the whole world (italics added)—* he was thrown down to the earth, and his angels were thrown down with him. (Revelation 12:9)

The book of Revelation informs us that Satan is also called the devil, the ancient serpent, and the dragon. He lied to Eve to tempt her to sin against God and destroy both her and Adam's relationship with God and God's plan for mankind. The Bible later informs us that the devil did this out of envy:

> For God formed us to be imperishable; the image of his own nature he made us. *But by the envy of the devil, death entered the world, and they who are allied with him experience it.* (Wisdom 2:23–24)

The serpent said to Eve (summary), "Did God actually tell you not to eat from any tree in the garden?"

Eve responded, "God said that we shall not eat from the fruit of the tree in the middle of the garden, or we will die."

The serpent said, "You will not die. God told you that because he knows that if you eat from it, your eyes will be opened and you will be like God, knowing good and evil" (Genesis 3:5).

Eve went against what God told her, and she ate from the tree. She then gave fruit from this tree to Adam, and he ate from it too. Adam and Eve's eyes were opened, and they knew that they were naked. They made themselves loincloths out of fig leaves to hide their nakedness. They heard the sound of God walking in the garden, and they hid themselves from him.

God called out to them, "Where are you, Adam and Eve?"

Adam said (summary), "I heard you coming in the garden, and I was afraid because I was naked, so I hid from you."

God responded (summary), "How did you know that you were naked? Did you eat from the tree that I forbid you to eat?"

Adam blamed Eve and God for this, saying (summary), "It was the woman that *you* gave me to be with that gave me the fruit to eat, so I ate it."

God said to Eve, "What have you done?"

Eve blamed the serpent, claiming that it tricked her into eating the forbidden fruit (Genesis 3:7–13).

Who is Satan, or the devil, and what exactly did he tempt Adam and Eve to do? A great thing about the Bible is that it often gives more information about a topic that is in one part of the Bible in another part of the Bible. The Prophetic Books in the Old Testament reveal who Satan is a bit more. In the book of Ezekiel, God calls Satan the King of Tyre and says this about him:

> You were the signet of perfection, full of wisdom and perfect in beauty. *You were in Eden, the garden of God; (italics added)* every precious stone was your covering, sardius, topaz and diamond, beryl, onyx, and jasper, sapphire, emerald and

carbuncle; and crafted in gold were your settings and your engravings. *On the day you were created they were prepared. You were an anointed guardian cherub. I placed you; you were on the holy mountain of God; in the midst of the stones of fire you walked (italics added).* You were blameless in your ways from the day you were created, till unrighteousness was found in you. In the abundance of your trade you were filled with violence in your midst, and you sinned; so I cast you as a profane thing from the mountain of God, and I destroyed you, O guardian cherub, from the midst of the stones of fire. *Your heart was proud because of your beauty; you corrupted your wisdom for the sake of your splendor (italics added).* (Ezekiel 28:12–17)

I highlighted important points in the above Bible verse. Satan was an anointed guardian cherub who was created and placed by God. He was in the garden of Eden. He became full of self-pride over the beauty and splendor *that God gave to him (italics added).* It was not inherently his and/or he did not earn it; God created it for him. Because of his pride, he became corrupted. What exactly did Satan do that caused him to fall? This is detailed in the book of Isaiah in the Bible:

How you are fallen from heaven, O Day Star, son of Dawn! How you are cut down to the ground, you who laid the nations low! You said in your heart, "I will ascend to heaven; above the stars of God I will set my throne on high; I will sit on the mount of assembly in the far reaches of the north; I will ascend above the heights of the clouds; I will make myself like the Most High." But you are brought down to Sheol, to the far reaches of the pit. (Isaiah 14:12–15)

Satan was cast down because he wanted to be like God and take over as God. What did Satan say to Eve when she told him that God said to her that if she or Adam ate of the tree of the knowledge of good and evil that they would surely die? Satan said,

> You will not surely die. For God knows that when you eat of it your eyes will be opened, *and you will be like God (italics added),* knowing good and evil. (Genesis 3:4–5)

Out of envy that God man imperishable and in the image of God's own nature (Wisdom 2:23–24), Satan tempted Eve with the desire that caused him to fall: wanting to be like God. The temptation worked.

The Bible further details what will eventually happen to Satan. Although for us it is an event in the future, God is outside of time. It is detailed in the Bible in the past tense, an event that has already happened for God. Continuing from the above passage in the book of Ezekiel:

> Your heart was proud because of your beauty; you corrupted your wisdom for the sake of your splendor. I [God] cast you to the ground; I exposed you before kings, to feast their eyes on you. By the multitude of your iniquities, in the unrighteousness of your trade you profaned your sanctuaries; so I brought fire out from your midst; it consumed you, and I turned you to ashes on the earth in the sight of all who saw you. All who know you among the peoples area appalled at you; you have come to a dreadful end and shall be no more forever. (Ezekiel 28:17–19)

Returning to the events with Adam and Eve—God then cursed the serpent (the devil) for tempting Adam and Eve to sin which caused them to fall. He also gave a prophecy of a Savior, who will be a man, that will go to war with the serpent, which is the devil, saying,

> I will put enmity between you and the woman, and between your offspring and her off-spring; he shall bruise your head, and you shall bruise his heel. (Genesis 3:15)

This Savior will also bear the sins of man on himself to save man: God told Adam that because he listened to Eve and ate from the tree that God forbid him to eat from, the ground would be cursed because of him. He shall eat of it in pain for the rest of his life, and it will produce thistles and thorns for him. What was placed on and pushed into Jesus's head during the crucifixion events? A crown of thorns. Jesus would have the curse of the sins of man placed on him during his crucifixion (in more ways than just this). God also told Adam that he will work in sweat to make bread to eat until he returns to the ground as dust, from where he came from. God told the Eve that because of what she did, she will have painful childbirth, and she will desire her husband, and he will rule over her. They were both cast out of the Garden of Eden. God still cared for them however. He made them clothes out of animal skins, and he looked out for them (Genesis chapter 3).

CAIN AND ABEL

Adam and Eve were husband and wife, and they had a son and named him Cain. They then had a second son, and named him Abel. Cain became a farmer, and Abel became a shepherd of sheep. Since God loved them and took care of them, Cain and Abel brought offerings to God. Abel brought the firstborn of his flock to God as an offering, while Cain brought an offering of things that he grew. For an unspecified reason, God liked Abel's gift, but he did not like the gift Cain presented to him. Cain became very angry about this. God said to Cain,

> Why are you angry, and why has your face
> fallen? If you do well, will you not be accepted?
> And if you do not do well, sin is crouching at the
> door. It's desire is for you, but you must rule over
> it. (Genesis 4:6–7)

Cain then spoke with his brother Abel. When they were in the field, Cain killed his brother Abel. This was the first murder in history (Genesis 4:1–8).

God said to Cain (summary), "What did you do? You killed your brother! Because of this, you will be cursed and will wander around the earth."

Cain pleaded with God for mercy. God still loved Cain even though he killed his brother, and he watched over Cain so that nothing bad would happen to him. God made a wife for Cain, and they had children. Adam and Eve, Cain's parents, also had more children. Back then, God allowed people to live to be over nine hundred years old. People kept having children, and over time, the earth was full of people (Genesis 4:9–25 and Genesis 5:1–32).

NOAH AND THE ARK

People multiplied greatly on the earth. Over time the people became increasingly evil. God shortened their lives to a maximum of 120 years because of this. People continued to get progressively evil however.

> The Lord saw that the wickedness of man
> was great in the earth, and that every intention of
> the thoughts of his heart was only evil continu-
> ally. (Genesis 6:5)

Mankind got so bad that God became sorry that he made people. He decided that he would destroy everything alive on earth with a flood—people, animals, and plants—because the entire world was exceedingly evil. However, there was a man named Noah who found favor with God.

> Noah was a righteous man, blameless in his generation. Noah walked with God. (Genesis 6:9–10)

God decided he would save him from the flood and repopulate the earth from his offspring (Genesis 6:1–8). God came to Noah and revealed to him that due to the violence that man filled the earth with, he would destroy all flesh in the world with a flood. God made his covenant with Noah, because he found Noah to be righteous before him. He told Noah to make a boat called an ark. He told him to put his family in the ark, along with one male and one female of every animal on earth, and bring food to feed everyone and every animal. It took Noah several decades to build the ark, but one day it was finally finished. God sent all the animals to Noah to put on the ark, and Noah and his family got in the ark and God sealed the door so the water would not get in. God then sent rain to the earth for forty days and forty nights, and the world was flooded. He also caused water to spring up from inside the earth. The water was so high that it covered all the mountaintops. All the people in the world drowned because they were so evil, but God saved Noah and his family. Noah and his family floated in the ark for 150 days. Finally, the flood started to go away. The ark landed on the top of a mountain called Mount Ararat. Noah, his family, and all the animals got out of the ark. God made a promise to Noah that he would never again send a worldwide flood. He sent a rainbow to Noah and told him that every time we see a rainbow, it is God remembering that he would never again wipe out mankind with a flood. God also increased the life span of man once again from the 120-year restriction he put on it due to their evil hearts. Noah lived to be 950 years old (Genesis 6:9–22, 7:1–24, 8:1–19, 9:1–28).

THE TOWER OF BABEL

After Noah's family came out of the ark, they had children, grandchildren, and great-grandchildren, etc. and became many people (Genesis 10:1–32). Everybody at this time spoke the same language. Many settled in one place in the land of Shinar. They said,

> Come, let us build ourselves a city and a tower with its top in the heavens, and let us make a name for ourselves, lest we be dispersed over the face of the whole earth. (Genesis 11:4)

When God saw the city and tower that humans built, he said,

> Behold, they are one people, and they have all one language, and this is only the beginning of what they will do. And nothing that they propose to do will now be impossible for them. (Genesis 11:6)

God confused everyone's language so that they could not understand each other. When they tried to speak with each other, it sounded like they were babbling. This caused them to call the tower that they built the Tower of Babel. It also caused the people to abandon the tower and the city and spread out from each other and fill the earth, like God wanted them to (Genesis 11:1–9).

CHAPTER 3

GOD STARTS THE JEWISH/ CHRISTIAN FAITH WITH ABRAHAM

After the fall of the Tower of Babel, people spread out over the earth and multiplied. There was a man named Abram in the land of Haran. God came to Abram and told him to go from his country and take his family to a land that God would show him. If he did this, God promised to bless him and make a great nation from his descendants, and his name would be great. His descendants will be as numerous as the sand grains on the seashore, and "in you, all the families of the earth shall be blessed" (Genesis 12:3). Abram went as God told him. He was seventy-five years old at the time. He took his wife, Sarai, and his nephew, Lot, with him on their journey to the land of Canaan. When they arrived at the land of Canaan, God told Abram that he would give this land to Abram's offspring. At the time, the Canaanites were in the land. Abram built an altar there but kept moving on to the land of Negeb, where God instructed him to go (Genesis chapters 11 and 12:1–9).

There was a famine in the land that Abram was in, so Abram went down to Egypt due to the famine. Abram told his wife, Sarai, that because she was beautiful, he feared the Egyptians would kill him and take her if they found out he was her husband. So he instructed Sarai to tell them that she was Abram's sister, which she did. News about her beauty eventually reached Pharaoh, who took her into his home and dealt well with Abram. But God afflicted Pharaoh and his house with severe plagues because he took another man's wife. Pharaoh angrily called in Abram and asked why he told him that Sarai was his sister instead of his wife. Pharaoh then sent both Abram and Sarai away (Genesis 12:10–20). On another occasion years later, Abram did the exact same thing, telling King Abimelech that Sarai was his sister instead of telling the truth that she was his wife.

Abraham eventually went up from Egypt back to the land of Negeb with Sarai and his nephew, Lot. Both Abram and Lot were rich in possessions and livestock to the point that the land could not support the herds of both. Abram decided they needed to split up, because they could no longer fit in the same land together. Abram gave Lot first choice of where he would settle. Lot settled in a city called Sodom, because it was well-watered everywhere like Egypt was. Abram settled in the land of Canaan (Genesis 13:1–13). At one point, there were battles between the kings of the surrounding areas. Abram's nephew, Lot, was captured during one of the battles. Abram gathered 301 men and rescued Lot, his people, and his possessions. When Abram returned, he was blessed by Melchizedek, the king of Salem, priest of God Most High. Melchizedek blessed Abram, saying,

> Blessed be Abram by God Most High,
> Possessor of heaven and earth; and blessed be
> God Most High; who has delivered your enemies
> into your hand! (Genesis 14:19–20)

Abram then gave Melchizedek one-tenth of everything that he owned.

God appeared to Abram and told him that he will have a son, who will be his heir. He told him that his offspring will be as numerous as the stars. God then gave Abram the following prophecy:

> Know for certain that your offspring will be
> sojourners in a land that is not theirs and will
> be servants there, and they will be afflicted for
> four hundred years. But I will bring judgment

on the nation that they serve, and afterward they
shall come out with great possessions. And they
shall come back here in the fourth generation, for
the iniquity of the Amorites is not yet complete.
(Genesis 15:12–14 and 16)

At this time, there were two cities that did very evil things. The
cities names were Sodom and Gomorrah. God told Abram that he
would destroy these two cities because they were overwhelmingly
evil. This made Abram sad. He asked God if God could find just ten
people who were not evil in these cities, would he not destroy them?
God said that he would not destroy the cities if he could find ten good
people in them. God looked as hard as he could, but he could not
find ten people who were not evil, so he had to destroy the cities. God
allowed Abram to save his nephew, Lot, and his family from Sodom
before he destroyed it. Before God destroyed Sodom and Gomorrah,
he sent down two angels to the cities to meet the people who lived
there to make sure that they were as evil as God believed them to be.
When the two angels arrived, the people were so evil that they tried
to sexually assault the angels. God had seen enough. He rained fire
and brimstone down on Sodom and Gomorrah, completely destroying both cities (Genesis 18:1–33 and Genesis 19:1–29).

ABRAM AND THE BIRTH OF HIS TWO SONS

When God first appeared to Abram, he told him that he would
give Abram and his wife, Sarai, children. Abram was now eighty-
five, Sarai was seventy-five, and they did not have any Children yet
(Genesis 16:15). Sarai believed that God prevented her from having any children. Because of this, Sarai told Abram that he should
take her servant, Hagar, as a second wife and have children with her.
Abram did. Abram had a son with Sarah's servant, and God told them
to name him Ishmael. Having a second wife caused a lot of conflict
between Hagar and Abram's first wife, Sarai. Sarai then began to mistreat Hagar. The angel of the Lord came to Hagar, who was miserable

because of this. He told her that her son, Ishmael, would have count-less offspring, but he himself would be a wild, rebellious man when he grew up (Genesis chapter 16).God appeared to Abram when he was ninety-nine years old. He told him again that if he followed God, he would make a great nation of his descendants. Kings would be his offspring, and God would give them the land of Canaan as their everlasting possession. God made a covenant with Abram on this promise. For Abram's part, every male offspring would be cir-cumcised throughout generations. God then changed Abram's name to Abraham and Sarai's name to Sarah. God told Abraham that he would have a son with his wife, Sarah, who was ninety. This is the son that God would establish his covenant through of making a great nation. The next year Sarah had Abraham's son. They named their son Isaac. Abraham was one hundred years old, and Sarah was ninety years old at this time (Genesis chapters 17, 18, and 21).

Isaac grew as a young child. Hagar, Abraham's second wife, remained living with them along with her son, Ishmael. Sarah became jealous and commanded Abraham to cast out Hagar and Ishmael, because Sarah did not want Ishmael to be an heir along with Isaac. Abraham did not want to do this to his son Ishmael. God appeared to Abraham and told him it was ok to tell Hagar and Ishmael to go. God promised that he would also make a great nation out of Ishmael, because Ishmael was Abraham's offspring. Therefore, Abraham sent Hagar and Ishmael away. God looked after and took care of the both of them (Genesis 21:8–21).

GOD PUTS ABRAHAM TO A GREAT TEST TO SEE IF ABRAHAM WILL TRUST AND FOLLOW GOD

Abraham's son Isaac grew into an older boy, and Abraham and Sarah loved Isaac very much. God put Abraham to a very difficult test to see if Abraham would follow God's instructions. God told Abraham to take his son Isaac into the mountains in the land of Moriah and, once they were there, to offer him as a sacrifice to God.

Abraham was extremely sad about this. But he listened to God and trusted him that somehow God would make everything okay.

Abraham took Isaac his son, whom he loved very much, on the several-day journey to the place God instructed him to offer up Isaac as a sacrifice. When they got there, Abraham bound Isaac, laid him on the altar that he made, and pulled out a knife to kill him like God told him to do. As Abraham lifted up his knife to kill Isaac, God immediately went to Abraham and said, "Abraham, Abraham!" And Abraham said, "Here am I."

God said,

> Do not lay your hand on the boy or do anything to him, for now I know that you fear God, seeing that you have not withheld your son, your only son, from me. By myself I have sworn, declares the Lord, because you have done this and have not withheld your son, your only son, I will surely bless you, and I will surely multiply your children and grandchildren as the stars of heaven and as the sand that is on the seashore. And in your children and grandchildren shall all of the nations of the earth be blessed because you have obeyed my voice. (Genesis 22:11–18)

Because Abraham trusted God and tried to do this most difficult task that God told him to do, which was offer up his only son to God, God would make it so that Abraham's children and grandchildren would be the ones who would found the country of Israel. Additionally, one of Abraham's descendants would be Jesus, who would save the world from their sins.

ISAAC HAS TWIN SONS: ESAU AND JACOB

Abraham's son, Isaac, grew into a man and married a woman named Rebekah. Rebekah was unable to have any children, so Isaac prayed to God that he would grant them children. God answered Isaac's prayer, and Rebekah became pregnant with twin sons. The sons fought with each other inside Rebekah's womb. She asked God why this was so. God answered Rebekah's prayer, telling her,

> Two nations are in your womb, and two peoples from within you shall be divided; the one shall be stronger than the other, the older shall serve the younger. (Genesis 25:23)

At the twin's birth, the first one came out covered in red hair, and they named him Esau. The second son came out holding Esau's heel, and they named him Jacob. As they grew up, Esau became an outdoorsman and a skilled hunter, while Jacob was a quiet man who dwelled in tents. Isaac loved Esau because of the food he hunted, but Rebecca loved Jacob.

One day Jacob was cooking stew. Esau came in and was very hungry and asked for some stew. Jacob said he would give him stew only if Esau gave him his birthright for it. Esau said he felt like he was starving to death, so what good was a birthright to him? He therefore gave Jacob his birthright in return for some stew.

> Thus, Esau despised his birthright. (Genesis 25:34)

Isaac became very old and grew blind, and he believed that he may die soon. He called in his firstborn son, Esau, and told him to go and hunt and make him a meal out of it, and afterward he would give him the blessing due to the firstborn son. Isaac's wife, Rebekah, heard the conversation. She told Jacob what his father said to his brother, Esau, and then she gave Jacob the following instructions: She told him to go and get two young goats from their flock. She would make a meal out of them. Jacob would give them to Isaac, and since he was blind, he would think it was Esau and give Jacob the blessing in place of Esau.

Jacob did not think this would work. Esau was hairy, and Jacob had smooth skin. He said that if his father Isaac touched him, he would feel that he was Jacob and not Esau and curse him instead of bless him. Rebekah made the meal, dressed Jacob in Esau's clothes so that he would smell like Esau, and put animal pelts on his arm so he would feel hairy like Esau. When Jacob brought the food in to Isaac and asked for the blessing for the firstborn son, Isaac who was blind said that Jacob felt like Esau but sounded like Jacob. Jacob reassured Isaac that he was, in fact, Esau, and Isaac gave Jacob the blessing meant for the firstborn son. This was the blessing:

> May God give you the dew of heaven and the fatness of the earth and plenty of grain and wine. Let peoples serve you, and nations bow down to you. Be lord over your brothers, and may your mother's sons bow down to you. Cursed be everyone who curses you, and blessed be everyone who blesses you! (Genesis 27:26–29)

As soon as Jacob received the blessing from his father Isaac and left, his brother Esau came in from hunting. He prepared his father a meal and brought it in to him and asked for the firstborn blessing. Isaac said, "Who are you? I already was given a meal from my son Esau and gave him my blessing."

Esau said, "I am your son, Esau! Jacob tricked me!" Esau cried out in bitter agony and asked for a blessing also from his father.

Isaac said that he made Jacob lord over Esau in his blessing, and he does not have another blessing for Esau. Esau wept for a blessing from Isaac, and Isaac answered him and said:

> Behold, away from the fatness of the earth shall your dwelling be, and away from the dew of heaven on high. By your sword shall you live, and you shall serve your brother; but when you grow restless you shall break his yoke from your neck. (Genesis 27:39–40).

Esau hated Jacob because he tricked their father Isaac into giving him the firstborn blessing that belonged to Esau. Esau said that after their father dies, he will kill his brother, Jacob. Rebekah found out about Esau's intentions. She sent Jacob to live with her brother Laban in the land of Haran until his brother's anger subsides (Genesis 27:30–46).

Esau later married a daughter of Ishmael, the son of Abraham and Hagar who was cast out. God came to Jacob in a dream and told him that he made a promise to his grandfather, Abraham, that his descendants would be many and would form a great nation, starting with Jacob's sons. Through a series of deceitful acts by Jacob's uncle Laban, Jacob wound up marrying two women instead of just one. They were Laban's daughters, who were sisters, named Leah and Rachel. Through the both of them, Jacob had twelve sons. These twelve sons would go on to form twelve tribes which would become the country of Israel. Israel is the country in which Jesus would later be born in when he came to earth from heaven (Genesis chapters 29–31).

God came to Jacob one night in the form of a man, and Jacob began to wrestle with him. Jacob and God wrestled all night long. When God saw that Jacob would not give up, he touched Jacob's hip socket and caused it to pop out of joint. This caused Jacob to limp for the rest of his life to remind him of the day he wrestled with God. Jacob still would not stop wrestling with God until God blessed him. God asked Jacob his name, and he said, "Jacob." Then God said to Jacob,

> Your name shall no longer be called Jacob,
> but Israel, for you have striven with God and
> men and have prevailed. (Genesis 32:27–28).

This is where the country of Israel began. Jacob became the first person to form Israel, and his twelve sons would go on to form the twelve tribes that would make up Israel. God then finally blessed Jacob as he asked him to (Genesis 32:22–32). God later appeared to Jacob and reaffirmed what he told Jacob on the night that they wrestled. God said,

Your name is Jacob; no longer shall you be called Jacob, but Israel shall be your name. I am God almighty: be fruitful and multiply. A nation and a company of nations shall come from you, and kings shall come from your own body. The land that I gave to Abraham and Isaac I will give to you, and I will give the land to your offspring after you. (Genesis 35:9–12)

CHAPTER 4

GOD USES JOSEPH'S DIFFICULT TRIALS FOR GOOD

Jacob had twelve sons. Their names were Reuben, Simeon, Levi, Judah, Issachar, Zebulun, Joseph, Benjamin, Dan, Naphtali, Gad, and Asher. Joseph was the second youngest son of Jacob. Jacob loved Joseph the most out of all his sons because he was the first son from his wife Rachel, the wife that he loved more than his other wife, Leah. The fact that Jacob loved Joseph more than his other brothers bothered these other brothers greatly. Jacob made Joseph a robe of many colors, which Joseph wore. When his brothers saw this, they became envious and hated Joseph (Genesis 37:1–4). When Joseph was seventeen years old, he had two dreams. He told his brothers the first dream. Joseph said,

> "Behold, we were binding sheaves of wheat in the field, and my sheaf arose and stood upright. And behold, your sheaves gathered around it and bowed down to my sheaf." His brothers said, "Are you indeed to reign and rule over us?" His second dream was, "Behold, the sun, the moon, and eleven stars were bowing down to me." (Genesis 37:6–9)

Both his father and his brothers criticized Joseph for these dreams that he had.

One day Joseph's older brothers were watching a flock of sheep in a field far away. Joseph's father Jacob sent Joseph to them to see if they needed his help. His brothers saw Joseph coming from a distance. They were envious of him and plotted to kill him. His oldest brother, Reuben, said it would be very wrong to kill their brother. He said they should put him in a pit until they figured out what to do with him. They grabbed him, took off his robe of many colors, and put him in a pit. While Reuben was away working, a bunch of Ishmaelite slave traders passed by. His other brothers decided to sell Joseph to the slave traders for twenty pieces of silver, which they did. Then they took Joseph's robe, ripped it up, and put animal blood on it. They went home and told their father Jacob that a fierce wild animal killed Joseph. Jacob was heartbroken over this for many years because he loved his son Joseph very much (Genesis 37:12–36).

Joseph was taken to Egypt as a slave. He was bought by a man named Potiphar, who was captain of the Pharaoh's guard. God was with Joseph and blessed everything that he did. As a result, Joseph was successful at all tasks that he did in his service to Potiphar. Potiphar noticed that Joseph was successful at everything he was involved with, so he made Joseph overseer of his house and put him in charge of all that he had (Genesis 39:1–6). Joseph was a handsome man, and Potiphar's wife was attracted to him. Day after day, she would ask Joseph to sleep with her. Joseph responded,

> Behold, because of me my master has no concern about anything in the house, and he has put everything that he has in my charge. He is not greater in this house than I am, nor has he kept back anything from me except yourself, because you are his wife. How then can I do this great wickedness and sin against God? (Genesis 39:8–9)

Potiphar's wife persisted in pursuing Joseph, but Joseph would not listen to her.

One day when no one was in the house except for Joseph and Potiphar's wife, she grabbed him by his shirt and yelled, "Sleep with me!"

He refused because it was wrong and a sin. She would not let him go, so he pulled away, and it ripped his shirt off. She got angry because Joseph rejected her. She had his shirt in her hand, and she lied to the guards, saying that Joseph tried to force himself on her and she ripped his shirt off as she tried to get away. She also told her husband, Potiphar, this lie when he got home from work. He had Joseph arrested and put in prison. However, God was with Joseph and blessed everything he did in prison so that it would be successful. As a result, Joseph was put in charge of all the prisoners in the prison (Genesis 39:11–23).

While Joseph was in prison, the Pharaoh's cupbearer and baker were accused of stealing from the Pharaoh, and they were put in prison with Joseph. Both of them had dreams while they were sleeping and were troubled by them because they did not know what they meant. They told their dreams to Joseph, and God told Joseph the meanings of their dreams. God told Joseph that the cupbearer's dream meant that in three days he would be declared innocent of his crime and would be released from prison. The baker's dream meant that in three days he would be found guilty of his crime and would be put to death for it. That is exactly what happened. The cupbearer was very happy that he was released from prison. At Joseph's request, he promised Joseph that he would speak to the Pharaoh about getting Joseph out of prison because Joseph was innocent of the crime that placed him there. But once the Pharaoh's cupbearer was released from prison, he forgot about Joseph. Joseph remained in prison for two more years (Genesis 40:1–23).

Two years later, the Pharaoh had two troublesome dreams. In the first dream, seven healthy cows walked out of the Nile River. Shortly after that, seven skinny and sickly cows walked out of the Nile River and ate the healthy cows. In the second dream, seven plump and healthy ears of corn grew out of the ground. Right after that, seven diseased and dried-up ears of corn grew up and ate up the healthy ears of corn. When the Pharaoh woke up, he was very upset about these dreams. He asked all the wise men of Egypt if they could tell him what these dreams meant, but no one could (Genesis 41:1–8).

The chief cupbearer then remembered that Joseph interpreted his dream two years ago when they were both in prison. He told the Pharaoh that Joseph might be able to interpret his dreams. The Pharaoh sent for Joseph and told Joseph his two dreams. Joseph said that God would interpret the dreams and tell him what they meant. Joseph said that the dream about the healthy and sickly cows and the healthy and sickly corn meant the same thing. There would be seven years of great crops, followed by seven years of severe famine in which the crops would not grow and there would be no food. He told the Pharaoh that during the seven years of good crops, he needed to take one-fifth of the crops and store them up to be used during the seven years of famine after that so that they would have food during the famine. The Pharaoh was extremely pleased that God told Joseph what the Pharaoh's dreams meant. The Pharaoh said that because God was clearly with Joseph in everything that he did, the Pharaoh made Joseph second-in-command over all of Egypt behind him, and everyone in Egypt had to do whatever Joseph said (Genesis 41:37–45).

Joseph was thirty years old when he was placed second-in-command over Egypt. The Pharaoh's dreams came true just as God told Joseph they would. There were seven years of plenty, during which the Egyptians saved up one-fifth of their crops each year in storehouses. After this came seven years of famine in which crops would not grow. Joseph opened up the storehouses and sold the saved food to the people during the famine. He sold this food not only to the Egyptians, but also to neighboring countries hit by the famine. The famine also came to Joseph's father, Jacob (Israel), and his eleven brothers living in Canaan who sold him to the slave traders several years ago. Jacob (Israel) instructed his ten of his sons to go to Egypt to buy food because they had none due to the famine. Jacob kept his youngest son, Benjamin, home with him. When the ten brothers got there, they had to go to Joseph because he was in charge of distributing the food. Joseph recognized his brothers and had his guards take them to the prison, accusing them of being spies. They did not recognize Joseph, and they were very afraid. They believed that they were finally being punished for selling Joseph into slavery thirteen years ago because they were very envious of him. They were sorry for doing this and said they deserve whatever punishment they got now for doing this to Joseph. After Joseph had them frightened for a few days that he would keep them as prisoners for believing they were spies, he finally said to them,

> Take a good look at my face. I am your brother Joseph, who you sold into slavery. I am now second in command of all of Egypt. (Genesis 43:1–34, 44:1–34)

Joseph's brothers were dismayed at his presence. Joseph did not punish them. He said,

> [Summary] God allowed everything to happen the way that it did so that I can save people's lives. Although you sold me to the slave traders and meant it for bad, God meant it for good. He made everything I did be successful, and it eventually put me second in charge of Egypt where I saved up food to survive the famine. I love you brothers, and do not be afraid of me.

The brothers were overjoyed that Joseph was alive and doing well. Joseph sent for his father, Jacob. Jacob was overwhelmed with joy that his son, Joseph, was actually alive. Jacob (Israel) and his eleven other sons moved to Egypt and lived with Joseph for the rest of their lives (Genesis 41:1–28, 46:1–26).

CHAPTER 5

MOSES AND THE ISRAELITES

THE BOOK OF EXODUS

As time passed, Jacob's (Israel's) twelve sons had children, grand-children, great-grandchildren, and so on while living in Egypt. Because of Joseph's wise plan given to him by God on what to do during the famine, Egypt was the only country in the area that had food. They became a great many people called the Israelites, who were living in Egypt. Over time, a new Pharaoh was in charge of Egypt who never heard of Joseph. He became afraid of the large number of Israelites living in Egypt, that they might one day turn against him. The Pharaoh instructed the commanders beneath him to turn the Israelites into slaves and to treat them harshly. The Israelites helped build cities for the Pharaoh as slaves. The more the Pharaoh oppressed the Israelites, however, the more they multiplied. The Pharaoh then instructed the midwives that delivered babies that if an Israelite or Hebrew woman gave birth to a boy, they were to kill the baby boy, but if it was a girl, they would let the girl live. This was done by the Pharaoh to reduce the number of Israelites living in Egypt. The midwives refused to do this, and God blessed the mid-wives for refusing. Pharaoh then gave an order that every boy that was born of a Hebrew woman would be thrown into the Nile River to drown, but Hebrew daughters may live (Exodus 1:1–22)

THE BIRTH OF MOSES

One day, a Hebrew (Israelite) woman gave birth to a boy in Egypt. She hid him for three months so that the authorities would not drown him in the Nile River. As he got bigger, she could no longer hide him well. She put the baby in a basket at the edge of the river. The baby's sister hid and watched what would happen to him. The Pharaoh's daughter came down to the river to take a bath in it. She found the basket with the baby inside. She realized it was a Hebrew baby, but she felt sorry for it and adopted it as her own son. The baby's sister approached Pharaoh's daughter and asked her,

> "Shall I go and call you a nurse from the Hebrew women to nurse the child for you?" And Pharaoh's daughter said to her, "Go." (Exodus 2:7–8)

The baby's sister went and got their actual Hebrew mother and brought her to Pharaoh's daughter. Pharaoh's daughter told the baby's mother that she would pay her to nurse him. The baby was nursed by his own Hebrew mother in the house of Pharaoh's daughter. The Pharaoh's daughter named the boy Moses, which means,

> I drew him out of the water. (Exodus 2:1–10)

Moses grew into a man. One day he saw an Egyptian beating a Hebrew slave, one of his own people. Moses killed the Egyptian and hid him in the sand. The Pharaoh found out about this and wanted to kill Moses because of it. Moses was afraid and ran away to a land called Midian. Moses found a wife there named Zipporah, and they had a son named Gershom. Moses lived in Midian for forty years (Exodus 2:11–22).

GOD HEARS ISRAEL'S GROANING

The people of Israel groaned for many years because of their slavery to Egypt, and they cried out to God for help. God heard their groaning and cries. He remembered his promise to Abraham, Isaac, and Jacob that he would make their descendants as numerous as the sand on the seashore, so he decided to help. At the time, Moses was tending the flock of his father-in-law, Jethro, in the land of Midian. God appeared to Moses in the form of a bush that was burning yet was never consumed. He told Moses that he had seen the affliction of his people in Egypt and he heard their cry due to the suffering from their Egyptian taskmasters. God said that he would send Moses to the Pharaoh of Egypt to bring the Hebrews out of Egypt and into a land flowing with milk and honey that God was setting aside for them. Moses was afraid to do this. God therefore told him that he would strengthen him and give him whatever power he needed to bring the Hebrews out of slavery in Egypt and in to a new promised land (Exodus 3:1–22, Exodus 4:1–17).

> Moses asked God, "If I come to the people of Israel and say to them, 'The God of your fathers has sent me to you,' and they ask me, "What is his name?' What shall I say to them?" God said to Moses, "I AM WHO I AM." And he said, "Say this to the people of Israel, 'I AM has sent me to you.'" (Exodus 3:13–14).

Moses was afraid that the Israelites in Egypt would not believe him that God sent him to free them. God gave Moses the ability to do miracles in front of the Israelites to prove that God sent him. Moses then told God that he spoke poorly and did not think he was able to do what God was telling him to do. God reminded him that it was he who made everyone's mouth and gave them the ability to speak. He will surely give Moses the ability to speak powerfully when the time comes. He also told Moses that if it would make him feel better, he could take his brother Aaron with him. Aaron was a Levite who spoke very well. God said that he would be with both of them when they speak. Moses agreed (Exodus 4:1–17).

Moses returned to Egypt with his family. Moses went to the Pharaoh and told him that God said that the Pharaoh needs to let the Israelites go for three days to worship God in the wilderness. Pharaoh became angry at this. He asked,

> Who is the Lord, that I should obey his voice
> and let Israel go? I do not know the Lord, and
> moreover, I will not let Israel go. (Exodus 5:2)

He said not only would he not let the Israelites go to worship God, but he would give the Israelites much harder work to do, because they had free time on their hands to go worship. Before this, the Egyptian taskmasters would provide the straw needed for the Israelite slaves to make bricks. The Pharaoh ordered the taskmasters to stop giving the Israelites straw. The Israelites must now find their own straw to make bricks, yet the amount of bricks demanded of the Israelites to make would not be reduced. Moses complained to God and asked him why he told him to tell the Pharaoh to let his people go worship, which resulted in the Pharaoh punishing the Israelites. God said to Moses that he would now see what God would do to the Pharaoh for being harsh to the Israelites. He told Moses to tell the Israelites that God would free them from being slaves to the Egyptians, he would give them their own land, and he would be their God (Exodus 5:1–23, 6:1–8).

Moses was eighty years old and his brother Aaron was eighty-three when they spoke with the Pharaoh. God said to Moses,

> See, I have made you like God to Pharaoh,
> and your brother Aaron shall be your prophet.
> You shall speak all that I command you, and your
> brother Aaron shall tell Pharaoh to let the people
> go out of his land. (Exodus 7:1–2)

Moses went with his brother Aaron to Pharaoh and said, "God said: Let my people go." The Pharaoh refused. Moses threw the staff he had in his hand on the ground, and it became a snake. The Pharaoh had his magicians do the same thing. However, Moses's snake attacked and ate all the magicians' snakes. The Pharaoh was surprised at this but still would not let the Israelites go. Moses said to Pharaoh that he would come back again and demand in the name of God that the Pharaoh let the Israelites go. Each time the Pharaoh said "no," God would send a plague on the Egyptians until they could take it no longer and finally let the Israelites go.

The first time Pharaoh said no, God had Moses turn the water of the Nile River into blood. All the fish died, and the river stank. Pharaoh's magicians were also able to do this with their secret arts. The second time Pharaoh refused to let the Israelites Go, God had Moses send a plague of frogs into Egypt. Frogs got into the people's houses and were everywhere. The Pharaoh's magicians were able to do this too. The third time the Pharaoh said no, God had Moses send a plague of gnats (little flies) all over the Egyptians. Pharaoh's magicians could not do this, or any of the miracles that Moses did from this point on. The fourth time the Pharaoh said no, God had Moses send a plague of flies onto the Egyptians. The fifth time the Pharaoh said no, all the livestock of the Egyptians died (cows, horses, camels, etc.), but the livestock of the Israelites were untouched. The sixth time the Pharaoh said no, God sent a plague of boils and sores on the skin of the Egyptian people. The Pharaoh's magicians could not stand before Moses because they too were covered with painful boils. The seventh time the Pharaoh said no, God had Moses send huge hail onto Egypt that killed any person or animal that was outside. The eighth time the Pharaoh said no, God had Moses send a plague of locust (grasshoppers) all over Egypt, but they did not bother the Israelites. The ninth time the Pharaoh said no, God had Moses send three days of complete darkness over Egypt so they couldn't see anything, but the Israelites had light in their homes. With each plague sent by God, the Pharaoh would tell Moses that he sinned against God and he would let the Israelites go if Moses stopped the plague. Each time Moses asked God to stop the plague, which God would do, the Pharaoh's heart would become hardened, and he would once again refuse to let the Israelites go (Exodus chapters 7, 8, 9, and 10).

THE PASSOVER

The final plague was the worst one. God had Moses tell the Pharaoh that if he did not let the Israelites go, God would kill the firstborn child and animal of everyone in Egypt. The Pharaoh said he would not let the Israelites go. God told each Israelite family to kill a lamb and paint a stripe of its blood across the doorway of each house. This way, God would know which houses are those of the Israelites, and he would pass over that house and not kill the firstborn person or animal of that house. At midnight, God killed the firstborn of every family that did not have the lamb's blood over its doorpost, including the Pharaoh's first son.

> And there was a great cry in Egypt, for there
> was not a house where someone was not dead.
> (Exodus 12:30)

The Israelites had lamb's blood over all their doorposts, so their firstborn children and animals were spared. The Egyptians were so upset that the Pharaoh finally told the Israelites that they could leave Egypt (Exodus 12:1–32).

THE EXODUS AND THE PARTING OF THE RED SEA

A few days after the Israelites left Egypt, the Pharaoh changed his mind about allowing them to leave. He gathered his army and chased after the Israelites, intending to capture them and once again turn them into slaves of the Egyptians. The Egyptian army surrounded the Israelites on three sides. On the fourth side was the Red Sea. God told Moses to raise his arms in the air. When he did, the Red Sea parted, and the Israelites crossed over the dry sea floor with huge walls of water on each side. When the Israelites crossed the Red

Sea, the Egyptian army began to cross the floor of the Red Sea after them. When the Israelites were safely on the other side and all the Egyptian army was on the dry sea floor, God told Moses to raise his arms in the air again. When he did, the walls of water of the Red Sea came crashing down on the Egyptian army and drowned the entire army, saving then Israelites. Finally, God saved the Israelites from being slaves of the Egyptians, and he moved them out of Egypt after being slaves there for 430 years (Exodus 12:33–42, Exodus 14:1–31).

After being saved by God from the Egyptian army, Moses and the Israelites were walking around outside of Egypt, waiting for God to show them where he would have them live. They got hungry, so God rained down bread from heaven each day like snowflakes. It was called manna, and the people would gather it up each day and eat it. The people also wanted meat to eat, so each evening God made birds called quail fly down and land in the Israelites' camp for the people to cook and eat. When the people got thirsty, God had Moses strike a rock with a stick that he had in his hand, and water would flow out of the rock for the people to drink (Exodus chapters 16 and 17).

GOD GIVES MOSES AND THE ISRAELITES THE TEN COMMANDMENTS

One day God told Moses to climb to the top of Mt. Sinai. There, God wrote the Ten Commandments personally, engraving his words on both sides of the two stone tablets. The Ten Commandments are ten rules that God insists that all of us follow. The Ten Commandments are the following:

1. I am the Lord your God. You shall have no other gods before me.
2. You shall not make and worship a carved image.
3. You shall not take the name of the Lord your God in vain (don't curse).
4. Remember the Sabbath day (Sunday) and keep it holy.
5. Honor your father and mother and you will have a long life.
6. You shall not murder.

7. You shall not commit adultery.
8. You shall not steal.
9. You shall not bear false witness against your neighbor (do not lie).
10. You shall not covet your neighbor's house; you shall not covet your neighbor's wife, or his male servant, or his female servant, or his ox, or his donkey, or anything that is your neighbor's (Exodus 20:1–17).

God then gave the Hebrews a collection of rules and laws that said what he did and did not want them to do. This is called the Law. God also told the Israelites where he was going to have them settle down and live. God told them to make an Ark (a very fancy box) where they would store the stone tablets with the Ten Commandments on them. This is called the Ark of the Covenant (Exodus chapters 20–31).

THE ISRAELITES REBEL AGAINST GOD

Moses was up on Mt. Sinai for several days talking with God and getting the Ten Commandments from him. The people went to Moses's brother, Aaron, and said (summary), "Why is Moses taking so long? Maybe something bad happened to him. He might not come back. We want you to make us new gods that we can follow."

Aaron agreed with their request. He told the Israelites to give him any gold that they had, which they did. Aaron melted the gold down and made a gold statue of a calf. All the people started to worship the golden calf as a god and said that it was the golden calf that saved the Israelites from the Egyptians and brought them out of Egypt, not God. Meanwhile, God told Moses on Mt. Sinai what the Israelites were doing. God asked Moses if he wanted God to wipe out all the Israelites because they were so bad and start over with a new nation from Moses's descendants. Moses told God not to kill them. God listened to Moses about this because God and Moses were friends. Moses came down from the mountain and was furious at the Israelites. He smashed the two stone tablets with the Ten Commandments out of anger, and he melted the golden calf that the people made. Moses asked who was on the side of God, and all the sons of the Tribe of Levi stepped forward, signifying they were on the side of God. Moses had them kill three thousand people who rejected God and instead chose to make a golden calf as their god to follow. This act of loyalty to God by the Tribe of Levi helped make it so that God later chose members of only the Tribe of Levi to be the priests for the Nation of Israel. God also sent a plague against the people who rejected God and followed a golden calf that they made as their god (Exodus 32:1–35).

Moses made a tent that he would go into and talk with God. When Moses would go into the tent, God would come down in the form of a cloud stand at the entrance of the tent and talk with Moses.

> Thus, the Lord used to speak with Moses face to face, as a man speaks to his friend. (Exodus 33:11)

Moses would then tell the Israelites what God said. God had Moses cut two new stone tablets, and God rewrote the Ten Commandments on those tablets to replace the ones Moses smashed out of anger when the Israelites were worshipping the golden calf as their god.

THE BOOK OF LEVITICUS

In the book of Leviticus, God gave the Israelite people and the Israelite priests many laws and rules that he wanted them to follow in their lives. (Remember—in the Old Testament, God gave the people many laws and rules to follow so they would know right from wrong. If they followed them perfectly they would be sinless, but they were too weak to follow them perfectly.) In this summary, God's laws that would come to be a major theme later on throughout the Bible will be presented.

LAWS FOR ALL ANIMAL OFFERINGS

God would only accept as a sacrifice an animal without blemish, and its blood must be spilled against the sides of the altar (Leviticus chapter 1). This reveals the standard for the only kind of sacrifice God would later accept to save mankind from their sins: an unblemished (sinless) man, whose blood must be spilled. Jesus was the only sinless man who would ever live, and therefore, he is the only one who could have been accepted by God as a sacrifice for us. And in this sacrifice, his blood must be spilled (crucifixion). For all the sin offerings of animals, they would only atone for sins that were unintentional or accidental. They could not atone for any intentional sin by people. Only Jesus can do that.

CLEAN AND UNCLEAN ANIMALS

God spoke to Moses and Aaron and told them which animals were clean and which ones were unclean. This became the basis of Jewish dietary laws, which would come into play in other parts of the Bible such as the book of Daniel and the New Testament. God forbade the Israelites from eating the following animals because he deemed them to be unclean: the camel, the rock badger, the pig, any seafood that does not have fins or scales, vultures, kites, falcons, ravens, the ostrich, nighthawks, seagulls, hawks, owls, storks, herons, hoopoes, and bats. They may eat locusts, crickets, and grasshoppers, but no other winged insects that walk on all fours. If a person ate these, they would be unclean until evening. God also forbade them to eat rats, mice, and lizards. No one was allowed to eat a clean animal that died on its own from sickness or any other reason (Leviticus chapter 11).

Male children were to be circumcised eight days after birth. Laws about how to handle people who had leprosy were given. Laws about hygiene were presented to the people. Laws about presenting a variety of sacrifices to God by both the priests and offerings by the people were detailed. People were forbidden to eat the blood of any animal. God said this is because the life of living things resides in its blood. This may also explain why Jesus was required to shed his blood for us (Leviticus chapters 12–17).

LAWS ABOUT SEXUAL RELATIONS

God gave the people his laws concerning sexual relations. He forbade the people from viewing any close relative naked. There should not be sexual relations with multiple people. They were forbidden to commit adultery. It was forbidden to offer their children as sacrifices to the false god Molech, which was a profanity to God. Men were forbidden from lying with men, and sex with an animal was forbidden (Leviticus chapter 18).

> And the Lord spoke to Moses, saying, "Speak to all the congregation of the people of Israel and say to them, You shall be holy, for I the Lord God am holy. Every one of you shall revere his mother and his father, and you shall keep my Sabbaths: I am the Lord your God. Do not turn to idols or make for yourselves any gods of cast metal: I am the Lord your God." (Leviticus 19:1–4)

LOVE YOUR NEIGHBOR AS YOURSELF

God gave his people the following laws on how to treat other people: When farming, do not take everything that grows. Leave some remnants of food in your fields for the poor and the travelers. Do not steal or deal falsely with others. Do not lie to others or take false oaths. Do not oppress others. Pay others immediately for work they have done for you. Do not take advantage of the deaf and the blind, but fear God. Do not be unfair or unjust in court. Do not favor the rich and judge against the poor just based on money. You must judge others righteously. Do not slander other people. Do not hate others in your heart, but reason frankly with them. To do otherwise would be a sin.

> You shall not take vengeance or bear a
> grudge against the sons of your own people, but
> you shall love your neighbor as yourself: I am the
> Lord. (Leviticus 19:18)

God forbade the people from turning to mediums or necromancers. People were forbidden from having false weights, balances, or measurements to cheat others.

CHILD SACRIFICE IS FORBIDDEN

God stated that anyone found in Israel giving a child to Molech would be stoned to death by the people of the land (that practice was giving a burnt offering of a child to this false God, Molech). God himself would set his face against any person that did this and he would cut that person off from his people. If anyone closed his eyes and did not put to death the person who sacrificed a child, then God would turn his face against the man who overlooked it and his entire clan, and he would cut them off from among their people (Leviticus chapter 20). As you will see, this will come into play in a big way in future chapters. The people of Israel will fall into the grave sin of sacrificing children to false gods and demons. This is a major reason why Israel will have to be punished severely by God in the future in the Old Testament.

DO NOT DO THE PAGAN PRACTICES OF THE OTHER PEOPLES AROUND YOU

God instructed the Israelites to keep all his rules and statutes that he was now giving them when they entered the land of Canaan where he was bringing them. If they did not, they would be expelled from the land. He gave them this clear warning:

And you shall not walk in the customs of the nation that I am driving out before you, for they did all these things, and therefore I detested them. (Leviticus 20:23)

This is the major reason why God will punish the Israelites in future chapters. They will fall into the horribly sinful practices of the pagan peoples around them, and they will stop following God and his laws. It will lead to them being exiled, as God said would be the punishment for this, and their land destroyed (Leviticus 20:22–26).

LAW ABOUT THE SABBATH

> Six days shall work be done, but on the seventh day is a Sabbath of solemn rest, a holy convocation. You shall do no work. It is a Sabbath to the Lord in all your dwelling places. (Leviticus 23:3)

As you will later see, the Pharisees used this against Jesus in an attempt to condemn him, accusing him of doing work on the Sabbath because he was found healing the sick on that day, which they said was unlawful. Jesus responded that it is lawful to do good on *any* day, including the Sabbath

LAW OF BLASPHEMY

There was a fight between two young men in the Israelite camp. During the fight, one man cursed God (blasphemed). The people brought this to Moses, and Moses inquired of God about how this should be handled. God told Moses to tell the people,

> Whoever curses his God shall bear his sin. Whoever blasphemes the name of the Lord shall surely be put to death. All the congregation shall

stone him. The sojourner as well as the native, when he blasphemes the Name, shall be put to death. (Leviticus 24:15–16)

This is important. In the New Testament, what the Pharisees eventually used to condemn Jesus to death was they claimed that he blasphemed, and this is the actual account:

The high priest asked Jesus, "Are you the Christ, the Son of the Blessed?" And Jesus said, "I am, and you will see the Son of Man seated at the right hand of Power and coming with the clouds of heaven." (Mark 14:61–62)

For this, they charged Jesus with breaking the law of blasphemy and condemned him to death. On closer inspection, Jesus did not curse God; he answered their question, and he did so truthfully. Additionally, the Pharisees did not kill him by the prescribed punishment by God for this, which was stoning. They crucified him.

The book of Leviticus gives details on being good to the poor and how God will bless the crops and protect the Israelites from their enemies if they are obedient to his commands, and he will walk among them and be their God and they will be his people. But if they turn away from him and refuse to turn back, they will suffer increasing disciplines from God until they finally repent and return to him. He gave them clear warnings that if they refuse to stop rebelling against God and his ways and persist in worshipping pagan gods and their dreadful practices, God will eventually allow them to be conquered by the horrible pagan people whose sinful practices they idolize in place of following God. However, after suffering greatly under the hands of their pagan destroyers whose ways they once worshipped, if they repent and turn back to God, he will show mercy on them and rescue them (Leviticus chapter 26).

THE BOOK OF NUMBERS

Remember that the nation of Israel started with the twelve sons of Jacob. Over 430 years later, by the time that Moses saved the Israelites from the Egyptians, the Israelite people were numerous. God told Moses to take a census of all the men age twenty and older, who were able to go to war. The number of men was 603,550. That did not take into account any females or males under the age of twenty (Numbers 1:1–46). The tribe of Levi were excluded from the census of men able to go to war. Instead, God assigned the men of the tribe of Levi to guard over the tabernacle of testimony and were assigned to later be priests under Aaron (Numbers 1:47–54, 3:1–39).

God would hover over the tent of the tabernacle that was set up in the midst of the Israelites. In the day God hovered over the tent in the form of a cloud. At night God would hover over the tent in the form of fire. As long as the cloud of God sat over the tent, the people camped and stayed in that spot. When the cloud moved, the people would follow the cloud. Where it stopped, that was where they would set up camp until it moved again (Numbers 9:15–23). One day God told Moses to send twelve men, one prince from each tribe of Israel, into the land of Canaan to act as spies. They were instructed by God through Moses to find out...

> What kind of land is it? Are the people living there strong or weak, few or many? Is the country in which they live good or bad? Are the towns in which the dwell open or fortified? Is the soil fertile or barren, wooded or clear? (Numbers 13:17–20)

God did *not* instruct the Israelites to check out the inhabitants of the land that he was going to give them, and if they thought they were too strong for God to move them out, they could decide to abandon God's plan to give them the land.

It was a test by God to see if they would trust him. Canaan was the land that God intended to give to the Israelites to live in.

However, it was presently inhabited by people who God said were evil and sinful (the Canaanites). They would have to be moved out of the land for the Israelites to enter it and live there as God wanted them to.

When the spies returned after gathering information about the land of Canaan for forty days, this was their report: All of them said the land of Canaan was very good land, flowing with milk and honey. However, all except one said the people there were strong, the cities were fortified, and there were men of giant height living there. One of the spies, named Caleb, however, told the people that they should enter and seize the land of Canaan, and he assured them that the Israelites would be able to do so. The other spies kept insisting to the people that they would fail in their attempt to take the land of Canaan as God instructed them to do because the people living there were too strong (Numbers 13:1–33).

The Israelites decided to believe that God could not or would not help them defeat the people that lived in Canaan, even though God was the one who told them that he would give them the land of Canaan. They became angry at Moses and God, not remembering that God could save them from anyone that he wanted to because he was all-powerful. These were the same people that witnessed God do many miracles against the Pharaoh in Egypt. Because the Israelites revolted against God's instructions to them to take over the land of Canaan for themselves, God told them to turn around and not enter the land he promised them. Instead, God had them wander around the wilderness for forty years until all the people who rebelled against God's instructions to take the land of Canaan died off. Their children were the ones who would be given the land promised to them by God. Some of them revolted against this too. Instead of following God's instructions to remain in the wilderness and not enter Canaan, some of the Israelites on their own went against what God said and tried to take the land of the Canaanites by force. God was not with them, so they were soundly defeated (Numbers 14:1–45).

While the Israelites were in the land of Shittim during their forty years of wandering, they began to intermarry with the daughters of Moab. The Moabites invited the Israelites to the sacrifices of their gods, and some of the Israelites began to worship the gods of

Moab. Israel became yoked to Baal of Peor. God got very angry with Israel because of this. God instructed Moses to hang any of the men who were involved with Baal worship. A plague on the Israelites was released for their worship of Baal that killed twenty-four thousand people. This is the first time that Baal worship appears in the Bible. It will become a major issue between the Israelites and God in the future generations (Numbers chapter 25).

One day the Israelites were thirsty, and they complained to Moses about it. God told Moses to strike a rock with his staff once, and water would come out of it for the people to drink. Moses was angry with the people for complaining about the water, because they complained to him about everything for decades. He yelled at them and then slammed his staff down on the rock, and water came out of it for the people to drink. God told Moses that because he made it look to the people that God was angry with them when he was not, he would not let Moses enter the land that God was giving to the Israelites. He would be able to see it, but he would die before entering it. God told Moses that an Israelite named Joshua would take over his role as leader of the Israelites when he died. Finally, after forty years in the wilderness, the Israelites entered the land of Canaan. This later became the country of Israel, which God had promised them (Numbers 20:1–12).

THE BOOK OF DEUTERONOMY

The book of Deuteronomy goes into more detail about Moses and the Israelites while they were in the wilderness before God gave them a land to live in. The book of Deuteronomy gives the Hebrews additional directions that God wanted them to live by. For example, God stated what the greatest commandment is:

> You shall love the Lord your God with all your heart, with all your soul, and with all your might. (Deuteronomy 6:5)

He told the Israelites that he would bless them if they follow him. God informed the Israelites,

> It is the Lord your God you shall fear. Him you shall serve and by his name you shall swear. (Deuteronomy 6:13)

> You shall not put the Lord your God to the test. (Deuteronomy 7:16)
> Man does not live by bread alone, but by every word that comes from the mouth of the Lord. (Deuteronomy 8:3)

(These three scriptures in Deuteronomy were what Jesus would later quote to defend himself against Satan's attempts to tempt him to sin in the wilderness in the gospels.)

God reminded the Israelites that he took care of them well when they were in the wilderness before they would come into the land of Canaan that he would soon give to them. He told them that when they become successful, to remember that it is God who blessed them and allowed them to be successful. Also, God told them not to think that they were getting good things because they were superior people. They were not; they had all sinned, like everyone else had. They were getting good things because he said, "I love being kind to those who love me. If you love me, I will take care of you well, give you good things, and give you everything that you need" (paraphrased).

God also chose them as his special people due to a covenant he made with their fathers, Abraham, Isaac, and Jacob (Deuteronomy chapters 1–8).

God said do not worship other gods because there are no other gods; he is the only God. Some of his messages to his people included the following:

> [Summary] I am the only God, and the rest are false, and it makes me very upset when people worship false gods instead of me. If you see peo-

ple that are poor or are in need of something, you need to help these people and be happy about helping them, and I will bless you for it. You must be honest and truthful when dealing with people. Do not lie about other people.

God gave the Israelites many, many other laws, rules, or directions to follow in the book of Deuteronomy (Deuteronomy chapters 9–30). (Remember, in the Old Testament, God gave us the law to teach us right from wrong. The Law by itself was unable to keep us sinless or save us once we have sinned, because people we were too weak to follow them all the time.)

In the end of the book of Deuteronomy, God took Moses to the top of Mount Nebo. He showed Moses the land that he would now give to the Israelites to live in. Moses saw it, but he was not allowed to go into the land because he disobeyed God by misrepresenting him as angry toward the Israelite people when God was not. Moses then died, he was buried, and Joshua took over Moses's position of leader of the Israelites (Deuteronomy chapters 31–34).

THE BOOK OF JOSHUA

After Moses died, God appointed Joshua to take over as the leader of the Israelites. God had Joshua lead the army of Israel to take land of Canaan from evil groups of people that lived there and turn it into the land that they would live in. In order to possess the land of Canaan as God wanted them to, they had to conquer the Canaanites, Hittites, Hivites, Perizzites, Girgashites, Amorites, and the Jebusites who lived there. Joshua and the Israelites came to the river Jordan and had to cross it. God made it so that the river parted and allowed the Israelites cross it, as he did formerly with the Red Sea (Joshua chapter 3).

One of the cities that God wanted the Israelites to take for themselves was called Jericho. The city of Jericho was surrounded by a big wall. God told the Israelites to march around the entire city, once each day for six days, and the priests who were carrying the Ark of the Covenant (the box with the Ten Commandments in it) would blow their horns as they walked around the city. On the seventh day, they would march around it seven times with the priests blowing their horns. After they stopped marching, the people were told to let out a loud shout, and God would knock Jericho's walls down for them. The Israelites did what God told them to do, the walls fell down, and they captured he city to live in as God instructed them to (Joshua 6:1–27).

God led Joshua and the Israelite troops. When they followed God's instructions, they conquered and took over cities and lands to live in through the power of God. When they did not listen to God, they were defeated in battle. God at times did miracles in the battles of the Israelites, such as making the sun and the moon stand still until Israel took vengeance on its enemies (Joshua 10:12–13). Many lands and peoples were conquered by the Israelites as they took the land that God promised them. After the Israelites conquered land and moved into it, Joshua divided this land among the twelve tribes of Israel, which were founded by Jacob's twelve sons. When this was accomplished, Israel's leader, Joshua, died at the age of 110 years old. The country of Israel was finally established to the descendants of Abraham, as God had promised him (Joshua chapters 7–24).

CHAPTER 6

THE BOOK OF JUDGES

U nder Joshua, when the Israelites were conquering land to turn it into the country of Israel in which they would live, God told them to drive out all the people that they conquered because they were evil. The Israelites disobeyed God and did not do this. They let some of the conquered people stay in the land and live with them. God warned them, telling them that these people "shall become thorns in your sides, and their gods shall be a snare to you" (Judges 2:3).

After Joshua died, Israelites disobedience to God became worse. The Israelites began to follow the evil ways of these people that they did not evict as God instructed them to. Many Israelites stopped following God and started to follow false gods. This included following the Baals, who required human sacrifice as part of their worship, and the Ashtaroth, which included sexual fertility acts in worship. The Israelites were doing many evil things that God told them not to do, and they ignored God when he told them to stop doing these things. God therefore became angry with the Israelites. God gave them over to plundering people, who conquered and mistreated them. God was against the Israelites due to their rebellion against him, so everything they did in battle failed and they were in terrible distress (Judges 2:11–15).

God eventually had compassion on the Israelites, and he wanted to help them. He raised up *judges*—who were mighty, often-supernatural warriors—to save the Israelites from the people who conquered them. The problem was, after each time the judges saved the Israelites, the Israelites began to act evil again very quickly and turn away from God. This caused God to remove his protection from them, and without God's help, other nations conquered them. They would cry out to God, he would have compassion on them and save them with a judge, and then they would soon become disobedient again. This cycle happened repeatedly (Judges 2:16–23). God said that one of the reasons why he allowed other countries to conquer Israel when Israel abandoned following God was,

> They were for the testing of Israel, to know
> whether Israel would obey the commandments
> of the Lord, which he commanded their fathers
> by the hand of Moses. (Judges 3:4–6)

Here are the stories of some of the judges that God raised up to save the Israelites. Because the Israelites "forgot the Lord their God and served the Baals and the Ashtaroth" (Judges 3:7), God allowed them to be conquered by the Mesopotamians. They were ruled by them for eight years and cried out to God for help. He raised up a judge named Othniel.

> The Spirit of the Lord was upon him, and
> he judged Israel. (Judges 3:10)

Othniel went to war with the Mesopotamians, conquered them, freed the Israelites, who then had peace for forty years.

Othniel then died, and the Israelites once again did what was evil in the sight of the Lord. The Lord allowed the armies of the King of Moab to conquer the Israelites for eighteen years. The Israelites complained to God, so he raised a judge named Ehud. Ehud personally assassinated the King of Moab. He then he led an Israelite rebellion against the Israelite captors, the Moabites. The Lord allowed the Israelites to win their battles, and they became free again (Judges 3:12–30).

Once again, the Israelites acted evil and were conquered by the Philistines. They cried out to God, who raised up a judge named

Shamgar. In one battle, Shamgar killed six hundred Philistines with an ox bone, and he eventually freed Israel (Judges 3:31).

Once free, the Israelites did not learn their lesson, "and the people of Israel again did what was evil in the sight of the Lord" (Judges 4:1). God allowed the Israelites to be conquered by a king named Jaban, the king of Canaan, for twenty years because of this. God rose up two judges: a woman named Deborah and a man named Barak. Deborah was a prophetess.

> She used to sit under the palm of Deborah
> between Ramah and Bethel in the hill country of
> Ephraim, and the people of Israel came up to her
> for judgment. (Judges 4:5)

She summoned a man named Barak and told him that God said he needed to gather ten thousand Hebrew men. She (Deborah) would draw out the general of the Canaanite army, named Sisera, and Barak as leader of these ten thousand Hebrews would conquer the Canaanites. Barak said he would only do this if Deborah went with him. She told Barak she would go with him, but he needed to know that a woman would get the glory for defeating general Sisera, not him. Barak agreed. God was with the Israelites in Battle. Under Barak as leader, the Israelites routed the huge and well-armed army of the Canaanites. General Sisera escaped on foot and hid. A woman named Jael tricked and killed General Sisera. These two Judges, Barak and Deborah, helped the Israelites become free from their oppressors, and they were at peace for forty years (Judges chapters 4 and 5).

Over time, the Israelites again did things that made God angry. He allowed the Midianites to overpower Israel and rule over them in a cruel way for seven years. The Midianites would routinely raid the farms of the Israelites, taking all their crops and livestock so they had no food. The Israelites cried out to God to help them. God heard their cries (Judges 6:1–10). He rose up one of the most famous judges named Gideon to save them. Gideon was from the weakest tribe of Israel, and he was the weakest one in his tribe.

63

God appeared to Gideon and told him that he was with him, that Gideon would be a mighty man of valor, and God was sending him to defeat their Midianite oppressors. Gideon found this hard to believe because he was shy and weak. God instructed Gideon to tear down an altar made to Baal and the Ashtaroth and replace it with an altar of God. Gideon did this. The townspeople wanted him put to death for doing this. Gideon's father said,

> Will you contend for Baal? Or will you save him? Whoever contends for him shall be put to death by morning. If he is a god, let him contend for himself, because his altar has been broken down. (Judges 6:32)

> The breaking down of the altar to Baal and the Ashtaroth caused Gideon to get respect from his people. Gideon was now filled with the Spirit of God. The people of many tribes of Israel came out and followed Gideon. (Judges 6:33–35)

Gideon asked God if he could put God to two tests, to make sure it was actually God who was appearing to Gideon and telling him to save Israel. God agreed to let Gideon put him to two tests, and he passed both of the tests. Once Gideon was convinced that it was God that was telling him to defeat the Midianites, he agreed to do whatever God told him to do (Gideon 6:36–40). Gideon gathered thirty-two thousand men of Israel to fight the Midianites, who had a much larger force of soldiers. God said that Israel had too many soldiers for the battle. If they beat the Midianites, they would think they did this because they were great soldiers in sufficient number, not because God was the one that won the battle. God instructed Gideon to tell the soldiers that if there were any of them that did not want to be there, they could go home. Twenty-two thousand soldiers left and went home, leaving just ten thousand to fight against the Midianites. God then told Gideon that he still had too many soldiers. God told Gideon to send the soldiers to the river to drink. There were 9,700 who scooped up water in their hands to drink, while 300 men lapped up the water as a dog drinks. God told Gideon to send the 9,700 soldiers that scooped up water in their hands home. Gideon would use only the 300 soldiers to fight the huge Midianite army. Now, there would be no way that the Israelites would believe they could defeat the Midianites just because they were "great" soldiers. To defeat the Midianites, the 300 Israelites needed a miracle from God (Judges 7:1–8).

God told Gideon to give each of his soldiers a horn and divide them into three companies of one hundred soldiers each. When Gideon gave the signal, the three hundred soldiers blew their horns and yelled,

> A sword for the Lord and for Gideon! (Judges 7:20).

As soon as they yelled this, God caused confusion among all the Midianite troops, and they began to attack each other. The entire Midianite army wiped themselves out. Gideon's army of three hundred did not even have to fight: God did all the fighting for them. Once again the Israelites were free (Judges chapters 7 and 8).

After Gideon's death, God sent several Judges to help Israel after they *once again turned (italics added)* away from God and had bad things happen to them. One of the judges was the most famous judge of all named Samson. He actually was not famous; he was infamous. He was well-known for doing bad things. However, God used Samson's unruly behaviors as a tool to defeat the Philistines for the Israelites, which was Samson's purpose as a judge.

Because Israel did evil things and refused to follow God's warnings to stop, God allowed them to be conquered by the Philistines for forty years. God came to a woman of the tribe of the Danites, who had no children. He told her that she would have a son and he would save Israel from the Philistines. This child was to be a Nazarite to God, and he was forbidden to cut his hair. (The Nazirite vow obliged the person to abstain from strong drink or cutting his hair.) The woman had a son and she named him Samson (Judges 13:1–25).

The Spirit of God was within Samson, and this caused him to become powerful as he got older. Once, Samson was attacked by a huge lion. With God's strength in him, he picked up the lion and tore it to pieces. Samson got extremely strong because of God, but he did not always do what God told him to do. He was mischievous, and he would start fights with groups of men when he should not have. In one of his fits of rage, he set fire to the fields of the rulers of the Israelites, the Philistines. His own townspeople tried to capture him to turn him over to their enemy, the Philistines, to prevent punishment from the Philistines for the things Samson did to them. Samson allowed the men of Judah to capture him and deliver him to the Philistines. When he was in the presence of the Philistines, he easily broke out of his restraints. He then picked up the bone of a dead donkey nearby and killed one thousand Philistine men with his great strength. Samson judged Israel in the days of the Philistines for twenty years (Judges chapters 14 and 15).

Samson was engaging in inappropriate relationships with women (Judges 16:1–3). At one point, he was in love with a woman named Delilah, and she was a troublemaker like Samson. Samson's enemies, the Philistines, came up to her and said they would give her 1,100 pieces of silver if she could find out the secret of Samson's strength so they could capture him. Delilah later said to Samson,

> Please tell me where your strength lies, and
> how you might be bound, that one could subdue
> you. (Judges 16:6)

He told her that if she tied him up with seven fresh bowstrings that had not been dried, he would lose his strength. She tied him up with fresh bowstrings when he was sleeping, but he still had his strength. The same thing happened with new ropes that were not used, and with other fabrics, but they did not work. Delilah became upset that he was lying to her. She bugged him every day to tell him the secret of his strength. He finally said that if his head was shaved, all of God's power would leave him. One day when Samson fell asleep, Delilah shaved part of his head. When she did this, all of God's strength left him. She yelled for his enemies, the Philistines. They came in and grabbed him. He tried to get away, but he no longer had any super strength. They tied him up in chains, blinded him, and locked him in a prison and forced him to grind grain (Judges 16:7–21).

Over time, Samson's hair began to grow back. God gave Samson his power through his unshaved head. The Philistines had a party in a large building to worship their false god, Dagon. They offered sacrifices to Dagon and thanked him for delivering Samson their enemy into their hands. During the Philistine group worship of Dagon, they brought Samson out to make fun of him to entertain the crowd. There were several thousand Philistines in the large building. Samson found his way to two pillars that held up the building. Then Samson called to the Lord and said,

> O Lord God, please remember me and please strengthen me only this once, O God, that I may be avenged on the Philistines for my two eyes. (Judges 16:28)

Samson put his hand on the pillars to the right and the left of him. He said to God,

> Let me die with the Philistines. (Judges 16:30)

Samson pushed each pillar with all his strength, and the building fell down and killed all the Philistines in it along with Samson. He killed more of the Philistines that oppressed Israel in this one event than he did during the rest of his life. His family took Samson's body and buried him. Israel was once again free and at peace. There were other judges after Samson, and Israel went through periods of good and evil, war and peace in the time of the judges (Judges chapters 17 to 21).

THE BOOK OF RUTH

The book of Ruth takes place during the times of the judges, so it is included in this chapter of the judges. During the time when the judges ruled, there was a famine in the land. There was a family consisting of a father named Elimelech, a mother named Naomi, and two sons named Mahlon and Chilion. They were from Bethlehem in the land of Judah but moved to the country of Moab. While in Moab, Elimelech, the father, died. Her two sons later got married. Their wives' names were Oprah and Ruth. Within ten years of living in the country of Moab, both sons died. The mother-in-law and both daughters-in-law were now all widows (Ruth 1:1–5).

Naomi heard that the Lord had visited his people back in her home of Judah and given them food. She and her two daughters-in-law set out to move back to Judah because of this. Naomi instructed her daughters-in-law, Oprah and Ruth, to return to the homes of their original families. They were from the country of Moab, which they were now leaving. They refused, choosing to remain living with Naomi. Naomi pleaded with them to return to their families. She told them that she has no more sons, and if they stayed with her, they would deprive themselves of having a husband and children for the remainder of their lives. They were all sad about this. Oprah decided to leave Naomi and return home to her original family. Ruth, however, was determined to remain living with Naomi as a daughter of hers. Ruth was a Moabite and told Naomi that Naomi's people (Israelites living in Judah) would become her people and Naomi's God would become Ruth's God. When Naomi saw Ruth's determination to remain with her, she allowed it (Ruth 1:6–18).

Naomi and Ruth returned to Naomi's home of Bethlehem. A relative of Naomi's deceased husband was a worthy man named Boaz. One day Ruth was gleaning ears of grain in the field that belonged to Boaz. Boaz took a liking to Ruth and was very kind to her as his servant. Upon Naomi's suggestion, Ruth asked Boaz if he could be her redeemer, since he was in position to be. Boaz told her he would like to be her redeemer, but there was one man whose position to do this was ahead of his. If the other man was willing to redeem her, she would need to go with him. If he was not willing to redeem her, Boaz would redeem her (Ruth 2:1–23, 3:11–8).

Boaz approached this other man and explained the situation of redeeming Ruth. The other man said, "I cannot redeem her for myself, lest I impair my own inheritance. Take my right of redemption for yourself, for I cannot redeem her." Boaz then took Ruth as his wife. Naomi was very happy with this. Ruth could have left and returned to her home of Moab when she became a widow. But she loved Naomi and became like a daughter to her. Ruth and Boaz had a son whom they named Obed. Naomi now happily had a grandson. Obed was no ordinary grandson. He became the father of Jesse, who became the father of David, who would become the greatest king in the history of Israel (Ruth 4:1–22). One of David's descendants, who is also one of Obed's descendants, would be Jesus Christ. None of this would have happened if Ruth did not decide to stay with Naomi when their husbands died and become a daughter to her.

CHAPTER 7

ISRAEL'S FIRST KINGS

There was a man named Samuel, who God made in to a prophet. A prophet is a person who God tells things to, and that person then tells the people what God said. One day the Israelites were at war with the Philistines, and the Philistines defeated the Israelites in battle. When they did, they took the Ark of the Covenant, which was the fancy box that held the two tablets with the Ten Commandments on them.

The Philistines took the Ark of God and put it in the temple of their false god, Dagon, next to a big statue of Dagon. When the Philistines woke up the next day, they found the statue of Dagon knocked down on its face before the Ark of God. They put Dagon's statue back up, but the next day they found it on the ground again before the Ark of God with its hands and head cut off (God did this to show them that he is the only true God). The Philistines who lived near where they were storing the Ark of God broke out in tumors. The Philistines moved the Ark of God to the city of Gath, and the people there too broke out in tumors and they panicked. They then moved it to the city of Ekron, and the same thing happened. The Philistines decided to not harden their hearts against the God of Israel (God) like the Egyptians did who were struck by plagues from God. They said,

They have brought around to us the Ark
of the God of Israel to kill us and our people.

> Send away the Ark of the God of Israel, and let it
> return to its own place, that it may not kill us and
> our own people, for there was a deathly panic
> throughout the whole city. (1 Samuel 5:10–11)

The Philistines sent the Ark of God, the beautiful and richly decorated container containing the two tablets with the Ten Commandments in it, back to the Israelites. They filled it with gold as a guilt offering to God, hoping it would stop his anger toward them (1 Samuel chapters 4–6).

At this time, there were still judges over Israel, like Gideon and Samson. God made Samuel the prophet a judge over Israel. When Samuel became old, he made his own two sons judges over Israel. Samuel's sons were not honest as judges. They took bribes and perverted justice to benefit themselves. The Israelites became upset over this. The Israelites came to Samuel and said, "Instead of judges, give us a king to rule over us." This was against what God wanted. God wanted to be the only king over Israel. However, God told Samuel that if the Israelites want a king, they could have a king. He warned them, though, that they would have problems with a king. The Israelites told God and Samuel that they wanted a king anyway so they could be like the other countries that had kings. God allowed what the Israelites wanted. God told Samuel to anoint a man named Saul to be their king. Saul was a very tall and handsome man (1 Samuel 8:1–22).

When Saul became king of Israel, Israel was at war with a people called the Philistines. The people of Israel were very afraid of being at war with the mighty Philistines, and they were starting to scatter. The prophet Samuel was supposed to make a burnt offering and a peace offering to God on a particular day on behalf of the Israelites. Samuel did not show up for this when King Saul wanted him to. King Saul became impatient. He took matters into his own hands, and he made the offerings to God when God instructed that the prophet Samuel was to be the only person to do this. As soon as King Saul finished doing this, the prophet Samuel arrived. Samuel told King Saul that because of his disobedience, God would remove him from being king. He would anoint another man king, who was after God's own heart (1 Samuel 13:8–14). Even after this, King Saul would often not follow what God told him to do. God regretted that he made Saul the king of Israel, because he was very disobedient to God. Once again, God had the prophet Samuel tell King Saul that God would replace him with a better king, one who would always do what God told him to do. King Saul was greatly upset by this.

Samuel the prophet was sad that Saul was rejected by God as king. God told Samuel that he should not be upset and that God would choose a new king of Israel. He sent Samuel to a man who lived in Bethlehem named Jesse. God would make one of Jesse's sons the new king over Israel. Jesse had many strong, handsome sons. Samuel thought one of these would be chosen as king. God told Samuel that he does not judge people by their appearance but he judges people by their heart (God knows if people have good or bad intentions). God chose the youngest of Jesse's sons to be the future king of Israel. He was a shepherd boy, and his name was David. Samuel anointed David to be Israel's next king. The Spirit of God was with David from that day forward (1 Samuel 16:1–13).

DAVID AND GOLIATH

During the time that David was a young man, Israel was at war with the Philistines. On one occasion, the Philistines set up a camp on a mountain that was on one side of a valley in preparation to battle Israel. The Israelites under King Saul set up their armies on a mountain that was on the other side of this valley. The Philistines sent out their champion warrior named Goliath. He was nine feet, nine inches tall. He had a huge sword and spear, and he was covered in bronze armor. Goliath yelled out to the Israelites, "Send out your best warrior. If he can beat me, we will be your servants. If I beat him, you will be our servants." The Israelites had no one to send out to face Goliath. No one in the Israelite army could match Goliath's size and fierceness (1 Samuel 17:1–11).

Goliath came out into the valley and yelled and cursed at the Israelite army for forty days, challenging them to send a man out to fight him. Three of David's brothers were in Israel's army camp facing the Philistines. One day Jesse told his son David to bring some food to his brothers. When David reached his brothers at the Israelite army camp, he heard Goliath cursing at the Israelite army.

David began to say out loud,

> What shall be done for the man who kills this Philistine and takes away the reproach from Israel? For who is this godless Philistine that he should defy the armies of the living God? (1 Samuel 17:26).

King Saul heard that this boy was questioning about Goliath, so he sent for him. David told King Saul not to worry, because he would fight the Philistine. King Saul did not think this was a good idea, because David was just a teenager, and Goliath was a giant that had been fighting his entire life. David told King Saul that he had worked as a shepherd and lions and bears had taken his sheep at times. David chased the lions and bears down, got into battles with them, killed them, and saved the sheep. He told King Saul that he would do the same to Goliath, the godless Philistine giant, because he defied the armies of the living God. King Saul said to David,

> Go, and the Lord be with you! (1 Samuel 17:37)

When David went out to fight Goliath, he wore no armor. The only weapon he had was a slingshot and five smooth stones that he took from a stream. When Goliath saw David coming out to fight him, he was insulted that the Israelites would send out a boy to fight a great champion like himself. Goliath began to curse at David and the Israelites. David said to Goliath,

You come to me with a sword and with a
spear and with a javelin, but I come to you in
the name of the Lord of hosts, the God of the
armies of Israel, whom you have defied. This
day the Lord will deliver you into my hand, and
I will strike you down. All the earth will know
that there is a God in Israel, for the battle is the
Lord's, and he will give you into our hand. (1
Samuel 17:45–47)

When Goliath approached to meet David, David ran quickly
at Goliath. David pulled a stone out of his bag, put in in his slingshot, and slung it at Goliath. The stone hit Goliath in the forehead
so hard that it sank into his forehead. Goliath fell facedown on the
ground. Since David had no weapons other than his slingshot, he
took Goliath's huge sword, killed him with it, and cut off his head.
David defeated the Philistine giant Goliath with the power of God
behind him. When the Philistines saw what happened, they became
very afraid and ran away from the Israelites (1 Samuel 17:48–58).

After David defeated Goliath, King Saul moved David into the
king's castle with him. There, God made it so that King Saul's son,
Jonathan, became best friends with David. Because God was with
David, he was successful at every task King Saul asked him to do.
King Saul eventually made him a commander in his army. Because
God was with David, the Israelites won every battle that David was a
part of. One day, after David won a battle, the women of Israel were
singing in the streets,

Saul has struck down his thousands, and
David his ten thousands. (1 Samuel 18:7)

This meant that the people believed that David was a greater
warrior than King Saul. This made King Saul envious of David from
that day on.

The next day, King Saul was tormented by a spirit sent by God.
(Remember, God had rejected Saul as King of Israel because he dis-

obeyed God several times in the past.) While King Saul was irritated, on two occasions he picked up a spear and threw it at David with the intentions to kill him. Each time, David ducked out of the way. King Saul repeatedly tried to kill David because he was envious of him. King Saul's son, Jonathan, was David's best friend. Whenever he heard that his father was going to try to kill David, he would warn David so he could escape (1 Samuel chapters 18–20).

David was now on the run from King Saul, who clearly intended to kill David. One day David entered a town called Nob and met with a priest named Ahimelech. He asked the priest for food for he and his men and a sword for himself. The head priest gave David these things, because he knew David was a good man. He did not know that King Saul was trying to kill David. When King Saul heard that the priests helped David, He summoned Ahimelech the priest, and eighty-five other priests from the town of Nob went with him to meet King Saul. Saul asked Ahimelech the priest why he helped David, when David was an enemy of his. Ahimelech said he did not know that David was an enemy of King Saul. He believed that David was a loyal servant of King Saul. In a fit of evil rage, King Saul had Ahimelech and the other 85 priests put to death. Then he sent his soldiers into Nob, the city of the priests, and killed everyone and everything that was alive in the town. King Saul was becoming extremely evil. He was trying to hold onto his power as king even though God rejected him. He was now killing everyone that he felt got in his way (1 Samuel chapters 21 and 22).

On two occasions, David snuck up secretly on King Saul when Saul was looking for David to kill him. David could have easily killed King Saul. Each time, however, David let King Saul go. He said that it was God who anointed Saul as king, and David should never lay a hand against someone that God anointed. He believed that when God decided it was time for Saul to stop being king, God would get rid of Saul himself. David made King Saul twice aware that he snuck up on him and could have killed him, but he had no bad intentions toward his king. King Saul twice thanked David for sparing his life, and he said that he would no longer come after David. However, his promises to leave David alone never lasted long. He was overcome quickly by his envy of David (1 Samuel chapters 24 and 26).

Around this same time, the prophet Samuel died. The Israelites were presently fighting with the Philistines. King Saul tried to ask God what he should do in battles. God would not answer King Saul because he rejected Saul as king for his evil and rebellious ways. Therefore, King Saul went to a fortune teller (a medium). He told her to contact the spirit of the prophet Samuel, who had died, to ask him what to do in battle. God said we should never go to mediums. The medium contacted the spirit of Samuel, and Samuel was mad that King Saul did this. Samuel told King Saul that because he kept rebelling against God to serve his own purposes, the kingdom would be torn out of his hand and given to David. God said that King Saul would die tomorrow in a battle with the Philistines. That is exactly what happened. The next day, King Saul and his forces were in a battle with the Philistines. King Saul was killed, along with his son, Jonathan, who was David's best friend (1 Samuel chapters 28 and 31).

BOOK 2 OF SAMUEL

David was brought the news that King Saul and his son, Jonathan, who was David's best friend, were killed in battle with the Philistines. This made David very sad. After King Saul's death, David was anointed king over the territory of Judah, while a son of King Saul named Ish-bosheth was anointed king over another part of Israel. Without David knowing, and strongly against David's wishes, two followers of David assassinated King Ish-bosheth, viewing him as an enemy to David. David was greatly upset that they did this and had these two men put to death for doing it. Eventually, all of Israel anointed David as king over the entire country, as God said would happen, when he had Samuel anoint David as future king when David was a shepherd boy. David was thirty years old when he became King of Israel, and he ruled as king for forty years (2 Samuel chapters 4 and 5).

When David became king of Israel, the Ark of God with the Ten Commandments inside of it was sitting in a tent. King David said to

Nathan the prophet, "I live in a house of cedar wood, yet the Ark of God is only in a tent." David wanted to build a temple for the Ark of God. Nathan the prophet asked God if King David should build a temple for the Ark of God. God told Nathan the prophet to tell King David that it was acceptable for the Ark of God to be in a tent up to this point, because it could be easily moved around to wherever the Israelites were. God said that one of David's sons who would be king (future King Solomon) would be the one who would build a beautiful temple for the Ark of God. As for King David, God said that he would make King David a great name for all eternity. He would protect him and Israel from their enemies so that they would not bother them. King David's descendants would last forever, and the kingdom of Israel under David's name would also last forever (2 Samuel 7:1–17). This came true. The Jewish people are still here. Additionally, the flag of the country of Israel today is a white flag with a big six-pointed star in the middle of it, which is called the Star of David. However, it was a conditional covenant between God and David and his descendants. God would be with them, prosper them, and protect them *as long as they continued to follow God's ways (italics added).* If they stopped following God's ways, the covenant was broken that God made with David and his descendants who would be kings.

From this point on, David's armies defeated anyone that tried to attack Israel. David was a kind, honest, and fair king. God said that King David was a man after God's own heart. Everything was going very well for David and Israel because David was a good man that followed whatever God said. That was until David committed a great sin. At that point, things fell apart for King David because he did something very evil and sinful

DAVID AND BATHSHEBA

One day, King David stayed back at his palace while his armies were out in battle. He was walking across the rooftop of his palace when he looked down and noticed a very beautiful woman named Bathsheba. Bathsheba was the wife of Uriah the Hittite, one of

David's best soldiers and a very good man. King David was made aware that Bathsheba was Uriah's wife by one of David's servants. King David had Bathsheba brought to him. He slept with her, which was a great sin because she was the wife of Uriah. Shortly after, Bathsheba informed King David that she was pregnant with his baby (2 Samuel 11:1–5).

King David tried to cover this up. He brought Uriah home from the battle and told him to spend some time with his wife, Bathsheba, because he deserved it for being such a good soldier. He was hoping Uriah would sleep with his wife, Bathsheba, so he would think her baby was his. However, Uriah was a man of good character. He refused to go visit his wife Bathsheba. He said, "How can I spend time in comfort, when my soldiers are fighting in a battle?" Instead, he slept on the ground in front of King David's palace. King David tried to do this again with Uriah, but Uriah still refused to go to his home. When King David realized that he could not cover up his sin by making Bathsheba's baby look like it was her husband Uriah's, he decided to kill Uriah. David wrote a sealed message and gave it to Uriah himself to deliver it to the generals. The sealed message said that when they were in a fierce battle, they were to put Uriah at the front of the battle. Then, the soldiers were instructed to back away and leave Uriah by himself in the battle so he would be killed. This is what happened. Not only was Uriah killed, but several other of Israel's soldiers were killed due to King David's order to foolishly engage Uriah's group of soldiers in an ill-advised fierce battle. King David took the news very lightly that many soldiers along with Uriah were killed in battle due to his treacherous orders, saying to the messenger of the news,

> Do not let this matter trouble you, for the sword devours now one and now another. (2 Samuel 11:25)

The only thing King David cared about was making sure that Uriah was killed to cover up his own grave sin with Uriah's wife. After Uriah was killed in battle as King David ordered, King David then took Uriah's wife, Bathsheba, and made her his own wife. All this angered God greatly (2 Samuel 11:6–27).

God sent the prophet Nathan to tell King David that God knew all about the series of evil sins that David committed against Bathsheba, Uriah, and God himself. David crumbled in the presence of the prophet Nathan when he told him that God knows about everything that he did. God told the prophet Nathan to tell King David that due to David's breaking the covenant they made in which God would protect and prosper David and his descendants *if he walked in God's ways (italics added),* from this point on David would frequently have trouble in his life. The son that he would have with Bathsheba would die shortly after birth, which did happen. He would have strife from his own household, which also happened: one of his own sons tried to kill him, and he no longer had much peace in his life. David was very sorry for the sins he committed against God, Uriah, and Bathsheba. He repented and asked God for forgiveness. God forgave David, and he no longer held his sins against him. However, David now had to deal with the consequences that were caused by his grave sins. He would struggle with problems in his life for as long as he would live. David had another son with Bathsheba. He named him Solomon, and he would be the future king of Israel after King David died (2 Samuel 12:1–25).

King David had a son named Amnon and a daughter named Tamar. They were children of King David but had different mothers (King David now had multiple wives). Amnon was strongly attracted to his half sister, Tamar. One day he sexually assaulted her. This made Tamar's full brother, Absalom, very angry. At one point, Absalom killed his half brother Amnon for what he did to his sister Tamar. This whole series of incidents made their father, King David, very sad. After Absalom killed his brother, he ran to another land and hid for three years. After three years, King David allowed Absalom to return home to Jerusalem. However, when Absalom returned, his father, King David, did not handle the situation well. He ignored Absalom and refused to speak to him. This caused Absalom to grow to hate his father, King David (2 Samuel chapters 13 and 14).

Absalom's hatred for his father increased over time. He became power-hungry, and he wanted to get rid of his father, King David, so that he could become king. Absalom began to tell lies to the people, making himself look good and his father, King David look bad. Many people believed these lies, and they began to follow Absalom as their leader instead of King David. At one point, King David and his friends had to flee their castle because they were afraid that Absalom would attack it and try to kill the king. Sure enough, Absalom brought an army with him and invaded King David's castle in Jerusalem with the intent to kill him so that he could be king. David ran away before this, so he was not there when Absalom invaded and tried to kill him (2 Samuel chapters 15–17).

At one point, King David gathered his army, and his son Absalom gathered his army, and they went into battle with each other. During the battle, Absalom was killed. Even though Absalom was trying to kill his father, King David was extremely heartbroken when he heard of the death of his son, Absalom, because he was his son, and he loved him. As God foretold, David had serious consequences in his life due to his series of sins of killing Uriah and stealing his wife, Bathsheba: His first son with Bathsheba died at birth; his son Amnon hurt his daughter, Tamar; another son Absalom killed Amnon, his brother, because of this; Absalom tried to kill King David; and he himself was killed. King David lost his peace as the consequence of willfully engaging in very serious sins.

CHAPTER 8

ISRAEL'S NEXT GROUP OF KINGS AND PROPHETS

(BOOKS OF 1 AND 2 KINGS)

When King David was very old, he anointed one of his sons to be the next king of Israel after him. His son's name was Solomon. Solomon was another son that King David had with Bathsheba now that she was his wife. King David gave Solomon instructions to always follow the ways, laws, rules, and testimonies of God. If he did, King David assured Solomon that he would prosper in whatever he does, and he would always have a descendent on the throne of Israel (1 Kings 2:1–4). King David died, and his son Solomon took his place as king.

One night, God appeared to King Solomon in a dream. He told King Solomon to ask him for whatever he wanted and God would give it to him. King Solomon said that because God made him king, he asked God to Give him wisdom to be a good king for the Israelites and so that he would always make good decisions as their king. This pleased God that Solomon asked him for this. God said,

> Because you have asked this, and have not
> asked for yourself long life or riches or the life of
> your enemies, but have asked for yourself under-

standing to discern what is right, behold, I now do according to your word. Behold, I give you a wise and discerning mind, so that none like you has been before you and none like you shall arise after you. I give you also what you have not asked, both riches and honor, so that no other king shall compare with you, all your days. *And if you walk in my ways, keeping my statutes and my commandments, as your father David walked, then I will lengthen your days (italics added).* (1 Kings 3:10–14)

God greatly blessed King Solomon. God made him the wisest man in the world at the time and gave him great riches. People from different nations came to Israel to hear King Solomon speak because of his wisdom. God instructed King Solomon to build him a temple. Solomon gathered almost two hundred thousand men to work to help build the temple for God in Israel. It took Solomon seven years to build the temple, and it was very fancy and beautiful. King Solomon then built a palace for himself, which took thirteen years to build. This was also fancy and beautiful. Solomon brought the Ark of the Covenant of God and put it in the temple. This was the ornate box which held the two stones with the Ten Commandments on them (1 Kings chapters 6–8). As soon as King Solomon finished building a temple for God, God appeared to Solomon. He told King Solomon that *if he was a man who followed God with integrity of heart and uprightness, doing whatever God commanded him to, and keeping Gods laws and rules,* then God will establish King Solomon's royal throne over Israel forever, as he promised Solomon's father King David (1 Kings 9:1–5).

However, God warned King Solomon that if he or his children turned away from following God, and do not keep God's commandments and his laws that he set before King Solomon, but go and serve other gods and worship them, then God would cut off Israel from the land that he had given them, and he would cast the temple out of his sight, and Israel would be cursed by all peoples. Solomon's palace would become a heap of ruins (1 Kings 9:6–8). People would ask why God did this to Israel and to King Solomon's house? And they would say,

> Because they abandoned the Lord their God
> who brought their fathers out of the land of Egypt
> and laid hold of other gods and worshipped them
> and served them. Therefore the Lord has brought
> all this disaster on them. (1 Kings 9:9).

One day, the queen of a country called Sheba heard of the great riches and blessings that God had given King Solomon. She took a journey to visit King Solomon to see if the reports were true. She asked King Solomon very difficult questions. He was able to answer every one beyond her expectations. The wisdom, wealth, and blessings that God had given King Solomon took the Queen of Sheba's breath away. King Solomon and the Queen of Sheba exchanged exceedingly valuable gifts, treasures, and riches with each other. The Queen of Sheba then went back to her own land (1 Kings 10:1–13).

Despite King Solomon being the wisest man in the world, as he got older he began to go against what God told him to do. God told Solomon to not marry any women who worshipped other gods, because they would pull Solomon away from God to worship their gods. Also, a man is supposed to have only one wife. Solomon had seven hundred wives and princesses and three hundred girlfriends (concubines). Many of these women followed other gods, and they pulled King Solomon away from following God to follow their gods. Some of these "gods" involved demon worship, which included extremely evil things, such as human sacrifices. What King Solomon did greatly angered God. God said that because Solomon disobeyed him and was worshipping false gods and demons, God would take eleven out of the twelve kingdoms that King Solomon now ruled out of the hands of his son in the future, and other people would rule them. Up until this point, King Solomon had total peace in his kingdom. Because of King Solomon's rebellion against God's direct instructions to him, God took his protection of King Solomon away. This allowed numerous enemies of King Solomon to rise up and give him trouble. King Solomon ruled Israel for forty years. He started out following God and all went exceptionally well for him. He turned away from following God, and he then had major problems. King Solomon died, and his son, Rehoboam, replaced him as king of Israel (1 Kings 11:1–43).

KING REHOBOAM

When Rehoboam was anointed king of Israel, the people came to him and said,

> Your father [King Solomon] put on us a
> heavy yoke. If you now lighten the harsh service
> and the heavy yoke your father imposed on us,
> we will serve you. (1 Kings 12:1–4).

King Rehoboam told the people he will give an answer to their request to lighten their burdens in three days. King Rehoboam asked advice from the elders who had been in service for his father, King Solomon. They advised him to follow the people's request to lighten their burdens, and in return, the people would serve King Rehoboam forever. King Rehoboam ignored their advice. He then asked the advice of young men who he grew up with and were in his service. They advised him to do the opposite: tell the people he will be much harder on the them than his father, King Solomon, ever was.

Following their advice, King Rehoboam answered the people's request to lighten their load by saying:

> My father put on you a heavy yoke, but I
> will make it heavier. My father beat you with
> whips, but I will beat you with scorpions. (1
> Kings 12:14).

This prompted ten out of the twelve tribes of Israel to decide to no longer follow Rehoboam as their king. It therefore caused a once-united Israel to split into two kingdoms. The tribes of Judah and Benjamin remained following King Jeroboam's rule and became the southern kingdom of Judah. The ten other tribes stopped following King Rehoboam as their king and became the northern kingdom of Israel. This northern kingdom of Israel anointed their own king, King Jeroboam, to rule them (1 Kings 12:1–20). This is as God prophesied would happen to King Solomon. Throughout the following years, the kingdoms of Judah and Israel had many kings. Some followed the instruction of God, and some abandoned God, followed other gods, and did many things that were evil in the eyes of God (books of 1 Kings and 2 Kings).

PROPHETS OF ISRAEL DURING THIS TIME: ELIJAH AND ELISHA

God raised up a prophet named Elijah in the kingdom of Israel. God Gave Elijah the power to do mighty miracles so that the people would believe that he was a prophet sent by God. At this time, many of the people of Israel were following God. However, many of the Israelites were following a false and evil god named Baal. Some of the Israelites were following both God and Baal. Elijah said to the people, "How long will you people go back and forth deciding which god to follow? If God is the real God, then follow him. If Baal is the real god, then follow him."

Elijah put the followers of Baal to a test in front of the Israelite people to see who was the real god, God or Baal. He said, "I am the only prophet of God here, but Baal has 450 men here who are prophets of Baal. Let's have a contest. I will kill a bull, and the 450 prophets of Baal will kill a bull, and we will each put our bull on a pile of wood. The prophets of Baal can call out to Baal to send fire down from the sky to set their bull and wood on fire, and I will call out to God to send down fire from the sky to set my bull and wood on fire. Whichever God does this is the true God." The prophets of Baal and the people of Israel agreed to this.

The 450 prophets of Baal went first. They killed a bull and put it on a big pile of wood and cried out to Baal form morning until noon for him to send fire down from the sky. They yelled for so long that they were losing their voices and were limping. Nothing happened. Elijah said to them "Cry out loud, for he is a god. Either he is goofing off, or he is going to the bathroom, or he is on a journey, or perhaps he is asleep and must be awakened." The ranted and raved on until later in the day. By this point, they were passing out from exhaustion from crying out to Baal, but absolutely nothing happened.

Elijah now called the people of Israel over to his pile of wood with a bull on it. He laid twelve stones around his pile, representing the twelve tribes of Israel. He then had the people completely soak his pile of wood and the bull with water, so it would be impossible for a person to set it on fire. Then Elijah said,

> Oh Lord, the God of Abraham, Isaac and Jacob [Israel], let it be known this day that you are God in Israel, and that I am your servant, and that I have done all these things at your word. Answer me, O Lord, answer me, that this people may know that you, O Lord, are God, and that you have turned their hearts back. (1 Kings 18:36–37)

As soon as Elijah finished saying this, God rained down an immense fire from heaven on bull, the wood, and the water, and it burned everything up. When the people saw it, they fell on their faces and said,

> The Lord, he is God; The Lord, he is God.
> (1 Kings 18:39)

Elijah had the people grab the prophets of the false god Baal and get rid of them (1 Kings 18:1–40).

Shortly after this, the prophet Elijah became very tired and depressed because he felt like he was the only person in Israel who had a true love for God. (This was not true, but it was how Elijah felt.) God appeared to Elijah in his time of sorrow. He assigned the prophet

Elijah a person to take his place as the prophet in Israel. The new prophet that Elijah anointed as per God's directions was named Elisha (1 Kings 19:9–21). During Elijah's life as a prophet, God gave him power to do many miracles so that the people would believe he was a prophet of God. One day God told Elijah that he would take him up to heaven while he was still alive. Elijah asked his replacement Elisha if he could do anything for him before God took him to heaven. Elisha asked Elijah if he could give him a double portion of his spirit.

Elijah said that was up to God to do, but it was okay with him if God did that. While they were talking, God sent down chariots of fire and horses of fire that separated the two of them. God then took Elijah up to heaven in a whirlwind while he was still alive. Elijah was one of the only people in the Bible who did not have to die: he was taken up by God while he was still alive (2 Kings 2:1–12). The other person to go up to heaven while still alive was Enoch, who was the grandfather of Noah. When Elijah went up to heaven, a double portion of his spirit was given to Elisha like he asked. Now Elisha also had the power to do great miracles. The miracles God Gave Elisha the power to do included parting a body of water and walking through on the dry ground as Moses did with the Red Sea during the Exodus, causing water to appear out of nowhere and form pools so the people had water to drink, causing food to keep appearing in a poor woman's house to prevent her and her son from starving, making it so a childless woman gave birth to a son, bringing a boy back to life who had died, removing the poison from poisoned food so the people could eat it, and healing a man of leprosy (2 Kings chapters 2–6).

During Elisha's time as a prophet of Israel, the king of Syria was at war with Israel. He wanted to capture Elisha the prophet, because Elisha was able to warn Israel whenever Syria intended attack them because God would tell him this. The king of Syria sent an army and surrounded Elisha and his friends. God sent an army of soldiers, horses, and chariots of fire from heaven to protect Elisha. The armies of the king of Syria saw this and reported it back to their king. Out of fear of God, the king of Syria stopped conducting raids in the land of Israel, and he never went after Elisha again (2 Kings 6:8–23).

CHAPTER 9

THE FALL AND EXILES OF ISRAEL AND JUDAH

During this period of the kings, there were many good kings over Israel and Judah, but even more bad ones who did not follow what God instructed them to do. They ignored God's instructions and did what they wanted to do. Sometimes their actions were very sinful. Eventually, God ran out of patience with these bad kings of Israel and Judah. Israel, however, was much worse than Judah in rebelling against God and following the false gods of other countries instead of God. God warned them many times through the prophets to stop doing this and return to him, but they would not listen. Since the kings and people of Israel did not want to follow God's instructions, God took his help and protection away from Israel. They were conquered by the Assyrians and taken away to Assyria as captives in an exile.

> And this occurred because the people of Israel had sinned against the Lord their God, who had brought them up out of the Land of Egypt from under the hand of Pharaoh king of Egypt, and had feared other gods and walked in the customs of the nations whom the Lord drove out before the people of Israel, and in the customs

that the kings of Israel had practiced. And the
people of Israel did secretly against the Lord their
God things that were not right. (2 Kings 17:7–9)

Some of the practices the people of Israel engaged in included
sacrificing their own sons and daughters to Baal and other false gods.
This upset God greatly.

Therefore the Lord was very angry with Israel
and removed them out of his sight. None was left
but the tribe of Judah only. (2 Kings 17:18)

Over time, the kingdom of Judah also greatly offended God by
following the evil practices of the pagan nations around them. One
king of Judah was particularly evil, whose name was King Manasseh.
He rebuilt temples to worship false gods and demons. He put
altars to these false gods in the holy places of Judah and instructed
the people of Judah to worship these other gods. King Manasseh
burned his own son alive a sacrifice to these other evil false gods
(2 Kings 21:1–9). As a consequence, God took his protection away
from the kingdom of Judah. The kingdom of Judah was captured
by the very powerful king of Babylon, King Nebuchadnezzar. The
people of the kingdom of Babylon were called the Chaldeans. King
Nebuchadnezzar brought back to Babylon all the important and
skilled people of Judah, only leaving the very poorest people behind.
He also carried back to Babylon all of Judah's treasures and riches.

King Nebuchadnezzar appointed a man named Zedekiah
as king over Judah. King Zedekiah soon rebelled against king
Nebuchadnezzar. King Nebuchadnezzar of Babylon and the
Chaldeans invaded Jerusalem because of this. They killed or captured everyone who was in the city except for the poorest of the
people, whom they left alone. King Nebuchadnezzar burned all the
important buildings in the kingdom to the ground, broke down the
walls that surrounded Jerusalem, and carried anything of value back
to Babylon. These series of events are called the Babylonian Exile (2
Kings chapters 24 and 25).

THE BOOK OF EZRA

Within a few decades after the kingdom of Juda was conquered by the Chaldeans and its citizens were exiled to Babylon, the Babylonian kingdom transitioned into the kingdom of Persia. The Persians had a king named Cyrus. God stirred the spirit of King Cyrus to help the captured people of Judah and return them to their home. King Cyrus made a proclamation that the people formerly of Judah that were now exiled in Persia were to return to Judah to "rebuild the house of the Lord, the God of Israel—he is the God who is in Jerusalem" (Ezra 1:3). The temple was destroyed by Nebuchadnezzar of Babylon when his army conquered Jerusalem in the territory of Judah. The people of the tribes of Judah and Benjamin, and the priests and the Levites were stirred up by God to return to Jerusalem to rebuild the temple of God. King Cyrus of Persia returned all the precious items that former King Nebuchadnezzar carried away to Babylon when he conquered Judah. Several thousand people and their descendants who were in exile in Persia as a result of King Nebuchadnezzar's conquering of Judah now returned to Judah under the proclamation of King Cyrus to rebuild the house of God (Ezra chapters 1 and 2).

After a delay in rebuilding the temple due to interference from enemies of the people of Judah, the temple was finally finished. God sent a man named Ezra to teach the Israelites about God.

> He was a scribe skilled in the Law of Moses
> that the Lord, the God of Israel, had given, and
> the king granted him all that he asked, for the
> hand of the Lord was on him. (Ezra 7:6)

> For Ezra had set his heart to study the Law
> of the Lord, and to do it and teach his statutes
> and rules in Israel. (Ezra 7:10)

Ezra was now both a priest and a scribe. King Artaxerxes of Persia instructed Ezra to appoint magistrates and judges who might judge the people in areas of Juda and to teach them the laws of Ezra's God.

BIBLE SUMMARY FOR ADULTS AND STUDENTS

Ezra took several hundred men with him from Babylon and went to the rebuilt temple in Jerusalem as King Artaxerxes had instructed him. Ezra became the head priest at the temple in Jerusalem, and he served the Jews that returned to Judah from the exile in that capacity. The main issue that Ezra had to deal with was the forbidden inter-marrying of the Jews with pagans from other nations who did not follow God (Ezra chapters 7 and 8).

THE BOOK OF NEHEMIAH

When King Nebuchadnezzar of the Chaldeans captured the city of Jerusalem and carried the people of Judah off into exile to Babylon, he broke down Jerusalem's protective walls and burned down its important buildings. There was a Jewish man named Nehemiah who was still in exile under King Artaxerxes of Persia. King Artaxerxes was a king whom God inspired to allow the exiled Jews to rebuild the Jewish temple in Jerusalem and also appoint Ezra to be the high priest to the Jews there. Nehemiah was the cupbearer to King Artaxerxes (Nehemiah chapter 1).

Nehemiah heard that for the remnant of people living in Jerusalem, the wall of the city remained torn down and its gates destroyed. Nehemiah prayed to God that God would fix this situation. While Nehemiah was serving the king as his cupbearer, the king noticed that Nehemiah looked sad. King Artaxerxes said to Nehemiah,

> Why is your face sad, seeing you are not
> sick? There is nothing but sadness in your heart.
> (Nehemiah 2:2)

Nehemiah became afraid at this. However, he gathered his courage and said to the king,

> Let the king live forever! Why should not
> my face be sad, when the city, the place of my

> fathers' graves, lies in ruins, and its gates have
> been destroyed by fire? (Nehemiah 2:3)

The king asked Nehemiah what he wanted from him. Nehemiah asked the king if he would send Nehemiah to Judah so he could rebuild his homeland. The king asked him how long he would be gone and when he would return. When Nehemiah told him how long he thought it would take for him to do this, the king granted Nehemiah's request. The king also wrote letters to rulers of territories under his dominion to give Nehemiah the building materials he would need to rebuild the walls of Jerusalem and parts of the city.

> And the king granted me what I asked,
> for the good hand of my God was upon me.
> (Nehemiah 2:1–8)

Nehemiah gathered a group of Jewish men, and they began to rebuild the walls and gates of Jerusalem that had been destroyed by King Nebuchadnezzar of Babylon years earlier. They encountered opposition and threats of violence from several people who did not want the Israelites to rebuild their Jerusalem. Nehemiah and his men also faced oppression from local officials as they worked. Throughout this, they prayed to God for guidance and protection, and he provided both for them. With God's help, it took Nehemiah and his men only fifty-two days to rebuild the wall all around Jerusalem. The enemies of the Jews rebuilding the wall were astounded that it only took them fifty-two days to rebuild it. They realized that God was helping them do his. Out of fear of God, they no longer tried to stop the Jews from rebuilding Jerusalem. Although the wall around the city was now complete, there were only a few people living within Jerusalem, and none of the houses that were destroyed by King Nebuchadnezzar were rebuilt (Nehemiah chapters 3–6). Shortly after the wall around Jerusalem was rebuilt, 42,360 people returned from the Babylonian exile back to the areas of Jerusalem and Judah, along with approximately 7,500 male and female servants. All the people gathered together, and Ezra, the scribe and priest, read the book of the Law of Moses to them. Nehemiah became the governor of the area. Jewish religious worship practices to God finally began once again in the areas of Jerusalem and Judah (Nehemiah chapters 7–13).

THE BOOK OF ESTHER

The book of Esther takes place during the time that the Israelites were exiled in the Media-Persia Kingdom. The Israelites in the exile during this particular period were ruled by King Ahasuerus of the kingdom of Media-Persia, which encompassed 127 provinces ranging from India to Ethiopia. The king had a huge party for the army, the princes, and the governors of the kingdom that lasted for many days. After seven days of partying, the king ordered that his queen, Queen Vashti, be brought to the party to show her off to everyone there because she was very beautiful. Queen Vashti refused to come as the king ordered. King Ahasuerus became enraged that the queen refused his order to come to the party. The king spoke with his consultants on how to handle this. They said that the queen needed to be replaced by another woman as queen for disobeying the king. They feared that if nothing was done, all women in the kingdom would follow Queen Vashti's actions and not listen to their husbands. Queen Vashti therefore had her title as queen removed. Young men who were attendants of King Ahasuerus suggested to him that he should have all the beautiful young single women from across the kingdom be brought to him so that he may choose a new queen from among them. The king agreed to their suggestion and made it so (Esther 1, 2:1–4).

At this time, there was a good Jewish man named Mordecai. He was living in the Media-Persia kingdom ruled by King Ahasuerus. His great-grandfather was brought to this kingdom by King Nebuchadnezzar, the former king of Babylon (now the Medio-Persian Kingdom), along with many other Jews in the Babylonian Exile. Mordecai was raising up a young woman named Esther. Esther's parents died when she was young. Mordecai was an older cousin of Esther, and he adopted her as his own daughter because she had no parents. Esther was a very beautiful young woman. When the king's order was sent out to bring beautiful women to the palace to select a new queen, Esther was brought to the palace along with many other women (Esther 2:5–11).

Esther was the nicest and most beautiful of all the women brought to the king's palace. Over time, she became the favorite of King Ahasuerus and he eventually made her queen to replace Queen Vashti who disobeyed him. Each day during this time, Esther's father, Mordecai would walk in front of the palace to find out how Esther was doing and what was happening to her. Esther did not tell anyone that she was Jewish and from Israel ancestry, because Mordecai told her not to. One day when Mordecai was standing at the king's gate to hear how Esther was doing that day, two of the king's servants became angry with the king and were making plans to kill him. Mordecai overheard this. Mordecai told this to Queen Esther, his daughter, who then told the king what Mordecai discovered. The two men were arrested for trying to kill the king. Mordecai might have saved the king's life (Esther 2:19–23).

There was an official in this kingdom named Haman. The king promoted Haman to be second-in-charge in the kingdom behind the king. Everyone who Haman passed had to bow down to Haman under the king's orders. Mordecai would never bow down to Haman. He said that he was Jewish, and under Jewish law, God was the only person that people should bow down to. ("Jewish" was a name given to the people of Israel. Remember, they were captured and living in this other country at this time.) Haman became very angry at this. He decided that he would not only kill Mordecai for not bowing down to him, but he would kill every Jewish person in the whole kingdom (Esther 3:1–6).

Haman went to the king and said,

> [Summary] There are a group of people living in this kingdom called the Jews. They are not following your laws and commands, and I think it would be in the best interest of the kingdom if they be destroyed.

The king said to Haman,

> Do whatever you think is the right thing to
> do with them.

A letter was sent out by Haman to all the officials of the king-dom that on December 13, all the Jews in the kingdom were to be killed. Mordecai heard about this plan, and he was extremely upset. Mordecai told his daughter, Queen Esther, that Haman planned to kill all the Jewish people in the kingdom, even her, because she was Jewish. He asked Esther to do something to save the Jews and herself, because she too was Jewish. He told her,

> And who knows whether you have not
> come to the kingdom for such a time as this?
> (Esther 4:14).

Queen Esther sent a message to all the Jews in the kingdom to fast for three days (do not eat or drink anything) and keep praying to God to save them. Queen Esther then came up with a plan to try to save her people (Esther 3:7–15 and Esther chapter 4).

Queen Esther went to the king and asked if a banquet could be held, and to make sure that Haman was there. The king agreed. Haman was happy that he was invited to this banquet. He was later talking to his wife about it. Haman's wife reminded him that Mordecai would not bow down to him, and she suggested that a seventy-five-foot pole be put up and Mordecai would be hanged on it at the banquet. Haman agreed (Esther chapter 5).

The night before the banquet, the king could not sleep. He asked that his servants read to him reports of things that happened recently in the kingdom. In the reports, he discovered that Mordecai saved his life by reporting that two of the king's servants were plan-ning to kill the king. The king asked, "What was done to reward Mordecai for saving my life?"

"Nothing," they replied. The king called in Haman, who just finished building the seventy-five-foot pole to hang Mordecai. The king asked Haman, "What should be done to honor a man that I like?"

Haman assumed the king was going to honor him. Haman said (summary),

> Put the king's robes on the man, put him
> on the king's horse, and put the king's crown on
> his head, and parade him through the city saying,
> "This is what happens to a man that the king
> honors."

Then the king said, "That is a great idea. Do all that for Mordecai the Jew, because he saved my life, and I want to honor him."

Haman became terrified. He did all those great things for Mordecai: he put the king's robes on him, put him on a horse with the king's crown on his head, and paraded Mordecai through the streets saying, "This is what happens to a man that the king honors."

Haman then he ran and hid, because the king now loved Mordecai, and Haman was trying to kill him (Esther chapter 6).

At the banquet, Queen Esther told the king that Haman planned not only to kill Mordecai, who saved the king's life, but he wanted to kill all the Jewish people, including her, because she was also a Jew. The king became enraged at Haman. The king was told that Haman just built a seventy-five-foot pole and planned to hang Mordecai on it that day.

The king said (summary), "Oh really? Well, go and hang Haman on that pole that he built to kill Mordecai who saved my life."

Haman was hanged on that pole, and Mordecai and Queen Esther saved the Jews from destruction. The king stopped all the plans that Haman set to kill all the Jews on December 13. Because Mordecai saved the king's life, he was promoted to a very powerful position in the kingdom, and he was loved by everyone in the land (Esther chapters 7, 8, and 9).

CHAPTER 10

THE WISDOM BOOKS OF THE BIBLE

T he next series of writings fall under the category of the Wisdom
Books in the Bible. In them, God conveys messages to humanity
of wise ways to think and act in our daily lives. There are five
books described as Wisdom Books in the Bible. They are Job, Psalms,
Proverbs, Ecclesiastes, and Song of Solomon.

THE BOOK OF JOB

Job was a man that had great faith in God. He worshipped God
daily and always followed God's instructions. Job was also the richest
and most successful man in the East in his time. He had abundant
land, herds of animals, possessions, and seven sons and three daughters (Job 1:1–5).

One day God and Satan were having a conversation. God asked
Satan what he had been doing lately. Satan said he had been roaming
the earth observing things. God asked Satan what he thought about
Job. God told Satan that Job was the most blameless and upright
man on earth. He feared God, and turned away from evil. Satan
said that Job was only good to God because God protected Job and
all that he had. God also blessed Job so that everything he did was
successful. Satan said that if this protection and blessings were taken
away and very difficult trials hit him, Job would curse God to his

face. God said he would take his protections and blessings away from Job so Satan could test him. God put one restriction on Satan: he could not touch Job himself (Job 1:6–12).

Satan caused horrible tragedies to hit Job so that he lost all his treasures in one day. Two different groups of robbers attacked properties that Job owned, taking all his possessions and killing the people that worked there. Satan caused fire to come down from the sky that burned up a farm that Job owned, killing his animals and the people that worked for him there. Finally, a huge wind knocked down a house that Job's ten children were in, killing all of them. In all this, Job did not curse God to his face as Satan said he would, and he still worshipped God (Job 1:13–22).

Satan and God met and had another conversation about Job. God told Satan that even after Satan caused all these terrible tragedies to happen to Job, Job still worshipped and followed God. Satan said that was because nothing bad actually happened to Job himself. Bad things happened to Job's possessions and the people around him. He said if something bad happened directly to Job, he would curse God to his face. God told Satan that he would remove his protection from Job himself so Satan could test him. Satan caused loathsome sores to appear from the sole of Job's feet to the top of Job's head (Job 2:1–10).

These horrible sores, along with losing so many people and possessions in his life, pushed Job over the edge. Job quickly went into a downward spiral of anger, frustration, and hopelessness. Over just a few days' time while conversing with his friends, Job wished that he was never born. Next, he wished that God would kill him so that he would not have to go through this horrible grief. Then, he got angry at God, saying that he (Job) never did anything wrong and he did not deserve for these tragedies to happen to him. Next, he said that God is an unfair God; he did these bad things to him when he should not have, because Job thought he was so good. (He did not realize that Satan did these things to him, not God.)

Job then stated that God does not cause tragedies to hit evil people like he caused them to hit him. Therefore, God must favor evil people over good people. Next, Job said that he wished that he himself was an evil person. He believed that evil people had it good in life. He thought that they had fun and did not experience the tragedies that he was experiencing, so he wished that he was an evil person. Finally, Job's hidden pride was exposed. He said that what he missed most about losing everything was not losing his kids or being separated from God. He used to be an important big shot that everyone looked up to. That was what he missed and wanted back more than anything (Job chapters 3–37).

It was at this point that God appeared to Job. He reminded Job that God was God and Job was not God. God created everything that exists. Everything Job had was because God created it and gave it to him. It was not right that Job was acting like the things that he lost were things that he himself created and were rightfully his. They were gifts from God. In the presence of God, Job became humbled. He asked God for forgiveness for his arrogance, and for turning first away from, and then against God in his trial. God forgave Job. He also restored Job. He doubled all the possessions that Satan took away. Additionally, he gave Job ten more children. These children were the most beautiful children in all the land. Job lived to happy ripe old age, and he died in peace (Job chapters 38–42).

THE BOOK OF PSALMS

The book of Psalms is a very dense and complicated book. It consists of 150 writings, each typically a few paragraphs in length. King David wrote more psalms than anyone else, approximately 73 out of the 150 psalms that chronicle his life experiences and prayers to God. Other authors of psalms include Asaph (12 psalms), the sons of Korah (11 psalms), King Solomon (2 psalms), Moses (1 psalm), and Heman (1 psalm). There are 48 psalms that have anonymous authors. Many of the psalms are prayers to God in both circumstances of happiness and sorrow. Several of the psalms are hymns. Christians around the world use the psalms extensively in prayer and worship. Many psalms are good models to use as prayers because they may identify with our life circumstances and emotions.

The 150 psalms cover a wide range of unique topics and situations. The book of Psalms is an extremely deep and diverse collection of writings. A summary of the Psalms cannot do them true justice. Please read them in the Bible for yourself. What I will present now is one sample each of a variety of different categories that the Psalms tend to fall under.

PSALMS OF WISDOM

Blessed is the man who walks not in the counsel of the wicked, nor stands in the way of sinners, nor sits in the seat of scoffers; but his delight is in the law of the Lord, and on his law he meditates day and night. He is like a tree planted by streams of water that yields its fruit in its season, and its leaf does not wither. In all that he does, he prospers. The wicked are not so, but are like chaff that the wind drives away. Therefore the wicked will not stand in the judgment, nor sinners in the congregation of the righteous; for the Lord knows the way of the righteous, but the way of the wicked will perish. (Psalm 1:1–6)

PSALMS ASKING GOD FOR HELP
A PSALM OF DAVID

O Lord, rebuke me not in your anger, nor discipline me in your wrath. Be gracious to me, O Lord, for I am languishing; heal me, O Lord, for my bones are troubled. My soul is greatly troubled. But you, O Lord—how long? Turn, O Lord, deliver my life; save me for the sake of your steadfast love. For in death there is no remembrance of you; in Sheol who will give you praise?

I am weary with my moaning; every night I flood my bed with tears; I drench my couch with weeping. My eyes wastes away because of grief; it grows weak because of all my foes. Depart from me, all you workers of evil, for the Lord has heard the sound of my weeping. The Lord has heard my plea; the Lord accepts my prayer. All my enemies shall be ashamed and greatly troubled; they shall turn back and be put to shame in a moment. (Psalm 6)

PSALMS TESTIFYING TO THE GREATNESS OF GOD A PSALM OF DAVID

Ascribe to the Lord, O heavenly beings, ascribe to the Lord glory and strength. Ascribe to the Lord glory due his name; worship the Lord in the splendor of holiness. The voice of the Lord is over the waters; the God of glory thunders, the Lord, over many waters. The voice of the Lord is powerful; the voice of the Lord is full of majesty. The voice of the Lord breaks the cedars; the Lord breaks the cedars of Lebanon; He makes Lebanon skip like a calf, and Sirion like a young ox. The voice of the Lord flashes forth flames of fire. The voice of the Lord shakes the wilderness; the Lord shakes the wilderness of Kadesh. The voice of the Lord makes the deer give birth and strips the forests bare, and in his temple all cry, "Glory!" The Lord sits enthroned over the flood; the Lord sits enthroned as king forever. May the Lord give strength to his people! May the Lord bless his people with peace! (Psalm 29)

PSALMS OF MOURNING
A MASKIL OF THE SONS OF KORAH

As a deer pants for flowing streams, so pants my soul for you, O God. My soul thirsts for God, the living God. When shall I come and appear before God? My tears have been my food day and night, while they say to me all the day long, 'Where is your God?' These things I remember, as I pour out my soul: how I would go with the throng and lead them in procession to the house of God with glad shouts and songs of praise, a multitude keeping festival. Why are you cast down, O my soul, and why are you in turmoil within me? Hope in God; for I shall again praise him, my salvation and my God. My soul is cast down within me; therefore I remember you from the land of Jordan and of Hermon, from Mount Mizar. Deep calls to deep at the roar of your waterfalls; all your breakers and your waves have gone over me. By day the Lord commands his steadfast love, and at night his song is with me, a prayer to the God of my life. I say to God, my rock: 'Why have you forgotten me? Why do I go mourning because of the oppression of my enemy?' As with a deadly wound in my bones, my adversaries taunt me, while they say to me all the day long, 'Where is your God?' Why are you cast down, O my soul, and why are you in turmoil within me? Hope in God; for I shall again praise him, my salvation and my God. (Psalm 42)

PSALMS OF PRAISE TO GOD

Shout for Joy in the Lord, O you righteous! Praise befits the upright. Give thanks to the Lord with the lyre; make melody to him with the harp of ten strings! Sing to him a new song; play skillfully on the strings with loud shouts. For the word of the Lord is upright, and all his work is done in faithfulness. He loves righteousness and justice; the earth is full of steadfast love to the Lord. (Psalm 33:1–5)

PSALMS OF TRUST IN GOD
A PSALM OF DAVID

Fret not yourself because of evildoers; be not envious of wrongdoers! For they will soon fade like the grass and wither like the green herb. Trust in the Lord and do good; dwell in the land and befriend faithfulness. Delight yourself in the Lord, and he will give you the desires of your heart. Commit your way to the Lord; trust in him, and he will act. He will bring forth your righteousness as the light, and your justice as the noonday. Be still before the Lord and wait patiently for him; fret not yourself over the one who prospers in his way, over the man who carries out evil devices! Those who wait for the Lord will inherit the land. The meek shall inherit the land and delight themselves in abundant peace. He is ever lending generously, and his children become a blessing. For the Lord loves justice; he will not forsake his saints. They are preserved forever, but the wicked shall be cut off. (Psalm 37:1–28)

PSALMS OF PROPHECY OF FUTURE EVENTS

There are many psalms which are psalms of prophecy. A psalm of prophecy is one in which it reveals something that will happen in the future. There are many psalms which reveal things that God will do in the future from when the psalm was written. Quite a bit of the prophetic psalms deal with the future life of Jesus. Many of these psalms tell the reader about things that Jesus will do in both his First and Second Coming. The following psalm was written by King David. He lived roughly one thousand years before the arrival of Jesus to earth. Yet this psalm details several events, which would clearly happen in Jesus's life later on. Remember, the author of the Bible is God. Through the Holy Spirit, God guided the writers of the Bible to write exactly what God wanted written. God knows everything that will happen form the beginning to the end. I put in italics the events in this psalm that refer to things that would later happen in the life of Jesus. Can you identify these events that later actually happened in Jesus's life?

A PSALM OF DAVID

My God, my God, why have your forsaken me? Why are you so far from saving me, from the words of my groaning? Oh my God, I cry by day, but you do not answer, and by night, but I find no rest. Yet you are holy, enthroned on the praises of Israel. In you our fathers trusted; they trusted, and you delivered them. To you they cried and were rescued; in you they trusted and were not put to shame. But I am a worm and not a man, *scorned by mankind and despised by the people. All who see me mock me; they wag their heads; 'He trusts in the Lord; let him deliver him; let him rescue him, for he delights in him!'* Yet you are he who took me from the womb; you made me trust you at my mother's breasts. On you I was cast from my birth, and from my mother's womb you have been my God. Be not far from me, for trouble is near, and there is none to help. *Many*

*bulls encompass me; strong bulls from Bashan sur-
round me; they open wide their mouths at me, like
a ravening and roaring lion. I am poured out like
water, and all my bones are out of joint; my heart is
like wax; it is melted within my breast; my strength
is dried up like a potsherd, and my tongue sticks
to my jaws; you lay me in the dust of death. For
dogs encompass me; a company of evildoers encircles
me; they have pierced my hands and my feet—I can
count all of my bones—they stare and gloat over me;
they divide my garments among them, and for my
clothing they cast lots.* (Psalm 22:1–18)

THE BOOK OF PROVERBS

Most of the proverbs in the book of Proverbs were written by
King Solomon, the son of King David of Israel, whom God made the
wisest man who ever lived. He wrote twenty-nine out of the thirty-one
chapters in the book of Proverbs. Other Proverb authors include a man
named Agur, who wrote chapter 30, and King Lemuel, who wrote
chapter 31. But the real author of everything in the Bible is God. He
guided the authors of the proverbs to write what he wanted to be written. King Solomon stated that his reason for writing the proverbs was,

> To know wisdom and instruction, to under-
> stand words of insight, to receive instruction in
> wise dealing, in righteousness, justice, and equity;
> to give prudence to the simple, knowledge and
> discretion to the youth—Let the wise hear and
> increase learning, and the one who understands
> obtain guidance, to understand a proverb and
> saying, the words of the wise and their riddles.
> The fear of the Lord is the beginning of knowl-
> edge; fools despise wisdom and instruction.
> (Proverbs 1:2–7).

I wanted to include some of the proverbs from the book of Proverbs in this Bible summary because they help teach us how God wants us to live. Additionally, it will give you an idea about what the book of Proverbs in the Bible is like. It would benefit you greatly to read the entire book of Proverbs for yourself. They truly are gems of wisdom that you can benefit from in your daily life. All the following proverbs were taken from the book of Proverbs:

> My son, do not despise the Lord's discipline or be wary of his reproof, for the Lord disciplines who he loves, as a father the son in whom he delights. (Proverbs 3:11–12)
>
> The fear of the Lord is the hatred of evil. (Proverbs 8:13)
>
> Wisdom loves those who love her, and those who seek her diligently find her. (Proverbs 8:17)
>
> A wise son makes a glad father, but a foolish son is a sorrow to his mother. (Proverbs 10:1)
>
> Treasures gained by wickedness do not profit, but righteousness delivers you from death. (Proverbs 10:2)
>
> Hatred stirs up problems, but love covers all offenses. (Proverbs 10:12)
>
> What the wicked dreads will come upon him, but the desire of the righteous will be granted. (Proverbs 10:24)
>
> When pride comes, then comes disgrace, but with the humble people is wisdom. (Proverbs 11:2)
>
> The righteous is delivered from trouble, and the wicked walks into it instead. (Proverbs 11:8)
>
> Whoever criticizes his neighbor lacks sense, but a person of understanding remains silent. (Proverbs 11:12)
>
> One gives to others generously, yet grows richer, another withholds what he should give

and is always poor. (Proverbs 11:24) [God blesses and helps those who are generous to others.]

Whoever trusts in his riches will fall, but those who trust in God will prosper. (Proverbs 11:28)

A person who is kind benefits himself, but a cruel person hurts himself. (Proverbs 11:17)

Be assured, an evil person will not go unpunished, but the children of the righteous will be delivered. (Proverbs 11:21)

The desire of the righteous ends only in good; the expectation of the wicked in wrath. (Proverbs 11:23)

Whoever brings blessing will be enriched, and one who waters will himself be watered. (Proverbs 11:25)

Whoever loves discipline loves knowledge, but he who hates being corrected is stupid. (Proverbs 12:1)

A good person obtains favor from the Lord, but a person of evil devices is condemned by God. (Proverbs 12:2)

The way of a fool is right in his own eyes, but a wise man listens to advice. (Proverbs 12:15)

Whoever guards his mouth preserves his life; but he who opens wide his lips comes to ruin. (Proverbs 13:3)

Whoever despises the Word of God brings destruction on himself, but he who reveres the commandments will be rewarded. (Proverbs 13:13)

Whoever walks with the wise will become wise, but the companion of fools will suffer harm. (Proverbs 13:20)

The righteous has enough to satisfy his appetite, but the belly of the wicked always wants more. (Proverbs 13:25)

Leave the presence of a fool, for there you do not meet the words of knowledge. (Proverbs 14:7)

One who is wise is cautious and turns away from evil, but a fool is reckless and careless. (Proverbs 14:16)

Whoever despises his neighbor is a sinner, but blessed is he who is generous to the poor. (Proverbs 14:21)

In all work there is profit, but mere talk leads only to poverty. (Proverbs 14:23)

In the fear of the Lord one has strong confidence, and his children will have a place of safety. (Proverbs 14:26)

Whoever is slow to anger has great understanding, but he who has a hasty temper is a fool. (Proverbs 14:29)

A peaceful heart gives life to the body, but envy makes the bones rot. (Proverbs 14:30)

Whoever oppresses a poor person insults the poor person's Maker, which is God. But he who is generous to the needy honors God. (Proverbs 14:31)

A soft answer turns away wrath, but harsh words stirs up anger. (Proverbs 15:1)

The sacrifice of the wicked is an abomination to the Lord, but the prayer of the upright is acceptable to him. (Proverbs 15:8)

Better is a little with the fear of the Lord than great treasure and trouble with it. (Proverbs 15:16)

Better is a dinner of just salad where love is, than a full course meal and hatred with it. (Proverbs 15:17)

Without counsel plans fail, but with many advisers they succeed. (Proverbs 15:22)

Whoever is greedy for unjust gain troubles his own household, but he who hates bribes will live. (Proverbs 15:27)

The Lord is far from the wicked, but he hears the prayers of the righteous. (Proverbs 15:29).

Whoever ignores instruction despises himself, but he who listens to correction gains intelligence. (Proverbs 15:32)

It is better to have a little with righteousness than a lot of money with injustice. (Proverbs 16:8)

How much better to get wisdom than gold! To get understanding is to be chosen rather than silver. (Proverbs 16:16)

Pride goes before destruction, and a haughty spirit before a fall. (Proverbs 16:18)

It is better to be of a lowly spirit with the poor than to divide riches with the proud. (Proverbs 16:19)

Whoever gives thought to God's word will discover good, and blessed is the person who trusts in the Lord. (Proverbs 16:20)

Whoever is slow to anger is better than the mighty, and he who rules his spirit is better than he who takes a city. (Proverbs 16:32)

A joyful heart is good medicine, but a crushed spirit dries up the bones. (Proverbs 17:22)

A fool takes no pleasure in understanding, but only in expressing his opinion. (Proverbs 18:2)

A false witness will not go unpunished, and he who breathes out lies will not escape. (Proverbs 19:5)

Whoever is generous to the poor lends to the Lord, and God will repay him for his good deed. (Proverbs 19:17)

Do not say "I will repay evil." Wait for the Lord and he will deliver you. (Proverbs 20:22)

To do righteousness and justice is more acceptable to the Lord than sacrifice. (Proverbs 21:3)

Whoever closes his ear to the cry of the poor will himself call out someday and not be answered. (Proverbs 21:13)

Whoever pursues righteousness and kindness will find life, righteousness, and honor. (Proverbs 21:21)

A good name is to be chosen rather than great riches, and favor is better than silver or gold. (Proverbs 22:1)

The rich and the poor will meet together; the Lord is the maker of them all. (Proverbs 22:2)

The reward for humility and fear of the Lord is riches and honor and life. (Proverbs 22:4)

Train up a child in the way he should go; even when he is old he will not depart from it. (Proverbs 22:6)

Do not envy sinners, but continue to love the Lord always. (Proverbs 23:17)

Never say "I will do bad to him as he has done to me; I will get back at the person for what he has done." (Proverbs 24:29)

If your enemy is hungry, give him something to eat. If he is thirsty, give him something to drink. For this will heap burning coals on his head, and the Lord will reward you. (Proverbs 25:21–22)

Due to a lack of wood a fire goes out, and where there is no gossiping, fighting stops. (Proverbs 26:20–21)

Let another praise you, and not your own mouth; a stranger, and not your own lips. (Proverbs 27:2)

The prudent sees danger and hides himself, but the foolish walk into it and suffer for it. (Proverbs 27:12)

Iron sharpens iron, and one man sharpens another. (Proverbs 27:17)

The wicked flee when no one pursues, but the righteous are as bold as a lion. (Proverbs 28:1)

Better is a poor man who walks in his integrity than a rich man who is crooked in his ways. (Proverbs 28:6)

Whoever misleads upright people into an evil way will fall into his own pit, but the blameless will have a goodly inheritance. (Proverbs 28:10)

Whoever hides his wrongdoings will not prosper, but he who confesses and forsakes them will receive mercy. (Proverbs 28:13)

A fool gives vent to his spirit, but a wise man quietly holds it back. (Proverbs 29:11)

One's pride will bring him low, but he who is humble in spirit will obtain honor. (Proverbs 29:23)

Every word of God proves true; he is a shield to those who take refuge in him. (Proverbs 30:5)

Give me neither poverty nor riches; If I am rich, I may say "Who needs God?" If I am poor, I may steal and dishonor the name of my God. (Proverbs 30:8–9)

THE BOOK OF ECCLESIASTES

It is often believed that King Solomon was the author of the book of Ecclesiastes, but there is some debate to this, as the author never identifies himself specifically. However, there is enough evidence in the writing of the author that King Solomon can be assumed to be the author of Ecclesiastes. For example, the author claims to be the king of Israel, the son of David, and having acquired wisdom that surpassed all who lived in Jerusalem before him.

Ecclesiastes is the story of a man who identifies himself as the king of Israel. He claimed to be the wisest man ever to live in Jerusalem, who indulged in as many pleasures, activities, and experiences in his life as he could. He is reporting in the book of Ecclesiastes what he found to be useful, and what he found to be useless (which he repeatedly calls "vanity"). The writer evolves throughout the book from a man who is worried about what will happen to all the material possessions that he collected in life when he dies, to a man who realizes that material possessions are not important; enjoying each day that God gave him is what is important. One thing that is very important in reading the book of Ecclesiastes—whether the writer was King Solomon or someone else—is that the writer lived before Jesus came as our Savior. At the time of this writer, no one could get into heaven; Jesus did not arrive yet to make that possible. Therefore, the writer is looking at his life at the time when one's life while alive on earth was all that there was. Even though this person identified himself as the King of Israel, and the richest, most successful, and wisest person that ever lived up to that point in Jerusalem, he realized (summary), "What is the point? Even though I am the richest, wisest, and most successful person that ever lived in Jerusalem, I will die one day like everyone else and all that I accumulated cannot go with me."

Christians today have something that the richest, wisest, most successful man in Jerusalem in his day did not have: a Messiah that opened the doors to heaven for an eternal life with God in paradise after this life on earth is over. He only had this life on earth, and he realized that one day it would all end. The following is a summary of his conclusions of observing the life that he led.

The writer finds that there is nothing new under the sun. What is discovered by people in life now has been discovered by people in former generations. People came and went, and so will he (Ecclesiastes 1:1–11).

He believes that the more wisdom a person collects, the more sorrow he may have (Ecclesiastes 1:12–18). (King Solomon did not use the wisdom he was given by God properly. He had seven hundred wives and three hundred girlfriends, he followed their evil gods, all which resulted in a sorrowful end to his life.)

The writer examined the result of filling his life with pleasure. He drank wine and observed its effects. He also engaged in "folly" in his life and observed its results. He built many structures, had male and female slaves, had great riches, and numerous women. His riches surpassed all that came before him in Jerusalem. He reported that he indulged in every pleasure that his heart desired. At the end of all this, he concluded:

> All was vanity and a striving after the wind, and there was nothing to be gained under the sun. (Ecclesiastes 2:11).

The author believed that living wisely was better than living foolishly, just as it is better to be in the light than in darkness. Then he realized that the people who live wisely and foolishly both will die one day, and after time neither will be remembered here on earth. This caused him to hate his life, because no matter what he did in life, he would still die and his earthly treasures would be lost to him forever (Ecclesiastes 2:12–17).

The writer came to hate doing productive work, because whatever he produced would be left to the people after him when he died. What if the people mishandled and wasted all that he built up? He became full of despair, realizing that a person who toiled with great knowledge, wisdom, and skill must leave it all to another person to enjoy who did not work for it. This realization led the writer's days and nights to be full of sorrow (Ecclesiastes 2:18–23).

The writer came to a conclusion that he should enjoy just living day to day, appreciating what God has given him daily, and not be concerned with gathering wealth and who may get it after he dies.

> There is nothing better for a person than that he should eat and drink and find enjoyment in his toil. This also, I saw from the hand of God, for apart from him who can eat or who can have enjoyment? For to the one who pleases him God has given wisdom and knowledge and joy, but to the sinner he has given the business of gathering and collecting, only to give to one who pleases God. (Ecclesiastes 2:24–26)

> I perceived that there is nothing better for people than to be joyful and to do good as long as they live; also that everyone should eat and drink and take pleasure in all his toil—that is God's gift to man. (Ecclesiastes 3:12–13)

In the second half of Ecclesiastes, the writer gave brief bits of wise observations, much in the format of the book of Proverbs. Here is a sample of his observations in life:

The author of proverbs lamented over evil in the world.

The author was upset that the rich and powerful oppressed the poor and powerless (Ecclesiastes chapter 4).

He believed that we should fear and respect God (Ecclesiastes chapter 5).

Striving after riches was viewed as a waste of time and possibly a destructive endeavor. A person striving after riches is never satisfied (Ecclesiastes chapter 5 and 6).

The completion of a task (and a life) is better than the beginning of a task (and a life).

Wisdom gives a person great strength.

Do not let what people say about you offend you.

Although death comes to us all, it is better to be alive than to be dead (Ecclesiastes 9:1–6).

Enjoy living the life that you have, with the spouse that you have been given (Ecclesiastes 9:7–9).

Remember God your Creator when you are young before life gets difficult and you get discouraged (Ecclesiastes 12:1–8).

> Fear God and keep his commandments, for
> this is the whole duty of man. For God will bring
> every deed into judgment, with every secret thing,
> whether good or evil. (Ecclesiastes 12:13–14)

THE SONG OF SOLOMON

In the book the Song of Solomon, the author describes God's love for his people using the relationship of the love between a man and his wife as an illustration of this.

CHAPTER 11

THE PROPHETIC BOOKS: THE BOOK OF ISAIAH

The Prophetic Books are a series of books focusing on four major and twelve minor prophets in Israel and Judah's history. The terms *major* and *minor* refer to the length of the books, not to how important each prophet was. A prophet was an intermediary between God and his people. God would give messages to prophets that he wanted relayed to the people by the prophet. These messages often consisted of what he wanted his people to do, warnings to the people, teachings for the people, and information of things to come in the future. Each prophetic book is named after the prophet that God gave messages to that he wanted given to his people.

BOOK OF ISAIAH

The book of Isaiah is a prophetic book. It has more prophecies about both the First and Second Coming of Jesus to earth than any other book in the Bible. Those prophecies about Jesus in the book of Isaiah will be placed in the upcoming chapter "Prophecies about Jesus in the Old Testament." There is much more to the book of Isaiah than the numerous prophecies about Jesus. The following is a summary of the book of Isaiah that does not include future prophecies about Jesus, which will be included in that later chapter.

In the days of King Hezekiah, there was a man named Isaiah who received a vision from God. God told him that the people of Jerusalem and Judah, his own people, have turned away from God and became wicked. God stopped accepting the sacrifices and prayers from these people because they routinely lived wickedly. God told Isaiah that if the people repented of their sins and turned back to him, they would be forgiven and all would be well with them. But if they did not, they would be devoured by the sword. Without repentance, strong discipline from the Lord would be coming (Isaiah chapter 1).

Isaiah was shown by God that because Jerusalem and Judah rebelled against God and loved to sin, God would take away food, water, and supplies from them. People would mistreat and disrespect each other as a result of the scarcity. The women were acting in seductive and sinful manners. Therefore, God would take away all their seductive attire and jewelry in a time of scarcity. Because the people of Jerusalem and Judah turned their backs on God and abandoned him, they were prophesied to go into exile. Their towns would be abandoned, being inhabited by nomads and wild animals.

God once again appeared to Isaiah in a vision. Isaiah saw God sitting upon his throne, and the train of his robe filled the entire temple. Seraphim stood above God who was sitting on the throne. The seraphim said,

> Holy, holy, holy is the Lord of hosts; the whole earth is full of his glory! And the foundations of the thresholds shook at the voice of him who called, and the house was filled with smoke, and Isaiah said: "Woe is me! For I am lost; for I am a man of unclean lips, and I dwell in the midst of a people of unclean lips; for my eyes have seen the King, the Lord of hosts!" Then one of the seraphim flew to me, having in his hand a burning coal that he had taken with tongs from the altar. And he touched my mouth and said: "Behold,

this has touched your lips; your guilt is taken away, and your sin is atoned for." (Isaiah 6:3–7)

In the days of King Ahaz of Judah, the kings of Syria and Israel banded together and tried to attack Jerusalem. (At this point in time, Israel and Judah were separate kingdoms. Jerusalem was the capital of the kingdom of Judah.) This made the people of Jerusalem anxious and fearful. God told Isaiah to take his son and go and give a message from God to King Ahaz of Judah. He told them to have firm faith in God, and within sixty-five years, many of the people who want to attack you now would be destroyed. God told Isaiah that because the people of Judah lacked trust in God but instead greatly feared their enemies, Assyria would come with a strong force and attempt to invade Judah. God warned Isaiah not to be like the people of Judah, who did not trust in God to take care of them but instead fear their enemies. God told Isaiah that he and his sons would be signs for Judah from God. God told Isaiah to not listen to the people when they advised others to turn to consulting mediums, soothsayers, and ghosts looking for answers to their problems instead of turning to God (Isaiah chapters 7 and 8).

In Isaiah 14:12–17, information is given about what Satan did that got him banished from heaven and some of the destruction he caused on earth:

How you have fallen from heaven, O Day Star, son of Dawn! How you are cut down to the ground, you who laid the nations low! You said in your heart, "I will ascend to heaven; above the stars of God I will set my throne on high; I will sit on the mount of assembly in the far reaches of the north; I will ascend above the heights of the clouds; I will make myself like the Most High." But you are brought down to Sheol, to the far reaches of the pit. Those who see you will stare at you and ponder over you: "Is this the man who made the earth tremble, who shook kingdoms,

who made the world like a desert and overthrew
its cities, who did not let his prisoners go home?"

God next gave Isaiah numerous prophecies about what will
happen to the sinful and godless countries involved with Judah and
Israel in the future. It is prophesied that the Medes would completely
destroy Babylon. God would restore Israel. The Assyrians would be
defeated by the power of God. Famine and death would come to
the land of the Philistines. Due to pride, arrogance, and insolence,
devastation and wailing were decreed for Moab. At some point in
our future, the city of Damascus, Syria, would cease to be a city and
become a heap of ruins (this has not happened yet). (Isaiah 17:1).
Because the people had forgotten the God of their salvation and forgotten the Rock of their refuge, many cities would become desolate
places. However, this would cause the people to turn back to God,
the Holy One of Israel, and away from their false idols (Isaiah chapter 17). Fearsome people who are tall and smooth from a land in
which the rivers divide will come by sea and take the people of Cush
to their land (Isaiah chapter 18).

At some point in the future of the writing of Isaiah, it is prophesied that God would stir up the Egyptians to fight each other, and
there would be chaos and civil war across Egypt. The Egyptians
would consult their idols, sorcerers, mediums, and necromancers for
a solution to their problems. God would hand them over to a fierce
king who would rule them harshly. Much of the waters of Egypt
would dry up, and the people would mourn because of this. Wise
men of Egypt would be consulted to no avail. The people would be
frightened and weak because of this. The result of all these calamities that would take place in Egypt is some of the people of Egypt
would turn to God to be their God. When these people who would
then follow God cry out to him, he would send them a Savior and
Defender to deliver them. God would make himself known to the
Egyptians, and the Egyptians would turn to God. God would both
discipline and heal Egypt, and would will listen to their pleas for
mercy and heal them. Egypt would lead the Assyrians to also worship God. In that day, Israel, Egypt, and Assyria would worship God

together. God would bless them, and they would be a blessing to that area of the earth (Isaiah chapter 20).

Jerusalem was called to repent of their sins by God. Instead, they celebrated and ignored God's commands. It is prophesied that God would shake the people of Jerusalem and replace their leaders with ones that God would appoint because of this (Isaiah chapter 22).

God would lay waste the city of Tyre due to their pompous pride and the undeserved glory they bestowed on themselves. The strongholds of the city of Tarshish would be destroyed. However, Tyre would be restored by God after seventy years of desolation. Her merchandise would supply abundant food and fine clothing for those who dwelled before the Lord (Isaiah chapter 23).

The book of Isaiah has many prophecies about a future time in which God would restore Israel. God was using, and he would continue to use, multiple exiles of his people to progressively turn Israel and Judah away from their sins and back to God. It is prophesied that one day, all the Jewish people would return to Israel and worship the Lord on the holy mountain in Jerusalem (Isaiah 25–27).

God warns one of the tribes of Israel, the tribe of Ephraim, that they would be trodden under foot because they were drunkards, lovers of wine, which included the priests and the prophets.

God warns Jerusalem in prophecy that they would be under siege by many nations, and would will be trampled down by them for a time. However, God would visit them at some point. He would quickly end the attacks of many nations against Jerusalem.

God reveals that he would stop giving prophecies to the prophets and seers. They would not be able to understand anything that came from God, including understanding the reading of scripture. Wisdom of the wise men would disappear, and discernment would be hidden from them. This is because…

> This people draw near to me with their mouth and honor me with their lips, while their hearts are far from me, and their fear of me is a commandment taught by men. (Isaiah 29:13)

God describes his foolish people as a clay pot saying about its potter "he did not make me," or a thing that is formed saying to he who formed it "he has no understanding." However, one day once again the deaf shall hear, and the blind shall see, and the meek will obtain fresh joy in God, and the poor of mankind will exult the Holy One of Israel. Yet the ruthless and the scoffers and those who seek to do evil will be cut off (Isaiah chapter 29).

God warns his people not to trust in and rely on Egypt to help them. That is not God's plan for them, and he did not tell them to do that. Seeking Pharaoh to protect them would turn into shame for God's people, because that was not what God wanted them to do. God says that his people, the Israelites, were a rebellious people. They were unwilling to hear God's instruction. They refused to accept what God's prophets told them. They instructed the prophets to tell them pleasant things that they wanted to hear instead of the hard truth from God. Since they despised the word of God and instead rely on perverse Egypt to protect them, they would be destroyed quickly and comprehensively. However, if the Jews returned to following God instead of relying on Egypt, they would be saved. God would give them rest, quietness, and he would return their strength because they once again trusted in him. If they returned to following God, he would be gracious to them. Although they would first have adversity and affliction for turning away from God, God would return as their Teacher once more. Their crops and livestock would be prosperous. God would bind up the brokenness of his people and heal the wounds inflicted by the blows of his discipline (Isaiah chapter 30).

God once again warns his people against going down to Egypt for help, trusting in Egypt's strong army instead of consulting with the God of Israel about what to do. The Egyptians were men and not God. If the Lord stretched out his hand, Egypt would stumble and Israel would fall and they would perish together. God does not fear any enemies of Israel. If they turned to him instead of Egypt as a protector, he would protect, deliver, spare, and rescue Jerusalem. God commands his people who had revolted against him to turn back to him. If they did this, God himself would defeat the Assyrians whom Israel feared. He would rout them, and they would be a threat to Jerusalem no more (Isiah chapter 31).

In the fourteenth year of the reign of King Hezekiah, King Sennacherib of Assyria captured the fortified cities of Judah. The king of Assyria approached representatives of King Hezekiah of Judah with a great army. He sent a representative to King Hezekiah with the following message:

> [Paraphrased] The great King of Assyria wonders who you put your trust in to save you? Is it in Egypt, that broken reed that pierces any hand that leans on it? Is it in your God, the God whose high places and alters your King Hezekiah has removed? It was your God that appeared to me and said "Go up against the land of Judah and destroy it." Then the representative of the king of Assyria made an announcement to the people of the town within listening distance of his voice: "Do not listen to King Hezekiah because he cannot deliver you. Do not believe him when he says 'God will surely deliver us.' Has any of the gods of the nations that went against the King of Assyria delivered them out of his hand? No, the King of Assyria defeated all of them. Instead, make your peace with the King of Assyria and come out to him. If you do, you will be granted peace in your own land until a time in which you will be exiled to a good land like your own, full of food, wine, farms, and vineyards." (Isaiah chapter 36)

When the representatives of King Hezekiah brought the message from the King of Assyria to him, King Hezekiah tore his clothes, covered himself with sackcloth, and went into the house of God. He sent representatives, also covered in sackcloth, to Isaiah the prophet. They said to Isaiah,

This is a great time of trouble for all of us. May our God hear the words of the King of Assyria, who mocks and rebukes our God. Please pray for the remnant that is left of our people.

God gave the prophet Isaiah a message, which he told to the representatives of King Hezekiah. God said,

Thus say the Lord: Do not be afraid because of the words you have heard, with which the young men of the king of Assyria have reviled me. Behold, I will put a spirit in him, so that he shall hear a rumor and return to his own land, and I will make him fall by the sword in his own land. (Isaiah 37:6–7)

The king of Assyria got messages that two different kings of foreign lands were preparing to go to war with him. The king of Assyria sent a message back to King Hezekiah of Judah, saying,

Do not trust that your God can save you from me. You have heard that I devoted to destruction all of the kingdoms that I went up against, and their gods could not deliver them from my hand.

When King Hezekiah got this message from the king of Assyria, he went to the house of God and spread out the message from the king of Assyria before God. He then prayed to God, saying that God was the Creator and Ruler of everything. He asked God to listen to the king of Assyria who was mocking God. He told God that the king of Assyria destroyed all other nations and their false gods that he came up against. He asked God to save them from the hand of the king of Assyria, so that all the kingdoms of the world would know that he alone is God (Isaiah 37:8–20).

God gave the prophet Isaiah a message, which he relayed to King Hezekiah: God said the king of Assyria was mocking God, because up to this point, that king had defeated every nation and their false gods that he went up against.

> It was I, God, that allowed him to con-
> quer those nations. Now that he is raging against
> me, I will drag him into a position that I want
> him to be in. I personally will defend my city
> of Jerusalem, and no attack from him against it
> will take place; I will send the King of Assyria
> back the way he came. At that point the angel of
> the Lord went out and struck down one hundred
> and eighty-five thousand soldiers of the Assyrian
> army. King Sennacherib of Assyria then returned
> home and lived in Nineveh. When he was wor-
> shipping in the house of his god, Nisroch, two of
> his own sons came in and killed him with swords.
> (Isaiah 37:21–38)

Around that time, King Hezekiah of Juda became terminally ill. Isaiah the prophet told him to get his affairs in order because he would die from this illness. King Hezekiah offered this prayer to God:

> "Please, O Lord, remember how I have
> walked before you in faithfulness and with a
> whole heart, and have done what is good in your
> sight." And Hezekiah wept bitterly. (Isaiah 38:3)

God responded through the prophet Isaiah to King Hezekiah, telling him that God heard his prayer and saw his tears. He will add fifteen years to his life, defend the city, and deliver him out of the hand of the king of Assyria. King Hezekiah was restored to health by God, for which he was exceedingly thankful (Isaiah chapter 38).

During this time, the king of Babylon heard that King Hezekiah of Judah was very sick. The king of Babylon sent envoys with letters and a gift to King Hezekiah. King Hezekiah welcomed them gladly and showed them all the treasures of his kingdom. When the envoys left, the prophet Isaiah asked King Hezekiah what these envoys from Babylon saw in the king's house. King Hezekiah told Isaiah that he showed them all his treasures. Isaiah gave King Hezekiah a prophecy that in the time of his son's reign, all his riches, including some of his own sons, would be captured and carried off to Babylon as spoil. This news *pleased (italics added)* King Hezekiah, because he thought "that will be my sons' problems. At least I will have peace and security during my life" (Isaiah chapter 39).

God revealed that he authorized Cyrus to be a great conquering leader from another land. Although Cyrus does not know God, God would use Cyrus to rebuild Jerusalem and the temple there (Isaiah 44:28 and 45:1–4).

The last several chapters in the book of Isaiah detail how God will save and restore both the country of Israel and any individual who followed him as their God.

God informs his people that if they regularly practiced sinful deeds, God would not hear and answer their prayers to him (Isaiah chapter 59).

Through the prophet Isaiah, God predicts that one day the country of Israel would be a blessing to the entire world. The nations would come to her to pay homage and to seek guidance from God there. In those days Israel would never again be conquered by foreign peoples.

CHAPTER 12

THE PROPHETIC BOOKS: THE BOOKS OF JEREMIAH AND LAMENTATIONS

Jeremiah was a priest in the land of Benjamin. God came to Jeremiah and made him a prophet beginning under the rule of King Josiah of Judah, through the end of the reign of King Zedekiah of Judah, which finished with the captivity of the city of Jerusalem by the King of Babylon and the second Babylonian exile (Jeremiah 1:1–3).

God appeared to Jeremiah the priest and said,

> "Before I formed you in the womb I knew you, and before you were born I consecrated you; I appointed you a prophet to the nations. To all to whom I send you, you shall go, and whatever I command you, you shall speak. Do not be afraid of them, for I am with you to deliver you," declares the Lord. Then the Lord put out his hand and touched my mouth. And the Lord said to me, "Behold, I have put my words in your mouth. See, I have set you this day over nations and over kingdoms, to pluck up and break down, to destroy and overthrow, to build and to plant." (Jeremiah 1:4–10)

God told the prophet Jeremiah that the people of Jerusalem were an evil people. They had forsaken God, and they worshipped false gods and idols that they made with their own hands. As a result of this, out of the north will come conquering armies that would set their thrones at the entrance gates of Jerusalem, and against its walls and against all the cities of Judah. God told Jeremiah to get dressed for work. He was instructed to say everything that God commanded him to say to the kings, the priests, and the people of Judah. Jeremiah was warned that the people of Judah would fight against him and his messages. However, God would make him a fortified city against all the people and leaders of Judah, and they would not prevail over Jeremiah because God would be with him to deliver him (Jeremiah chapter 1).

God instructed Jeremiah to give the people of Jerusalem this message from God:

> [Summary] I am angry with them. I established them as a country, and took loving care of them. Yet they abandoned me to chase after the false gods of other countries and to sacrifice to the Baals. Only in time of great trouble to they turn back to me and cry out "Save us!" Why don't you cry out to your false gods to save you in time of trouble? You will not accept my correction, and you killed the prophets that I sent you. Have I not been good to Israel? Then why do my people say they want to be free from me and no longer come to me? You have forgotten me as your God for countless days. You have killed the innocent and the poor, yet you proclaim, "I am innocent. God will not get angry with me." I will bring judgement on you for saying that you have not sinned. If a woman leaves her husband and becomes another man's wife, would the first husband then take her back as his wife? She has become polluted. And you have become polluted

by leaving me to worship other Gods. (Jeremiah chapters 2 and 3)

In the days of King Josiah, God appeared to the prophet Jeremiah with messages for both the kingdoms of Judah and Israel:

[Summary] Israel left me to chase after other Gods. I thought that after she did all this she would return to me, but she did not. And her treacherous sister, Judah, saw her do this. Judah saw me send away Israel with a divorce decree because of her worshipping other gods. Yet, Judah had no fear of me and she too went after worshipping other gods. She worshipped false idols of nature. She then returned to me only superficially, but not with her whole heart. Faithless Israel has been more righteous than treacherous Judah. Now, Jeremiah, go and proclaim to Israel to return to me, and I will no longer be angry with them because I am merciful. Only Israel must acknowledge your guilt of rebelling against me and following foreign people and other gods. If you do, I will provide you shepherds after my own heart who will give you understanding and knowledge. Jerusalem in the future will be called the throne of the Lord, nations will come to it in the presence of God, and Israel and Judah will once again be joined together. (Jeremiah 3:6–24)

God stated through Jeremiah that even though he disciplined Jerusalem and Judah, they refused to repent of their rebellion against God. They had forsaken God and turned to worshipping false gods. Their prophets prophesy falsely, saying things that God never told them to say to the people and the king. The people refuse to listen to the instruction from God. The people are full of sinful behaviors. God took great care of them, but they turned to worship others. The people believed that God would not judge them for their rebellion. Because of this, God was bringing fierce nation from far away in the north to conquer Jerusalem and Judah. But God would not make a complete end to them; he would leave a remnant of his people to survive.

> And when your people say, "Why has the Lord our God done all these things to us?" you shall say to them, "As you have forsaken me and served foreign gods in your land, so you shall serve foreigners in a land that is not yours." (Jeremiah 5:19)

God came to the Prophet Jeremiah and told him to go to the gates of the temple and tell the people the following message:

> [Summary] Repent of your evil ways and I will let you remain in this land. Do not trust that you will be saved just because my temple is located here. If you change your ways and are just with each other; you do not oppress strangers, widows, and the fatherless; if you do not murder, or follow other gods, then I will let you remain in this land that I gave to your fathers forever. Do you think you can steal, murder, commit adultery, swear falsely, give offerings to Baal, worship other gods, and then come to this temple and say "We are delivered!" only to continue to do all of these abominations? Because you did not listen to me when I persistently spoke to you, and you would not answer when I called you, I will cast you out of my sight. And Jeremiah, do not pray for these people or feel bad for them. They all spend their days worshipping false gods instead of following me. They have set detestable idols in my house. They built altars to burn their own children as sacrifices to false gods. I did not com-

mand them to do this, nor was it anything that I would even think of having them do. Because of the exceedingly evil practices of the people of Judah and Jerusalem and their refusal to repent of them, I will take some of their lives and lay waste to their land. (Jeremiah 7:1–34)

God revealed how sad and heartbroken he was due to his people abandoning him and he having to discipline them because of this [summary]:

I lost my joy, I am full of grief, my heart is sick inside me. I hear my people crying "Where did God go?" Why did they provoke me by worshipping carved images and foreign idols as gods? My heart aches because my people ache. I am in mourning because of them. I feel like crying day and night over the slain of my people! I wish I had a place to go to get a respite from my people. They are all adulterers, treacherous liars. They go from one evil to the next and they do not know me. They lie to each other continually and cannot be trusted. They refuse to know me. I will test and refine my people. What else can I do? Shall I not punish them for continually sinning against each other and myself? I will weep for the land and its animals because it will be laid waste due to my sinful people. The cities of Judah will become desolate without inhabitants. And I will have to do this because my people forsook my law that I gave them, not obeying my voice or walking in accord with it. Instead they stubbornly followed their own impulses and worshipped the Baals as their fathers taught them to do. Instead of boasting in their pride, my people should boast that they know and understand me, that I am God who practices steadfast love, righteousness and justice in the earth. These are the things that I delight in. (Jeremiah chapter 9)

God let the prophet Jeremiah know that there was a group of people that were planning to kill Jeremiah because they did not like the prophecies he was giving to them from God. God let Jeremiah know that he would punish these people who were planning to kill him. God then informed Jeremiah that although he planned to discipline Judah for turning away from him and worshipping the evil Baals as their gods, he would one day have compassion on his people and restore them when they turned back to him (Jeremiah chapters 11 and 12).

God gave a warning that all of Judah would go into exile, conquered by invaders from the north. This would happen because of the greatness of their iniquity against God. They forgot God and trusted in false gods (Jeremiah chapter 13).

God gave Jeremiah a prophecy that Judah would experience a drought and resulting famine because of their iniquity. He let Jeremiah know that the prophets of Judah were lying to the people in the prophecies they are giving them. They were telling the people that everything would be fine; they would not experience war or famine but would have peace in the land. God did not send these self-titled "prophets," and he never spoke to them. Because these false prophets were telling the people that the sword and famine should not come upon the land, they themselves would die by sword and famine. The people who listen to these lying prophets would also die by sword and famine. God instructed Jeremiah to inform the people of Judah that this was what they would be faced with if they did not return to God and stop listening to their lying prophets and leaders that God never sent (Jeremiah chapter 14).

Jeremiah became despondent and sad. The people hated him and were turning against him because of the prophecies of all the discipline God will inflict on them because of their continued sinfulness. God encouraged Jeremiah and assured him that he would strengthen Jeremiah and protect him as he was called by God to bring this news to the people of Judah (Jeremiah chapter 15).

God once again had the prophet Jeremiah proclaim to the house of Israel that he would send disaster upon them because of their evil ways. However, if the people turned from their evil ways, he would chose to not bring disaster upon the people of the house of Israel. God revealed that the people would not follow his warning. They would not return to following God, instead choosing to continue to follow false gods and their abominable practices. God knew that they were planning to kill the prophet Jeremiah, believing that they would be safe in abandoning the directions of God because they had the law and priests and prophets. Upon hearing this from God, Jeremiah pleaded to God to protect him from their plans to harm him, since the reason why they were planning to silence him was because he was faithfully proclaiming God's prophecies to them as God told him to do (Jeremiah chapter 18).

God sent the prophet Jeremiah to make another announcement to the kings and inhabitants of Judah and Jerusalem. He told them that God will bring famine and destroying armies to them because…

> The people have forsaken me [God] and
> have profaned this place by making offerings in it
> to other gods whom neither they nor their fathers
> nor the kings of Judah have known; and because
> they have filled this place with the blood of the
> innocents, and have built the high places to Baal
> to burn their sons in the fire as burnt offerings to
> Baal, which I did not command or decree, nor
> did it come into my mind. (Jeremiah 19:4–5)

And because the people stiffened their necks and refused to hear God's warnings about these things.

Pashhur the priest, who was the chief officer of the house of the Lord, heard this message from the prophet Jeremiah and became enraged at him for delivering it. He beat Jeremiah and put him in the stocks. Pashhur then released Jeremiah from the stocks the following day. When released from the stocks, Jeremiah told Pashhur that the people close to him would fall by the sword as he looked on. The king of Babylon would capture the land of Judah. He would carry people into captivity in Babylon and kill many with the sword. The king of Babylon would also carry all the riches and treasures of Judah back to Babylon as spoil. Jeremiah told Pashhur that he himself and all that lived in his house would also be taken to Babylon in captivity. He and all his friends whom he prophesied to falsely would die and be buried there (Jeremiah chapter 20).

At this point, Jeremiah cried out to God in anguish that God made him a prophet. Everyone was mocking him and turning against him because all his messages are about violence and destruction decreed for the land of Judah. He tried not to tell the people the messages God gave to him to the people, but it is of no avail. God's word burned inside him, and it burst forth even though he tried to keep it in. He knew that the people all hate him, and he wished that he died because of his negative prophecies to the people from God. Yet he also knew that God was protecting him because God chose him to be his messenger to his people. Jeremiah regretted the day that he was born out of the stress that he was under at this point in the book (Jeremiah 20:7–18).

God let it be known to Jeremiah that he was very upset with people calling themselves "prophets" when God gave them no message to tell the people. They were telling the people lies that "all would be well" when all would not be well with them. They were also telling people dreams they had and claiming they were messages from God. They were not messages from God, just random dreams. God instructed Jeremiah to warn both the prophets and the priests to stop telling the people messages they made up themselves and saying God gave them these messages for the people. (Jeremiah chapter 23).

During the time of King Jehoiakim of Judah, God came to the prophet Jeremiah. God told Jeremiah to get a scroll and write down all the things he ever told Jeremiah that God has against Israel, Judah, and other nations since the time he began speaking to Jeremiah in the days of King Josiah. He told him to present this to the people of Judah, in hopes that they would hear of all the disaster God intends to do to them, so that they would all turn from their evil ways and God would forgive their iniquity and sin. Jeremiah was banned from going to the temple, so he had a man named Baruch read the scroll in the temple and to all the men of Judah. It was hoped that they might give pleas of mercy to God and turn from their evil ways, so God would relent in his anger and wrath that he had pronounced for them. A man named Micaiah was one of the people in the crowd that heard the reading of the scroll. He went to King Jehoiakim's chamber and reported to the king's officials the message from God that was read from the scroll. The officials sent for Baruch, the man who read the scroll to the people, and commanded him to read it to the king's officials, which he did. The officials became frightened at the message from God. They told Baruch and Jeremiah to hide and not let anyone know where they were.

The scroll was then brought and read to King Jehoiakim of Judah. After every three or four sections were read, King Jehoiakim would cut that section off and throw it into the fireplace until the entire scroll was burned up. He and his servants were not afraid of the message from God, and they did not repent. The king commanded that Baruch and Jeremiah be captured and brought to him, but God hid them. God then instructed Jeremiah to rewrite everything that was on the scroll. He told him to add a message to King Jehoiakim, saying,

> [Summary] Because you burned the scroll with my warnings on it to you and your people, the king of Babylon will certainly come and destroy the land. You will never have an heir to the throne, and your body will be thrown on the ground to rot. You, your offspring, and your servants shall be punished for your iniquity. I will bring the disaster upon you and the inhabitants of Judah that I pronounced against them, but everyone refused to hear. (Jeremiah chapter 36)

God gave the prophet Jeremiah a message for all the inhabitants of Judah and Jerusalem, which he gave to them.

[Summary] For twenty-three years, the word of God has come to me, which I persistently spoke to you, but you have not listened. I routinely gave you God's message instructing you to turn away from your evil deeds, to not go after other gods and serve them, and to not make evil things with your own hands. God now says to you, "Because you have not obeyed my words, I will send all of the tribes of the North, and King Nebuchadnezzar of Babylon against the inhabitants of this land and the surrounding nations. You will all be punished severely, and you will serve the king of Babylon for seventy years. After the seventy years are completed, I will punish the king of Babylon and that nation of the Chaldeans for their iniquity. I will make their land a waste, and their peoples will become slaves of other nations." (Jeremiah 25:1–14)

God came to Jeremiah and instructed him to give the following message to all cities of Judah that worship in the house of the Lord.

[Summary] If you walk in my law that I set before you, and listen to the words of my prophets that I urgently sent to you; if you all turn away from your evil ways, then I may relent of the disaster that intend to do to you because of your evil deeds. However, if you do not listen to me, I will make this city desolate without inhabitants; a curse for all of the nations of the earth. (Jeremiah 26:1–6)

There was great debate among the officials, priests, and townspeople as to whether Jeremiah should be put to death for giving these grim prophecies, or if the people should listen to him and follow what he said to do (Jeremiah chapter 26).

God gave insight to Jeremiah about his upcoming plan for his people of Judah. Some of the people of Judah were previously exiled to Babylon by King Nebuchadnezzar, including Jeconiah, the former king of Judah, with his officials, craftsmen, and metalworkers. These people from Judah were purposely exiled away to protect them from God's wrath to come on the land. He would later bring them back to the land of Judah, and he said,

> I will build them up, and not tear them down; I will plant them, and not uproot them. I will give them a heart to know that I am the Lord, and they shall be my people and I will be their God, for they shall return to me with their whole heart. (Jeremiah 24:6–7)

As for the current king of Judah, King Zedekiah, he and his officials and all who remained in the city, who would disobey God's instructions to surrender to King Nebuchadnezzar, would be completely destroyed by the sword, famine, and pestilence (Jeremiah chapter 24).

King Zedekiah sent Pashhur the priest to Jeremiah to get a prophecy from God about how things would turn out in an impending war with Nebuchadnezzar, the King of Babylon. (King Nebuchadnezzar of Babylon placed Zedekiah as king of Judah, and Zedekiah rebelled against Nebuchadnezzar. Nebuchadnezzar's armies were already attacking the walls around Judah for King Zedekiah's rebellion against him.) King Zedekiah was hoping to get a message from God through Jeremiah that God would help them in their war with King Nebuchadnezzar of Babylon.

God sent Jeremiah to give a message to the kings of all the nations who had relationships with Judah:

> [Summary] I, God have made the earth and everything that lives on it. I give it to whomever it seems right to me. I have now given all of these lands into the hand of Nebuchadnezzar, king of

Babylon. All the nations shall serve him, his son, and his grandson until the time I decreed for his rule is up. Then, other nations shall make him their slave. Any nation that I addressed that does not submit to king Nebuchadnezzar's rule, I will allow him to destroy it by the sword, famine, and pestilence. Do not listen to your prophets, fortunetellers, or sorcerers who tell you that you will not serve the king of Babylon. It is a lie, and if you follow it you will be destroyed. But any nation that submits to the rule of king Nebuchadnezzar, I will allow to remain and live on his own land.

Jeremiah then gave king Zedekiah of Judah a similar message from God:

[Summary] Serve King Nebuchadnezzar of Babylon and live. If you do not, you will also die by the sword, famine, and pestilence. Do not listen to your lying prophets who are saying to you "You shall not serve the king of Babylon." It is a lie, and I did not send them.

Then Jeremiah gave this message to the priests and the people of the land from God:

[Summary] Do not listen to your lying prophets saying you will defeat the King of Babylon. You will not. Serve the king of Babylon and live. If you do not, this city will become a desolation. (Jeremiah chapter 27)

God made a promise that one day in the future, he would rebuild Israel, and the Jews that were scattered in exiles would return to their homeland. People would live happily and securely in Israel in those days. Then the descendants of God's people would be countless, and Israel would never again be overthrown (Jeremiah chapter 31).

At this point in time, the city of Jerusalem was under siege from the armies of king Nebuchadnezzar of Babylon. This is because King Nebuchadnezzar handpicked Zedekiah to be king of Judah, but King Zedekiah then rebelled against King Nebuchadnezzar. King Zedekiah had the prophet Jeremiah imprisoned within his palace. He did this because Jeremiah kept giving prophecies from God that said that Jerusalem would be conquered by Nebuchadnezzar and everyone, including King Zedekiah, would be taken back to Babylon as captives in an exile (Jeremiah chapter 32).

God told the prophet Jeremiah to give the following message to King Zedekiah of Judah:

> [Summary] The Babylonians [Chaldeans] will in fact conquer and enter this city. I will bring them in and fight against you people myself because I have decreed this city to destruction. The people of this city will die of great pestilence, famine, and the sword. The people who are left, including King Zedekiah, will fall into the hand of King Nebuchadnezzar and his armies and will be struck down by the edge of the sword without pity. However, I will give you an option to choose life or death when you start to see this happen. All of the people who choose to remain in this city when it is under attack by King Nebuchadnezzar will die by the sword, famine, and pestilence. In contrast, anyone who goes out and surrenders to King Nebuchadnezzar shall live and be carried into exile and live in Babylon, including King Zedekiah. Whatever you do choose, this city itself will in fact be given into the hand of the King of Babylon and it will be burned with fire. (Jeremiah chapter 21)

God let it be known that he would burn the city with fire, because the people of the city were burning their own children as grotesque sacrifices to the false god Baal, among other offerings they were making to false gods.

God sent Jeremiah the prophet to King Zedekiah of Judah with the following message:

> This says the Lord: Behold, I am giving this city into the hand of the king of Babylon and he shall burn it with fire. You shall not escape from his hand but shall surely be captured and delivered into his hand. You shall see the king of Babylon eye to eye and speak with him face to face. And you shall go to Babylon. (Jeremiah 34:2–3)

King Zedekiah did not listen to the words from God spoken through Jeremiah the prophet. One day he approached Jeremiah and asked him to pray to God for he and his people. Jeremiah gave him a message from God.

> [Summary] Pharaoh's army from Egypt, who you believe will help you against the Chaldeans [Babylonians], are about to return to Egypt and leave you. The Chaldeans will capture this city and burn it with fire. Do not deceive yourself by believing that the Chaldeans will not capture this city and burn it down. (Jeremiah 37:6–10)

When there was a break in the action in the battle between the Chaldeans and Jerusalem, Jeremiah left Jerusalem and went to the land of Benjamin. He was accused by a century at the gate of deserting the people of Judah and joining the Chaldeans. Jeremiah denied this. The officials there became enraged at Jeremiah. They beat him and imprisoned him. Jeremiah remained in prison for many days. Eventually, King Zedekiah had him removed from prison and brought to him. King Zedekiah asked Jeremiah if he had any messages for him from God. Jeremiah did. He told King Zedekiah that he would be delivered into the hand of the King of Babylon. King Zedekiah did not return him to prison. He kept Jeremiah in the court of the guard, and a loaf of bread was given to him daily until all the bread from the city was gone due to the siege of King Nebuchadnezzar (Jeremiah chapter 37).

The prophet Jeremiah was giving the following message from God to the people:

> Thus says the Lord: He who stays in the city shall die by the sword, by famine, and by pestilence, but he who goes to the Chaldeans shall live. This city shall surely be given into the hand of the army of the king of Babylon and be taken. (Jeremiah 38:2–3)

The officials petitioned King Zedekiah to put Jeremiah to death, because his negative prophecies were weakening the morale of the soldiers and the people of Jerusalem. King Zedekiah gave them permission to do with Jeremiah as they saw fit. They cast Jeremiah into a cistern. There was no water in the cistern, so he sank into its mud. An Ethiopian eunuch reported to King Zedekiah that Jeremiah was placed in a dry cistern, and if he wasn't removed, he would die from starvation. King Zedekiah ordered that Jeremiah be removed from the cistern and returned to the court of the guard (Jeremiah 38:7–13).

King Zedekiah sent for Jeremiah to hear the latest message about what would happen in the Battle of Jerusalem from God. Once again, Jeremiah gave the following message from God to King Zedekiah:

> If you surrender to the officials of the King of Babylon, then your life shall be spared, and this city shall not be burned with fire, and you and your house shall live. But if you do not surrender to the officials of the king of Babylon, then this city shall be given into the hands of the Chaldeans,

and they shall burn it with fire, and you shall not
escape from their hand. (Jeremiah 38:17–18)

King Zedekiah ordered Jeremiah to tell no one about this message he had received from God.

King Zedekiah and his officials did not follow the repeated
instructions given to them by God to surrender to King
Nebuchadnezzar of Babylon and they would live. After a two-year
siege of Jerusalem by King Nebuchadnezzar, a breach was made
into the city. When this happened, King Zedekiah fled from the
city at night with some of his soldiers. The army of the Chaldeans
pursued them and captured them. He was brought to face King
Nebuchadnezzar of Babylon. King Nebuchadnezzar passed sentenced
on him. King Nebuchadnezzar killed all the sons of King Zedekiah
before his eyes, along with all the nobles of Judah. He then put out
the eyes of King Zedekiah and brought him in chains to Babylon.
The Chaldean soldiers burned down the king's house, the houses of
the people, and broke down the walls around Jerusalem. All the treasures of the temple of God were carried away to Babylon. The rest of
the people of Jerusalem were brought to Babylon as captives. Just the
poorest of the people who owned nothing were allowed to remain in
the land of Judah and were given vineyards and fields. Concerning
Jeremiah the prophet, King Nebuchadnezzar gave the command to
treat him well, do him no harm, and do with him whatever Jeremiah
told them to do. Jeremiah chose a man named Geldaliah to stay with,
and he remained in Jerusalem and lived among the few people that
were left (Jeremiah chapters 39 and 52).

God gave a message to Jeremiah for the remaining people in Judah.
He told them to stay in the land of Judah and he would make them greatly
prosper there. They did not have to be afraid of King Nebuchadnezzar
of Babylon. God would protect them from him and he would do them
no harm. God warned them to not go to Egypt as some were planning
because they believed they would be protected there. God would protect
them in their own land of Judah. If they went to Egypt, everyone that
would go would die by the sword and famine there, and they would
never see the land of Judah again (Jeremiah chapter 42).

The men of Judah rebelled against the message the prophet Jeremiah gave to the remaining people of Judah. They said God did not give him that message. He was lying, and he wanted the remnant of Judah to be captured or killed by the Chaldeans. The remnant of Judah left Judah and went to Egypt, bringing Jeremiah along with them (Jeremiah chapter 42). God gave Jeremiah a message for the rebellious people of Judah who were now in Egypt against God's command. God said that he would send Nebuchadnezzar against Egypt and he would conquer it. He would destroy much of the territory. Many would die by the sword, famine, and pestilence, and many would be taken into captivity (Jeremiah chapter 43).

The people of Judah who went to Egypt against God's direct command began to worship the false gods of Egypt. Jeremiah gave them a message from God to stop worshipping the false gods of Egypt. The people replied to Jeremiah that they would not stop worshipping the gods of Egypt. They believed that by worshipping the gods of Egypt, the prosperity that they once had in Judah would return to them. This was after God made it clear to them multiple times that the reason why he allowed Nebuchadnezzar to conquer Judah was to discipline them for abandoning God to worship false gods. The people returned to making abominable offerings to the queen of heaven as they did back in Judah. God informed them through Jeremiah that he would wipe almost all of them out in Egypt through an invasion by King Nebuchadnezzar, and only a few stragglers would return to Judah alive (Jeremiah chapter 44).

THE BOOK OF LAMENTATIONS

The book of Lamentations is a collection of five poems which express the grief and mourning of the survivors of the destruction of Jerusalem by King Nebuchadnezzar in 587 BC.

The first chapter mourns about the empty city that used to be full of people. Almost all the people were taken away in an exile to Babylon by King Nebuchadnezzar's forces. This is because of Judah's many and repeated sins against God and rejection of his instructions to turn back to him and away from sin. The people that were left in Jerusalem were groaning in lamentations as they search for food. The people were in the hands of their conquering enemies. Much crying and sorrow was experienced without any relief or comfort (Lamentations chapter 1).

Chapter 2 of Lamentations describes God's angry destruction of his people because of their refusal to listen to him and their continued grave sinning. The people of Jerusalem now lay in ruins with their destroyed city. The people followed false prophets who said, "All will be well," instead of following the true word from God, which said,

> Turn away from your sin and your follow-
> ing false gods and turn back to me or else I will
> destroy you.

People were fainting from hunger in the streets (Lamentations chapter 2).

The writer of chapter 3 laments about how God was greatly punishing him, which was causing him exceeding pain and anguish. He then details that although God was punishing him now, he would not punish him forever. God would eventually show his steadfast love and have mercy on him. The writer then grieves about how he was suffering at the hands of his enemies. He asks God to avenge him and punish his enemies for what they were doing to him (Lamentations chapter 3).

Chapter 4 details how the temple is destroyed. People were sick and dying in Jerusalem from hunger. The rich and the fine nobility now wandered around the streets starving, and they were covered with soot. People were resorting to eating other people who had died due to starvation. God's anger was due to the sins of the prophets and priests, who shed the blood of the righteous in the open in Jerusalem (Lamentations chapter 4).

The author tells God all the hardships the people of Jerusalem were going through at the cruel hands of their conquerors. The people had no hope. He asks God to please have mercy on the people of Jerusalem and restore them (Lamentations chapter 5).

CHAPTER 13

THE PROPHETIC BOOKS: THE BOOK OF EZEKIEL

E zekiel was a priest, and he was one of the people taken away from Israel to the land of the Chaldeans in the Babylonian exile. This was the first Babylonian exile in which King Jehoiakim of Judah was captured and brought to Babylon along with many of his people. One day the word and hand of God came upon Ezekiel the priest.

God gave Ezekiel a great vision. He saw four fantastic creatures emerging from a great cloud. Each creature had four sides, and each side had a face. Each had a human face on the front, a lion's face on the right side, the face of an ox on the left side, and the face of an eagle on the back side. Each creature also had two wings. Their appearance was like a bright, burning fire, and lightning came out of the fire. The creatures darted around and appeared like flashes of lightning. As Ezekiel continued to look, he saw a wheel on the earth beside each of the four living creatures. The wheels looked like gleaming beryl, and their construction was a wheel within a wheel. The tall, awesome rims of each wheel were full of eyes all around them. The wheels went along side wherever the four living creatures went. Both the creatures and the wheels went wherever the spirit wanted them to go; the spirit of the living creatures were in the wheels. The wings of the four creatures had the sound of many waters, the sound of a great army, the sound of God Almighty. Above their heads was an expanse, and a voice came from above the expanse over their heads. Above this expanse over their heads was a likeness of a throne appearing like sapphire. Above the throne was the likeness of a human. Above his waist was gleaming metal that had fire enclosed around it. Below his waist was fire, and there was brightness around him, which appeared to be some kind of rainbow. This was the appearance of the likeness of the glory of God. When Ezekiel saw it, he fell on his face. He then heard God speak to him (Ezekiel chapter 1).

God spoke to Ezekiel, and the Holy Spirit entered him as this happened. God said,

> [Summary] I am sending you to the people of Israel, sinners who rebelled against me and continue to do so. They will be aware that you are a prophet of God. You will speak my words to them, whether they choose to hear them or choose to ignore them. Do not be afraid of what they say and do, because they are a rebellious people.

A hand then handed him a scroll with words of lamentations, mourning, and woe written on the front and back of it. God instructed Ezekiel to eat the scroll, which he did. God then said,

> [Summary] The house of Israel will not be willing to listen to you because they are not willing to listen to me out of stubbornness. I will make you more stubborn than they are. Go to the exiles and say "Thus says the Lord God" and tell them what I tell you to say to them, whether they listen to you or not.

Then the Holy Spirit lifted Ezekiel up and brought him to the exiles at Tel-abib. He sat there overwhelmed among them for seven days due to his encounter with God and the four creatures of God (Ezekiel chapters 2 and 3:1–15).

After seven days, the word of God came to Ezekiel. He said,

> [Summary] Ezekiel, I have made you a watchman for the house of Israel. Whenever you hear a message from me, you must give it to them. I will hold you fully responsible for giving them whatever message I give to you for them. (Ezekiel 3:16–27)

God gave the message to the people in the Babylonian exile through Ezekiel. He told them that the city of Jerusalem would be under siege. Israel would be under God's punishment for 390 years and Judah for 40 years. When Jerusalem was under siege, they would run out of food and water. God said that Jerusalem was more wicked and rebellious than the pagan nations around her. The people of Jerusalem rejected God's rules and laws. Therefore, God was against Jerusalem, and he would judge the city. It would fall into starvation. Whoever survived that would be scattered among the nations. This would happen because God was withdrawing his protection of his people due to their continued abominations against him. All in all, one-third of Jerusalem would die from famine and pestilence, one-third would die by the sword, and one-third would be scattered to the winds. There would be an end to God's fury and jealousy one day, and because of it, his people would know that he was the Lord (Ezekiel chapter 5).

God showed Ezekiel all the abominations that the people did throughout the land. God then instructed Ezekiel to pass through the city and put a mark on the forehead of all the people who were disgusted with the abominations that the other people were doing against God. God then instructed Ezekiel to pass through the people once again with a group of executioners and execute everyone who did not have this mark on their forehead (Ezekiel chapters 8 and 9).

Ezekiel was very worried that God would completely wipe out the remnant of Israel. God reassured Ezekiel that even though he scattered the people of Israel throughout other countries, he had been a sanctuary to them in those places. God would once again gather his people that he had scattered and give them back the land of Israel. The people would then remove all the abominations in the land of Israel. God would give them one heart, and he would put a new spirit in them. They would then obey God's rules and ways, and they would be his people and he would be their God. Ezekiel then went and told all the Israelites who were now exiles in Chaldea all the things that God showed him (Ezekiel chapter 11).

God gave Ezekiel a prophecy to tell the exiles that Ezekiel was with in Babylon. He let them know that back home, Jerusalem would be captured by an invading Babylonian army. The prince of Jerusalem would try to escape at night through a hole in the wall, but he would will be captured. He would be brought to Babylon, the land of the Chaldeans, and he would die there, along with his helpers and his troops. Many in Jerusalem would die from famine, the sword, and pestilence. Only a small number of people would escape death. This would be allowed so they could declare all their abominations among the nations in which they would be scattered, so those nations would know that God was the Lord. This is exactly what would happen shortly to King Zedekiah of Judah, who would rebel against King Nebuchadnezzar of Babylon, the ruler over Judah (Ezekiel chapter 12).

God reminded Jerusalem through Ezekiel that they were not a nation until God made them one. He made them everything that they were and gave them all the land, food, clothes, and supplies that they needed to survive as a nation. They responded to his planting and nourishing them by abandoning him to follow the gods of other nations. They killed his sons and daughters as offerings to these false gods and demons.

> [Summary] You were never satisfied with the amount you chased after the false gods of other nations. Therefore, I will gather all of the nations that you chased after and they will become your enemies and conquers. Your sins are worse than those of Sodom, who I completely destroyed because of their sins. However, I will

remember the covenant I made with you in the
days of your youth. You will become ashamed of
your sins. I will establish my covenant with you.
I will atone for all of the sins that you committed
and you will know that I am the Lord. (Ezekiel
chapter 16)

God informed Ezekiel that he would surely punish sinners.
However, he stated twice that he took no pleasure in punishing anyone because of their sins. What he wanted everyone to do was turn
away from their sinning so that they might live (Ezekiel chapter 18).

God told Ezekiel that if the people of Jerusalem asked him who
he thought he was by judging their city, he was to declare to them
the sins they had committed against God: shedding innocent blood,
making idols to defile themselves, treating their parents with con-
tempt, extorting travelers, wronging orphans and widows, despising
God's holy things and profaning his Sabbaths, slandering in order
to murder, worshipping other gods, very grave sexual immoralities,
taking bribes to shed blood, extorting one's neighbor to make financial gain, false prophets conspiring to tell lies to the people resulting
in the loss of life and giving people false words from God, priests
doing violence to God's laws and profaning his holy things, princes
destroying lives to get dishonest gain, and many of the people forgetting God. God sought out a man among them who should build up
the wall and stand in the breach before God for the land so he would
not destroy it, but he could not find any. As a result of this, they
would be profaned by their own doing in the sight of other nations.
Jerusalem would be destroyed with the sinners in it, and then his
people would know that God was the Lord (Ezekiel chapter 22). In
the tenth month of the ninth year of the reign of King Zedekiah over
Jerusalem, King Nebuchadnezzar of Babylon began his siege against
Jerusalem as God said he would (Ezekiel chapter 24).

God then gave Ezekiel a pattern of prophecies against nations
that harmed Judah and Israel in some way. In all these prophecies he
mentioned the countries or lands, which included Ammon, Moab,
Seir, Edom, Philistia, Tyre, Sidon, and Egypt. He then told them the

harmful things they did to Israel and Judah. Next, he gave a prophecy to each country through the prophet Ezekiel of exactly what kind of tragedy would befall the people of that country because of their evil acts toward Israel and Judah. He would then end the prophecy to each country with this statement:

Then they will know that I am the Lord.

It appears that God may be using his prophecies about the tragedies to each country and then allowing that tragedy to happen exactly as prophesied, as a way for foreign nations to recognize him as God. They are told what would happen to them by Ezekiel, God's prophet. When the tragedy happened, they would remember Ezekiel's God said this would happen, realize that he was in fact God, and possibly follow him as God (Ezekiel chapters 25–32). God actually does this numerous times throughout the book of Ezekiel, with prophecies of both good and bad things that will happen to various peoples in the future. God will give a specific prophecy to a specific group of people. The prophecy of a future event often ends with the saying, "Then you will know that I am the Lord." It appears that prophecies from God spoken about in scripture, when they actually come to pass as he said they would cause the people to whom they happen realize God is true and they would come to recognize him and/or follow him as God.

God told Ezekiel to say the following to the house of Israel:

[Summary] What I am about to do for you is not for your sake, but for the sake of my holy name which you have profaned among the nations in which you encountered. I will take you from the nations in which you are dispersed and I will bring you back to your own land. I will cleanse you from all of your idol worship and I will deliver you from all uncleanness. I will give you a new heart, and I will put a new spirit within you. I will also put my Spirit in you which will cause you to carefully obey my laws and rules. You will dwell in the land I gave to your fathers, and you will be my people and I will be your God. I will make your crops abundant, and you will never again experience famine. You will hate all of your former evil ways. I will cause your cities to once again be inhabited, and your waste places will be rebuilt. Desolate land will become lush vegetation, which will astonish the world. Your people will increase in their land like a flock and your land will be full of its people. Then the nations around you will know that I am the Lord when they see your deserted and destroyed homeland completely rebuilt. (Ezekiel 36:22–36)

God informed the prophet Ezekiel of things that would happen far in the future. God would one day reunite the tribes of Israel and the tribes of Judah. God would take the people of Israel who were scattered among the nations, and he would bring them back to their own land. He would make them one nation in their land, and one king would be king over all. They would no longer be two nations (Israel and Judah) but one (Israel). They would no longer defile themselves with idols and detestable practices. God would cleanse them and protect them from all their backslidings. They would be God's people, and he would be their God. David would once again be king over them, and they would have one shepherd. God's sanctuary would be in their midst forever, God's dwelling place would be with them, and God would make a covenant of peace with them (Ezekiel 37:15–28).

God then gave Ezekiel a vision of the complete design of a future temple of Israel and instructions on how worship would be conducted in it. He also gave instructions to Ezekiel about how the future land of Israel should be divided as an inheritance among the twelve tribes of Israel. The new name of the land at that time would be "The Lord Is There" (Ezekiel chapters 40–48).

CHAPTER 14

THE PROPHETIC BOOKS: THE BOOK OF DANIEL

When God allowed the Babylonians (Chaldeans) to conquer the kingdom of Judah because its people kept going against what God told them to do, the people of Judah were taken away as captives to the land of Babylon. When they got there, the most promising of the exiles were educated for three years in the customs of the Chaldeans. After that, they would stand before the king to see if they were worthy to become part of the Chaldean society. During these three years, they were given daily servings of Chaldean food and drink (Daniel 1:1–7).

A young man from Judah living as a Babylonian exile was named Daniel. Daniel refused to eat the king's food and drink, because some of the food he was given was prohibited by God for the Jews to eat. The king's servants said to Daniel that if he did not eat the king's food given to him, he would become weak and sick, and they would get in trouble because it would look like they were not feeding Daniel. Daniel told the king's servants to test him and his three friends for ten days. He told them to just give them vegetables and water for ten days. At the end of ten days, the king's servants would inspect their health. If they were healthy, then they would not have to eat the king's food. If they were not healthy, then they would eat the king's food. The king's servants agreed to this. At the end of ten days,

Daniel and his three friends were healthier than all the other young men there. God was taking care of them because they followed God.

> As for these four youths, God gave them learning and skill in all literature and wisdom, and Daniel had understanding in visions and dreams. (Daniel 1:17)

This was discovered by King Nebuchadnezzar when they stood before the king to be tested after their three years of training in Chaldean culture. The king often asked them for advice on important matters, and their advice was better than that of the other men in the kingdom (Daniel 1:18–21).

At one point, King Nebuchadnezzar had a troublesome dream. He put out an order to all the magicians, enchanters, sorcerers, and Chaldeans in the kingdom of Babylon that he wanted them not to just interpret what his dream meant but to also tell him what his secret dream was. If they could not do this, he ordered them to be put to death. He did this to see if the wise men truly had special abilities and to prevent them from fabricating any interpretation of his dream. No one could tell the king what his dream was. Because Daniel was obedient to God, God allowed Daniel to tell the king of the dream that he had and its interpretation. Daniel's revealing of the king's dream, and the interpretation of it was completely accurate. King Nebuchadnezzar was amazed.

> Then King Nebuchadnezzar fell upon his face and paid homage to Daniel, and commanded that an offering and incense be offered up to him. The king answered and said to Daniel, "Truly your God is God of gods and Lord of kings, and a revealer of mysteries, for you have been able to reveal this mystery." (Daniel 2:46–47)

Because he was the only one of the king's men who could do this, the king made Daniel ruler over the whole province of Babylon and chief perfect over all the wise men of Babylon. In turn, Daniel appointed his three friends, Shadrach, Meshach, and Abednego over all the affairs of the Babylon province (Daniel chapter 2)

DANIEL'S FRIENDS AND THE FIERY FURNACE

One day King Nebuchadnezzar, the king of Babylon, made a golden statue ninety feet high and nine feet wide. King Nebuchadnezzar commanded all the people of Babylon that they were to fall on their knees and worship the statue whenever any kind of music was played. It was reported to the king that Daniel's three friends would not bow down and worship the golden statue whenever music was played. The names of Daniel's three friends were Shadrach, Meshach, and Abednego. The king became extremely angry. He brought Shadrach, Meshach, and Abednego to his palace. He told them that if they did not bow down and worship the golden statue whenever the king played music or blew a horn, they would be thrown into a fiery furnace. The three men said to the king:

> Our God is able to deliver us from your
> fiery furnace. But even if he does not, we will not
> serve your gods or worship the golden statue that
> you set up. (Daniel 3:16–18)

The king went into an angry rage when they said this. He demanded that the furnace be heated seven times hotter than usual. He ordered soldiers to tie up Shadrach, Meshach, and Abednego and throw them into the burning fiery furnace. When the soldiers tied the three men up and threw them into the furnace, the fire was so hot that it killed the soldiers that threw them into the fire. As King Nebuchadnezzar looked on, he jumped up in astonishment.

He said to his followers "Did we not cast three men bound into the fire?"

They said, "Yes we did, king."

The king said,

> But I see four men, untied walking around
> in the middle of the fire, and they are not hurt;
> and the appearance of the fourth one is like the
> son of God. (Daniel 3:24–25)

King Nebuchadnezzar came close to the fiery furnace and yelled,

> Shadrach, Meshach, and Abednego, ser-
> vants of the Most High God, come out and come
> here! (Daniel 3:26)

The three men came out of the fire, and everyone saw that the fire did not hurt them at all. King Nebuchadnezzar then said,

> Blessed be the God of Shadrach, Meshach
> and Abednego, who has come and saved these
> three men who trusted in him, and ignored my
> command and risked their lives rather than serve
> and worship any god except their own God.
> (Daniel 3:28)

King Nebuchadnezzar then made a law that no one could speak anything bad against the God of these three men because their God was the only true God. Additionally, Shadrach, Meshach, and Abednego were promoted to very important positions in Babylon. God used these three men to convince the King Nebuchadnezzar of Babylon that our God is the only true God.

DANIEL INTERPRETS MORE VISIONS FOR THE KINGS OF BABYLON

One night, King Nebuchadnezzar had a dream that made him afraid. He called in all the wise men, magicians, enchanters, and astrologers. He told them his dream and asked them for an interpretation of it, but none of them could do so. He then brought in Daniel, knowing that the spirit of God was with him and he would be able to do it. The dream was as follows: King Nebuchadnezzar dreamed of a giant tree in the middle of the earth, whose height reached up into the heavens. It was visible to the whole earth. Then a holy watcher from heaven came down and chopped down the tree, cut off its branches, stripped off its fruit, and put an iron and bronze band around the stump that was still in the ground.

The watcher from heaven then said,

> Let his portion be with the beasts in the grass of the earth. Let his mind be changed from a man's, and let a beast's mind be given to him; and let seven periods of time pass over him. This is that the living may know that the Most High rules the kingdom of men and gives it to whom he will and sets over it the lowliest of men. (Daniel 4:15–17)

Daniel was dismayed when he heard the dream. King Nebuchadnezzar asked him kindly to tell him what the dream meant. Daniel told Nebuchadnezzar that he was the tree in the dream, who had grown strong, whose greatness reached heaven, and whose dominion covered the earth. God has decreed that King Nebuchadnezzar would be driven from among men, and he would live with the beasts of the field. He will eat grass like an ox, and he would be like this for seven years, until he knew that God ruled the kingdom of men and he gave it to whom he willed. When he fully knew that God in heaven ruled everything, he would once again return to his position as king. Daniel gave King Nebuchadnezzar advice, saying to end his sins by practicing righteousness and by showing mercy to the oppressed, and possibly his sentence would be reduced (Daniel 4:19–27).

This is exactly what happened to King Nebuchadnezzar one year later. He was walking on the roof of his royal palace in Babylon and said,

> Is not this great Babylon, which I have built
> by my mighty power as a royal residence and for
> the glory of my majesty? (Daniel 4:30)

As the last word was still in his mouth, a voice came down from heaven,

> O King Nebuchadnezzar, to you it is spo-
> ken: The kingdom has departed from you, and
> you shall be driven from among men, and your
> dwelling shall be with the beasts of the field. And
> you shall be made to eat grass like an ox, and
> seven periods of time shall pass over you, until
> you know that the Most High rules the kingdom
> of men and gives it to whom he will. (Daniel
> 4:31–32)

This happened immediately. King Nebuchadnezzar was driven from among men. He ate grass like an ox, his body was wet with the dew from heaven, his hair grew as long as eagles' feathers, and his nails were like birds' claws. After seven years, Nebuchadnezzar lifted his eyes to heaven, and his reason returned to him. He blessed God, praised, and honored him, acknowledging that God is ruler of everything. When his reason returned to him, he was restored by the counselors and nobles as king of Babylon. This time, he ruled it under humble submission to God (Daniel chapter 4).

Sometime after this, Nebuchadnezzar's son, Belshazzar, was the king of Babylon. One day during a great feast with his nobility, he commanded that the religious items that his father took away from the Jewish temple during the siege and exile to be brought out for the people from the festival to drink from. This took place. Immediately, the fingers of a human hand appeared. It wrote on the wall of the king's palace, and King Belshazzar became very afraid. He called all the enchanters and wise men to his palace to decipher the meaning of the writing on the wall made by the mysterious hand that appeared out of nowhere. None could do so. The queen informed the king that Daniel had previously interpreted messages for his father, King Nebuchadnezzar, because God was with Daniel. Daniel was summoned by the king to do so. Daniel was brought to the king, and he was asked to interpret the mysterious writing on the wall. God gave Daniel the ability to do so.

Daniel told King Belshazzar that God gave his father, King Nebuchadnezzar, great power as a king, and the world feared and respected him. Yet he became proud. Therefore, his kingship was taken from him and he was driven from mankind, living like an animal. He then acknowledged that Most High God ruled the kingdom of mankind and set over it whom he willed.

> As his son, King Belshazzar, you knew all this. Yet, you have not humbled your heart, but instead you have lifted up yourself against the God of heaven. You took the holy articles from God's house and drank from them at your party and worshipped idols.

Therefore, God sent the hand that wrote MENE, MENE, TEKEL, and PARSAN (Daniel 5:1–23) This means:

> MENE, God has numbered the days of your kingdom and brought it to an end; TEKEL, you have been weighed in the balances and found wanting; PERES, your kingdom is divided and given to the Medes and Persians. (Daniel 5:26–28)

> That very night Belshazzar the Chaldean was killed. And Darius the Mede received the kingdom, being about sixty-two years old. (Daniel 5:30)

DANIEL AND THE LION'S DEN

God helped Daniel in many ways because Daniel listened to God and followed what he said to do in his life. Daniel rose to a high position in the Babylonian government because of this. He was about to be named ruler over all the other leaders in the entire kingdom by King Darius "because an excellent spirit was in him" (Daniel 6:3). The other leaders of the government became envious of Daniel. They were searching for a way to get him in trouble so they could get rid of him. They convinced King Darius to make a law that for thirty days that no one should make a petition to any god or man besides King Darius. If they did, they would be thrown in to a lions' den. They did this because they knew that Daniel prayed to God every day. The king agreed to this. He did not know they were trying to get rid of Daniel, whom the king liked (Daniel 6:1–9).

When Daniel heard about this new law, he got down on his knees and prayed to God like he usually did. The men who were envious of Daniel were spying on him, knowing that he prays to God every day. When they saw him praying to God, they went to the king and said "King Darius, did you not make a law that if anyone prayed to any god over this thirty-day period, they would be thrown in a lions' den?" The king said "Yes, I did agree to that law." The envious men said to the king "Daniel, who is one of the exiles from Judah, pays no attention to you or your law, because we saw him praying to his God three times every day." (Daniel 6:10–13)

The king was very upset about this because he liked Daniel. He tried to save Daniel from being thrown into a lions' den. However, in that culture when a king made a law it could not then be changed, even by the king himself. The king was tricked by these evil men into making this irrevocable law. The king was unable to save Daniel, and he was cast in to the lions' den. Before he went in, the king said to Daniel, "May your God, who you serve continually, deliver you from the lions!" A big stone was placed over the entrance of the lions' den so Daniel could not escape. The king went back to his castle and fasted from food and drink all night, hoping that Daniel's God would save him. (Daniel 6:14–18)

In the morning, the king went to the lions' den. He yelled out in sadness "O Daniel, servant of the living God, has your God, whom you serve continually, been able to deliver you from the lions?" (Daniel 6:20)

Then Daniel said to the king "O king, live forever! My God sent his angel and shut the lions' mouths, and they have not harmed me, because I was found blameless before him; and also before you, O king, I have done no harm." (Daniel 6:21–22)

The king was very happy that Daniel was not hurt at all by the lions. Daniel was taken out of the lions' den completely unharmed because he trusted God. Then the king gathered up all the envious men who tricked the king into making a law that would throw Daniel into the lions' den. The king threw these evil men into the lions' den in the place of Daniel. The lions jumped up and ate the men before they even reached the ground. As a result of God saving Daniel from the lions, King Darius declared to his whole kingdom that Daniel's God is the one true God, and the whole kingdom must love and follow him. God used Daniel being put in a lions' den to

convince the whole kingdom that he is the only true God, who saves
those that trust in him (Daniel 6:19–28).

The book of Daniel ends with many symbolic prophecies about
the events that will happen to various future kingdoms.

CHAPTER 15

THE PROPHETIC BOOKS: THE MINOR PROPHETS

The following are summaries of the books of the minor prophets in the Bible. They are called the minor prophets because the books are short in length relative to the books of Isaiah, Jeremiah, Ezekiel, and Daniel. The term *minor prophets* has nothing to do with the significance of the prophets.

THE BOOK OF HOSEA

God began to speak to a man named Hosea and made him a prophet between God and his people. Hosea lived during the kings Uzziah, Jotham, Ahaz, Hezekiah of Judah, and King Jeroboam of Israel. God instructed Hosea to choose a prostitute for a wife and have children with her. He told him to do this because his own people were prostituting themselves to other nations and their false gods. He therefore married a prostitute named Gomer, and they had children. Hosea named his children after the names God instructed him to name them. He named his son Jezreel, because God would soon punish the house of Jehu for shedding blood at Jezreel, and he would bring an end to the kingdom of the house of Israel. They had a daughter and Hosea named her Not-Pitied, because God would no longer felt pity for the house of Israel. He would feel pity for the house of

Judah and he would save them by God's own hand. They then had a son and named him Not-My-People because Israel was no longer God's people and he was no longer their God (Hosea chapter 1).

God compared his people to a woman who becomes a prostitute who leaves her husband to go after other men. God was the one who gave his people all the grain, oil, wine, and gold, which they then used to make sacrifices to Baal. Therefore, God would take back all the riches that he gave to his people. They would be laid bare before all the foreign nations that they wrongfully chased after, while forgetting their true God. God then stated,

> One day, however, my people will turn back
> to me. On that day I will once again love them
> and take care of them as a husband does a loving
> and faithful wife. (Hosea chapter 2)

God sent a message through Hosea that he was very angry with the priests and the so-called "prophets." God's people were ruined because the priests and prophets were lacking in knowledge of God. Therefore, God would reject them as serving as priests to the people because they had forgotten God's law. Their sinfulness increased against God. They were greedy and fed on the sin of the people. They abandoned God to follow the ways of false gods and to worship idols. God would punish them for these things (Hosea chapter 4).

God let his wayward people know that he desired steadfast love and not sacrifice. He wanted them to have knowledge of God rather than giving burnt offerings (Hosea 6:6).

God was angry at Israel because they chose kings and princes that were not from God. Their princes were rebels, and the people made detestable idols. They had mixed in with and followed the ways of other nations. They followed Assyria to their demise. They erected altars for other gods. They thought they would be safe in Egypt. Their prophets were fools; they did not fear God. God would remember their sins and discipline them for it. Israel had forgotten their Maker. Therefore, God would depart from them. He would reject them because they had not listened to him. Judah had built fortified cities, but God would devour them by fire (Hosea chapters 8, 9 and 10).

Through the prophet Hosea, God instructed his people to sow righteousness for themselves and they would reap steadfast love. If they sought God, he might come and rain righteousness on them. God said that when Israel was a child, God loved them. However, the more God called them, the more they went away, sacrificing to the Baals and making burnt offerings to idols. God was the one who raised them as a Father raises a child and he healed them, although they did not know it. God gave them cords of kindness with bands of love. He eased their burdens, and he bent down to feed them. They left God and refused to return. Now, they would be servants to the king of Assyria. The sword should rage against them for following their own sinful counsels instead of following God. Israel was bent on turning away from God, but God loved them. His heart recoiled within him because of the suffering they were going through from their own doing. He is God, and he will withhold some of his anger toward them because he is holy and not a man. The people of Israel would one day return to God. He would roar like a lion, and his children would return to him in fear and trembling from the countries in which they were scattered. God would return them to their homes (Hosea chapters 10 and 11).

God told Israel that they had fallen because of their iniquity. He wanted them to return to him and ask for forgiveness of sins and admit that they inappropriately trusted other countries and false idols to save them. If they did these things, God would heal them from their turning away from him. He would love Israel freely and stop his anger toward them. Israel would then flourish under God's loving care, and he would protect them (Hosea chapter 14).

THE BOOK OF JOEL

The word of God came to a man named Joel, the son of Pethuel. Swarms of various types of locust ate the vegetation of the land, and there was not much of the crops, if any, left. Joel instructed the priests to mourn in sackcloth, and he called for a fast of the people. God sent his people a message through the prophet Joel. He instructed his people to return to following God with all their heart. To mourn, weep, and fast in front of him. To return to God because he is gracious and merciful, slow to anger, and he abounds in steadfast love. He relents disasters. God told Joel to gather all the people and have them ask God for mercy to spare them from this famine caused by the locust. The people did this. God then became jealous for his land, and he had pity on his people. He told them that he would send them grain, wine, and oil and they would be satisfied. He would return all their vegetation to them that the locust ate.

THE BOOK OF AMOS

Amos was a shepherd in the land of Tekoa when God appeared to him. He gave him visions and messages to give to God's people. Amos lived during the time of King Uzziah of Judah and King Jeroboam of Israel.

In the first part of the book of Amos, God gave Amos prophecies about things that would happen in various countries and lands in and near Israel. God said that he would punish the city of Damascus for threshing Gilead with sledges of iron and for devouring the strongholds of Ben-hadad. He would send fire upon the wall of Gaza and destroy the strongholds Philistia because they exiled an entire population, handing them over to Edom. God would do the same thing to Tyre for the same reason. He would punish Ammon and send their king and princes into exile for killing innocent people. God would destroy the ruler and princes of Edom for burning to ashes the bones of Edom's king (Amos chapter 1).

God would send fire upon Judah and devour the strongholds of Jerusalem because Judah spurned the instruction of God and did not keep his laws. They were led astray by following lies instead of the true God. God accused Israel of many sins against him. The people of Israel persecuted their neighbors for financial gain, they oppressed the poor and the lowly, they engaged in sexual immorality, and they misused wine in the temple. God destroyed the enemies of Israel and brought them out of the land of Egypt where they were slaves. He raised up prophets among their children and Nazirites among their young men. Yet the Israelites compelled the Nazirites to drink and told the prophets to not give prophesy. God was groaning, burdened with the sins of Israel against him. Therefore, battle would come to Israel and they would not be victorious in it (Amos chapter 2).

God informed Israel:

> Indeed, the Lord God does nothing without revealing his plan to his servants the prophets. (Amos 3:7)

God sent a message through the prophet Amos to Samaria (a territory of Israel).

> [Summary] Samaria—you oppress the needy and do not follow my ways. I made food scarce for you, yet you did not return to me. I withheld the rain from you so cities were staggering for lack of water, yet you did not return to me. I caused plagues of disease and insects to destroy your crops, yet you did not return to me. I sent death to your people through disease like that of Egypt and through the sword, yet you did not return to me. I overthrew you like I did with Sodom and Gomorrah, yet you did not return to me. Therefore Israel, prepare to meet me: the one who forms mountains and creates winds, who gives thoughts to mortals, who makes the dawn turn into darkness and strides upon the heights of the earth. Prepare to meet the Lord, the God of hosts! (Amos chapter 4).

Amaziah, the priest of Bethel, sent a letter to king Jeroboam of Israel, complaining that Amos was prophesying that King Jeroboam would die by the sword and Israel would be exiled from their land. Then Amaziah the priest approached Amos and said,

> Off with you, seer, flee to the land of Judah
> and there earn your bread by prophesying! But
> never again prophesy in Bethel; for it is the king's
> sanctuary and royal temple. (Amos 7:12–14)

Amos responded to Amaziah by saying that he was a shepherd, and God personally took him from being a shepherd and told him to go and prophesy to the people of Israel. Because Amaziah was now telling him to not prophesy against Israel and preach against the house of Isaac, which was in contrary to God's instructions to Amos, tragedy would befall Amaziah, his family, his land, and the country of Israel (Amos 7:10–17).

THE BOOK OF JONAH

Jonah was an Israelite man. One day God appeared to Jonah and said,

> Arise, go to Nineveh, that great city, and call
> out against it, for their evil has come up before
> me. (Jonah 1:2)

Nineveh was a huge, pagan city (they did not follow our God). It was located in modern-day Iraq, and it had 120,000 people living in it. God wanted Jonah to go to Nineveh and tell them to repent of their sinful ways or God would destroy the city.

Jonah did not want to do this. The city of Nineveh was the capital of the Assyrian Empire, an enemy of the Israelites. Jonah did not want to go there, and he did not want God to save the city. Instead of heading to Nineveh as God told Jonah to do, he turned around and headed in the completely opposite direction. He found a ship heading to Tarshish and boarded it. Tarshish was west of where Jonah was at; Nineveh was east (Jonah 1:1–3).

God created a massive storm surrounding the ship that Jonah was on. Everyone onboard panicked, and they thought they were going to die. They yelled out to everyone onboard to call to the various gods that they worshipped, to see if any would help them in this deadly storm. Things got progressively worse for the people on Jonah's ship. They decided to cast lots to see who might have been responsible for this storm being sent against them. The lots fell on Jonah. Jonah revealed that he was a Hebrew and God was sending this storm at them because he was running away from directions God gave him to do. Jonah told them this was all his fault. He said that if they threw him into the sea and got rid of him, the God of the Hebrews (our God) would stop the storm. The sailors tried on their own to navigate through the storm, but it was no use and they were about to die. They came to the conclusion that they would have to throw Jonah overboard to save themselves.

> They called out to the Lord, "Oh Lord, let us not perish for this man's life, and lay not on us innocent blood, for you, O Lord, have done as it pleased you." They then picked up Jonah and hurled him into the sea, and the sea ceased from raging. Then the men feared the Lord exceedingly, and they offered a sacrifice to the Lord and made vows. (Jonah 1:14–16)

Jonah now found himself sinking to his death in the ocean. God appointed a great fish to swim up to Jonah and swallow him. Jonah was alive and unharmed in the belly of the great fish for three days and three nights. Jonah was actually very relieved and thankful to be alive and well inside of the huge fish, rather than drowning in the ocean, which was what he thought would happen to him. While inside the fish, Johan offered up a prayer of thanksgiving to God for saving his life. After these supernatural series of events, Jonah was now willing to obey God's instructions to him (Jonah chapter 2).

After three days and nights, God freed Jonah from the belly of the great fish.

> And the Lord spoke to the fish, and it vomited Jonah out upon dry land. (Jonah 2:10)

> Then the word of the Lord came to Jonah the second time, saying, "Arise, go to Nineveh, that great city, and call out against it the message that I tell you." (Jonah 3:1–2)

> Jonah went to Nineveh and walked through it, shouting "Yet forty days, and Nineveh shall be overthrown!" (Jonah 3:4)

Due to the preaching of Jonah, the people of Nineveh believed God, and they repented of their sinful ways.

> They called for a fast and put on sackcloth, from the greatest to the least of them. (Jonah 3:5)

News of this reached the king of Nineveh. He ordered the whole kingdom to repent of their evil ways and to call out to God to have mercy on them.

> When God saw what they did, how they turned from their evil way, God relented of the disaster that he said he would do to them, and he did not do it. (Jonah 3:10)

Jonah was actually very upset that God saved the people of Nineveh. They were the enemies of Israel, and Jonah did not want God to save them. God responded to Jonah,

> [Summary] Why should I not feel bad for the people in Nineveh? There are 120,000 people in that city who do not know me, and therefore,

they do not even know that they are doing things that are wrong against me. (Jonah chapter 4)

THE BOOK OF MICAH

The word of God came to a man named Micah during the reign of Kings Jotham, Ahaz, and Hezekiah. God gave him prophecy concerning Samaria and Jerusalem.

God said he would make Samaria a ruined field. He would destroy its idols and carved images. A conquering people would come and take its inhabitants away in an exile (Micah chapter 1).

God condemned the people for coveting fields and houses that belonged to others and taking them.

> [Summary] Therefore, captors will take your possessions and divide them among themselves in front of their eyes. You tell me not to preach these things to you; you contend that shameful things will not happen to you. Do I not promise good things to one who walks in justice? But you rise up against my people as if they were an enemy. You rob from the peaceful people. (Micah chapter 2)

God said,

> [Summary] You rulers of the house of Israel and leaders of Jacob: Is it not your duty to know what is right? Instead, you hate what is good and love what is evil. You horribly oppress and take advantage of the poor and powerless. You pervert all that is right and you abhor justice. You fill Zion with bloodshed and Jerusalem with wickedness. Your leaders make judgments based on bribes. Priests teach for money and prophets give messages for pay. And you think that no harm

can come to you because you believe you are relying on the Lord, which you are not. Zion shall be
plowed like a field and Jerusalem will be reduced
to rubble. The mount of the temple will become
a forest ridge. I will not hear your voice when
you cry out to me. Regarding the prophets: you
lead my people astray. You manipulate war and
peace for your own profit. Therefore, you will get
no messages from God, and you will be put to
shame. (Micah chapter 3)

God then gave the prophet Micah wonderful prophecies about
the future of Israel. It would be discussed more in depth in the chapter on the prophecies about Jesus in the Old Testament. But in a brief
summary, God told Micah to tell the people that one day the land
of Zion would actually have God dwelling in it, and it would be the
most revered place in the world because God would be there. People
would come from all over the world to the Lord's mountain to hear
instructions from God. All the tools of war of the nations would be
changed into farming tools. The weak would be assembled by God
there, and the people would live in peace. Micah informed them that
in the meantime, the people of Zion would be exiled to Babylon for a
while, but God would rescue them and redeem them from the hand
of their enemies (Micah chapter 4).

Many nations are now gathered against you,
but God will protect you from them and you will
defeat them.

God stated that a ruler whose origin was from ancient times
will come out of Bethlehem and rule Israel. He should be a shepherd
by the strength of God. His greatness should extend to the ends of
the earth, and he should be peace. In that time the remnant of Jacob
would be among many nations and many peoples. The enemies of
Jacob would be destroyed. However, at some earlier time before this,
God would in vengeance and wrath destroy the cities of his peo-

ple because of their sorcery, soothsaying, and worshipping of idols (Micah chapter 5).

In the above prophecy, it is possible that what is stated is that when Jesus returns, he may bring a resurrected David with him to rule Israel. These are two other Bible prophecies that seem to possibly say that.

In Ezekiel, it is prophesied that Israel and Judah will one day join back together and form the nation of Israel. And it says,

> My servant David shall be king over them,
> and they shall have one shepherd. (Ezekiel 37:24)

In another Bible prophecy, it states,

> And it shall come to pass in that day, declares the Lord of hosts, that I will break his yoke from off your neck, and I will burst your bonds and foreigners shall no longer make a servant of him. But they shall serve the Lord their God and David their king, whom I will raise up for them. (Jeremiah 30:8–9)

King David is long dead by now in the Bible. For him to rule over God's people on earth in the future, God would have to bring him back to earth.

God told the people exactly what he always wanted from them:

> Only to do justice and to love goodness and
> to walk humbly with your God. (Micah 6:8)

However, the wealthy of his people are full of violence, and the inhabitants of God's land habitually lie and speak falsehoods. They have loved to do evil deeds, and therefore they will be disciplined by God (Micah chapter 6).

God announced that the faithful had vanished from the earth and there was no one who was just. People act treacherously against others, harming each other for personal gain. Judges are taking bribes, and the powerful do not care what they do to others. People even in one's own family cannot be trusted in these times. Micah concludes by putting trust in God. Although times may be difficult in the lives of God's followers, God does not stay angry forever but delights in the first chance to offer mercy. He will ultimately save those that follow his ways (Micah chapter 7).

BOOK OF NAHUM

God gave a man named Nahum visions and messages about the city of Nineveh, the capital of Assyria, enemies of Israel. The messages given to Nahum are as follows:

> God is all-powerful. He is slow to anger, but he is all powerful. When he decides to strike, he destroys as he wishes, and nothing or no one can resist what he does. Nineveh has plotted evil against God, and counseled people to do evil. God has humbled them in the past. He will humble them not a second time; he will destroy them. The false idols of its false gods will be abolished. (Nahum chapter 1)

Nineveh was a city that scattered its enemies, and it had done this to Israel. The Lord would restore Israel from this. God would arrive with warriors carrying crimson shields dressed in scarlet. They would siege Nineveh, and its inhabitants would be washed away, and the city would be plundered into desolation.

> I now come against you—oracle of the Lord of Hosts—I will consume your chariots in smoke, and the sword will devour your young lions. Your preying on the land I will bring to

an end, the cry of your lioness will be heard no more. (Nahum 2:14)

God described Nineveh as the bloody city, all lies, full of plunder that never stopped looting. It had many debaucheries, a charming mistress of witchcraft, who enslaved other nations with her witchcraft and prostitution. Therefore, God would shame the city in front of the other nations. Better and more powerful cities than Nineveh had been sent into exile as a punishment by God. This would be Nineveh's fate also. And all who heard this news of Nineveh would applaud, because of the countless people it had made suffer by its endless malice (Nahum chapter 3).

THE BOOK OF HABAKKUK

The prophet Habakkuk received a vision from God. Habakkuk questioned God why he did not stop the sinful evil that was taking place around him. God replied that at that very moment, he was working on raising up the Chaldeans, whom he would use to discipline the sinful people of Israel. Habakkuk then questioned God if it was the right thing to do to use the bloodthirsty Chaldeans as a means to discipline Israel. God let Habakkuk know that although the Chaldeans' conquering ways would discipline Israel, the peoples oppressed by Chaldea would one day turn the tables on Chaldea, and they would treat Chaldea as Chaldea treated them. He who treats other nations as his personal possession will one day be possessed by them. Their greed will lead to their destruction. Chaldea would be judged and punished for shedding innocent blood and pursuing evil gain for themselves. The way they harshly and unjustly treated others would cause God to treat them in the same manner. Praying to their false gods and idols would not save them in the day of God's judgment against the evil Chaldeans. Habakkuk then praised God for all the glorious things he had done as all-powerful God (Habakkuk chapters 1, 2, and 3).

BOOK OF ZEPHANIAH

The word of God came to Zephaniah, who lived in Judah during the reign of King Josiah. This was shortly before King Nebuchadnezzar of Babylon (the Chaldeans) invaded and destroyed Jerusalem and took the people to Babylon in an exile. God gave a prophecy that God would sweep away all things from the face of the land. He would stretch his hand our against Judah and Jerusalem because they worshipped Baal, whom the idolatrous priests had come to worship. The people also turned away from God, and in his place they worshipped the moon and stars as gods and Milcom, the false god of the Ammonites. The kings' officials and sons would be punished, who followed foreign customs not of God. People would wail, and merchants would be destroyed. People who believed God was powerless to either help or punish them would be destroyed by him. All their ill-gotten possessions would be given over to those who would come to plunder them. The day of the Lord was near, and it would arrive swiftly. The silver and gold that the people own would not be able to save them (Zephaniah chapter 1).

God then instructed the shameful people of Judah and Jerusalem to gather themselves together, humble themselves and observe God's law, and they might be sheltered from God's anger. God then let the people know that in the more distant future, the remnant of the house of Judah would rule over all the surrounding lands and nations. God would at some point destroy the nations that were the enemies of Israel, and the people of Israel would plunder and dispossess them. God would make all the false gods of the earth waste away. All nations would come to bow down to the Lord. God revealed that Assyria would be destroyed. He would make Nineveh a waste, and it would be as dry as a desert. Wild animals would live in the buildings that were once inhabited by its people. People would ask, "Is this the city that exulted itself, that was so secure, that asked if there was any other city as great as it?" It would become a waste, inhabited by wild animals. People who would go by would shake their fists at it and hiss (Zephaniah chapter 2).

God then gave a message to Jerusalem:

[Summary] You rebellious, tyrannical, polluted city! It will not listen to me, and accept my correction for it. It has not trusted me, or drawn near to me. It officials are roaring lions, its judges are desert wolves. Its prophets are reckless and treacherous people. Its priests profane things that are holy and do violence against the law. But God is in its midst who is just and does no wrong. I render judgment every morning, but the wicked here know no shame. I have cut down and devastated nations that were against me. I said, "Jerusalem will surely now fear me and you will accept my correction of you." They clearly see all I have brought upon them. Yet they increasingly do corrupt deeds, and they do so eagerly. (Zephaniah 3:1–7)

[Continued summary] One day I will gather all the nations and pour out my wrath on them. Then, I will purify the speech of the peoples that they may all call upon the name of the Lord to serve me with one accord. People from all over the world will then bring me offerings. You will no longer be ashamed of all of your rebellious deeds against me. I will remove all of the prideful braggarts and you will no longer exalt yourself on my holy mountain. I will leave a humble and lowly remnant in your midst, the remnant of Israel, who will take refuge in the name of God. They will speak no lies and do no wrong. They will lie down in peaceful pastures and no one will disturb them. Shout for joy, Zion, and sing joyfully in Israel! God has removed his judgement against you and protected you from your enemies. The King of Israel, God, is in your midst, you have nothing else to fear. On that day the people will worship God happily in Zion. I will rejoice with gladness over you and renew you in my love. I will protect you, and save the weak and the outcast. I will gather you and bring you home. You will be praised among all the peoples of the earth, when I restore you before your very eyes, says the Lord. (Zephaniah chapter 3)

THE BOOK OF HAGGAI

The word of God came through the prophet Haggai. Haggai lived during the rule of the Persian King Darius I, when some of the Babylonian exiles returned to Judah which was earlier destroyed by King Nebuchadnezzar. The returned exiles to Judah believed that it was not the right time to rebuild the temple that was destroyed by the Chaldeans. God told his people through Haggai that he wanted them to rebuild his temple. The returned exiles took the time and put in the effort to rebuild houses for themselves, but they left God's temple in ruins. Therefore, God declared a famine on the land because of this. The leaders, the high priest Joshua, and the people obeyed the words of Haggai, because he was speaking a message from God as God's prophet. God then stirred up the spirit of all the remnant of the people to go to work rebuilding God's temple (Haggai chapter 1).

Through the prophet Haggai, God spoke to Zerubbabel, the governor of Judah, to Joshua the high priest, and to the remnant of the people that returned to Judah. He said,

[Summary] This fallen temple is nothing like what it was in its former glory. Be strong, everyone in the land, and work! For I, God, am with you made a commitment to you when you came out of Egypt. My spirit remains here with you, so do not fear! In a little while, I will shake the heavens, the earth, and all of the nations so that the treasures of all of the nations will come in to you. And I, God, will fill this house with glory. I own all of the silver and gold. This house of mine will be more glorious than it was in its former days. And I will give you peace in this place. (Haggai 2:1–9)

On the day that the people were about to rebuild the temple, God told them,

[Summary] You have sinned against me and defiled the holy things. That is why even though you worked hard, you were not able to produce anything fruitfully. However, from this day on, I will bless you. (Haggai 2:10–19)

BOOK OF ZECHARIAH

The word of God came to the prophet Zechariah, who lived during the reign of King Darius of Persia. Through Zechariah, God made an announcement to the people:

I was very angry with your ancestors. If you return to me as my people, I will return to you as your God. Do not be like your ancestors who were told by the prophets to turn away from your wicked ways and return to me, but they did not listen. Look what had to happen to them before they finally repented. (Zechariah 1:1–6)

One day, God sent visions and words to the prophet Zechariah. Zechariah saw a vision of a man mounted on a red horse, and behind him were three other horses. The man on the horse told Zechariah that these were the ones that God sent to patrol the earth. They reported to the angel of the Lord that the whole earth now rested quietly. The angel of the Lord then asked God how much longer he would be without mercy on Judah and Jerusalem who had felt God's anger for seventy years. God replied with comforting, favorable words. God then said,

> [Summary] I am very jealous for Jerusalem and Zion. I return to Jerusalem in mercy. My house will be rebuilt in Jerusalem. My cities will once again have overflowing prosperity. I will comfort Zion again, and I will choose Jerusalem again. (Zechariah 1:7–17)

Zechariah then raised his eyes and saw another vision. Zechariah saw four horns. He was told that they were the horns that scattered Israel, Jerusalem, and Judah so that no one could raise their head anymore. He then saw four workmen. He was told that the four workmen have come to terrify those horns, to cut down the horns of the nations that scattered the land of Judah (Zechariah 2:1–4).

A third vision came to Zechariah. In it, a man had a measuring cord. An angel told Zechariah that the man was measuring Jerusalem to see how great its length and width were. Then God spoke to him through an angel and said that Jerusalem would be unwalled because of the abundance of people and beasts in it. God himself would be an encircling wall of fire, and he would be the glory in the midst of the city. He then told Zechariah that the Jewish people would return from Babylon. God will protect the land of Israel and would be there with the people, and they would be his people (Zechariah chapter 2).

Next, God gave Zechariah a vision about Joshua the high priest. Joshua was standing before the angel of the Lord while Satan was accusing him. The angel of the Lord said to Satan,

> May the Lord rebuke you, O Satan! The Lord who has chosen Jerusalem rebuke you! Is this not a brand plucked from the fire? (Zechariah 3:2)

Joshua was standing before the angel wearing filthy garments. The angel took his filthy garments off of him and said that he had taken his iniquity away from him and would clothe him in pure vestments and a clean turban. The angel of the Lord assured Joshua that if he walked in God's ways and followed his commands, he would rule God's house and be in charge of his courts and of the people (Zechariah chapter 3).

God had Zechariah make a gold crown and set it on the head of Joshua the high priest. Then God instructed Zechariah to say to him:

> Behold the man whose name is the Branch: for he shall branch out from this place, and he shall build the temple of the Lord. It is he who shall build the temple of the Lord and shall bear royal honor, and shall sit and rule on his throne. And there shall be a priest on his throne, and the counsel of peace shall be between them both. (Zechariah 6:12–13).

> And this shall come to pass, if you diligently obey the voice of the Lord your God. (Zechariah 6:14)

God let Zechariah know that because he sent so many messages to the people through the prophets about how he wanted them to live, but they refused to listen to him, that was why God refused to listen to their cries to him when they were in great distress (Zechariah chapter 7).

God told Zechariah that he was jealous for Zion. He had now returned to Zion and he was present among his people. Jerusalem would be called the faithful city and the mountain of the Lord of Hosts, the holy mountain. Old men and women would once again line the streets of Jerusalem, which would be full of boys and girls playing. They would be God's people, and he would be their God in righteousness and faithfulness. There would now be a sowing of peace for the remnant of this people. Crops would flourish, and rain would be plentiful. God would save them, and they would be a blessing. Just as God brought disaster to his sinful people, in these days he would bring good to the house of Judah and Jerusalem. God instructed his people:

> Speak the truth to one another; render in your gates judgments that are true and make for peace; do not devise evil in your hearts against one another, and love no false oath, for all these things I hate, declares the Lord. (Zechariah 8:16–17)

Instead, love truth and peace.

God said that in the future, people would happily come from all over the world to Jerusalem to seek God, because he would be there. God would protect Jerusalem from any enemies.

Zechariah 9:9–12 gives a prophecy about the future coming of Jesus on his triumphant entry into Jerusalem on Palm Sunday and how he would save people from their sins:

> Rejoice greatly, O daughter of Zion! Shout aloud, O daughter of Jerusalem! Behold, your king is coming to you; righteous and having salvation is he, humble and mounted on a donkey, on a colt, the foal of a donkey. I will cut off the chariot from Ephraim and the war horse from Jerusalem; and the battle bow shall be cut off, and he shall speak to the nations; his rule shall be from sea to sea, and from the River to the ends of the earth. As for you, because of the blood of my covenant with you, I will set your prisoners free from the waterless pit. Return to your stronghold, O prisoners of hope; today I declare that I will restore to you double.

God said that he would punish the bad shepherds who failed to lead his sheep. God cared for his flock, the house of Judah. He would make them a majestic people. From God would come the cornerstone. God would strengthen his people because he has compassion on them; he was their God, and he would answer them. The children would see it and be glad and rejoice. God would gather his people in because he had redeemed them. Though he previously scattered them among the nations, God would bring them back home from all the countries in which they were scattered. He would make his people strong in the Lord, and they would walk in his name (Zechariah chapter 10).

Another prophecy about Jesus was given in the book of Zechariah, about Judas betraying Jesus for thirty pieces of silver and the money then being used to buy potter's field:

> Then I said to them, "If it seems good to
> you, give me my wages; but if not, keep them."
> And they weighed out as my wages thirty pieces
> of silver. Then the Lord said to me, "Throw it to
> the potter—the lordly price at which I was priced
> by them." (Zechariah 11:12–13)

God lets us know that one day the people of Jerusalem will come to recognize Jesus as the Messiah and mourn for what they did to him:

> And on that day I will pour out on the house
> of David and the inhabitants of Jerusalem a spirit
> of grace and pleas for mercy, so that, when they
> look on me, on him whom they have pierced,
> they shall mourn for him, as one mourns for an
> only child, and weep bitterly over him, as one
> weeps over a firstborn. (Zechariah 12:10)

False prophets and idols will be removed from the land on that day. Another prophecy of Jesus is given, which Jesus would later quote concerning himself and the apostles abandoning him when he would be apprehended by the Roman soldiers:

> Awake, O sword, against my shepherd,
> against the man who stands next to me, declares

the Lord of hosts. Strike the shepherd, and the sheep will be scattered. (Zechariah 13:7)

The book of Zechariah ends with a lengthy prophecy about the Second Coming of Jesus (Zechariah chapter 14).

THE BOOK OF MALACHI

Through the prophet Malachi, God condemned the priests of his people. God said,

> [Summary] You say I am a Father, yet you do not honor me. If I am a master, you do not fear me. You priests, you despise my name. You offer polluted food upon my altar. You offer me blind animals as a sacrifice. Is that not evil? You offer me animals in sacrifice that are lame or sick. If you presented that to the governor, would he accept it? You give me that and you want me to show you favor and be gracious to you. With these kinds of gifts you give to me, will I show any favor to you? I have no pleasure in you, and I will not accept these offerings from you. My name will be great among the nations of the world, and in every place incense and a pure offering will be offered to my name. My name will be great among the nations. But you profane my name when you say my table is polluted and its food may be despised. But you say 'What a chore this is,' and you snort at it. You bring me animals that were killed by violence or that are lame or sick. And this is the offering you bring to me! Will I accept it from you? Cursed is the cheat that vows to bring me an unblemished animal, yet sacrifices to me one that is blemished. I am

a great King, and my name will be feared among the nations. (Malachi chapter 1)

This command is for you, priests. If you will not listen and take it to heart to give honor to my name, then I will curse you and your blessings. I have actually already cursed them, because you do not take it to heart. I will rebuke your offspring, I will spread dung on your faces and your offerings and you will be taken away with it. My covenant with Levi was one of life and peace, and I gave them to him. He feared me and stood in awe of my name. He gave true instruction and did not lie. He walked with me in uprightness and peace, and he turned many away from iniquity. The lips of a priest should guard knowledge, and people should seek instruction from him, because he is a messenger of God. You have turned aside from the way. You have caused many people to stumble by your instruction. You have corrupted the covenant of Levi. Therefore, I will make you despised and abased before all the people because you do not keep my ways but show partiality in your instruction. (Malachi 2:1–9)

God then said,

[Summary] Judah has been faithless. Abomination has been committed in Jerusalem and in Israel. Judah profaned the sanctuary of God, which he loves, and married the daughter of a foreign god. Additionally, you weep and groan because I no longer accept your offerings. This is because you have been faithless to the wife of your youth, even though she is your companion and your wife by covenant. Did I not make husband and wife one, with a portion of the Spirit in their union? And why did I do this? Because I want godly offspring. Therefore, guard yourselves and do not be faithless to the wife of your youth. For the man who does not love his wife but divorces her covers his garment with violence. Guard yourselves in your spirit and no longer be faithless. You weary me by saying, "Everyone who does evil is good in the sight of God, and he delights in them," and by asking, "Where is the God of justice?" (Malachi 2:10–17)

Behold, I send my messenger, and he will prepare the way before me. And the Lord whom you seek will suddenly come to this temple; and the messenger of the covenant in whom you delight, behold, he is coming, says the Lord of hosts. But who can endure the day of his coming, and who can stand when he appears? For he is like a refiner's fire and like a fuller's soap. He will sit as a refiner and a purifier of silver, and he will purify the sons of Levi and refine them like gold and silver, and they will bring offerings in righteousness to the Lord. Then the offering of Judah and Jerusalem will be pleasing to the Lord as in the days of old and as in former years. (Malachi 3:1–4)

[Summary] I will bring you to judgment. I will judge the sorcerers, the adulterers, the liars, those who oppress the hired worker in his wages, the fatherless and the widow, and the sojourner, and those who do not fear me. (Malachi 3:5)

[Summary] I God, do not change. Return to me, and I will return to you. You rob me in your tithes and contributions. Bring the full tithe into the storehouse so that there will be food in my house. Put me to the test in this. See if I will not open the windows of heaven for you and pour down a blessing on you until there is no more need. I will protect your crops so that they will always produce. Then all of the nations will call you blessed, and you will be a land of delight. You have insulted me. You say "It is vain to serve God. What is our profit in keeping his laws or walking humbly before him? We call the arrogant blessed. Evildoers prosper and they put God to the test and escape unharmed." (Malachi 3:6–15)

Then those who feared God spoke with each other and followed him. And God saw this. A book of remembrance was written before him with the names of those who feared God and esteemed his name.

They shall be mine, says the Lord of hosts, in the day when I make up my treasured possession, and I will spare them as a man spares his son who serves him. Then once more you will see the distinction between the righteous and the wicked, between one who serves God and one who does not serve him. (Malachi 3:17–18)

God then said that the day is coming when the wicked will be destroyed. But for those who fear his name, the sun of righteousness will shine on them and heal them. They will go out leaping for joy, and they will tread the wicked as ashes under their feet.

The book of Malachi, the last book in the Old Testament, ends with a command and a prophecy:

Remember the law of my servant Moses, the statutes and rules that I commanded him at Horeb for all Israel. Behold, I will send you Elijah the prophet before the great and awesome day of the Lord comes. And he will turn the hearts of fathers to their children and the hearts of children to their fathers, lest I come and strike the land with a decree of utter destruction. (Malachi 4:4–5)

CHAPTER 16

PROPHECIES ABOUT JESUS IN THE OLD TESTAMENT

Jesus is the most important figure in the Bible. In the Old Testament, the first people ever created, Adam and Eve, sinned. This damaged human nature, inclining us toward sin and death entered the world. Therefore, all of Adam and Eve's offspring, which is everyone who was ever born, also sinned. People are separated from God when they sin, and they cannot enter heaven when they die because no sin is allowed there, in God's home in the presence of God. In the Old Testament, there was no mechanism to forgive sin. There were sin offerings which took care of any unintentional sins of the people. Such as if a person did something sinful, who did not know it was sinful, and he or she had no actual intent of doing anything wrong. But there was nothing in the Old Testament that could forgive intentional sins, such as a man struck someone else out of envy or anger. Intentional sins are almost all the sins that are committed. With Jesus dying on the cross for us, from that point on, everyone had the opportunity to be forgiven of their sins. He paid the price for every sin that would ever be committed by mankind, and God the Father accepted the sacrifice of his Son as acceptable payment, or punishment for the sins of the world. If we follow Jesus along with God the father and God the Holy Spirit, we are now able to be forgiven of our sins and enter heaven when we die. Since Jesus is the only person/God that can save us from going to hell and bring us eternal life with God, he would be the central figure of the Bible. In fact, the whole Bible is about him. The Old Testament shows how a world lost in their sins desperately needed a Savior, Jesus, and he arrived in the New Testament. In the Old Testament, there are *numerous* prophecies not only about his first coming over two thousand years ago, but also about his Second Coming sometime in the future. Jesus himself spoke about him being mentioned all throughout the Old Testament:

On the day that Jesus rose from the dead after he was crucified, he appeared to two random men on the road walking to the village of Emmaus.

That very day two of them were going to a village named Emmaus, about seven miles from Jerusalem, and they were talking with each other about all these things that had happened. While they were talking and discussing together, Jesus himself drew near and went with them. But their eyes were kept from recognizing him. And he said to them, "What is this conversation that you are holding with each other as you walk?" And they stood still, looking sad. Then one of them, named Cleopas, answered him, "Are you the only visitor to Jerusalem who does not know these things that have happened there in these days?" And he said to them, "What things?" And they said to him, "Concerning Jesus of Nazareth, a man who was a prophet mighty in deed and word before God and all the people, and how our chief priests and rulers delivered him up to be condemned to death, and crucified him. But we had hoped that he was the one to redeem Israel. Yes, and besides this, it is now the third day since these things happened. Moreover, some women in our company amazed us. They were at the tomb early in the morning, and when they did not find his body, they came back saying they had even seen a vision of angels, who said that he was alive. Some of those who were with us went to the tomb and found it just as the women had said, but him they did not see." And he said to them, "O foolish ones, and slow of heart to believe all that the prophets have spoken! Was it not necessary that the Christ should suffer these things and enter into his glory?" *And beginning with Moses and all the Prophets, he interpreted to them in all the scriptures the things concerning himself (italics added).* (Luke 24:1–27)

They invited Jesus, who kept the two men from recognizing him, to their home for dinner.

When he was at the table with them, he took the bread and blessed and broke it and gave it to them. And their eyes were opened, and they recognized him. And he vanished from their sight. They said to each other, "Did not our hearts burn within us while he talked to us on the road, *while he opened us to the scriptures?" (italics added)* (Luke 24:30–32)

This chapter will look at several, but not all, the prophecies in the Old Testament which tell us about the First and Second Coming of Jesus. I cannot list all of them here because there are so many that they would fill up a book all by themselves. Please look for prophecies about Jesus in the Old Testament on your own in the actual Bible. They are exceedingly interesting.

The Lord God said to the serpent, 'Because you have done this, cursed are you above all livestock and above all beasts of the field; on your belly you shall go, and dust you shall eat all the days of your life. *I will put enmity between you and the woman, and between your offspring and her offspring; he shall bruise your head, and you shall bruise his heel (italics added)*. (Genesis 3:14–15)

Right after the serpent tempted Adam and Eve to sin, God gave a prophecy about Jesus confronting Satan in the future. Satan shall bruise the heel of Jesus (Jesus was hurt in the crucifixion, but he was raised from this blow), and Jesus will bruise Satan's head (the blow Jesus would strike against Satan would be a knockout blow). In case there is any doubt that the serpent in the garden of Eden in Genesis is actually the devil, the Bible clears this up later:

And the great dragon was thrown down, *that ancient serpent, who is called the devil and Satan, the deceiver of the whole world (italics added)*— he was thrown down to the earth, and his angels were thrown down with him. (Revelation 12:9)

The book of Revelation informs us that Satan is also called the devil, the ancient serpent, and the dragon.

And to Adam God said, "Because you have listened to the voice of your wife and have eaten of the tree which I commanded you, 'You shall not eat of it,' cursed is the ground because of you; in pain you shall eat of it all the days of your life; *thorns (italics added)* and thistles it shall bring you." (Genesis 3:17–18)

Adam's sin brought a curse to the ground. Thorns will grow from it instead of good fruit because of this. When Jesus was being abused during the crucifixion events, a crown of thorns was pushed into his head, literally taking the curse of the sin of all of mankind onto himself and being punished for us as a sacrifice acceptable to God the Father.

> If a man has committed a crime punishable by death and he is put to death, and you hang him on a tree, a man hanged on a tree is cursed by God. (Deuteronomy 21:22)

Jesus was hung on a tree—"a cross made out of wood"—and was cursed by God by taking all our sins on him and being punished in our place.

The book of Psalms was written mostly by King David who lived approximately one thousand years before Jesus was born. On many occasions, prophecies about what would happen to Jesus when he would come to earth in the future are found in the Psalms:

> Why do the nations rage and the peoples plot in vain? The kings of the earth set themselves, and the rulers take counsel together; against the Lord and against his *Anointed (italics added),* saying, "Let us burst their bonds apart and cast away their cords from us." He who sits in the heavens laughs; the Lord holds them in derision. He will speak to them in his wrath, and terrify them in his fury, saying, "As for me, I have set my *King on Zion, my holy hill." I will tell of the decree: The Lord said to me, "You are my Son; today I have begotten you. Ask of me, and I will make the nations your heritage, and the ends of the earth your possession. You shall break them with a rod of iron and dash them in pieces like a potter's vessel."* (italics added) Now therefore, O kings, be wise; be warned, O rulers of the earth. Serve the Lord with fear and rejoice with trembling. *Kiss the Son, lest he be angry, and you perish in the way, for his*

wrath is quickly kindled. Blessed are all who take refuge in him (italics added). (Psalm 2:1–12)

Jesus is the only begotten Son of God. Revelation chapter 20 explains that there will be a thousand-year period in the future in which Jesus will rule the nations of the world in person in Jerusalem.

My God, my God, why have you forsaken me? Why are you so far from saving me, from the words of my groaning? O my God, I cry by day, but you do not answer, and by night, but I find no rest (italics added). Yet you are holy, enthroned on the praises of Israel. In you our fathers trusted; they trusted and you delivered them. To you they cried and were rescued; in you they trusted and were not put to shame. *But I am a worm and not a man, scorned by mankind and despised by the people. All who see me mock me; they make mouths at me; they wag their heads; "He trusts in the Lord; let him deliver him; let him rescue him, for he delights in him!" (italics added)* Yet you are he who took me from the womb; you made me trust you at my mother's breasts. On you I was cast from my birth, and from my mother's womb you have been my God. *Be not far from me, for trouble is near, and there is none to help. Many bulls encompass me; strong Bulls of Bashan surround me; they open wide their mouths at me, like a ravening lion and roaring lion. I am poured out like water, and all my bones are out of joint; my heart is like wax; it is melted within my breast; my strength is dried up like a potsherd, and my tongue sticks to my jaws; you lay me in the dust of death. For dogs encompass me; a company of evildoers encircles me; they have pierced my hands and my feet—I can count all of my bones—they stare and gloat over me; they divide*

my garments among them, and for my clothing they
cast lots (italics added). (Psalm 22:1–18)

The above psalm is so rich in prophecies about future events in the life of Jesus. The multiple prophecies in this one psalm will now be explained individually:

My God, My God why have you forsaken me?

Jesus said this as he was hanging on the cross as he was dying for our sins (Mark 15:34).

I am scorned by mankind and despised by the people. All who see me mock me; they wag their heads; "He trusts in the Lord; let him deliver him; let him rescue him, for he delights in him." (Psalm 22:7–8)

As Jesus hung on the cross, the people that wanted him crucified mocked him, and said,

If you are really the Son of God, then Let God come down and save you from the cross! (Matthew 27:39–44, Luke 23:35–39, Mark 15:26–35)

Many bulls encompass me; strong Bulls of Bashan surround me; they open their mouths wide at me, like a ravening lion and roaring lion. (Psalm 22:12–13)

Jesus was surrounded by vicious enemies who were intent on crucifying him.

> I am poured out like water, all my bones are
> out of joint; my heart is like wax; it is melted in
> my chest, my strength is dried up line a potsherd
> and my tongue sticks to my jaws; you lay me in
> the dust of death. (Psalm 22:14–15)

When Jesus was on the cross, some of his bones were pulled out of joint due to the crucifixion. He had no strength, and his tongue was sticking to the inside of his mouth due to extreme thirst (John 19:28).

> For dogs encompass me, a company of evil-
> doers encircles me; they have pierced my hands
> and my feet—I can count all of my bones—they
> stare and gloat over me; they divide my garments
> among them, and for my garments they cast lots.
> (Psalm 22:16–18).

Jesus was surrounded by evil people who pierced his hands and his feet when they nailed him to the cross. He wore a valuable tunic that the people who took it from him gambled with each other (cast lots) to see who would keep it ("for my garments they cast lots") (John 19:17–24, Luke 23:32–39, Mark 15:21–32, Matthew 27:32–44).

Continuing with other prophecies about Jesus in the Old Testament...

> Into your hand I commit my spirit. (Psalm
> 33:5)

Jesus said this on the cross to God the Father the moment before he died (Luke 23:46).

> Even my close friend in whom I trusted,
> who ate my bread, he lifted his heel against me.
> (Psalm 41:9)

Judas, one of the apostles and a friend of Jesus, betrayed Jesus right after he ate bread with him at the Last Supper.

> For zeal for your house has consumed me,
> and the reproaches of those who reproach you
> have fallen on me. (Psalm 69:9)

"Zeal for your house will consume me" describes Jesus's actions of making whips and driving the money changers out of his Father's temple (John 2:13–17).

> I looked for pity and there was none, and
> for comforters, but I found none. They gave me
> poison for food, and for my thirst they gave me
> sour wine for drink. (Psalm 69:20–21).

When Jesus was on the cross, the people mocked him, harassed him, and gave him sour wine to drink (Mark 15:33–37, John 19:28–29).

> For he will command his angels concerning
> you to guard you on your ways. On their hands
> they will bear you up, lest you strike your foot
> against a stone. (Psalm 91:11–12)

Satan would later quote this Bible verse to Jesus when he was trying to tempt Jesus to follow his commands to leap off the temple to prove to Satan and others that he was the Son of God (Matthew 4:5–7).

> *The Lord says to my Lord: 'Sit at my right hand, until I make your enemies your footstool (italics added).* The Lord sends forth from Zion your mighty scepter. Rule in the midst of your enemies! Your people will offer themselves freely on the day of your power, in holy garments; from the womb of the morning, the dew of your youth will

be yours. The Lord has sworn and will not change his mind, *"You are a priest forever after the order of Melchizedek." (italics added)* (Psalm 110:1–4)

Jesus quoted the first part of this Psalm to question the Sadducees how the Messiah could be both a son of David and also a Lord over David. The second part of this prophecy in italics states that Jesus would be an eternal priest after the order of Melchizedek.

The stone that the builders rejected has become the cornerstone. (Psalm 118:22)

Jesus later quoted this psalm to describe himself as the Cornerstone (Matthew 21:42–44).

Blessed is he who comes in the name of the Lord. (Psalm 118:26)

This was what the people would say to Jesus upon his triumphant entry into Jerusalem on Palm Sunday, just days before the people turn against him and crucify him (Matthew 21:9).

Again the Lord spoke to Ahaz, "Ask for a sign of the Lord your God; let it be deep as Sheol or high as heaven." But Ahaz said, "I will not ask, and I will not put the Lord to the test." And he said, "Hear then, O house of David! Is it too little for you weary men, that you weary my God also? Therefore the Lord himself will give you a sign. *Behold, the virgin shall conceive and bear a son, and shall call his name Immanuel." (italics added)* (Isaiah 7:10–15).

God said in the book of Isaiah that he would give a great sign to the people, which would be that a virgin would give birth to a son who would be named Immanuel. That would be Mary giving birth to Jesus (Matthew 1:20–25, Luke chapters 1 and 2).

> But the Lord of hosts, him you shall honor as holy. Let him be your fear, and let him be your dread. *And he will become a sanctuary and a stone of offense and a rock of stumbling to both houses of Israel, a trap and a snare to the inhabitants of Jerusalem. And many shall stumble on. It. They shall fall and be broken; they shall be snared and taken (italics added).* (Isaiah 8:13–15)

Jesus used these words to describe what would happen to those who reject him, the Cornerstone, in Matthew 21:42–44. He said,

> The stone that the builders rejected has become the cornerstone; this was the Lord's doing, and it is marvelous in our eyes? … And the one who falls on this stone will be broken to pieces; and when it falls on anyone, it will crush him.
> For to us a child is born, to us a son is given; and the government shall be on his shoulder, and his name shall be called Wonderful Counselor, Mighty God, Everlasting Father, Prince of Peace. Of the increase of his government and of peace there will be no end, on the throne of David and over his kingdom, to establish it and to uphold it with justice and with righteousness from this time forth and forevermore. The Zeal of the Lord of hosts will do this. (Isaiah 9:6–7)

The above are many titles and names given to Jesus. "Increase of his government"—chapter 20 of the book of Revelation reveals that at one point in the future, there will be a thousand-year period in which Jesus would govern the entire world in person from Jerusalem.

There shall come forth a shoot from the stump of Jesse, and a branch from his roots shall bear fruit. And the Spirit of the Lord shall rest upon him, the Spirit of wisdom and understanding, the Spirit of counsel and might, the Spirit of knowledge and the fear of the Lord. He shall not judge by what his eyes see, or decide disputes by what his ears hear, but with righteousness he shall judge to poor, and decide with equity for the meek of the earth; he shall strike the earth with the rod of his mouth, and with the breath of his lips he shall kill the wicked. Righteousness shall be the belt of his waist, and faithfulness the belt of his loins. The wolf shall dwell with the lamb, and the leopard shall lie down with the young goat, and the calf and the lion and the fattened calf together; and the lion shall eat straw like the ox. The nursing child shall play over the hole of the cobra, and the weaned child shall put his hand on the adder's den. They shall not hurt or destroy in all my holy mountain; for the earth shall be full of the knowledge of the Lord as the waters cover the sea. In that day the root of Jesse, who shall stand as a signal for the peoples—of him shall the nations inquire, and his resting place shall be glorious. (Isaiah 11:1–10)

Jesus is a descendant of King David, whose father was Jesse. This passage describes attributes of Jesus as a judge in person on the earth and how the world will be completely at peace during his future reign. Even the animals who were now enemies would be at peace with each other once Jesus returned and established his kingdom on earth.

On this mountain the Lord of hosts will make for all peoples a feast of rich food, a feast of well-aged wine, of rich food full of marrow, of aged wine well refined. And he will swallow up on this mountain the covering that is cast over all peoples, the veil that is spread over all nations. He will swallow up death forever; and the Lord God will wipe away tears from all faces, and the reproach of his people he will take away from all the earth, for the Lord has spoken. It will be said on that day, "Behold, this is our God; we have waited for him, that he might save us. This is the Lord, we have waited for him; let us be glad and rejoice in his salvation." (Isaiah 25:6–9)

Jesus's payment for all our sins by his death on the cross took away spiritual death and gave eternal life for those who follow him. His paying for all our sins took away our reproach. The Israelites at the time the book of Isaiah was written were waiting for a savior promised to them by God. He later arrived as Jesus.

A voice cries: In the wilderness prepare the way of the Lord; make straight in the desert a highway for our God. Every valley shall be lifted up, and every mountain and hillside be made low; and the uneven ground shall become level, and the rough places a plain. And the glory of the Lord shall be revealed, and all people shall see it together. (Isaiah 40:3)

This is describing the coming of John the Baptist, who would announce to Israel the arrival of their Messiah, Jesus, using some of these very words (Matthew 3:1–12, Mark 1:1–8, Luke 3:1–21, John 1:19–34).

I gave my back to those who strike, and my cheeks to those who pull out my beard; I hid not my face from disgrace and spitting. (Isiah 51:3)

When Jesus would be crucified in the future, they would whip his back with whips, strike him in the face, and pull out parts of his beard (Matthew 26–27, Mark 14–15, Luke 22–23, John 18–19). (Remember, Jesus offered himself as a sacrifice for all the sins that would ever be committed in the world; that is why the treatment of him was very harsh.)

> As many were astonished at you—his appearance was so marred, beyond human recognition, and his body beyond that of human beings. (Isiah 52:13)

Jesus would be injured so badly during the crucifixion events that he could not even be recognized as being a human.

The following prophetic passage in the book of Isaiah is exceedingly full of prophecies about the future events in the life of Jesus:

> Who has believed what he had heard from us? And to whom has the arm of the Lord been revealed? For he grew up before him like a young plant, and like a root out of dry ground; he had no form or majesty that we should look at him. He was despised and rejected by men; a man of sorrows, and acquainted with grief; and as one from whom men hide their faces he was despised. And we esteemed him not. Surely he has borne our griefs and carried our sorrows; yet we esteemed him stricken. Smitten by God and afflicted. But he was wounded for our transgressions, he was crushed for our iniquities; upon him was the chastisement that brought us peace, and with his stripes we are healed. All we like sheep have gone astray; we have turned—every one—to his own way; and the Lord has laid on him the iniquity of us all. He was oppressed, and he was afflicted, yet he opened not his mouth.

By oppression and judgement he was taken away; and as for his generation, who considered that he was cut off of the land of the living, stricken for the transgression of my people? And they made his grave with the wicked and with a rich man his death, although he had done no violence, and there was no deceit in his mouth. Yet it was the will of the Lord to crush him; he has put him to grief; when his soul makes an offering for guilt, he shall see his offspring, he shall prolong his days; the will of the Lord shall prosper in his hand. Out of the anguish of his soul he shall see and be satisfied; by his knowledge shall the righteous one, my servant, make many to be accounted righteous, and he shall bear their iniquities. Therefore I shall divide him a portion with the many, and he shall divide the spoil with the strong, because he poured out his soul to death and was numbered with the transgressors; yet he bore the sins of many, and makes intercession for the transgressors. (Isaiah chapter 53)

"And a Redeemer will come to Zion, to those in Jacob who turn from transgression," declares the Lord. (Isaiah 59:20)

Jesus is our one and only Redeemer. He redeems those who repent of their sins and come to him for forgiveness.

Behold, the days are coming, declares the Lord, when I will fulfill the promise I made to the house of Israel and the house of Judah. In those days and at that time I will cause a righteous Branch to spring up for David, and he shall execute justice and righteousness in the land. In those days Judah will be saved, and Jerusalem will dwell securely. And this is the name by which it will be called: "The Lord is our righteousness." (Jeremiah 33:14–16)

In the Gospel of John, Jesus refers to himself as the True Vine, and the people in the world as branches:

I am the true vine and my Father is the vine-dresser. Every branch in me that does not bear fruit he takes away, and every branch that does bear fruit he prunes that it may bear more fruit. Abide in me, and I in you. As the branch cannot bear fruit by itself, unless it abides in the vine, neither can you, unless you abide in me. I am the vine; you are the branches. (John 15:1–5)

Additionally, Jesus is a descendant of David.

But you, O Bethlehem Ephrathah, who are too little to be among the clans of Judah, from you shall come forth for me the one who is to be ruler in Israel, whose coming forth is from of old, from ancient days... And he shall stand and shepherd his flock in the strength of the Lord, in the majesty of the name of the Lord his God. And they shall dwell secure, for now he shall be great to the ends of the earth. And he shall be their peace. (Micah 5:2 and 4)

The above prophecy reveals that the promised Messiah will be born in Bethlehem.

Rejoice greatly, O daughter of Zion! Shout aloud, O daughter of Jerusalem! Behold, your king is coming to you; righteous and having sal-vation is he, humble and mounted on a donkey,

on a colt, the foal of a donkey. I will cut off the
chariot from Ephraim and the war horse form
Jerusalem; and the battle bow shall be cut off,
and he shall speak peace to the nations; his rule
shall be from sea to sea, and from the River to
the ends of the earth. As for you also, because
of the blood of my covenant with you, I will
set your prisoners free from the waterless pit.
Return to your stronghold, O prisoners of hope;
today I declare that I will restore to you double.
(Zechariah 9:9–12)

There are many prophecies about events that will take place in
the future life of Jesus in the above Old Testament Bible Passage. The
one highlighted here is it predicted that the Messiah would enter
Jerusalem riding a donkey. This is exactly what Jesus did when he
entered Jerusalem on Palm Sunday (Matthew 21:1–11, Mark 11:1–
11, Luke 19:28–40, and John 12:12–19). Additionally, Jesus's death
made it so that people who would come to follow him would be saved
from being condemned to the waterless pit because of their sins.

So I became shepherd of the flock doomed
to be slaughtered by the sheep traders… Then
I said to them, "If it seems good to you, give
me my wages; but if not, keep them." And they
weighed out as my wages thirty pieces of silver.
Then the Lord said to me, "Throw it to the potter—the lordly price at which I was priced by
them." (Zechariah 11:1 and 12–13)

Judas betrayed Jesus for thirty pieces of silver. Judas then regretted what he did, and he hung himself. The thirty pieces of silver that
were given to Judas as the price to betray Jesus were later used to buy
potter's field (Matthew chapters 26–27).

> "Awake, O sword against my shepherd, against the man who stands next to me," declares the Lord of hosts. "Strike the shepherd and the sheep will be scattered." (Zechariah 13:7)

Jesus is the Good Shepherd, and he is at the right hand of God the Father. Jesus quotes this verse from Zechariah to Peter: "Strike the shepherd and the sheep will be scattered," telling Peter that he would abandon Jesus and deny him three times when Jesus would be apprehended by a throng of Roman soldiers. Peter assured Jesus he would never do that. He did.

In the Bible, Malachi is the last prophet to appear to the people on behalf of God until Jesus would come approximately four hundred years later. The following are some prophecies about Jesus from the book of Malachi.

> Behold, I send my messenger, and he will prepare the way for me. And the Lord whom you seek will suddenly come to his temple; and the messenger of the covenant in whom you delight, behold, he is coming, says the Lord of hosts. (Malachi 3:1)

God would send John the Baptist, who was Jesus's cousin, to tell all of Israel that their Savior was here and would be showing himself soon (Matthew 3:1–12, Mark 1:1–8, Luke 3:1–21, John 1:19–34).

> Behold, I will send you Elijah the prophet before the great and awesome day of the Lord comes. And he will turn the hearts of the fathers to their children and the hearts of children to their fathers' lest I come and strike the land with a decree of utter destruction. (Malachi 4:1)

A final prediction that God would send John the Baptist, who would have the spirit of Elijah, to prepare the way for the coming of God to earth, who would be Jesus Christ.

CHAPTER 17

THE NEW TESTAMENT: THE EARLY LIFE OF JESUS

The Bible is divided into two major sections. The New Testament is the second major section of the Bible. It is all about Jesus. It starts off with the birth of Jesus, tells about his whole life, and how the message of him spread after he rose from the dead and went back to heaven. The first four books in the New Testament are called the gospels. The gospels focus on Jesus's life while he was on earth. The four gospel books are Matthew, Mark, Luke, and John. Many events in the life of Jesus are told multiple times across some or all the four gospel books, while other events appear in only one of the gospel books. As the author of this Bible summary, I went through all four gospels and presented the events in the life of Jesus in a chronological order. If an event was told in multiple gospels, I selected the one which had the most detail of the event. Remember—although Jesus did many great things here on earth, his main reason for coming here was to be a sinless sacrifice for the sins of the world (crucified). His offering himself as a sacrifice for us, which was acceptable to God the Father, now allows us to be forgiven of sins we commit, if we confess them and repent of them. This was not possible without the death of Jesus as a sacrifice deemed acceptable by God the Father for our sins. We will now begin with the events in the life of Jesus while he was on earth.

JOHN THE APOSTLE'S TESTIMONY ABOUT JESUS

In the beginning was the Word, and the Word was with God, and the Word was God [Jesus is the Word of God]. He was in the beginning with God. All things were made through him, and without him was not anything made that was made [Jesus made everything that exists before he came down to earth to become both God and man simultaneously]. In him was life, and the life was the light of men. The light shines in the darkness, and the darkness has not overcome it. (John 1:1–5)

There was a man sent from God, whose name was John [Jesus's relative: John the Baptist]. He came as a witness, to bear witness about the light, that all might believe through him. John was not the light, but came to bear witness about the light. (John 1:6–8)

The true light, which enlightens everyone, was coming into the world. He was in the world, and the world was made through him, yet the world did not know him. He came to his own, and his own people did not receive him. But to all who did receive him, who believed in his name, he gave the right to become children of God, who were born, not of blood nor of the will of the flesh nor of the will of man, but of God. (John 1:9–13)

And the Word became flesh and lived among us, we have seen his glory, glory as of the only Son from the Father, full of grace and truth. [Jesus became a man while still being God and came to earth and lived with the people of Israel for thirty-three years. John bore witness about him, and cried out, "This is the one of whom

I said 'He who comes after me ranks before me, because he was before me.'"] And from his fullness we have all received grace upon grace. For the law was given through Moses; grace and truth came through Jesus Christ. No one has ever seen God; the only God, who is at the Father's side, he has made him known. (John 1:14–18)

Matthew 1:1–17 and Luke 3:23–38 show how Jesus came from a family whose ancestors included Adam, Seth, Enoch, Noah, Abraham, Isaac, Jacob, Judah, Ruth, Jesse, King David, King Solomon, and eventually Joseph, the husband of Mary, who was Jesus's mother. Remember, because Abraham and David trusted God, God promised that their children would form a great nation and people. What could be greater that one of your great-great-great-great...grandsons being Jesus, who is God that became man to save all of us from our sins!

THE BIRTH OF JOHN THE BAPTIST

The birth of Jesus is given in the most detail in the book of Luke, one of the four gospel books that was written about Jesus when he came to earth. Jesus's mother, Mary, was related to a woman named Elizabeth. Elizabeth was older and did not have any children, and she prayed to God that he would give her a child. One day an angel of God came to her husband, Zechariah. He told Zechariah that God heard their prayers, and he would make his wife Elizabeth pregnant with a son. He would be named John. John would be great before God, and he would be filled with the Holy Spirit. He would turn many of the children of Israel to the Lord their God, and he would go before God in the spirit and power of Elijah, to turn the hearts of the fathers to the children, and the disobedient to the wisdom of the just, to get the people ready for the coming of God (Jesus) (Luke chapter 1). John the Baptist's father questioned how this could be, since he and his wife, Elizabeth, were old and past childbearing years. The angel then identified himself to Zechariah as the angel Gabriel. Due to Zechariah's unbelief, the angel Gabriel told him that he would not be able to speak until the birth of his son, whom he was instructed to name John. This came to pass as the angel Gabriel told Zechariah it would. Prophets in the Old Testament predicted that John the Baptist would come to tell the people at their Savior, Jesus, has arrived. For example, four hundred years earlier, the prophet Malachi sent a message from God to the Israelites:

> Behold, I send my messenger, and he will prepare the way for me. I will send you Elijah the prophet before the great and awesome day of the Lord comes. And he will turn the hearts of fathers to their children, and the hearts of children to their fathers. (Malachi 4:5–6)

Jesus himself later reveals to his apostles at his transfiguration that John the Baptist was actually the coming of Elijah spoken about in the above prophecy from Malachi:

> And the disciples asked him [Jesus], "Then why do the scribes say that Elijah must first come?" He answered. "Elijah does come, and he will restore all things. But I tell you that Elijah has already come, and they did not recognize him, but they did to him whatever they pleased. So also the Son of Man will certainly suffer at their hands." Then the disciples understood that he was speaking to them about John the Baptist. (Matthew 17:10–13)

THE BIRTH OF JESUS

God sent the angel Gabriel to a young woman named Mary who lived in a small town in Israel Galilee named Nazareth. Mary was engaged to marry a man named Joseph. The angel Gabriel said to Mary that God was pleased with her. God would make her pregnant with a son, and she would name him Jesus.

> He will be great and will be called the Son of
> the Most High. And the Lord God will give to him
> the throne of his ancestor, King David, and he will
> rule over the house of Jacob forever, and there will
> be no end to his kingdom. (Luke 1:32–33)

Mary told the Angel Gabriel that she would do whatever God asked her to do. Mary became pregnant with Jesus as the angel Gabriel told her she would. Her husband, Joseph, looked to divorce her quietly to not put her to shame that she was pregnant from someone else. But an angel of the Lord appeared to Joseph in a dream saying,

> Joseph, son of David, do not fear to take
> Mary as your wife, for that which is conceived in
> her is from the Holy Spirit. She will bear a son,
> and you will call his name Jesus, for he will save
> his people from their sins. (Matthew 1:20–21)

Joseph did as the angel told him to do; he kept Mary as his wife. During Mary's pregnancy, she visited her relative Elizabeth. Elizabeth was pregnant with a boy that would be John the Baptist, the man that God would send to announce the coming of the Savior, Jesus. The angel Gabriel earlier informed Mary that her relative Elizabeth would be pregnant in her old age because nothing was impossible with God. When Elizabeth saw Mary, baby John the Baptist leaped for joy in Elizabeth's womb. Elizabeth said to Mary,

> Blessed are you among women, and blessed
> is the fruit of your womb!

During this time in history, Israel—along with much of Europe, Africa, and Asia—had been conquered by the Romans and was part of the Roman Empire. At this time, Caesar Augustus, the emperor of the Roman Empire, declared that a census must be taken in everyone's hometown to see how many people were living in each area of the Roman Empire. Mary, the woman who was pregnant with Jesus, went with her husband, Joseph, to Bethlehem for the census. Joseph had to get registered in Bethlehem because he was a descendant of King David, who was also from Bethlehem (Luke 2:1–5). You would see shortly how God used the census to fulfill his plan for Jesus to be born in Bethlehem instead of Nazareth, to protect Jesus from those who would want to kill him.

> And while they were there, the time came for Mary to give birth. And she gave birth to her firstborn son, and named him Jesus, and wrapped him in swaddling clothes and laid him in a manger, because there was no place for them in the inn. (Luke 2:6–7)

There was a prophecy that a special star would rise in the sky when the savior was born, and this happened. Wise men from the east saw this star and came to Jerusalem looking for the savior. They came to the king of Israel, King Herod, in the city of Jerusalem. They said to King Herod (summary), "Where is the one who is born king of the Jews? We saw his star rise, and we came to worship him."

This bothered King Herod. He did not want anyone to be king except him. He asked the priests and the scribes where the Savior was to be born. In the scripture book of Micah, it said that he would be born in Bethlehem. King Herod told the wise men to go to Bethlehem and find the baby that was born who would be the Savior. Then come back and tell King Herod where he was at so he could also go and worship him. The wise men followed the star in the sky until they came to a manger right beneath it where Jesus, Mary, and Joseph was. They worshipped the baby Jesus and gave him gifts of gold, frankincense, and myrrh. On the way back, God came to them in a dream and told them not to go back to King Herod and tell him where Jesus was because he wanted to kill Jesus. Therefore, they went home another way (Matthew 2:1–12).

After the wise men left Jesus, an angel came to Joseph in a dream. He told Joseph to take Jesus and Mary to Egypt and hide there because King Herod would try to kill Jesus because he was envious of him. Joseph took Jesus and Mary quickly by night to Egypt. When King Herod realized that the wise men were not coming back to tell him where Jesus was, he became furious. King Herod did not know which child was Jesus. Therefore, he sent in the army which killed *all* the boys in Bethlehem age two and under, in an attempt to get rid of Jesus. King Herod died sometime later. At that time an angel appeared to Joseph in a dream, instructing him to return to Israel with Jesus and Mary because the people who wanted to kill Jesus were dead. Jesus, Mary, and Joseph returned to Israel and settled in Nazareth. No one was looking for Jesus in Nazareth because they thought he would be living in Bethlehem. Jesus was only born in Bethlehem, when Joseph and Mary had to go there for the census. This helped protect Jesus because no one was looking for him in Nazareth (Matthew chapter 2).

THE BOY JESUS IN THE TEMPLE

Every year, Jesus, Mary, and Joseph went to the city of Jerusalem with a big group of other people to celebrate the Passover feast. One year when Jesus was twelve, he stayed behind in Jerusalem after his parents headed back to Nazareth. They eventually realized Jesus was not with the group, so they returned to Jerusalem to look for him. It took them three days to find him. He was in the temple, which was where the Jewish people worshipped God. Jesus was talking with the priests, and everyone who heard him was amazed at how much he knew about everything. His parents asked him why he would get them so upset by staying behind after they left to return home. Jesus said,

> Why were you looking for me? Did you not know that I must be in my Father's house? (Luke 2:49)

CHAPTER 18

JESUS BEGINS HIS MINISTRY

Nothing was written in the Bible about Jesus when he was between the ages twelve to thirty. Although he was one-hundred-percent God and one-hundred-percent man, it is assumed that he lived the life of a regular person during this time. It is believed that he was a carpenter like his stepfather, Joseph. Sometime during the time between when Jesus was twelve and thirty, his stepfather, Joseph, died, but no details were given about that.

At age thirty, Jesus began a three-year period, which ended with him taking all our sins on him and dying on the cross. During this time, he stopped being a carpenter, and he began his mission to save the world from our sins. He went out and told all of Israel that the time of salvation was near. He did countless spectacular miracles to prove beyond a doubt that he was God. He also taught the people all about God and how God wanted them to live their lives. This three-year period is called Jesus's ministry.

At the time when Jesus began his ministry, John the Baptist was the biggest preacher in the land. He would stand out in public and talk about God. He told the people to stop sinning and turn back to following God. He also told him that the Savior, or Messiah, would be coming very soon to save the people from their sins. The Old Testament stated in many places that a man would come to announce the coming of the Savior, and that man was John the

Baptist. One day John the Baptist was baptizing people, and Jesus walked up to him.

> When John saw Jesus, he said, "Behold, the Lamb of God, who takes away the sin of the world! This is he of whom I said 'After me comes a man who ranks before me, because he was before me.' I myself did not know him, but for this purpose I came baptizing with water, that he might be revealed to Israel. God, who sent me, showed me who he is. And I have seen and born witness that this is the Son of God." (John 1:29–34)

Therefore, John the Baptist, to whom everybody in his area in Israel listened, told Israel that Jesus was the Son of God who came here to take away the sins of the world. Jesus asked John to baptize him, which John was honored to do. When John the Baptist baptized Jesus in front of the crowd, the heavens were opened, and the Holy Spirit came down on Jesus in the form of a dove, and the voice of God came from heaven,

> You are my beloved Son; with you I am well pleased. (Matthew 3:17)

THE CALLING OF THE DISCIPLES

The first thing that Jesus did when he began his ministry was to gather disciples. People that followed Jesus were called his disciples. One way Jesus did this was by approaching particular men—such as Peter, James, John, and Levi (Matthew)—and saying, "Follow Me," which they did. He also began to teach and perform miracles publicly. This caused other people to begin to follow Jesus. One night Jesus went to the mountain and prayed all night long. When the day came, he called his disciples, and out of them he chose twelve to be his apostles. The apostles would come to be with Jesus throughout his three-year ministry. The twelve apostles that Jesus chose were Peter, James, John, Andrew, Philip, Bartholomew, Matthew, Thomas, a second James, Thaddaeus, Simon, and Judas. Out of the twelve apostles, there were three that Jesus was closest to: James, John (who was Jesus's best friend), and Peter (Mark 1, 2, 3; Luke 5, 6).

THE WEDDING AT CANA

Jesus was at a wedding with his mother Mary and his disciples. They ran out of wine at the wedding. Mary told Jesus to do something to help. Jesus said no, because it was not time for him yet to start doing miracles. She disregarded what Jesus told her and insisted that he helped. Jesus told the waiters to fill six big jars with water. Jesus turned the water into wine. The people at the wedding did not know where the wine came from, but they were astonished at the excellent quality of it. This was the first miracle that Jesus ever did as a man on earth (John 2:1–12)

THE TEMPTATION OF JESUS BY THE DEVIL

Jesus was led by the Holy Spirit into the wilderness to be tempted by the devil. He did this to prepare for his mission to save us from sin. He fasted for forty days and nights (did not eat food), and he was hungry. At that time, the devil came to tempt him to sin and said,

> If you are the Son of God, command these
> stones to become loaves of bread. (Matthew 4:3)

God the father told Jesus to fast (not eat), and the devil tried to get Jesus to disobey God the father. Jesus answered,

> It is written, man shall not live by bread
> alone, but by every word that comes from the
> mouth of God. (Matthew 4:4)

Then the devil took Jesus to the top of the Jewish temple and said,

> If you are the Son of God, throw yourself down, for it is written, "He will command his angels concerning you, and in their hands they will catch you so your foot will not strike against a stone." (Matthew 4:5–6)

Jesus said to the devil,

> Again it is written, "You shall not put the Lord your God to the test." (Matthew 4:7)

And the devil took him up and showed him all the kingdoms of the world in a moment of time and said to him,

> To you I will give all this authority and their glory, for it has been delivered to me, and I give it to whom I will. If you, then, will worship me, it will all be yours.

Then Jesus said to him,

> Be gone Satan! For it is written, "You shall worship the Lord your God and him only shall you serve." And when the devil had ended every temptation for Jesus to sin, he left him, waiting for another opportunity to destroy Jesus. Then angels came to Jesus and took care of him (Matthew 4:8–11 and Luke 4:5–8).

An important point to note in Satan's temptation of Jesus. If Satan was successful in his temptations and Jesus sinned, the salvation plan for man would have failed. God the Father would only accept a sinless, unblemished sacrifice to atone for the sins of all of us. If Jesus was successful and never sinned by the time he crucifixion ended, Jesus would have defeated Satan, death, and received back on behalf of man the authority over the world that was delivered to Satan when Adam and Eve (and every human after them) sinned against God (Luke 4:5–7). This was Satan's only direct confrontation with Jesus while Jesus was on earth, and everything was on the line. Therefore, both Jesus and Satan were using their most powerful weapons and defenses against each other in this confrontation. When Satan tempted Jesus, the only thing Jesus used to defend himself against Satan's temptations was scripture. Jesus quoted scripture to Satan as a response to each of Satan's temptations.

> It is not by bread alone that people live, but by all that comes forth from the mouth of the Lord. (Deuteronomy 8:3)

> You shall not put the Lord, your God, to the test. (Deuteronomy 6:16)

> The Lord, Your God, shall you fear; him shall you serve. (Deuteronomy 6:13)

When Satan saw that Jesus was using scripture as a defense, he tried to use scripture as a weapon against Jesus.

> No evil shall befall you, no affliction come near your tent. For he commands his angels with regard to you, to guard you wherever you go. With their hands they shall support you, lest you strike your foot against a stone. (Psalm 91:10–12)

Both Jesus and Satan know of the power in sacred scripture, which is the Bible. It is, in fact, the Word of God. We all have access to the Bible. We need to read it, know it, and use it.

THE MIRACLES OF JESUS

Jesus performed many, many miracles for the people of Israel. He did this for two main reasons: (1) He loved the people, and in many of his miracles, he healed them from illnesses and problems that they had. (2) He did these miracles so that everyone would know, without a doubt, that he was God. No man could do any of the miracles that Jesus did. Only God could do them. Here are some of the many miracles Jesus performed.

JESUS HEALS A MAN WITH LEPROSY

A man came to Jesus who had leprosy, which is a terrible skin disease. He said to Jesus, "Lord, if you will, you can make me healed." Jesus said, "I will; be healed." Immediately, the man's leprosy was healed. (Matthew 8:1–3)

JESUS HEALS THE SICK FROM A DISTANCE

One day a centurion (a Roman soldier) came up to Jesus. He told Jesus that a servant of his was paralyzed back at home and was suffering greatly. He asked Jesus if he could heal him. Jesus said, "I will come and heal him" (Matthew 8:7). The centurion said the he was not worthy to have Jesus enter his home, but if Jesus just said the word, he knew that his servant would be healed. He said that he knew that Jesus had authority over everything, and he had the power to heal his servant from where ever he was at. Jesus said that he had never come across anyone in Israel that had faith in him as strong as this centurion.

And to the centurion Jesus said, "Go; let it be done for you as you have believed." And the servant was healed at that very moment. (Matthew 8:13)

JESUS HEALS A PARALYTIC

Some people brought a paralyzed man to Jesus to be healed. When Jesus saw their faith, he said,

> Take heart, my son; your sins are forgiven.
> (Matthew 9:2)

The man stood up and went home. When the crowds saw it, they were afraid, and they glorified God, who had given such authority to Jesus. Jesus healed paralyzed people who came to him on multiple occasions

JESUS RAISES THE DEAD AND HEALS THE SICK

Jesus was talking to a group of people. A man came up to him and said,

> My daughter has just died, but come and
> lay your hand on her and she will live. (Matthew
> 9:18)

Jesus went to the man's house. He held the hand of the little girl, and she came back to life. When Jesus was on the way to raise the little girl who died, a woman who was sick with a disease for twelve years came up behind him and touched the fringe of his garment, believing that if she just touched his clothes, she would be healed. Jesus turned and said to her,

> Take heart, daughter, your faith has made
> you well. (Matthew 9:22)

The woman was instantly healed. A report of these events went through all that town.

JESUS MAKES THE BLIND SEE

When Jesus was leaving the neighborhood of the girl he brought back to life, two blind men followed him, yelling, "Have mercy on us, Son of David!" (Matthew 9:27)

Jesus touched their eyes and they could then see. Jesus healed people who were blind on more than one occasion

JESUS CAST OUT A DEMON

As the blind men were walking away, a demon-possessed man who could not speak because of it was brought to Jesus. Jesus cast the demon out and the man spoke. The Pharisees who heard about this said,

He casts out demons because he is a demon. (Matthew 12:22–32)

The Pharisees were envious that Jesus was getting a lot of attention. The Pharisees became enemies of Jesus, who would be responsible for getting him sentenced to death.

JESUS MULTIPLIED FIVE LOAVES AND TWO FISH TO FEED THOUSANDS

On one occasion, Jesus was speaking to a crowd of several thousand. There was no food there, and people were starting to get hungry. The apostles only had five loaves of bread and two fish. Jesus looked up to heaven and blessed it, and God multiplied it so there was enough food to feed the several thousand people, and they had twelve baskets of food leftover. Jesus did the exact same thing a little bit later when a large crowd he was speaking to was hungry and there was no food to feed them (Matthew 14:13–21).

JESUS WALKS ON WATER

After they fed the people, Jesus sent the disciples away in a boat and he went up a mountain to pray. Later in the night, Jesus walked out on the water toward the apostles who were in the boat. They thought it was a ghost, and they were afraid.

He said to them, "Take heart; it is I. Do not be afraid." When Peter saw him, he said, "Lord, if it is you, command me to come to you on the water." Jesus said, "Come." Peter got out of the boat and walked on the water toward Jesus. He then noticed the wind, became afraid, and started to sink. He yelled "Lord, save me!" Jesus grabbed him and said, "O you of little faith, why did you doubt?" The apostles began to worship him saying "Truly you are the Son of God." (Matthew 14:27–33)

JESUS HEALS THE DEAF AND THE MUTE

People brought a man to Jesus who was deaf and also unable to speak. They begged Jesus to heal him. Jesus put his fingers into the man's ears and touched the man's tongue and said, "Be opened." He immediately could hear and speak. The crowd was amazed and said, "Jesus has done all things well. He even makes the deaf hear and the mute speak." (Mark 7:32–37)

JESUS HEALS ALL

Jesus went on from here and sat down on a mountain. People were brought to him who were blind, crippled, could not speak, and those that had other diseases and illnesses, and Jesus healed them all

JESUS CASTS OUT MANY DEMONS

The most frequent healing and miracle that Jesus did was he cast demons out of people. There are multiple accounts across the four gospels of Jesus doing this. One was cited above. The demons caused a variety of severe problems for the people that they possessed. At times, Jesus would speak with the demons before he cast them out. The demons proclaimed out loud that Jesus was the Son of God, and they begged Jesus to either not cast them out of the possessed person, or to have mercy on them. Jesus told the evil spirits they had to leave each person and never come back. Jesus has power over everything, even demons and devils, so they had to listen to him. The evil spirits left the people and they were well. The people who witnessed this were amazed (Matthew 8:28–34; Mark 5:1–20, 9:14–29; Luke 4:31–37, 8:26–39, 9:37–43, 11:14–23, 13:10–17).

JESUS CALMS A STORM

One day, Jesus got into a boat with his disciples and he said to them "Let us go across to the other side of the lake." So they set out, and as they sailed, Jesus fell asleep. A windstorm came down on the lake, and the boat was filling with water and they were in danger. Then disciples woke Jesus, saying "Master, Master, we are perishing!" Jesus awoke and rebuked the wind and the waves and they ceased, and there was a calm. He said to them "Where is your faith?" And they were afraid and they marveled, saying to one another, "Who then is this, that he commands even the winds and water, and they obey him?" (Luke 8:22–25)

THE TRANSFIGURATION

One day, Jesus took the three apostles he was closest to—Peter, James, and John—with him to a mountaintop. There, Jesus transfigured, or turned into, what he looks like when he is in heaven. His face glowed like the sun, and his clothes became white as light. Then Moses and Elijah came down from heaven, and they were talking with Jesus. All of a sudden, a bright cloud hovered over all of them. God the Father spoke out of this cloud and said,

> This is my beloved Son, with whom I am
> well pleased; listen to him. (Matthew 17:6–7)

When the apostles heard this, they fell on their face and were terrified. Jesus came and touched them, saying,

> Rise and have no fear. (Matthew 17:7)

When they lifted up their eyes, they saw no one but Jesus with them.

JESUS RAISES LAZARUS FROM THE DEAD

There was a man named Lazarus, who was a friend of Jesus. Lazarus's sisters were named Martha and Mary, and they were also friends of Jesus. One day Lazarus became very sick. Martha and Mary sent a message to Jesus, letting him know that his friend Lazarus was sick. Jesus responded by saying,

> This Illness does not lead to death. It is for
> the Glory of God, so that the Son of God may be
> glorified through it. (John 11:4)

Jesus loved Martha, Mary, and Lazarus. When he heard Lazarus was sick, he purposely waited two days until he went to see Lazarus. After two days, Jesus said to his disciples,

> Let us go to Judea. Our friend Lazarus has fallen asleep, but I go to awaken him. (John 11:11)

The disciples said that if he fell asleep, that was good, because it would help Lazarus get better. They did not understand that he actually died. Jesus then said to them,

> Lazarus has died, and for your sake I am glad that I was not there, so that you may believe. But let us go to him. (John 11:14)

(If Lazarus was just sick and Jesus made him better, that would be a minor miracle. If Jesus brought him back from the dead, that would be a *major* miracle, and lead witness of this to believe Jesus was God.)

When Jesus arrived, Lazarus had already been dead and buried in a tomb for four days. Martha ran out to Jesus when he arrived. She said,

> Lord, it you had been here, my brother would not have died. But even now I know that whatever you ask from God, God will give you. (John 11:21–22)

> Jesus said to Martha, "I am the resurrection and the life. Whoever believes in me, though he die, yet shall he live, and everyone who lives and believes in me shall never die. Do you believe this?"

> Martha said "Yes Lord; I believe that you are the Christ, the Son of God, who is coming into the world." (John 11:25–27)

> Mary came out of the house along with a crowd of people to meet Jesus. Mary said to Jesus, "Lord, if you had been here, my brother would not have died." (John 11:32)

Everyone was crying. Jesus was greatly moved by this, and he cried along with his friends. Jesus and the crowd went to the tomb where Lazarus had been buried for four days. It was a cave, with a stone placed over the covering. Jesus told them to take away the stone. They were afraid of the smell that would come out, since Lazarus had been dead for four days.

> Jesus said, "Did I not tell you that if you believed, you would see the glory of God?" Jesus said, "Father, I thank you that you have heard me. I knew that you always hear me, but I said this on account of the people standing around that that they may believe that you sent me." Then Jesus said with a loud voice, "Lazarus, come out." (John 11:40–43)

Lazarus, who was dead for four days came out. His hands and feet were bound with linin strips, and his face wrapped with a cloth. Jesus told the people to untie Lazarus and let him go. Many of the witnesses of this came to believe that Jesus was the Christ.

CHAPTER 19

THE TEACHINGS OF JESUS

Jesus performed all the miracles stated above, along with additional others that were not listed here, to prove without a doubt that he was God. Another thing that Jesus did during his three-year ministry was, he taught the people about himself as God the Savior, about God the Father, about heaven, and about how we are to live our lives, among other things. These are some, but not all his teachings. To learn about all of Jesus's teachings, please read the gospels of Matthew, Mark, Luke, and John in the Bible.

JESUS SAYS THAT THE WAY TO LOVE HIM IS TO READ AND KNOW THE BIBLE (THE COMMANDS FROM GOD TO US) AND DO WHAT IT SAYS IN YOUR LIFE

Jesus said,

> Whoever has my commandments and keeps them, he is it who loves me. And he who loves me will be loved by my Father, and I will love him and manifest myself to him. (John 14:21)

Jesus said,

> If you love me, you will keep my commandments. And I will ask the Father, and he will give you another Helper, to be with you forever, even the Spirit if truth, whom the world cannot receive, because it neither sees him or knows him. You know him, for he dwells with you and will be in you. (John 14:15–17)

Jesus said,

> If anyone loves me, he will keep my word, and my Father will love him, and we will come to him and make our home with him. (John 14:23)

> Whatever we ask we receive from God, because we keep his commandments and do what pleases him. And this is his commandment, that we believe in the name of his Son Jesus Christ and love one another, just as he commanded us. Whoever keeps his commandments abides in God, and God abides in him. And by this we know that he abides in us, by the Spirit whom he has given us. (1 John 3:22–24)

Jesus said,

> You are my friends if you do what I command you. No longer do I call you servants, for the servant does not know what the master is doing, but I have called you friends, for all that I have heard from my Father I have made known to you. (John 15:14–15)

WHOEVER DOES THE WILL OF GOD WILL BE A FAMILY MEMBER OF JESUS

> While Jesus was still speaking to the people, behold, his mother and his brothers stood outside, asking to speak to him. But he replied to the man who told him, "Who is my mother, and who are my brothers?" And stretching out his hand to his disciples, he said "Here are my mother and my brothers! *For whoever does the will of my Father in heaven is my brother and sister and mother." (italics added)* (Matthew 12:46–50)

In Jesus's own words, he makes it clear that to love Jesus, to be his friend, to have God abide in us, and to be part of Jesus's family, we must follow his commandments and the will of God the Father. How do we know what Jesus commands us to do and what the will of God the Father is for us? He tells us in his Word to us, the Bible. We must read the Bible, know it, and follow it in our lives. If we do, Jesus said that is how we love him, he will become our friend, he will abide in us, and we will become a member of his immediate family.

THE BEATITUDES

Jesus went up on a mountain and taught the following to the crowd, which is called the beatitudes. The beatitudes describe some of the qualities of followers of Jesus:

> Blessed are the poor in spirit for theirs is the kingdom of heaven.
> Blessed are those who mourn, for they shall be comforted.
> Blessed are the meek, for they shall inherit the earth.

Blessed are those who hunger and thirst for righteousness, for they shall be satisfied.

Blessed are the merciful, for they shall receive mercy.

Blessed are the pure in heart, for they shall see God.

Blessed are the peacemakers, for they shall be called sons of God.

Blessed are those who are persecuted for righteousness sake, for theirs is the kingdom of heaven.

Blessed are you when others criticize you and persecute you and utter all kinds of evil against you falsely on my account. Rejoice and be glad, for your reward is great in heaven, because they persecuted the prophets who were before you. (Matthew 5:3–12)

WE ARE TO BE THE SALT AND LIGHT OF THE WORLD

Jesus said that Christians are to be good, consistent examples of followers of Christ to the rest of the world:
Jesus said,

You are the salt of the earth. But if salt has lost its taste, how shall its saltiness to be restored? It is no longer good for anything except to be thrown out and trampled under people's feet.

You are the light of the world. A city set on a hill cannot be hidden. Nor do people light a lamp and put it under a basket, but on a stand, and it gives light to all in the house. In the same way, let your light shine before others, son that they may see your good works and give glory to your father who is in heaven. (Matthew 5:13–16)

JESUS CAME TO FULFILL THE LAW

Jesus said,

> Do not think I came to abolish the Law or the Prophets; I have not come to abolish them, but to fulfill them. (Matthew 5:17–20)

DO NOT HAVE ANGER IN YOUR HEARTS BUT MAKE PEACE WITH EACH OTHER

[Summary] Jesus said that although the Law says if you murder you will be liable to judgement, Jesus says that having anger in your heart toward anyone is wrong and a sin. If you have anything against anyone in your heart, or you know of another person that has something against you, stop what you are doing, go to that person, and attempt to make peace with him or her. (Matthew 5:21–26)

AVOID LUST

[Summary] Jesus said that adultery is a sin. However, if you have lustful intents in your heart, that is also sinning. Do whatever you can do to avoid lustful thoughts to entice you. Do whatever you have to do to avoid the temptations that cause these lustful thoughts. (Matthew 5:27–30)

DIVORCE

Jesus said,

I say to you that everyone who divorces his wife, except on the ground of sexual immorality, makes her commit adultery, and whoever marries a divorced woman commits adultery. (Matthew 5:32)

DO NOT TAKE OATHS

[Summary] Jesus said to not take oaths in any form. Instead, say yes when you mean yes and no when you mean no and do not lie. (Matthew 5:33–36)

SEEK MERCY, NOT REVENGE

[Summary] Jesus said you must not try to get revenge against others that you believe have done wrong to you. Additionally, you should be very generous in your giving help to others who ask for it or are in need of it. (Matthew 5:38–42)

LOVE YOUR ENEMIES

Jesus said,

You have heard that it was said "You shall love your neighbor and hate your enemy." But I say to you, love your enemies and pray for those that persecute you, so that you may be the sons of your Father who is in heaven. For he makes the sun rise on the evil and the good, and sends rain on the just and the unjust. For if you love those that love you, what reward do you have? Do not even the tax collectors do the same? And if you greet only your brothers, what more are you doing than others? Do not even the gentiles do the same? You therefore must be perfect, as your heavenly Father is perfect. (Matthew 5:43–48)

BE GENEROUS TO OTHERS, BUT DO NOT DO IT TO SHOW OFF

Jesus said,

> Beware of practicing your righteousness before other people *in order to be seen by them (italics added),* for then you will have no reward from your father who is in heaven. Thus, when you give to the needy, sound no trumpet before you, as the hypocrites do in the synagogues and in the streets, that they may be praised by others. Truly I say to you, they have received their reward [the praise they got from others]. But when you give to the needy, do not let your left hand know what your right hand is doing, so that your giving may be in secret. And your Father who sees in secret will reward you. (Matthew 6:1–4)

JESUS GIVES US THE LORD'S PRAYER

Jesus said that when you pray, do not do it in a way to show off to be noticed by others. Pray in a personal way between you and God your Father. Also, when you pray, do not use a bunch of long, empty phrases. God is not impressed by how many words you use when you pray. Jesus said,

> Pray then like this:
> Our Father in heaven,
> Hallowed be your name.
> Your kingdom come,
> Your will be done,
> On earth as it is in heaven.
> Give us this day our daily bread,
> And forgive us our debts, a
> As we have also forgiven our debtors.
> And lead us not into temptation,
> But deliver us from evil. (Matthew 6:9–13)

Jesus then next said,

> For if you forgive others their trespasses, your heavenly Father will also forgive you, but if you do not forgive others their trespasses, neither will your Father forgive your trespasses. (Matthew 6:14–15)

DO GOOD THINGS TO LAY UP TREASURES FOR YOURSELF IN HEAVEN INSTEAD OF TREASURES ON EARTH

Jesus said,

> Do not lay up for yourselves treasures on earth, where moth and rust destroy and where thieves break in and steal, but lay up for yourselves treasures in heaven, where neither moth nor rust destroys and where thieves do not break in and steal. For where your treasure is, your heart will be also. (Matthew 6:19–23)

DO NOT WORRY ABOUT ANYTHING
IF YOU FOLLOW GOD, HE WILL TAKE CARE OF YOU

[Summary] Jesus said do not worry about your life, or what you eat or drink, or what you will wear. The animals and plants do not worry about these things, and God your Father takes care of all of them, and you are much more valuable to him than those. Can worrying about things help you in any way? God is your Father, and he knows you need these things, and he will supply them for you. Instead of worrying about all of the things of the world, seek out the kingdom of God and his righteousness. When you do, all of the worldly things will additionally be given to you. Additionally, do not worry about what will happen in the future. Focus on what you need to do today and the future will take care of itself. (Matthew 6:25–33)

DO NOT JUDGE OTHER PEOPLE
INSTEAD, FOCUS ON FIXING YOUR OWN FLAWS
SO YOU CAN BE A BETTER PERSON

Jesus said,

Judge not, that you be not judged. For with the judgment you pronounce you will be judged, and with the measure you use it will be measured to you. Why do you see that speck in your brother's eye, but you do not notice the log that is in your own eye? Or how can you say to your brother "Let me take the speck out of your eye," when there is a log in your own eye? You hypocrite, first take the log out of your own eye, and then you will see clearly to take the speck out of your brother's eye. (Matthew 7:1–5)

IF YOU ARE A CHILD OF GOD, HE WILL GIVE YOU GOOD THINGS THAT ARE ALIGNED WITH HIS WILL IF YOU ASK HIM

Jesus said,

> Ask, and it will be given to you; seek, and you will find; knock, and it will be open to you. For everyone who asks receives, and the one who seeks finds, and the one who knocks it will be opened. Or which one of you, if his son asks him for bread, will give him a stone? Or if he asks for a fish, will give him a serpent? If you then, who are evil, know how to give good gifts to *your children (italics added)*, how much more will your Father who is in heaven give good things and the *Holy Spirit (italics added)* to those who ask him! (Matthew 7:7–11 and Luke 11:9–13)

THE GOLDEN RULE

Jesus said,

> So whatever you wish that others would do to you, do also to them, for this is the Law and the Prophets. (Matthew 7:12)

READING THE BIBLE AND DOING WHAT IT SAYS WILL SHELTER YOU THROUGHOUT YOUR LIFE

Jesus said,

> Everyone who *hears these words of mine and does (italics added) them* will be like a wise man who built his house on the rock. And the rain fell, and the floods came, and the winds blew and beat on that house, but it did not fall, because it had been founded on the rock. And everyone who hears these words of mine *and does not do them (italics added)* will be like a foolish man who built his house on the sand. And then rain fell, and the floods came, and the winds blew and beat against that house, and it fell, and great was the fall of it. (Matthew 7:24–27)

JESUS CAME FOR THOSE WHO WANT HIM AND KNOW THEY NEED HIM

> Jesus saw a man who was a tax collector named Matthew [a bad thing to be in those days, because they were often corrupt]. Jesus said to him "Follow me" and Matthew rose and followed Jesus. Jesus was later with Matthew in a big house with a lot of guests. Many tax collectors and sinners were hanging out with Jesus and his disciples, because they knew they were sinners and needed Jesus to save them from their sins.
>
> When the Pharisees saw this, they said to Jesus disciples, "Why does your teacher eat with tax collectors and sinners?"
>
> Jesus heard this and said to them, "Those who are well do not need a doctor, but those who are sick do. Go and learn what this means, 'I

desire mercy, not sacrifice.' For I came not to call the righteous, but sinners." (Matthew 9:9–13)

The Pharisees thought they were holy and sinless and did not need Jesus, even though they needed him *the most* because of their pride and unforgiveness of others.

IF YOU COME TO JESUS, HE WILL GIVE YOU REST AND GUIDANCE

Jesus said,

> Come to me, all who labor and are heavy laden, and I will give you rest. Take my yoke upon you, and learn from me, for I am gentle and lowly in heart, and you will find rest for your souls. For my yoke is easy, and my burden is light. (Matthew 11:28–30)

HE WHO HEARS GOD'S WORD UNDERSTANDS IT AND DOES IT WILL BE PRODUCTIVE FOR GOD
THE PARABLE OF THE SOWER

Jesus told the crowds:

> A sower went out to sow. And as he sowed, some seeds fell along the path, and the birds came and devoured them. Other seeds fell on rocky ground, where they did not have much soil, and immediately they sprang up, since they had no depth of soil, but when the sun rose they were scorched. And since they had no root, they withered away. Other seeds fell among thorns, and the thorns grew up and choked them. Other seeds fell on good soil and produced grain, some

a hundredfold, some sixty, some thirty. He who has ears, let him hear. (Matthew 13:3–8)

The disciples asked Jesus to explain the parable of the sower to them, and this is what Jesus told them:

> When anyone hears the word of the kingdom and does not understand it, the evil one comes and snatches away what has been sown in his heart. This is what was sown along the path. As for what was sown on rocky ground, this is the one who hears the word and immediately receives it with joy, yet he has no root in himself, but endures for a while, and when tribulation or persecution arises on account of the word, immediately he falls away. As for what was sown among thorns, this is the one who hears the word, but the cares of the world and the deceitfulness of riches choke the word, and it proves unfruitful. As for what was sown on good soil, this is the one who hears the word and understands it. He indeed bears fruit and yields, in one case a hundredfold, in another sixty, and in another thirty. (Matthew 13:19–23)

PARABLES ABOUT HEAVEN

Jesus said,

> The kingdom of heaven is like treasure hidden in a field, which a man found and covered up. Then in his joy he goes and sells all that he has and buys that field. (Matthew 13:44)

Jesus said,

> Again, the kingdom of heaven is like a merchant in search of great pearls, who finding one pearl of great value, went and sold all he had and bought it. (Matthew 13:45–46)

JESUS GIVES US A GLIMPSE INTO THE AFTERLIFE

The following is a story Jesus gave about a rich man and a man named Lazarus. This may not be a parable but a story of an actual event. Jesus used parables, which were made-up stories intended to teach a point. In the parable of the rich man and Lazarus, Jesus uses the name of a specific person, Lazarus, in this story. He did not do this in his parables. In the following story, it is not believed that the rich man was being punished after his death just because he was rich. Rather, he was rich and never helped Lazarus, who was suffering right outside the rich man's gate, when it was easy for the rich man to help him. Here is the story from Jesus:

> There was a rich man who was clothed in purple and fine linen and who feasted sumptuously every day. And at his gate laid a poor man named Lazarus, covered with sores, who desired to be fed with what fell from the rich man's table. Moreover, even the dogs came and licked his sores. The poor man died and was carried by the angels to Abraham's side. The rich man also died and was buried, and in Hades, being in torment, he lifted up his eyes and saw Abraham far off and Lazarus at his side. And he called out, "Father Abraham, have mercy on me, and send Lazarus to dip the end of his finger in water and cool

my tongue, for I am in anguish in this flame." But Abraham said, "Child, remember that you in your lifetime received your good things, and Lazarus in like manner bad things; but now he is comforted here, and you are in anguish. And besides all this, between us and you a great chasm has been fixed, in order that those who would pass from here to you may not be able, and none may cross from there to us." And he said, "Then I beg you, father, to send him to my father's house— for I have five brothers—so he may warn them, lest they also come into this place of torment." But Abraham said, "They have Moses and the Prophets; let them hear them." And he said, "No, father Abraham, but if someone goes to them from the dead, they will repent." He said to him, "If they do not hear Moses and the Prophets, neither shall they be convinced if someone should rise from the dead." (Luke 16:19–31)

FOLLOW JESUS AND SAVE YOUR SOUL

Jesus told his disciples "If anyone would come after me, let him deny himself and take up his cross and follow me. For whoever would save his life would lose it, but whoever loses his life for my sake will find it. For what will it profit a man if he gains the whole world and forfeits his soul? Or what shall a man give in return for his soul? For the Son of Man is going to come with his angels in the glory of his Father, and then he will repay each person according to what he has done." (Matthew 16:24–27)

BEING HUMBLE, KIKE A CHILD, MAKES ONE GREAT IN HEAVEN

The disciples asked Jesus "Who is the greatest in the kingdom of heaven?" Jesus grabbed a child and said, "Truly I say to you, unless you turn and become like children, you will never enter the kingdom of heaven. *Whoever humbles himself like this is the greatest in the kingdom of heaven." (italics added)* (Matthew 18:1–6)

DO NOT CAUSE OTHERS TO SIN, ESPECIALLY CHILDREN

Jesus said,

Whoever receives one such child in my name receives me, but whoever causes one of these little ones who believe in me to sin, it would be better for him to have a great millstone fastened around his neck and to be drowned in the depth of the sea. (Matthew 18:5–6)

THE PARABLE OF THE UNFORGIVING SERVANT

The following parable demonstrates that since Jesus forgives *all* our sins when we follow him, should we not be grateful and follow his example and forgive the *few* sins others have committed against us?

Then Peter came up and said to Jesus, "Lord, how often will my brother sin against me, and I forgive him? As many as seven times?" Jesus said to him "I do not say to you seven times, but seventy times seven."
Therefore the kingdom of heaven may be compared to a king who wished to settle accounts

with his servants. When he began to settle, one was brought to him and owed ten thousand talents [a vast amount of money]. And since he could not pay, his master ordered him to be sold, with his wife and his children and all that he had, and payment to be made. So the servant fell on his knees, imploring him, "Have patience with me, and I will pay you everything." *And out of pity for him, the master of that servant released him and forgave him the debt (italics added).* But when the same servant went out, he found one of his fellow servants who owed him a hundred denarii [a small amount of money], and seizing him, he began to choke him, saying, "Pay what you owe." So his fellow servant fell down and pleaded with him, "Have patience with me, and I will pay you." He refused and went and put him in prison until he should pay the debt. When his fellow servants saw what had taken place, they were greatly distressed, and they went and reported to their master all that had taken place. Then his master summoned him and said to him, "You wicked servant! I forgave you all that debt because you pleaded with me. And should you not have had mercy on your fellow servant, as I had mercy on you?" And in anger his master delivered him to the jailers, until he should pay all his debt. So also my heavenly Father will do to every one of you, if you do not forgive your brother from your heart. (Matthew 18:21–35)

PARABLE OF THE LABORERS IN THE VINEYARD

God is generous in saving anyone who decides to follow God, no matter when they do it in their lifetime:

Jesus said,

> For the kingdom of heaven is like a master of a house who went out early in the morning to hire laborers for his vineyard. After agreeing with the laborers for a denarius a day, he sent them into the vineyard. And going out about the third hour he saw others standing idle in the market-place, and to them he said "You go into the vineyard too, and whatever is right I will give you." So they went. Going out again about the sixth hour and the ninth hour, he did the same. And about the eleventh hour he went out and found others standing. And he said to them, "Why do you stand here idle all day?" They said to him, "Because no one has hired us." He said to them, "You go into the vineyard too." And when evening came, the owner of the vineyard said to his foreman, "Call the laborers and pay them their wages, beginning with the last, up to the first." And when those hired about the eleventh hour came, each received a denarius. Now when those hired first came, they thought they would receive more, but each of them also received a denarius. And on receiving it they grumbled at the master of the house, saying "These last worked only one hour, and you have made them equal to us who have borne the burden of the day and the scorching heat." But he replied to one of them, "Friend, I am doing you no wrong. Did you not agree with me for a denarius? Take what belongs to you and go. *I choose to give to this last worker as I give to you. Am I not allowed to do what I choose with what belongs to me? Or do you begrudge my generosity?" (italics added)* So the last will be first, and the first will be last. (Matthew 20:1–16)

REPENTANCE

[Summary] Jesus posed a question to the people: "A man had two sons. He went to the first and said 'Son, go and work in the vineyard today.' The son answered 'I will not,' but afterward he changed his mind and went and worked. The father went to the second son and said the same. The son answered 'I will go dad,' but he did not go. Which one did the will of his father?" The crowd said, "The first." Jesus said to the crowd that many of them will not get into heaven because even though Jesus was telling them that they need to believe in him and follow him, many were not changing their minds and doing this. Or, they were just following Jesus with their words, but not with their actions. (Matthew 21:28–32)

LOVE GOD AND LOVE OTHERS

A Pharisee asked Jesus which is the greatest commandment. Jesus said,

> You shall love the Lord your God with all your heart, and with all your soul, and with all your mind. And a second is like it: You shall love your neighbor as yourself. On these two commandments depend all the Law and the Prophets. (Matthew 22:37–40)

JESUS CALLS THOSE WHO FOLLOW HIM HIS FRIENDS AND HE WANTS US TO LOVE EACH OTHER AS HE LOVES US

Jesus said,

> This is my commandment, that you love one another as I have loved you. Greater love has no one than this, that someone lay down his life for his friends. You are my friends if you do what I command you. No longer do I call you servants, for the servant does not know what his master is doing; but I have called you friends, for all that I have heard from my Father I have made known to you. You did not choose me, but I chose you and appointed you that you should go and bear fruit and that your fruit should abide, so that whatever you ask the Father in my name, he may give it to you. These things I command you, so that you will love one another. (John 15:12–17)

WE WILL BE JUDGED BASED ON HOW WE TREAT OTHERS

Jesus said,

> When the Son of Man comes in his glory, and all the angels with him, then he will sit on his glorious throne. Before him will be gathered all the nations, and he will separate people from one another as a shepherd separates the sheep from the goats. And he will place the sheep on the right, but the goats on the left. Then the King will say to those on his right, "Come, you who are blessed by my Father, inherit the kingdom prepared for you from the foundation of the world. For I was hungry and you gave me

food, I was thirsty and you gave me drink, I was a stranger and you welcomed me, I was naked and you clothed me, I was sick and you visited me, I was in prison and you came to me." Then the righteous will answer him saying, "Lord, when did we see you hungry and feed you, or thirsty and give you drink? And when did we see you a stranger and welcome you, or naked and clothe you?" And the King will answer them, "Truly, I say to you, as you did it to the least of these my brothers, you did it to me." (Matthew 25:31–46)

Then he will say to those on his left, "Depart from me, you cursed, into the eternal fire prepared for the devil and his angels. For I was hungry and you gave me no food, I was thirsty and you gave me no drink, I was a stranger and you did not welcome me, naked and you did not clothe me, sick and in prison and you did not visit me." Then they will also answer, saying "Lord, when did we see you hungry or thirsty, or a stranger, or naked or sick or in prison, and did not minister to you? And then he will answer them, saying, "Truly, I say to you, as you did not do it to one of the least of these, you did not do it to me." And these will go away into eternal punishment, but the righteous into eternal life. (Matthew 25:41–46)

CHRISTIANS MUST LOVE AND BE KIND TO EVERYONE, INCLUDING OUR ENEMIES

Jesus said,

But I say to you who hear, love your enemies, do good to those who hate you, bless those who curse you, pray for those who abuse you. To the one who strikes you on the cheek, offer the other also, and from one who takes away your cloak do not withhold your tunic either. Give to everyone who begs from you and from the one who takes away your goods do not demand them back. And as you wish others would do to you, do so to them.

If you love those who love you, what benefit is that to you? For even sinners love those who love them. And if you do good to those who do good to you, what benefit is that to you? For even sinners do the same. And if you lend to those from whom you expect to receive, what credit is that to you? Even sinners lend to sinners, to get back the same amount. But love your enemies, and do good, and lend, expecting nothing in return, *and your reward will be great, and you will be sons of the Most High, for he is kind to the ungrateful and the evil. Be merciful, even as your Father is merciful (italics added).* (Luke 6:27–36)

IF THE WORLD HATES YOU, REMEMBER THAT IT HATED JESUS FIRST BECAUSE BOTH JESUS AND CHRISTIANS ARE NOT OF THE WORLD

Jesus said,

If the world hates you, know that it has hated me before it hated you. If you were of the world, the world would love you as its own; but because you are not of the world, but I chose you out of the world, therefore the world hates you. Remember the word that I said to you: "A servant is not greater than his master." If they persecuted me, they will also persecute you. If they kept my word, they will also keep yours. But all these things they will do to you on account of my name, because they do not know him who sent me. If I had not come and spoken to them, they would not have been guilty of sin, but now they have no excuse for their sin. Whoever hates me hates my Father also. If I had not done among them the works that no one else did, they would not be guilty of sin, but now they have seen and hated both me and my Father. But the word that is written in their Law must be fulfilled: "They hated me without a cause." (John 15:18–25)

JESUS IS OUR RESURRECTION AND LIFE

Jesus said to Martha, the sister of Lazarus, before Jesus raised him from the dead,

> I am the resurrection and the life. Whoever believes in me, though he die, yet shall he live, and everyone who lives and believes in me shall never die. (John 11:25–26)

GOD CONSIDERS US GREAT WHEN WE SERVE OTHERS, JUST AS JESUS SERVED US

Jesus said,

> But whoever should be great among you must be your servant, and whoever would be first among you must be slave of all. For even the Son of Man came not to be served but to serve, and to give his life as a ransom for many. (Mark 10:43–45)

WE KNOW WE ARE FOLLOWERS OF GOD WHEN WE LOVE ONE ANOTHER

Jesus gave a new commandment to follow. He said,

> A new commandment I give you, that you love one another: just as I have loved you, you are also to love one another. By this all people will know that you are my followers, if you have love for one another. (John 13:34–35)

JESUS SAYS THAT *DOING* THE WILL OF THE FATHER IS WHAT MAKES ONE A CHRISTIAN

> Not everyone who says to me, "Lord, Lord," will enter the kingdom of heaven, *but the one who does the will of my Father who is in heaven (italics added)*. On that day many will say to me, "Lord, Lord, did we not prophesy in your name, and cast out demons in your name, and do many mighty works in your name?" And then I will declare to them, "I never knew you: depart from me, you workers of lawlessness." (Matthew 7:21–23)

JESUS WARNS THAT CHRISTIANS MAY FACE PERSECUTIONS IN THEIR LIVES

> Behold, I am sending you our as sheep in the midst of wolves, so be wise as serpents and innocent as doves. Beware of men, for they will deliver you over to courts and flog you in their synagogues, and you will be dragged before governors and kings for my sake, to bear witness before them and the Gentiles. When they deliver

you over, do not be anxious how you are to speak or what you are to say, for what you are to say will be given to you in that hour. For it is not you who speak, but the Spirit of your Father speaking through you. Brother will deliver brother over to death, and the father his child, and children will rise against parents and have them put to death, and you will be hated by all for my name's sake. But the one who endures to the end will be saved. When they persecute you in one town, flee to the next, for truly, I say to you, you will not have gone through all the towns of Israel before the son of man comes.

A disciple is not above his teacher, nor a servant above his master. It is enough for the disciple to be like his teacher, and the servant like his master. If they called the master of the house Beelzebul, how much more will they malign those of his household. (Matthew 10:16–25)

HAVE NO FEAR, BUT FOLLOW GOD

Jesus said,

So have no fear of them, for nothing is covered that will not be revealed, or hidden that will not be known. What I tell you in the dark, say in the light, and what you hear whispered, proclaim on the housetops. And do not fear those who kill the body but cannot kill the soul. Rather fear him who can destroy both soul and body in hell. Are not two sparrows sold for a penny? And not one of them will fall through the ground apart from your Father. But even the hairs of your head are numbered. Fear not, therefore; you are of more value than many sparrows. So everyone who acknowledges me before men, I also will acknowledge before my Father who is in heaven, but whoever denies me before men, I will also deny before my Father who is in heaven. (Matthew 10:26–33)

JESUS SAYS WE MUST PUT HIM FIRST IN OUR LIVES

Whoever loves father or mother more than me is not worthy of me, and whoever loves son or daughter more than me is not worthy of me. And whoever does not take up his cross and follow me is not worth of me. Whoever finds his life will lose it, and whoever loses his life for my sake will find it. (Matthew 10:37–39)

JESUS REAFFIRMS TO JOHN THE BAPTIST THAT HE IS THE CHRIST

Now when John the Baptist heard in prison about the deeds of the Christ, he sent word by his disciples and said to Jesus "Are you the one who is to come, or shall we look for another?" And Jesus answered them, "Go and tell John what you hear and see: the blind receive their sight and the lame walk, lepers are cleansed and the deaf hear, and the dead are raised up, and the poor have good news preached to them. And blessed is the one who is not offended by me." (Matthew 11:2–6)

THE PARABLE OF THE WEEDS

Jesus told the following parable:

The kingdom of heaven may be compared to a man who sowed good seed in his field, but while his men were sleeping, his enemy came and sowed weeds among the wheat and went away. So when the plants came up and bore grain, the weeds appeared also. And the servants of the master of the house came and said to him, "Master, did you not sow good seeds in your field? How then does it have weeds?" He said to them, "An enemy has done this." So the servants said to him, "Then do you want us to go and gather them?" But he said, "No, lest in gathering the weeds you root up the wheat along with them. Let both grow together until the harvest, and at harvest time I will tell the reapers, Gather the weeds first and bind them into bundles to be burned, but gather the wheat into my barn."

After Jesus left the crowds, his disciples asked him to explain the parable of the weeds to them. Jesus said, "The one who sows the good seed is the Son of Man. The field is the world, and the good seed is the sons of the kingdom. The weeds are the sons of the evil one, and the enemy who sowed them is the devil. The harvest is the close of the age, and the reapers are angels. Just as the weeds are gathered and burned with fire, so it will be at the close of the age. The Son of Man will send his angels, and they will gather out of his kingdom all causes of sin and all law-breakers, and throw them into the fiery furnace. In that place there will be weeping and gnashing of teeth. Then the righteous will shine like the sun in the kingdom of their Father. He who has ears, let him hear." (Matthew 13:24–30, 36–43)

JESUS SAID THAT WHAT COMES OUT OF YOUR HEART IS WHAT DEFILES YOU

The Pharisees and scribes came to Jesus and asked him why his disciples break the tradition of the elders by not washing their hands when they eat. Jesus responded,

> Hear and understand: it is not what goes into the mouth that defiles a person, but what comes out of the mouth that defiles a person. Do you not see that whatever goes into the mouth passes into the stomach and is expelled? But what comes out of the mouth proceeds from the heart, and this defiles a person. For out of the heart comes evil thoughts, murder, adultery, sexual immorality, theft, false witness, slander. These are what defiles a person. But to eat with unwashed hands does not defile anyone. (Matthew 15:10–20)

JESUS TELLS A PARABLE ABOUT HOW HE WILL BE KILLED BY THE ENVIOUS RELIGIOUS LEADERS

Jesus said to the crowd,

> Hear another parable. There was a master of a house who planted a vineyard and put a fence around it and dug a winepress in it and built a tower and leased it to tenants, and went into another country. When the season for fruit drew near, he sent his servants to the tenants to get his fruit. And the tenants took his servants and beat

one, killed another, and stoned another. Again he sent other servants, more than the first. And they did the same to them. Finally, he sent his son to them, saying, "They will respect my son." But when the tenants saw the son, they said to themselves, "This is the heir. Come, let us kill him and have his inheritance." And they took him and threw him out of the vineyard and killed him. When therefore the owner of the vineyard comes, what will he do to those tenants?" They said to him, "He will put those wretches to a miserable death and let out the vineyard to other tenants who will give him the fruits in their seasons." Jesus said to them, "Have you never read in the scriptures: 'The stone that the builders rejected has become the cornerstone, this was the Lord's doing, and it is marvelous in our eyes?' Therefore I tell you, the kingdom of God will be taken away from you and given to a people producing its fruits. And the one who falls on this stone will be broken to pieces; and when it falls on anyone, it will crush him."

When the chief priests and the Pharisees heard the parables, they perceived he was talking about them. And although they were seeking to arrest him, they feared the crowds, because they held him to be a prophet. (Matthew 22:33–45)

JESUS REVEALS THE SERIOUSNESS OF AVOIDING SIN IN ONE'S LIFE

Jesus said,

If your hand causes you to sin, cut it off. It is better for you to enter life crippled than with two hands to go to hell, to the unquenchable fire. And if your foot causes you to sin, cut it off. It is better for you to enter life lame than with two feet to be thrown into hell. And if your eye causes you to sin, tear it out. It is better for you to enter the kingdom of God with one eye than with two eyes to be thrown into hell, where the worm does not die and the fire is not quenched. (Mark 9:42–50)

JESUS INFORMS THE PRIDEFUL APOSTLES THAT IN ORDER TO BE GREAT, THEY MUST BE A SERVANT OF OTHERS

The apostles James and John, in a moment of ignorant pride, asked Jesus to let them sit at his right and left hands when he entered his kingdom of heaven. Jesus responded to their prideful request to be glorified,

You know that those who are considered rulers of the Gentiles lord it over them, and their great ones exercise authority over them. But it shall not be so among you. But whoever would be great among you must be your servant, and whoever would be first among you must be slave of all. For even the Son of Man came not to be served but to serve, and to give his life as a ransom of many. (Mark 10:35–45)

PEOPLE ARE JUDGED BY THE FRUIT THAT THEY ACTUALLY PRODUCE

Jesus said,

For no good tree bears bad fruit, nor again does a bad tree bear good fruit. For each tree is known by its own fruit. For figs are not gathered from thornbushes, nor are grapes picked from a bramble bush. The good person out of the good treasure of his heart produces good, and the evil person out of his evil treasure produces evil, for out of the abundance of the heart his mouth speaks. (Luke 6:43–45)

THE PARABLE OF THE GOOD SAMARITAN

When Jesus was speaking to the crowd, he told them that they must love God with all their heart, soul, strength, and mind, and they must also love their neighbor as themselves.

A man asked Jesus, "And who is my neighbor?"

Jesus answered his question with the following parable:

Jesus said, "A man was going down from Jerusalem to Jericho, and he fell among robbers, who stripped him and beat him and departed, leaving him half dead. Now by chance a priest was going down that road, and when he saw him he passed by on the other side. So likewise a Levite, when he came to the place and saw him, passed by on the other side. But a Samaritan, as he journeyed, came to where he was, and when he saw him, he had compassion. He went to him and bound up his wounds, pouring on oil and wine. Then he set him on his own animal and brought him to an inn and took care of him. And the next day he took out two denarii and gave them to the innkeeper, saying, 'Take care of him, and whatever more you spend, I will repay you when I come back.' Which of these three, do you think, proved to be a neighbor to the man who fell among the robbers?" He said, "The one who showed him mercy." And Jesus said to him, "You go, and do likewise." (Luke 10:25–37)

DO NOT EXALT YOURSELF

Jesus said,

> When you are invited by someone to a wedding feast, do not sit down in a place of honor, lest someone more distinguished than you be invited by him, and he who invited you both will come and say to you, "Give your place to this person," and then you will begin with shame to take the lowest place. But when you are invited, go and sit in the lowest place, so that when your host comes he may say to you, "Friend, move up higher." Then you will be honored in the presence of all who sit at table with you. For everyone who exalts himself will be humbled, and he who humbles himself will be exalted. (Luke 14:8–11)

JESUS WILL SET YOU FREE FROM THE SLAVERY OF SIN

Jesus said,

> Truly, truly, I say to you, everyone who commits sin is a slave to sin. The slave does not remain in the house forever; the son remains forever. So if the Son sets you free, you will be free indeed. (John 8:34–36)

MAKE LOVING GOD AND OTHERS YOUR TREASURE AND YOU WILL INHERIT THE KINGDOM OF GOD

Jesus said,

> Fear not, little flock, for it is your Father's good pleasure to give you the kingdom. Sell your possessions, and give to the needy. Provide yourselves with moneybags that do not grow old, with a treasure in the heavens that does not fail, where no thief approaches and no moth destroys. For where your treasure is, there will your heart be also. (Luke 12:32–34)

JESUS IS THE GOOD SHEPHERD, WE ARE HIS SHEEP

Jesus said,

> Truly, truly I say to you, I am the door of the sheep. All who came before me are thieves and robbers, but the sheep did not listen to them. I am the door. If anyone enters by me, he will be saved and will go in and out and find pasture. The thief comes only to steal and kill and destroy. I came that they may have life and have it abundantly. I am the good shepherd. The good shepherd lays down his life for the sheep. He who is a hired hand and not a shepherd, who does not own the sheep, sees the wolf coming and leaves the sheep and flees, and the wolf snatches them and scatters them. He flees because he is a hired hand and cares nothing for the sheep. I am the good shepherd. I know my own, and they know me, just as the Father knows me and I know the

Father; and I lay down my life for the sheep. And I have other sheep that are not of this fold. I must bring them also, and they will listen to my voice. So there will be one flock, one shepherd. For this reason the Father loves me, because I lay down my life that I may take it up again. No one takes it from me, but I lay it down of my own accord. I have authority to lay it down, and I have authority to take it up again. This charge I have received from my Father. (John 10:7–18)

My sheep hear my voice, and I know them, and they know me. I give them eternal life, and they will never perish, and no one will snatch them out of my hand. My Father, who has given them to me, is greater than all, and no one is able to snatch them out of the Father's hand. I and the Father are one. (John 10:27–30)

ALWAYS BE READY FOR THE COMING OF JESUS AND HE WILL REWARD YOU

Jesus said,

Stay dressed for action and keep your lamps burning, and be like men waiting for their master to come home from the wedding feast, so that they may open the door to him at once when he comes and knocks. Blessed are those servants whom the master finds awake when he comes. Truly, I say to you, he will dress himself for service and have them recline at table, and he will come and serve them… You must also be ready, for the Son of Man is coming at an hour that you do not expect. (Luke 12:35–40)

ALL OF HEAVEN REJOICES WHEN A SINNER COMES TO JESUS AND IS SAVED

Jesus said,

> What man of you, having a hundred sheep, if he has lost one of them, does not leave the ninety-nine in the open country, and go after the one that is lost, until he finds it? And when he has found it, he lays it on his shoulders, rejoicing. And when he comes home, he calls together his friends and his neighbors, saying to them, "Rejoice with me, for I have found my sheep that was lost." Just so, I tell you, there will be more joy in heaven over one sinner who repents than over ninety-nine righteous persons who need no repentance. (Luke 15:4–7)

JESUS WILL TAKE THOSE THAT FOLLOW HIM TO HEAVEN WITH HIM

Jesus said,

> Let not your hearts be troubled. Believe in God; believe also in me. In my Father's house there are many rooms. If it were not so, would I have told you that I go to prepare a place for you? And if I go and prepare a place for you, I will come again and will take you to myself, that where I am you may be also. And you know the way to where I am going. (John 14:1–3)

JESUS INFORMS THE APOSTLES THAT THEY AND ALL THE FOLLOWERS OF JESUS WILL BE REWARDED

On one occasion, the apostle Peter said to Jesus, "We have left everything and followed you. What then will we have?" Jesus said to the apostles, "Truly, I say to you, in the new world, when the Son of Man will sit on his glorious throne, you who have followed me will also sit on twelve thrones, judging the twelve tribes of Israel. And everyone who has left houses or brothers or sisters or father or mother or children or lands, for my name's sake, will receive a hundredfold and will inherit eternal life." (Matthew 19:27–29)

GOD THE FATHER WILL SAVE ANYONE THAT LOVES AND FOLLOWS HIS SON, JESUS

Jesus said to the crowds,

I am the bread of life; whoever comes to me shall not hunger, and whoever believes in me shall never thirst. But I said to you that you have seen me and yet do not believe. All that the Father gives me will come to me, and *whoever comes to me I will never cast out (italics added)*. For I have come down from heaven, not to do my own will but the will of him who sent me. And this is the will of him who sent me, that I should lose nothing of all that he has given me, but raise it up on the last day. *For this is the will of my Father, that everyone who looks on the Son and believes in him should have eternal life, and I will raise him up on the last day (italics added)*. (John 6:35–40)

261

JESUS REVEALS THE RELATIONSHIP BETWEEN HIM AND GOD THE FATHER

Jesus said,

> Truly, truly, I say to you, the Son can do nothing on his own accord, but only what he sees the father doing. For whatever the Father does, that the Son does likewise. For the Father Loves the Son and shows him all that he himself is doing. And greater works than these will he show him, so that you may marvel. For as the Father raises the dead and gives them life, so also the Son gives life to whom he will. The Father Judges no one, but has given all judgments to the Son, that all may honor the Son, just as they honor the Father. Whoever does not honor the Son does not honor the Father who sent him. Truly, truly, I say to you, whoever hears my word and believes him who sent me has eternal life. He does not come into judgment, but has passed from death to life.
>
> Truly, truly, I say to you, an hour is coming, and is now here, when the dead will hear the voice of the Son of God, and those who hear will live. For as the Father has life in himself, so he has granted the Son also to have life in himself. And he has given him authority to execute judgment, because he is the Son of Man. Do not marvel at this, for an hour is coming when all who are in the tombs will hear his voice and come out, those who have done good to the resurrection of life, and those who have done evil to the resurrection of judgment. (John 5:19–29)

Jesus said,

> Know and understand that the Father is in me and I am in the Father. (John 10:38)

JESUS AND GOD THE FATHER ARE ONE

Jesus said to his apostles,

> "I am the way, and the truth, and the life. No one comes to the Father except through me. If you had known me, you would have known my Father also. From now on you do know him and have seen him." Philip said to him, "Lord, show us the Father, and it is enough for us." Jesus said to him, "Have I been with you so long, and you still do not know me, Philip? Whoever has seen me has seen the Father. How can you say, 'Show us the Father?' Do you not believe that I am in the Father and the Father is in me? The words that I say to you I do not speak on my own authority, but the Father who dwells in me does his works. Believe me that I am in the Father and the Father is in me, or else believe on account of the works themselves. Truly, truly I say to you, whoever believes in me will also do the works that I do; and greater works than these will he do, because I am going to the Father. Whatever you ask in my name, this I will do, that the Father may be glorified in the Son. If you ask me anything in my name, I will do it." (John 14:6–14)

WHOEVER BELIEVES IN JESUS SHALL HAVE ETERNAL LIFE

Jesus said,

> I am the bread of life; whoever comes to me shall not hunger, and whoever believes in me shall never thirst. But I said to you that you have seen me and yet do not believe. All that the Father gives me will come to me, and whoever comes to me I will never cast out. For I have come down from heaven, not to do my own will but the will of him who sent me. And this is the will of him who sent me, that I should lose nothing of all that he has given me, but raise it up on the last day. For this is the will of my Father, that everyone who looks on the Son and believes in him shall have eternal life, and I will raise him up on the last day. (John 6:35–40)

Jesus said,

> Truly, truly, I say to you, whoever believes has eternal life. I am the bread of life. Your fathers ate the manna in the wilderness, and they died. This is the bread that comes down from heaven, so that one may eat of it and not die. I am the living bread that came down from heaven. If anyone eats of this bread, he will live forever. And the bread that I will give for the life of the world is my flesh. (John 6:47–51)

Jesus said,

> I am the resurrection and the life. Whoever believes in me, though he die, yet shall he live,

and everyone who lives and believes in me shall never die. (John 11:25–26)

JESUS STATES THAT HE CAME FROM GOD

Jesus said,

> You know me, and you know where I come from? But I have not come of my own accord. He who sent me is true, and him you do not know. I know him, for I came from him, and he sent me. (John 7:28–29)

JESUS WAS SENT BY GOD THE FATHER TO SAVE PEOPLE FROM DYING IN THEIR SINS

Jesus said,

> You are from below; I am from above. You are of this world; I am not of this world. I told you that you would die in your sins, for unless you believe that I am he you will die in your sins. I have much to say about you and much to judge, but he who sent me is true, and I declare to the world what I have heard from my Father. When you have lifted up the Son of Man, then you will know that I am he, and that I do nothing on my own authority, but speak just as the Father taught me. And he who sent me is with me. He has not left me alone, for I always do the things that are pleasing to him. (John 8:23–30)

JESUS IS THE TRUE VINE, WE ARE HIS BRANCHES

Jesus said,

> I am the true vine, and my Father is the vine-dresser. Every branch in me that does not bear fruit he takes away, and every branch that does bear fruit he prunes that it may bear more fruit. Already you are clean because of the word I have spoken to you. Abide in me, and I in you. As the branch cannot bear fruit by itself, unless it abides in the vine, neither can you unless you abide in me. I am the vine; you are the branches. Whoever abides in me and I in him, he is it that bears much fruit, for apart from me you can do nothing, if anyone does not abide in me he is thrown away like a branch and withers; and the branches are gathered, thrown in to the fire, and burned. If you abide in me, and my words abide in you, ask whatever you wish, and it will be done for you. By this my Father is glorified that you bear much fruit and so prove to be my disciples. As the father has loved me, so have I loved you. Abide in my love. If you keep my commandments, you will abide in my love, just as I have kept my Father's commandments and abide in his love. These things I have spoken to you, that my joy may be in you, and that your joy may be full. (John 15:1–11)

JESUS EXPLAINS THAT HE MUST DIE

Jesus said,

> The hour has come for the Son of Man to be glorified. Truly, truly, I say to you, unless a grain

of wheat falls into the earth and dies, it remains alone; but if it dies, it bears much fruit. Whoever loves his life loses it, and whoever hates his life in this world will keep it for eternal life. If anyone serves me, he must follow me; and where I am, will my servant be also. If anyone serves me, the Father will honor him. (John 12:23–26)

JESUS ANNOUNCES TO THE CROWD THAT HE WILL SOON DIE AND HIS DEATH WILL CAST THE DEVIL OUT OF THE WORLD

Jesus said to the crowd,

"Now is my soul troubled. And what shall I say? 'Father, save me from this hour?' But for this purpose I have come to this hour. Father, glorify your name." Then a voice came from heaven: "I have glorified it, and I will glorify it again." The crowd that stood there and heard it and said that it had thundered. Others said, "An angel has spoken to him." Jesus answered, "This voice has come for your sake, not mine. Now is the judgment of this world; now will the ruler of this world be cast out. And I, when I am lifted up from earth, will draw all people to myself." (John 12:27–32)

JESUS ANNOUNCES TO THE APOSTLES THAT HE IS RETURNING TO THE FATHER BUT THE HOLY SPIRIT WILL COME TO THEM

Jesus said to the apostles,

These things I have spoken to you while I am still with you. But the Helper, the Holy

Spirit, whom the Father will send in my name, he will teach you all things and bring to your remembrance all that I have said to you. Peace I leave with you; my peace I give to you. Not as the world gives do I give to you. Let not your hearts be troubled, neither let them be afraid. You have heard me say to you, "I am going away, and I will come to you." If you loved me, you would have rejoiced, because I am going to the Father and the Father is greater than I. And now I have told you before it takes place, so that when it does take place you may believe. I will no longer talk much with you, for the ruler of this world is coming. He has no claim on me, but I do as the Father commanded me, so that the world may know that I love the Father. (John 14:25–31)

Jesus said to the apostles,

I did not say these things to you from the beginning, because I was with you. But now I am going to him who sent me, and none of you asks me, "Where are you going?" But because I have said these things to you, sorrow has filled your heart. Nevertheless, I tell you the truth: it is to your advantage that I go away, for if I do not go away, the Helper will not come to you. But if I go, I will send him to you. And when he comes, he will convict the world concerning sin and righteousness and judgment: concerning sin, because they do not believe in me; concerning righteousness, because I go to the Father, and you will see me no longer; concerning judgment, because the ruler of this world is judged.

I still have many things to say to you, but you cannot bear them now. When the Spirit of truth comes, he will guide you into all the truth, for he will not speak on his own authority, but whatever he hears he will speak, and he will declare to you the things that are to come. He will glorify me, for he will take what is mine and declare it to you. All that the Father has is mine; therefore I said that he will take what is mine and declare it to you. (John 16:4–15)

JESUS HAS OVERCOME THE WORLD
THE FATHER LOVES US BECAUSE WE LOVE HIS SON

Jesus said,

I have said these things to you in figures of speech. The hour is coming when I will no longer speak to you in figures of speech but will plainly tell you about the Father. In that day you will ask in my name, and I do not say to you that I will ask the Father on your behalf; for the Father himself loves you, because you have loved me and have believed that I came from God. I came from the Father and have come into the world, and now I am leaving the world and going to the Father. I have said these things to you, that in me you may have peace. In the world you will have tribulation. But take heart, I have overcome the world. (John 16:25–33)

THE LAST PRAYER OF JESUS TO THE FATHER
BEFORE THE BEGINNING OF HIS CRUCIFIXION EVENTS

The following is the last recorded prayer in the Bible between Jesus and the Father before the beginning of the crucifixion events of Jesus. In much of his prayer, Jesus was praying to God the father about us and for us. Remember—the reason why he went through the horrible crucifixion events was to pay for our sins so that we could then be forgiven by God if we came to him.

Jesus prayed to the Father,

> Father, the hour has come; glorify your Son that the Son may glorify you, since you have given him authority over all flesh, to give eternal life to all you have given him. And this is eternal life, that they know you the only true God, and Jesus Christ whom you have sent. I glorified you on earth, having accomplished the work that you gave me to do. And now, Father, glorify me in your own presence with the glory that I had with you before the world existed.
>
> I have manifested your name to the people whom you gave me out of the world. Yours they were, and you gave them to me, and they have kept your word. Now they know that everything you have given me is from you. For I have given them the words that you gave me, and they have received them and have come to know in truth that I came from you; and they have believed that you sent me. I am praying for them. I am not praying for the world but for those you have given me, for they are yours. All mine are yours and all yours are mine, and I am glorified in them. And I am no longer in the world, but they are in the world, and I am coming to you. Holy Father, keep them in your name, which you have given me. I have guarded them, and not one of them has been lost except the son of destruction, that scripture might be fulfilled. But now I am coming to you, and these things I speak in the world, that they may have my joy fulfilled

in themselves. I have given them your word, and the world has hated them because they are not of the world, just as I am not of the world. I do not ask that you take them out of the world, but that you keep them from the evil one. They are not of the world, just as I am not of the world. Sanctify them in truth; your word is truth. As you sent me into the world, so I have sent them into the world. And for their sake I consecrate myself, so that they also may be sanctified in truth.

I do not ask for these only, but also for who will believe in me through their word, that they may all be one, just as you, Father, are in me, and I in you, that they may also be in us, so that the world may believe that you have sent me. The glory that you have given me I have given to them, that they may become one even as we are one, I in them and you in me, that they may become perfectly one, so that the world may know that you sent me and loved them even as you loved me. Father, I desire that they also, whom you have given me, may be with me where I am, to see my glory that you have given me because you have loved me before the foundation of the world. O righteous Father, even though the world does not know you, I know you, and these know that you sent me. I made known to them your name, and I will continue to make it known, that the love with which you have loved me may be in them, and I in them. (John 17:1–26)

The very next thing we see in the Bible is Jesus in the garden of Gethsemane, and he was arrested by a throng of soldiers to begin the crucifixion events. What love Jesus has for us.

THE MOST IMPORTANT PASSAGE IN ALL OF THE BIBLE

Jesus said,

> For God so loved the world, that he gave his only Son, that whoever believes in him should not perish but have eternal life. For God did not send his Son in to the world to condemn the world, but in order that the world might be saved through him. Whoever believes in him is not condemned, but whoever does not believe is condemned already, because he has not believed in the name of the only Son of God. And this is the judgment: the light has come into the world, and people loved the darkness rather than the light because their works were evil. For everyone who does wicked things hates the light and does not come to the light, lest his works should be exposed. But whoever does what is true comes to the light, so that it may be clearly seen that his works have been carried out in God. (John 3:16–21)

JESUS TELLS US ABOUT THE END OF THE AGE

> As Jesus sat on the mount of Olives, the disciples came to him privately, saying, "Tell us, when will these things be, and what will be the sign of your coming and of the close of the age?" And Jesus answered them, "See that no one leads you astray. For many will come in my name, saying, 'I am the Christ,' and they will lead many astray. And you will hear of wars and rumors of wars. See that you are not alarmed, for this must take place, but the end is not yet. For nation will rise against nation, and kingdom against king-

dom, and there will be famines and earthquakes in various places. All these are but the beginning of the birth pains.

"Then they will deliver you up to tribulation and put you to death, and you will be hated by all nations for my name's sake. And then many will fall away and betray one another and hate one another. And many false prophets will arise and lead many astray. And because lawlessness will be increased, the love of many will grow cold. But the one who endures to the end will be saved. And the gospel of the kingdom will be proclaimed throughout the whole world as a testimony to all nations, and then the end will come.

"So when you see the abomination of desolation spoken of by the prophet Daniel, standing in the holy place [let the reader understand]. Then let those in Judea flee to the mountains. Let the one who is on the housetop not go down to take what is in his house, and let the one who is in the field not turn back to take his cloak. And alas for women who are pregnant and for those who are nursing infants in those days! Pray that your flight might not be in winter or on a Sabbath. For there will be great tribulation, such as has not been from the beginning of the world until now, no, and never will be. And if those days had not been cut short, no human being would be saved. But for the sake of the elect those days will be cut short. Then if anyone says to you, 'Look, here is the Christ!' or 'There he is!' do not believe it. For false christs and false prophets will arise and perform great signs and wonders, so as to lead astray, if possible, even the elect. See, I have told you beforehand. So, if they say to you, 'Look, he is in the wilderness,' do not go out. If they say, 'Look, he is in the inner rooms,' do not believe it. For as the lightning comes from the east and shines as far as the west, so will be the coming of the Son of Man. Wherever the corpse is, there the vultures will gather.

Immediately after the tribulation of those days the sun will be darkened, and the moon will not give its light, and the stars will fall from heaven, and the powers of the heavens will be shaken. The will appear in heaven the sign of the Son of Man, and then all the tribes of the earth will mourn, and they will see the Son of Man coming on the clouds of heaven with power and great glory. And he will send out his angels with a loud trumpet call, and they will gather the elect from the four winds, from one end of heaven to the other." (Matthew 24:3–31)

NO ONE KNOWS THE DAY AND THE HOUR JESUS WILL RETURN

Jesus's apostles asked him what be the signs of his return will be. Jesus said,

But concerning that day and hour no one knows, not even the angels of heaven, nor the Son, but the Father only. For as were the days of Noah, so will be the coming of the Son of Man. For as in those days before the flood they were eating and drinking, marrying and giving in marriage, until the day when Noah entered the ark, and they were unaware until the flood came and swept them all away, so will be the coming of the Son of Man. Then two men will be on the field; one will be taken and one left. Two women will be grinding at the mill; one will be taken and one left. Therefore, stay awake, for you do not know on what day your Lord is coming. But know this, that if the master of the house had known in what part of the night the thief was coming, he would have stayed awake and would not let his house be broken into. Therefore you must also be ready, for the Son of Man is coming at an hour you do not expect. (Matthew 24:36–44)

CHAPTER 20

THE EVENTS THAT LED TO JESUS BEING CRUCIFIED

J esus, who always existed as God, also became man and came to earth to save us from sin and death. He did this by being completely obedient to God the Father for his entire life and, thus, being sinless his entire life. This made him the only sinless sacrifice that God the Father would accept as payment for the sins of the world. His payment for our sins would enable our sins to then be forgiven by God if we came to him in repentance and followed him in our lives. Therefore, Jesus came here to die as an unblemished sacrifice, acceptable to God the Father as payment for our sins. For Jesus to be a sacrifice for us, someone had to sacrifice him. This was accomplished by Jesus being crucified. What events led him to being crucified?

At the time, the Jewish religious leaders were following the Law given by God to the people, passed down through scripture and traditions. The Law taught the people right from wrong, and it punished people who did wrong (sinned) to avoid the people from falling into lawless anarchy, which seemed to have happened to the people before the flood of Noah. The Law was very strict, because sin is a serious matter. Sin could not be forgiven before Jesus came to earth. Very strict punishments might have been a deterrent from sinning, since there was no forgiveness available yet for intentional sin. The arrival of Jesus changed all this. By dying to pay for our sins, this enabled mankind to now be forgiven of their sins if they confessed them and repented of them. Jesus made everything new. The religious leaders did not understand this. Some saw Jesus as a heretic who was teaching new ways that were different from what was given to them in the first covenant by God (the Law). Some of the religious leaders that persecuted Jesus thought they were doing a good thing by getting rid of who they thought was a heretic because they were unable to understand what Jesus was doing. However, not all the religious leaders that persecuted Jesus did so with honestly good intentions.

Several of the religious leaders at the time were doing many things that God did not want them to do. They were adding their own man-made rules that God did not want on top of God's rules that he gave the people. They were also hypocrites. They demanded the people to follow these difficult rules, some of which they themselves did not follow. They did this to benefit themselves and not the people they were supposed to serve. Jesus harshly and frequently criticized the religious leaders for doing this. Additionally, some of the religious leaders were jealous of Jesus. He did unprecedented miracles and taught with unparalleled wisdom and authority (because he was actually God). Some people were turning away from the Jewish religious leaders and following Jesus. As we move forward through the gospels, Jesus progressively launched harsh public criticisms against the particular religious leaders that he knew were hypocrites and bad shepherds of God's people. In their lack of understanding and anger, many of (not all) the Jewish religious leaders decided to kill Jesus when they got the chance.

These are some of the events that the religious leaders used as reasons to kill Jesus. They are not necessarily in order as presented in the Bible:

One day a paralytic man was brought to Jesus to be healed. Jesus said to the man,

> Take heart my son, your sins are forgiven.
> (Mark 2:5)

MICHAEL KOTCH

Some of the religious leaders heard this and said,

> He is blaspheming! Who can forgive sins
> but God alone? (Mark 2:7)

(Jesus is God, but some of the religious leaders did not believe it.)

Jesus came to save us because we are all sinners. Therefore, Jesus spent a lot of time with people who were known to be big sinners, because he was teaching them to follow him and his ways and they would be saved from their sins. One day Jesus was at a gathering in a house, and he was reclining at a table.

> Many tax collectors and sinners came and were reclining with Jesus and his disciples. And when the Pharisees saw this, they said to his disciples, "Why does your teacher eat with tax collectors and sinners?" But when he [Jesus] heard it, he said, "Those who are well have no need of a physician, but those who are sick. Go and learn what this means, 'I desire mercy, and not sacrifice.' For I came not to call the righteous, but sinners." (Matthew 9:10–13)

Jesus was the doctor, helping those who came to him who were sick with sin. Some of the religious leaders of the time did not understand this. They did not speak with people whom they believed to be known sinners. They would become progressively upset and disgusted with Jesus for associating with sinners. Sinners were the people Jesus came to save—which is *all of us.*

One day Jesus cast a demon out of a man who was possessed. The people who witnessed it were amazed, and said,

> Can this be the son of David? (Matthew 12:23)

278

But when the Pharisees (religious leaders) heard it, they said that he has the power to cast out demons because he was given that power by Beelzebul, the prince of demons.

Jesus was in the synagogue in Nazareth, the town that he grew up in, on the Sabbath day. He read a scroll from the book of Isaiah that said that the Spirit of God was on him, that he was anointed by God to proclaim Good News to the poor, to bring sight to the blind, and to set the captives and oppressed free. He then said that the scroll was talking about him. The people marveled with glee at this good news. Jesus then told the people that prophets had been historically rejected by the Jewish people in their hometown (Jesus was now speaking to the people of his hometown of Nazareth), and therefore God rejected all those people who rejected the prophets that God sent them. Jesus said that during the time of the famine in Elijah's hometown, there were many widows who were in distress, but God only sent him to one widow in Sidon. There were many lepers in Israel during the time of Elisha, yet God only sent him to cleanse one leper, Naaman the Syrian. Jesus told them that undoubtedly his hometown would come to reject him, like the hometowns of the prophets before Jesus rejected them. Therefore, he would not save many of the people he was now speaking to in the synagogue, because they would come to reject him as the Messiah in the future.

> When they heard these things, all in the synagogue were filled with wrath. And they rose up and drove him out of the town and brought him to the brow of the hill on which their town was built, so that they could throw him down the cliff. But passing through their midst, he went away. (Luke 4:28–30)

Jesus said to the people,

> Beware of the scribes [some of the religious leaders at the time] who like to walk around in long robes and like greetings in marketplaces

and have the best seats in the synagogues and the places of honor at feasts, who devour widows' savings, and for money make long prayers. They will receive the greater punishment. This, of course, made the religious leaders very angry at Jesus. (Matthew chapter 23)

JESUS HARSHLY CONDEMNS THE RELIGIOUS LEADERS

While Jesus was speaking, a Pharisee asked him to dine with him, so he went in and reclined at table. The Pharisee was astonished to see that he did not first wash his hands before dinner. And the Lord said to him "Now you Pharisees cleanse the outside of the cup and of the dish, but inside you are full of greed and wickedness. You fools! Did not he who made the outside make the inside also? But give as alms those things that are within, and behold, everything is clean for you. But woe to you Pharisees! For you tithe mint and rue and every herb, and neglect justice and the love of God. These you ought to have done, without neglecting the others. Woe to you Pharisees! For you love the best seat in the synagogues and greetings in the marketplaces. Woe to you! For you are like unmarked graves, and people walk over them without knowing it."

One of the lawyers answered him, "Teacher, in saying these things you insult us also." And he said "Woe to you lawyers also! For you load people with burdens hard to bear, and you yourselves do not touch the burdens with one of your fingers. Woe to you! For you build the tombs of the prophets your fathers killed. So you are witnesses and you consent to the deeds of your fathers, for they killed them, and you build their tombs. Therefore also the wisdom of God said "I will send them prophets and apostles, some of whom they will kill and persecute, so that the blood of all the prophets, shed from the foundation of the world, may be charged against this generation, from the blood of Abel to the blood of Zechariah, who perished between the altar and the sanctuary. Yes, I tell you, it will be required of this generation. Woe to you lawyers! For you have taken away the key of knowledge. You did not enter yourselves, and you hindered those who were entering."

As he went away from there, the scribes and the Pharisees began to press him hard and to provoke him to speak about many things, lying in wait for him, to catch him in something he might say. (Luke 11:37–54)

One of the things the religious leaders used against Jesus as an excuse to kill him was Jesus was healing people and doing good works on the Sabbath. One of the Ten Commandments is to keep the Sabbath holy. In the commandment, it says,

Six days you shall labor, do all your work,
but on the seventh day you shall do no work.
(Exodus 20:8–9)

One day, on the Sabbath, Jesus came across a man who had been an invalid for thirty-eight years. Jesus felt compassion for the man, so he healed him and now the man could walk. The religious leaders began persecuting Jesus for healing people on the Sabbath. Jesus told them that the Sabbath was made by God for man so man could have a day to rest from his regular work. It was *never* meant to stop people from doing good for others on that day. People should do good things for others if necessary *on any day.* The religious leaders ignored this and held on to their statement that Jesus was breaking the law because he was doing work on the Sabbath by healing people.

Jesus responded,

> My Father is working until now, and I am working. (John 5:17)

> This is why the Jews were seeking all the more to kill Jesus, because not only was he breaking the Sabbath, but he was even calling God his own Father, making himself equal with God [which in truth, he was]. (John 5:18)

On another occasion, Jesus entered a synagogue, and there was a man there with a crippled hand. Jesus was about to heal the man. It was the Sabbath.

The Pharisees asked Jesus, "Is it lawful to heal a person on the Sabbath?" They did this because they wanted to accuse Jesus of breaking the commandment "You shall keep the Sabbath holy," which meant that not only should you worship God on the Sabbath, but you should not do work on that day. Jesus said to them,

> Which one of you who has a sheep, if it falls into a pit on the Sabbath, would not take hold of it and lift it out? Of how much more value is a man than a sheep! So it is lawful to do good on the Sabbath. (Matthew 12:11–12)

Jesus then healed the man with the crippled hand. The Pharisees got together and used this event in planning on how to destroy Jesus, claiming he broke the Law by healing this man (doing work) on the Sabbath.

One day the chief priests, scribes, and elders came to Jesus as he was walking in the temple and asked him in a critical way, "Who gave you the authority to say and do the things you are doing?"

Jesus answered them with this parable:

> A man planted a vineyard and put a fence around it and dug a pit for the winepress and built a tower, and leased it to tenants and went into another country. When the season came, he sent a servant to the tenants to get from them some of the fruit of the vineyard. And they took him and beat him and sent him away empty handed. Again he sent them another servant, and they struck him on the head and treated him shamefully. And he sent another, and him they killed. And so with many others: some they beat, and some they killed. He still had one other, a beloved son. Finally he sent him to them, saying, "They will respect my son." But those tenants said to one another, "This is the heir. Come, let us kill him, and the inheritance will be ours." And they took him and killed him and threw him out of the vineyard. What will the owner of the vineyard do? He will come and destroy the tenants and give the vineyard to others. Have you not read this scripture: "The stone that the builders rejected has become the cornerstone; this was the Lord's doing, and it is marvelous in our eyes?" And they [chief priests, scribes, and elders] were seeking to arrest Jesus but they feared the people, for they perceived that he told the parable against them. So they left him and went away. (Mark 12:1–12)

JESUS TELLS THE RELIGIOUS LEADERS THEY ARE FROM THEIR FATHER, THE DEVIL
JESUS THEN PUBLICLY DECLARES THAT HE IS GOD

Jesus and some of the religious leaders were increasingly at odds with each other. Those leaders were envious of Jesus. They hated him also because Jesus clearly, truthfully, and *publicly* criticized some of the religious leaders for not following God's instructions in the manner that God gave the instructions to them. Instead, they added human traditions to God's will that they used for their own benefit, at the expense of the people they were supposed to serve. Additionally, they rejected Jesus as the Savior, even though his works fulfilled the prophecies about the Savior. One day the religious leaders and Jesus were in a public argument. The following is the explosive statements Jesus made against them.

Jesus said to them,

> "I know you are offspring of Abraham, yet you seek to kill me because my words find no place in you. I speak of what I have seen with my Father, and you do what you have heard from your father." They answered him "Abraham is our father." Jesus said to them, "If you were Abraham's children, you would be doing the works Abraham did, but now you seek to kill me, a man who has told you the truth that I heard from God. This is not what Abraham did. You are doing the works your father did." They said to him "We are not born of sexual immorality. We have one Father—even God." Jesus said to them "If God were your Father, you would love me, for I came from God and I am here. I came not of my own accord, but he sent me. Why do you not understand what I say? It is because you cannot bear to hear my word. You are of your father the devil, and your will is to do your father's desires.

He was a murderer from the beginning, and has nothing to do with the truth, because there is no truth in him. When he lies, he speaks out of his own character, for he is a liar, and the father of lies. But because I tell the truth, you do not believe me. Which one of you convicts me of sin? If I tell the truth, why do you not believe me? Whoever is of God hears the words of God. The reason why you do not hear them is that you are not of God." (John 8:37–47)

The Jews responded by saying that Jesus was possessed by a demon and that was why he was saying these things. Jesus replied that he did not have a demon and anyone who kept his word would never see death. The Jews then said that Jesus must have a demon in him. All the prophets eventually died, including Abraham. They asked him who he thought he was and if he thought he was greater than Abraham? Jesus said that God is his father, and Abraham rejoiced that he would see the day of Jesus come.

The Jewish religious leaders said,

You are not yet fifty years old, how did you see Abraham? (John 8:57)

Jesus's next statement was the one the Pharisees would use against him as their main justification to crucify him: Jesus said,

Truly, truly, I say to you, *before Abraham was, I am (italics added)*. (John 8:58)

By Jesus saying "Before Abraham was, I AM," he was saying that he was God.

When God appeared to Moses and told him he would use him to set the Jewish people free, Moses asked God, "What shall I tell the people your name is?"

God responded, "I AM WHO I AM. Say this to the people of Israel, 'I AM has sent me to you.'" (Exodus 3:14)

Therefore, Jesus was calling himself the same name that God told Moses to call God. At hearing this, the Jewish religious leaders picked up stones to throw at Jesus, but Jesus escaped and left.

Later, other Jews were gathered around Jesus. They said to him "Don't keep us in suspense. Are you the Christ?" Jesus responded "I told you, and you do not believe. The works that I do in my Father's name bear witness about me, but you do not believe because you are not part of my flock. My sheep hear my voice and I know them, and they follow me. I give them eternal life and they will never perish, and no one will snatch them out of my hand. My Father, who has given them to me, is greater than all, and no one is able to snatch them out of the Father's hand. I and the father are one."

The Jews picked up stones again to stone him. Jesus answered them, "I have shown you many good works from the Father; for which of them are you going to stone me?" The Jews answered him "It is not for a good work that we are going to stone you, *but for blasphemy, because you, being a man, make yourself God.*" (John 10:24–33)

So Jesus was later put to death for telling the truth. They crucified him because Jesus said he was God. He is.

When Jesus triumphantly entered Jerusalem for the Passover feast a few days before he would be put to death, he entered the temple. There he drove out those who bought and sold in the temple. He overturned the tables of the money changers and those who sold pigeons.

> And he would not allow anyone to carry any-thing through the temple. He was teaching them and saying to them, "Is it not written, 'My house shall be called a house of prayer for all the nations'? But you have made it a den of robbers." And the chief priests and the scribes heard it and were seek-ing a way to destroy him, because all the crowd was astonished at his teaching. (Mark 11:16–18)

> But the chief priests and scribes and the principal men of the people did not find anything they could do, for all the people were hanging on his words. (Luke 19:47–48)

CAIAPHAS DECIDES JESUS MUST DIE

Many people were coming to believe in Jesus, which worried the Pharisees. The chief priests and Pharisees gathered together to discuss what to do. They said,

> What are we to do? For this man performs many signs. If we let him go on like this, everyone will believe in him, and the Romans will come and take away both our place and our nation. (John 11:47–48)

Caiaphas was the high priest that year. His statement in response to this is one of the most prophetic statements in the entire Bible. Caiaphas said,

> You know nothing at all. Nor do you under-stand that *it is better for you that one man should*

*die for the people, not that the whole nation should
perish (italics added).* (John 11:49–50)

Caiaphas did not realize it, but he was prophesying that it
would be better if one man die for the sins of the world, rather than
the whole world die because of their sins.

CHAPTER 21

THE DEATH AND
RESURRECTION OF JESUS

The chief priests and elders of the people gathered in the palace of the high priest, Caiaphas. They plotted together to arrest Jesus secretly and kill him. However, they did not want to do it during the Passover feast to avoid an uproar among the people (Matthew 26:3–5).

Jesus and his apostles and disciples entered Jerusalem for the Passover feast. Jesus knew this Passover feast would end with his crucifixion in a few days. Jesus had two disciples get him a donkey to ride on into Jerusalem. This was done to fulfill the Old Testament prophecy:

> Rejoice greatly, O daughter of Zion! Shout aloud, O daughter of Jerusalem! Behold, your king is coming to you; righteousness and having salvation is he, humble and mounted on a donkey, on a colt, the foal of a donkey. (Zechariah 9:9)

Most of the crowd spread their cloaks on the road and put palm branches down for Jesus to walk on so his feet would not touch the ground. People were walking before him and after him shouting,

> Hosanna to the Son of David! Blessed is he
> who comes in the name of the Lord! Hosanna in
> the highest! (Matthew 21:9)

The whole city was stirred up in joy and excitement at the entry of Jesus into Jerusalem. How things would change over the next few days.

Jesus told his apostles and disciples that he would soon be killed. For example, he told them that when they entered Jerusalem, he would soon be delivered over to the chief priests and scribes. They would condemn him to death and deliver him to the Gentiles (Roman soldiers). He would be mocked and flogged (brutally whipped) and then crucified. After this, he would be raised on the third day. For whatever reason, the apostles were unable to either understand or believe these things Jesus was telling them about his upcoming suffering and death (Matthew 26:1–2)

Jesus gave directions to his disciples on where they would prepare a room for the Passover. This would come to be known as the Last Supper. The apostles were directed to a large upper room for this. As they were eating, Jesus then told his twelve apostles that one of them would betray him. The apostles were all surprised, and they did not know which one of them it could be. John quietly asked Jesus who would betray him. Jesus revealed to John that it would be Judas. Judas previously went to the chief priests in order to betray Jesus to them. They promised to give him money for this, and Judas looked for an opportunity to betray Jesus (John 13:21–30).

> And as they were eating, he took bread, and
> after blessing it broke it and gave it to them, and
> said "This is my body." And he took a cup, and
> when he had given thanks he gave it to them,
> "This is the blood of the covenant, which is
> poured out for many. Truly, I say to you, I will
> not drink again of the fruit of the vine until that
> day when I drink it new in the kingdom of God."
> (Mark 14:22–25)

After the last supper, they all went out to the Mount of Olives.

> Jesus said to them, "You will all fall away, for it is written, 'I will strike the shepherd, and the sheep will be scattered.' [This was prophesied in Zechariah 13:7.] But after I am raised up, I will go before you to Galilee." Peter said to him, "Even though they all fall away, I will not." And Jesus said to him, "Truly, I tell you, this very night, before the rooster crows twice, you will deny me three times." But he said emphatically, "If I must die with you, I will not deny you." And they all said the same. (Mark 14:26–31)

Jesus went with his disciples to a place called Gethsemane to pray. He took Peter, James, and John alone with him. He told them,

> My soul is very sorrowful, even to death; remain here and watch with me. (Matthew 26:38)

Jesus walked away a little bit, fell on his face, and prayed,

> My father, if it is possible, let this cup pass from me; nevertheless, not as I will, but as you will. (Matthew 26:39)

Jesus returned and found the apostles asleep. He woke them up, told them to be on guard, and returned to praying. He said,

> My Father, if this cannot pass unless I drink it, your will be done. (Matthew 26:42)

Jesus returned to the apostles and found them sleeping again. He went and prayed to the Father a third time, saying the same thing.

He then returned to the apostles and told them to wake up, because his betrayer is at hand.

Judas knew where Jesus would be at because he was just at the Last Supper with Jesus and the other apostles. Judas came to the garden of Gethsemane with a band of soldiers and some officers from the chief priests and Pharisees. Judas drew near to kiss Jesus, which was his signal to the soldiers of identifying which one was Jesus. Jesus said to him,

> Judas, would you betray the Son of Man with a kiss? (Luke 22:48)

Jesus then walked forward and said to them, "Whom do you seek?"

They said, "Jesus of Nazareth."

Jesus said to them, "I am he" (John 18:4–5).

When Jesus said to them, "I am he," they drew back and fell to the ground (John 18:6). Jesus asked them again "Whom do you seek?"

They said, "Jesus of Nazareth."

Jesus said, "I told you I am he, so if you seek me, let these others go" (John 18:7–8).

They listened to Jesus. This fulfilled a prophecy that Jesus earlier gave:

> Of those whom you gave me I have not lost one. (John 18:9)

At this, to defend Jesus, Peter pulled out his sword and struck the high priest's servant and cut off his ear. Jesus told Peter to put his sword away, saying,

> Shall I not drink the cup that the Father has given me? (John 18:11)

Jesus then touched the ear of that wounded servant and he healed him (Luke 22:51). The band of soldiers and officers arrested Jesus and took him to the Jewish religious leaders that ordered Jesus's arrest. The head of this was Caiaphas, the high priest.

The chief priests and the whole council were looking for any kind of testimony they could use against Jesus to put him to death. Many false witnesses came forward, but their testimonies contradicted each other. Jesus remained silent during all the testimony against him. Remember, he came here to die for our sins, not to defend himself from that death sentence. The high priest then said to him,

> I adjure you by the living God, tell us if you are the Christ, the Son of God. Jesus said to him "You have said so, but I tell you, from now on you will see the Son of man seated at the right hand of Power and coming on the clouds of heaven." (Matthew 26:63–64)

The high priest tore his robes and said that Jesus uttered blasphemy, and they needed no more witnesses since everyone heard his blasphemy. He asked the religious leaders,

> "What is your judgment?" they answered "He deserves death." Then they spit in his face and struck him. And some slapped him saying "Prophesy to us, you Christ! Who is it that struck you?" (Matthew 26:65–68)

Earlier in the day, before Jesus was arrested, the apostles were arguing amongst themselves as to which one of them would be considered the greatest apostle. Jesus entered their prideful and arrogant conversation, and he confronted Peter. He told Peter that before the day was over, before the rooster crowed, he would deny knowing Jesus three times. Peter said this would absolutely not happen. He said he would follow Jesus anywhere he would go, even to death.

Jesus reaffirmed that Peter would, in fact, deny knowing him three times before the rooster crowed that day.

Now Jesus was being tried by the religious leaders inside an official building, while Peter waited outside with the crowd, warming himself by a fire.

A servant girl approached Peter and said, "This man was with Jesus."

Peter said he did not know what she was talking about, and he moved to another spot.

Then another servant girl recognized Peter and said, "This man was with Jesus."

Peter took an oath, swearing that he did not know Jesus.

Shortly after, some bystanders came up to him and said, "We can tell by your accent that you are one of the followers with Jesus."

Peter got angry and started swearing and cursing, saying, "I don't know the man!"

> And immediately, while he was still speaking, the rooster crowed. And Jesus looked at Peter. And Peter remembered the saying of the Lord, how he said to him, "Before the rooster crows today, you will deny me three times." And Peter went out and wept bitterly. (Mark 14:66–72 and Luke 22:60–62)

The men who were holding Jesus in custody were making fun of him as they spit on him and beat him. They blindfolded Jesus and kept asking him as they hit him,

> Prophesy to us, you Christ! Who is it that struck you? (Matthew 26:68)

And they said many other things against him as they hit him, blaspheming him.

Jesus was now brought before Pontius Pilate, the Roman governor who was ruler over Jerusalem. The religious leaders who brought

Jesus to Pilate told Pilate that they brought Jesus to him because he was misleading the nation of Israel, forbidding the people to pay taxes to Caesar (lies), and saying that he is the Christ and a king (the truth). Pilate questioned Jesus. *After thoroughly questioning him, Pilate then told the chief priests and the crowds that he did not find Jesus guilty of anything (italics added)* (Luke 23:1–5, John 18:28–38).

The religious leaders kept telling Pilate that Jesus was a trouble-maker and he was stirring up the crowds. Pilate found out that Jesus was from Galilee. King Herod was the ruler of Galilee. Pilate did not want to have anything to do with judging Jesus. He knew that Jesus was an innocent man and the Jewish religious leaders were doing all this because they were envious of Jesus. He told the Jewish religious leaders that since Jesus was a Galilean, he fell under King Herod's jurisdiction and Herod was the one that needed to hear their case against Jesus. The Jewish religious leaders brought Jesus to King Herod, hoping that Herod would find him guilty and sentence him to die.

King Herod was excited to see Jesus. He heard a lot about him, and he wanted to see Jesus perform miracles for him. Herod questioned Jesus, but Jesus remained silent. The chief priests and scribes kept making accusations against Jesus to Herod. No matter what was said to Jesus or about him, he remained silent. Remember, he came here to die to pay for our sins to save us. He did not want to get out of a death sentence. So he remained quiet and never defended himself during this whole ordeal. King Herod became upset that Jesus would not perform a miracle for him and he would not speak. He dressed Jesus in fancy clothes to make fun of him, and then he sent him back to Pilate (Luke 23:6–12).

> When Jesus was brought back to Pilate, he brought Jesus in to talk with him again. He asked Jesus, "Are you the King of the Jews? Your own nation and the chief priests have delivered you over to me. What have you done?" Jesus answered, "My kingdom is not of this world. If my kingdom were of this world, my servants would have been fighting, that I might not be

delivered over to the Jews. But my kingdom is
not from the world." Then Pilate said to him, "So
you are a king?" Jesus answered, "You say that I
am a king. For this purpose I was born and for
this purpose I have come into the world—to bear
witness to the truth. Everyone who is of the truth
listens to my voice." (John 18:33–37)

Pilate made an announcement to the chief priests and the
people,

You brought Jesus to me, accusing him of
misleading the people. I have thoroughly examined him. *I did not find this man guilty of any of
the charges you made against him. Neither did King
Herod. Nothing deserving death has been done by
Jesus (italics added).* Therefore, I will punish him,
and set him free. (Luke 23:13–17)

The religious leaders would not stop demanding that Pilate condemn Jesus to death. Pilate tried to set Jesus free. He knew that Jesus
was innocent of the charges of which the religious leaders accused
him, and they only wanted Jesus killed out of their envy of him.
Pilate gave the crowd a choice of one prisoner that he would set free
as a Passover tradition: either Jesus or a murderer and insurrectionist
named Barabbas. Pilate thought that the people would want Jesus set
free instead of Barabbas. The religious leaders convinced the crowd
to tell Pilate they wanted Barabbas released instead of Jesus, which
Pilate did (Matthew 27:15–23, Luke 23:18–25).

Pilate made another attempt to save Jesus's life from the envious
religious leaders and the bloodthirsty crowd they stirred up. He had
Jesus severely flogged or whipped. This split Jesus's back open. After
Jesus was flogged, the soldiers brought him inside the governor's
headquarters. They put a purple cloak on him to make fun of him
that he was a king. They made a crown of thorns and put it on his

head. They hit him in the head with a reed, spit on him, and made fun of him by bowing down and saying,

> Hail, King of the Jews! (Matthew 27:29)

When they were done whipping him and beating him, scripture says he was beaten so badly that he was not recognizable as a human being. A prophecy about Jesus's death in the book of Isaiah reveals this:

> As many were astonished at you—his appearance was so marred, beyond human semblance, and his form beyond that of the children of mankind. (Isaiah 52:14)

Pilate brought Jesus back out to the crowd. Jesus was beaten so badly that Pilate hoped the crowd would feel he was punished enough and they would not want him killed. Pilate showed Jesus to the crowd and shouted, "Behold the man!" (John 19:5), which meant "Look at him! Isn't he punished *enough?*"

The chief priests screamed out, "Crucify him!"

Pilate decided to release Jesus anyway because he found no guilt in him. Then the religious leaders backed Pilate into a corner.

They said, "Jesus says he is a king. We have no king but Caesar. If you release this man, you are no friend of Caesar" (John 19:12). Caesar was the supreme leader of Rome and its conquered territories (Israel). If it got out that Pontius Pilate released a man who claimed to be the king of Israel in place of Caesar, Caesar might have Pilate executed.

> So when Pilate saw that he was gaining nothing, but rather that a riot was beginning, he took water and washed his hands before the crowd, saying, "I am innocent of this man's blood; see to it yourselves." Then he delivered Jesus up to be crucified. (Matthew 27:24–26)

Jesus was led away by the Roman soldiers and made to carry his cross. They forced a man named Simon of Cyrene to help Jesus carry his cross. They brought Jesus, along with two other criminals who were to be crucified to a place called Golgotha, which means Place of a Skull. A great multitude of people and groups of women were following Jesus, grieving for him for what was happening to him. It was there that they crucified Jesus, along with one of the criminals on his right and one on his left. As they were crucifying Jesus, he said,

> Father forgive them, for they know not what they do. (Luke 23:34)

> Pontius Pilate wrote an inscription and put it on the cross of Jesus. It said, "Jesus of Nazareth, the King of the Jews." (John 19:19)

It was written in Aramaic, Latin, and Greek so everyone could read it. They offered him wine to drink mixed with gall, but when he tasted it, he would not drink it. The Roman soldiers divided Jesus's garments among them. But his tunic was seamless, woven in one piece from top to bottom. They could not tear it to divide it, so they cast lots for it, to see who would get it (Matthew 27:32–43, Mark 15:21–27, Luke 23:26–33, John 19:17–24). All these events had been prophesied about Jesus by the prophets in the Old Testament and can be found in the chapter in this Bible summary about the prophecies about Jesus in the Old Testament.

> The rulers mocked Jesus, saying, "He saved others; let him save himself, if he is the Christ of God, his Chosen one!" (Luke 23:35)

> Aha! You who would destroy the temple and rebuild it in three days, save yourself, and come down from the cross! (Mark 15:29–30)

The Roman soldiers and the two criminals crucified on both sides of Jesus said the same thing at first. One of the criminals then said, "If you are the Christ, save yourself and save us too!"

The other criminal came to believe in Jesus. He said, "Don't you fear God? We deserve our punishment for our bad deeds, but Jesus has done nothing wrong."

> The criminal then said, "Jesus, remember me when you come into your kingdom." And Jesus said to the criminal, "Truly, I say to you, today you will be with me in Paradise." (Luke 23:42–43)

> Standing by the cross of Jesus were his mother and his mother's sister, Mary the wife of Clopas, and Mary Magdalene. When Jesus saw his mother and the disciple whom he loved [the apostle John] standing nearby, he said to his mother, "Woman, behold your son!" Then he said to the disciple, "Behold, your mother!" And from that day on the Apostle John took her into his own home. (John 19:25–27).

Between the sixth and ninth hour, the sun's light failed, and there was darkness over the whole land. In the ninth hour, Jesus cried out with a loud voice, saying,

> My God, My God, why have you forsaken me? (Matthew 27:45–46)

One of the bystanders filled a sponge with sour wine and gave it to Jesus to drink, saying,

> Let's see if Elijah will come and take him down. (Mark 15:36)

After Jesus drank the sour wine, he said, "It is finished." (John 19:30)

Then Jesus, calling out with a loud voice, said, "Father, into your hands I commit my spirit!" And having said this he breathed his last. (Luke 23:46–47)

Since it was the day of Preparation, and so that the bodies would not remain on the cross on the Sabbath [for that Sabbath was a high day], the Jews asked Pilate that their legs might be broken and they might be taken away. So the soldiers came and broke the legs of the first, and of the other who had been crucified with him. But when they came to Jesus and saw that he was already dead, they did not break his legs. But one of the soldiers pierced his side with a spear, and at once there came out blood and water. For these things took place that the scripture might be fulfilled: "Not one of his bones will be broken." And another scripture prophecy says, "They will look on him who they pierced." (John 19:31–37)

As this happened, the curtain in the temple was split in two from top to bottom. There were earthquakes, and rocks split open. People who had died got out of their graves. After Jesus's resurrection, these people who got out of their graves walked around the city and appeared to many people. When the centurion and those who were with Jesus during all this saw the earthquakes and everything that took place, they were filled with awe and said,

Truly this was the Son of God! (Matthew 27:54)

Many in the crowd who saw all these events went home sad and mourning for what happened to Jesus. Many women were there who followed Jesus from Galilee, and other women who came up from Jerusalem, who had been ministering to him. These included Mary Magdalene and Mary, the mother of James and Joseph and the mother of the sons of Zebedee.

There was a rich man named Joseph from Arimathea, who was a member of the Council. He did not vote that Jesus was guilty, and he came to believe in Jesus. Joseph asked Pontius Pilate if he could have Jesus's body to bury it, and Pilate granted it to him. Joseph buried Jesus in his own tomb, which was a new tomb cut out of rock. The next day, the Pharisees went to Pontius Pilate. They told him that Jesus kept saying that he would rise three days after he died. They thought Jesus's disciples might steal Jesus's body to make it look like he rose from the dead. They asked Pilate if he could secure Jesus's tomb. Pilate gave them a guard of soldiers and told the Pharisees to make Jesus's tomb as secure as they could. They sealed a stone over the tomb and placed Roman soldiers around it to guard it (Matthew 27:57–66, Mark 15:42–47, Luke 23:50–56, John 19:38–42).

THE RESURRECTION OF JESUS

On the first day of the week, a group of women who knew Jesus went to his tomb with spices they prepared. When they got there, an earthquake took place because an angel of the Lord descended from heaven, rolled away the stone covering the tomb, and he was sitting on it. His appearance was like lightning, and his clothes were as white as snow. When this happened, "For fear of him the guards trembled and became like dead men" (Matthew 28:4). Jesus's body was gone from the tomb and it was empty. The angel said to the women,

> Do not be afraid, for I know that you seek Jesus who was crucified. He is not here, for he has risen, as he said. Come, see the place where he lay. Then go quickly and tell his disciples that he

has risen from the dead, and behold, he is going
before you to Galilee; there you will see him. See,
I have told you. (Matthew 28:5–7)

The woman ran with great joy to tell the apostles. Jesus appeared
to the women and said,

Greetings! Do not be afraid; go and tell my
brothers to go to Galilee, and there they will see
me. (Matthew 28:9–10)

The women grabbed Jesus and worshipped him, then they went
to tell the disciples.

The soldiers guarding the tomb came to the religious leaders
and told them what happened. The religious leaders gave them a
sufficient sum of money and told them to tell the people that Jesus's
disciples snuck in and stole his body while the guards were all asleep.
This was done to try to prevent the people from believing the news
that Jesus rose from the dead, but it didn't work well (Matthew
28:11–15). The apostles were gathered together, hiding out in fear of
the Jews that crucified Jesus. Jesus appeared in their midst. He said,

Peace be with You. As the Father has sent
me, even so I am sending you.

And when he had said this, he breathed on them and said to
them,

Receive the Holy Spirit. If you forgive the
sins of any, they are forgiven of them; if you withhold forgiveness from any, it is withheld. (John
20:21–22)

Thomas was not with the rest of the apostles when Jesus
appeared. He would not believe them that Jesus appeared to them.
He said unless he was able to see the nail marks in his hands and

place his hand in Jesus's side where he was pierced with a spear on the cross, he would not believe it was Jesus. Eight days later the apostles were together again, and Thomas was with them this time. Jesus appeared to all of them and said,

Peace be with you. (John 20:26)

He told Thomas to put his finger into the nail holes in his hands and his hand into his side.

Thomas answered him, "My Lord and My God!" Jesus said to him, "Have you believed because you have seen me? Blessed are those who have not seen and yet believed.' (John 20:28–29)

Jesus appeared to the apostles once again. He sat down and had a talk with Peter. When Jesus was arrested and under trial leading to his crucifixion, Peter denied knowing Jesus three times out of fear of also being arrested. In this conversation with Peter after Jesus was resurrected, Jesus said to Peter,

"Simon, son of John, do you love me more than these?" He said to him, "Yes, Lord; you know that I love you." He said to him, "Feed my lambs." He said to him a second time, "Simon, son of John, do you love me?" He said to him, "Yes, Lord; you know that I love you." He said to him, "Tend my sheep." He said to him a third time, "Simon, son of John, do you love me?" Peter was grieved because he said to him a third time, "Do you love me?" and he said to him, "Lord, you know everything; you know that I love you." Jesus said to him, "Feed my sheep. Truly, truly, I say to you, when you were young, you used to dress yourself and walk wherever you wanted, but when you are old, you will stretch out your hands, and another will dress you and carry you where you do not want to go." [This he said to show by what kind of death he was to glorify God.] And after saying this, he said to him, "Follow me." (John 21:15–19)

At another time when Jesus appeared to the apostles after he rose from the dead, he gave them the Great Commission. This is the instructions he wants his followers (us) to do. Jesus said:

All authority in heaven and on earth has been given to me. Go therefore and make disciples of all nations, baptizing them in the name of the Father and of the Son and of the Holy Spirit, teaching them do observe all that I have commanded you. And behold, I am with you always, to the end of the age. (Matthew 28:18–20)

Go into all the world and proclaim the gospel to the whole creation. Whoever believes and is baptized will be saved, but whoever does not believe will be condemned. (Mark 16:15–16)

What is interesting in the above passage is the authority over the kingdoms of the world was given back to Jesus after he completed his Father's will of dying as a sacrifice for us. Remember the previous statement Satan made to Jesus when he tempted him in the desert as Jesus began his ministry:

And the devil took Jesus up and showed him all the kingdoms of the world in a moment of time, and said to him, "To you I will give all this authority and their glory, *for it has been delivered to me, and I give it to whom I will." (italics added)* (John 4:5–7).

Jesus did not refute this statement of Satan at the time.

Now, after Jesus was crucified and rose from the dead, Jesus said in the above statement:

> All authority in heaven and on earth has been given to me. (Matthew 28:18)

Jesus defeated Satan through his crucifixion for us, as willed by the Father.

After Jesus rose from the dead, he appeared to the apostles and other people multiple times over a forty-day period. On one occasion, he appeared to a crowd of over five hundred people.

Jesus then told the apostles that he would now return to heaven. When he leaves, the Holy Spirit (God) would then come down and live inside each of them, giving them power, strength, and guidance. After Jesus said these things, as the apostles were looking at him, Jesus was lifted up and a cloud took him out of their sight. As the apostles were watching Jesus being lifted up into heaven, two angels appeared to them wearing white robes. They said,

> Men of Galilee, why do you stand looking into heaven? This Jesus, who was taken up from you into heaven, will come in the same way as you saw him go into heaven. (Acts 1:11)

CHAPTER 22

THE ACTS OF THE APOSTLES AND THE RISE OF THE CHRISTIAN CHURCH

S hortly after Jesus returned to heaven, the apostles were gathered together in a group. Suddenly, a sound came from heaven that sounded like a mighty wind, and a flame of fire hovered above each of the apostles' heads. It was the Holy Spirit, who came to live inside each of the apostles. The Holy Spirit is the third person of God (the Father, the Son [Jesus], and the Holy Spirit). The apostles began to speak in various languages that they previously did not know. The people who were around them who spoke these different languages became amazed that the apostles were suddenly able to speak their languages. The Holy Spirit gave the apostles strength, wisdom, power, and encouragement to go out and tell everybody who Jesus is and how everyone can be saved from their sins by following him (Acts chapters 1 and 2:1–13).

Peter immediately began to preach a sermon about Jesus to the people who were standing around him as the apostles were speaking in different languages. He spoke about God promising David that one of his descendants would sit on the throne, about the prophecies concerning the resurrection of the Christ, and this resurrected Christ was Jesus, whom the people of Jerusalem witnessed. Peter said that Jesus is now exalted at the right hand of God, and the Holy Spirit was poured out on the followers of Jesus as Jesus had promised he would be. The sudden speaking of different languages by the apostles was evidence of the Holy Spirit in them, and the people were witnessing it as Peter spoke. Peter then said,

> Let all the house of Israel therefore know for certain that God has made Jesus both Lord and Christ, this Jesus whom you crucified. (Acts 2:36)

The people who heard this were cut to the heart, and they asked Peter and the rest of the apostles what they should do. Peter said,

> Repent and be baptized every one of you in the name of Jesus Christ for the forgiveness of your sins and you will receive the gift of the Holy Spirit. For the promise is for you and for your children and for all who are far off, everyone whom the Lord our God calls to himself. (Acts 2:38–39)

Peter continued to give his witness testimony about Jesus, and about three thousand people were baptized and saved that day. The people devoted themselves to the teaching of the apostles and the fellowship and prayers. Many wonders and signs were being done by the apostles which brought awe to everyone who witnessed it. They began to sell their possessions and use the money to help those who were less fortunate and those who were in need. They gathered daily in the temple and in homes, breaking bread together and praising God with glad and generous hearts. The Lord God added the to their number day by day those who were being saved (Acts chapter 2).

One day the apostles Peter and John were going up to the temple. There was a man who was carried there daily. He had been lame from birth, and he would ask for alms from those entering the temple. Peter looked at him and said,

> [Summary] I do not have silver or gold for you, but I will give you what I do have: In the name of Jesus Christ of Nazareth, get up and walk!

The man was immediately healed, and he entered the temple with them walking, leaping, and praising God. The people who saw this were astonished. Peter then addressed these people, saying,

> [Summary] Why do you wonder how we made this man walk. It was not by our power, but by the power of Jesus, who you delivered to be crucified when Pilate had decided to release him. Jesus, the man who you killed gave us the power to make this lame man walk. I know you acted out of ignorance, as did the rulers who crucified him. Repent of your sins and turn to Jesus that he may forgive your sins. Jesus is the one who all the prophets spoke about his coming. (Acts chapter 3)

The priests and the captain of the temple and the Sadducees arrested them for teaching the people and proclaiming Jesus and the resurrection from the dead. Yet about five thousand men came to believe in Jesus because of what the apostles said. The next day they were questioned by the religious leaders by what power or name they said these things to the people.

> Then Peter, filled with the Holy Spirit, said to them, "Rulers of the people and elders, if we are being examined today concerning a good deed done to a crippled man, by what means this man has been healed, let it be known to all of you and to all the people of Israel that by the name of Jesus Christ of Nazareth, whom you crucified, whom God raised from the dead—by him this man is standing before you well. This Jesus is the stone that was rejected by you, the builders, which has become the cornerstone. And there is salvation in no one else, for there is no other

name under heaven given among men by which
we must be saved." (Acts 4:8–12)

The religious leaders were astonished by the boldness of Peter
and John, recognizing that they were uneducated, common men.
They saw that a miracle happened: the well-known lame man was
now walking. They did not know what to do. They decided to tell
Peter and John that they were forbidden to speak or teach in the
name of Jesus. Peter and John answered them,

> Whether it is right in the sight of God to
> listen to you rather than to God, you must judge,
> for we cannot but speak of what we have seen
> and heard. (Acts 4:19–20)

The religious leaders threatened them again to no longer speak
in the name of Jesus, but they could not do anything to them because
all the people were praising God for the miracle that had happened
to the lame man. They were released and gathered together and
prayed to God for boldness in proclaiming Jesus and for the ability to
do signs and wonders in Jesus's name. When they finished praying,
the ground shook, and they were filled with the Holy Spirit. They
continued to speak the word of God to the people with boldness
(Acts chapter 4).The apostles were regularly doing many signs and
wonders for the people. Because of this, more and more people were
becoming followers of Jesus every day. People would even bring the
sick out into the streets in hopes that Peter's shadow may fall on them
as he walked by so they could be healed. People from other towns
around Jerusalem brought the sick and the demon possessed to the
apostles, and they healed them all (Acts 5:12–16).

The high priest and the Sadducees were filled with envy over
the apostles. They rose up and put the apostles in public prison.

> But during the night an angel of the Lord
> opened the prison doors and brought them out
> and said, "Go and stand in the temple and speak

to the people all the words of this Life." And when they heard this, they entered the temple at daybreak and began to teach. (Acts 5:19–20)

The high priest arrived and summoned that the apostles be brought to him from the prison. The officers came back and said that the prison is securely locked, but the apostles were not in there. Then another person arrived and told the high priest that the men that he put in prison were in the temple teaching the people. The captain and the officers then brought the apostles to the high priest, but not by force, for they were afraid that if they did the people would stone them.

The apostles were brought before the council. The high priest rose and said that they were strictly instructed not to teach in Jesus's name, and they had broken this directive by filling Jerusalem with teaching about Jesus. Peter and the apostles answered,

We must obey God rather than men. The God of our fathers raised Jesus, whom you killed by hanging him on a tree. God exalted him at his right hand as Leader and Savior, to give repentance to Israel and forgiveness of sins. And we are witnesses to these things, and so is the Holy Spirit, whom God has given to those who obey him. (Acts 5:29–32)

When the council heard this, they were enraged and wanted to kill the apostles. But a very well-respected Pharisee named Gamaliel stood up and ordered the apostles be put outside while he talked with the council alone. He told them to be very careful with how they handle these apostles. There were several men before Jesus who rose up and gathered a following. The leader was killed, and in every case, the following fell apart and vanished forever. These men's leader, Jesus, was killed.

So leave these men alone. If their undertaking is of man, they will fail and their followers

will vanish like the numerous ones before them,
and we will not have to do anything about it. But
if this undertaking is from God, you will not be
able to overthrow them, and you might even find
yourself opposing God.

The council took the advice of Gamaliel. They then beat the
apostles and ordered them not to speak in the name of Jesus anymore, and they released them. The apostles left the council rejoicing
that they were counted worthy to suffer dishonor for the name of
Jesus. Every day they taught about Jesus as the Christ from house to
house and in the temple (Acts chapter 5).

There was a disciple of Jesus named Stephen. He was full of the
Holy Spirit and did great wonders and signs among the people. A
group of men belonging to the synagogue of the Freemen disputed
with Stephen, but they could not withstand the Spirit and the wisdom of which he was speaking. They began to spread false accusations
against him that he was blaspheming against Moses and God. They
stirred up the people against him. He was seized and brought before
the council where false witnesses accused him of teaching against
the holy place and the Law. Stephen was then given the opportunity
to answer the charges against him. Stephen gave a history of acts
of the Jewish patriarchs from Abraham through King Solomon. He
abruptly ended his speech by saying,

You stiff-necked people, uncircumcised in
your hearts and ears, you always resist the Holy
Spirit. As your fathers did, so do you. Which one
of the prophets did your fathers not persecute?
And they killed those who announced beforehand the coming of the Righteous One, whom
you have now betrayed and murdered, you who
received the law as delivered by angels and did
not keep it. (Acts 7:51–53)

Now when they heard these things they were enraged, and they ground their teeth at him. But he, full of the Holy Spirit, gazed into heaven and saw the Glory of God, and Jesus standing at the right hand of God. And he said, "Behold, I see the heavens opened, and the Son of Man standing at the right hand of God." But they cried out with a loud voice and stopped their ears and rushed together at him. Then they cast him out of the city and stoned him. And the witnesses laid down their garments at the feet of a young man named Saul. And as they were stoning Stephen, he called out, "Lord Jesus receive my spirit." And falling to his knees he cried out with a loud voice, "Lord, do not hold this sin against them." And when he said this, he fell asleep. (Acts 7:54–60)

Stephen was the first Christian martyr in the Bible.

And Saul approved his execution. (Acts 8:1)

On that day, a great persecution against the new church of the followers of Jesus in Jerusalem began. Saul was ravaging the church of the followers of Jesus. He went from house to house, dragging away followers of Jesus and putting them in prison. Yet the apostles and devoted disciples of Jesus kept preaching in his name and gathered followers. The message about Jesus was spreading from town to town, and believers in Jesus Christ were springing up in those towns (Acts chapter 8).

JESUS APPEARS TO SAUL (PAUL)

Saul was on a rampage to destroy the new church of the followers of Jesus. He was on his way to the synagogues in Damascus looking for any men or people in the Way (the name given to those following Jesus) so he could arrest them and bring them to Jerusalem. As he was on his way to Damascus, a light from heaven flashed around him.

> He fell to the ground, and he heard a voice that said, "Saul, Saul, why are you persecuting me?" and Saul said, "Who are you Lord?" and the voice said, "I am Jesus, whom you are persecuting. But rise and enter the city, and you will be told what you are to do." (Acts 9:4–6)

The men with Saul heard the voice, but they did not see anyone. Saul rose from the ground, but he was now blind. The men with him led him by the hand into Damascus. He was blind for three days, and he did not eat or drink during this time (Acts 9:1–9).

There was a disciple of Jesus in Damascus named Ananias. God spoke to him and told him to go into the street and he would find a man named Saul who would be praying. God told Ananias that he had given Saul a vision that Ananias would come to him and lay hands on him and his sight would be restored. Ananias told God that he had heard from many people about all the evil things Saul had done to God's saints in Jerusalem and that he was here to arrest followers of Jesus and bring them back to Jerusalem. God said to Ananias,

> Go, for he is a chosen instrument of mine to carry my name before the Gentiles and kings and the children of Israel. For I will show him how much he has to suffer for the sake of my name. (Acts 9:15–16)

Ananias went to Saul as God instructed him to. He laid hands on Saul and said,

> "Brother Saul, the Lord Jesus who appeared to you on the road by which you came sent me so that you may regain your sight and be filled with

the Holy Spirit." And immediately something
like scales fell from his eyes, and he regained his
sight. Then he rose and was baptized; and taking
food, he was strengthened. (Acts 9:17–19)

Saul stayed for some days in Damascus with disciples of Jesus.
He then went to the synagogues and proclaimed that Jesus was the
Son of God. The people who heard Saul preaching this were amazed.
They asked each other, "Isn't this the man who wreaked havoc in
Jerusalem against the followers of Jesus? Didn't he come to Damascus
to arrest followers of Jesus and drag them back to face the chief priests
in Jerusalem?"

But Saul increased all the more in strength,
and confounded the Jews in Damascus by prov-
ing that Jesus was the Christ. (Acts 9:22)

After several days had passed, the Jews plotted to kill Saul. They
were watching the gates of the city day and night with intent to kill
him. But Saul and the disciples became aware of their plans. The disciples took Saul at night and lowered him in a basket out of the city
through an opening in the wall (Acts 9:23–25).

Saul went to Jerusalem. He tried to join the disciples, but they
did not believe that he actually followed Jesus, and they were afraid
of him. A disciple named Barnabas took Saul to the apostles. He told
them all about how on the road to Damascus the Lord appeared to
Saul and spoke to him. As a result of this, Saul preached boldly in the
name of Jesus in Damascus. The accepted him as a disciple of Jesus.
He went out among them and preached boldly in the name of Jesus
in Jerusalem. He spoke out against the Hellenists, and they plotted
to kill Saul for it. When the brothers learned about this they brought
him down to Caesarea and sent him to Tarsus.

So the church throughout all Judea and
Galilee and Samaria had peace and was being
built up. And walking in the fear of the Lord and

in the comfort of the Holy Spirit, it multiplied. (Acts 9:31)

At the same time, Peter was traveling around, and he went to a town called Lydda. There was a man there named Aeneas who was paralyzed and bedridden for eight years. Peter came to him and said,

> Aeneas, Jesus Christ heals you; rise and make your bed. (Acts 9:34)

He immediately got up. The people of the towns of Lydda and Sharon saw him and turned to God because of it.

There was a good woman in the town of Joppa named Dorcas who became sick and died. Joppa was near the town of Lydda. The disciples heard that Peter was in Lydda, so they urgently summoned him. Peter entered the room where the dead woman Dorcas was laid. Peter Prayed to God and said, "Dorcas, arise." She opened her eyes, saw Peter, and sat up. He presented her alive once again to all the people in the house who were mourning over her. Word spread throughout Joppa about this, and many came to believe in the Lord (Acts 9:36–43).

One day Peter received a message from God that many of the animals that God forbade the Jews to eat were now made clean by God and could be eaten. He also told Peter that salvation of Jesus Christ has not just come to the Jews, but everyone who believes in Jesus will receive forgiveness of sins through the name of Jesus. This message came to Peter while he was in the company of several Gentiles that were sent to him by God to speak with Peter. As this was happening, the Holy Spirit came and fell on every one who was there with Peter, Jew and Gentile alike. The Jewish people who were there with Peter were amazed, because the gift of the Holy Spirit was poured out on the Gentiles too. The Gentiles began speaking in tongues and glorifying God in the presence of the disciples of Jesus. Peter then realized that salvation of Jesus Christ was given to everyone who would believe in Jesus, not just the Jews. He baptized everyone who was there, both Jews and Gentiles, in the name of Jesus Christ (Acts chapter 10).

The persecution of the followers of Jesus that started with the stoning of Stephen caused them to travel to Phoenicia and Cyprus and Antioch. They were only giving the message of Jesus Christ to the Jews. However, they encountered Hellenists and preached to them about Jesus. The hand of the Lord was with them, and the number of the followers of Jesus increased. A disciple of Jesus named Barnabas searched for Saul in Tarsus and brought Saul to Antioch. They taught the people in Antioch about Jesus for a year's time. It was during this teaching in Antioch that the disciples of Jesus were first called Christians (Acts 11:19–26).

At this time, King Herod persecuted some of the Christians. He killed James the apostle with a sword. This pleased the Jews, so he had Peter arrested also. While in prison, Peter had four squads of soldiers guarding him. But earnest prayer was made to God on his behalf by the church. That night Peter was bound with two chains, and he was sleeping between two soldiers with sentries at the door guarding the prison. An angel of the Lord appeared and stood next to Peter, and light shone in the cell. The angel woke up Peter and told him to get up quickly. The chains immediately fell off of Peter's hands. The angel led him out of the prison and onto the street. Peter immediately went to the home where several apostles and disciples were praying for him. When Peter knocked at the door, they were amazed. Peter told them all that had happened, and he left the area. There was a big commotion at the prison over the vanishing of Peter. The guards of the prison were examined by King Herod and then ordered to be put to death because Peter was missing.

One day King Herod put on his royal robes, took his seat upon the throne, and gave a speech to the people. The people were shouting at him,

> The voice of a god and not a man!'
> Immediately an angel of the Lord struck Herod
> down, because he did not give God the glory, and
> he was eaten by worms and breathed his last. But

the word of God increased and multiplied. (Acts 12:22–24)

A group of disciples were in the church at Antioch. The Holy Spirit appeared and told the group to set apart Saul and Barnabas for the work to which God had called them. The group fasted, prayed, laid hands on Saul and Barnabas, and sent them off. Being sent out by the Holy Spirit, Saul, Barnabas, and the apostle John went through several towns and came upon a false-prophet Jewish magician who opposed the work of the apostles and tried to turn the people away from God. Saul, who was now also called Paul by this time (and will be called Paul for the remainder of this Bible summary), confronted this deceitful person, and he immediately became blind. The people around them came to believe the teaching of Paul about Jesus because of this event (Acts 13:1–12).

Paul and Barnabas went from area to area teaching the message:

[Summary] Through Jesus forgiveness of sins is proclaimed to you, and by Jesus everyone who believes in him is freed from everything from which you could not be freed from the law of Moses.

The crowds to hear Paul speak became so large that on one Sabbath almost the whole city came out to hear Paul speak the word of the Lord to them.

But when the Jews saw the crowds, they were filled with jealousy and began to contradict what was spoken by Paul, reviling him. And Paul and Barnabas spoke out boldly, saying, "It was necessary that the word of God be spoken first to you. Since you thrust it aside and judge yourselves unworthy of eternal life, behold, we are turning to the Gentiles. For so the Lord has commanded us, saying, 'I have made you a light for the Gentiles, that you may bring salvation to the ends of the earth.'" And when the Gentiles heard this, they began rejoicing and glorifying the word of the Lord, and as many as were appointed to eternal life believed. And the word of the Lord was spreading throughout the whole region. But the Jews incited the devout women of high standing and the leading men of the city, stirred up persecution against Paul and Barnabas, and drove them out of their district. But they shook off the dust from their feet against them and went to Iconium. And the disciples were filled with joy and with the Holy Spirit. (Acts 13:45–52)

At Iconium, Paul and Barnabas entered the Jewish synagogue and preached about Jesus in a way that many Jews and Greeks came to believe. But the unbelieving Jews turned many Gentiles against Paul and Barnabas. They remained there a long time teaching about Jesus, bearing witness to him and performing signs and wonders. The people of the city became divided. Some of the people sided with the Jews, and some sided with the apostles. An attempt was made to have Paul and Barnabas stoned. They heard about it and fled to Lystra, where they continued to preach the Gospel (Acts 14:1–7).

In Lystra, there was a man who was crippled from birth and never walked. Paul looked at him and told him to stand upright on his feet, and the man did for the first time in his life and began walking around. When the crowds saw it, they yelled out that the gods came down to them in the likeness of men! They called Barnabas Zeus and Paul Hermes. The priest of Zeus came out of the Zeus temple and wanted to offer sacrifices to Paul and Barnabas. Paul and Barnabas tore their garments and rushed into the crowd, saying they were men just like everyone else. They were bringing Good News, and everyone should turn from their false gods to the one true God who made the heavens and the earth. Even with their own testimony that they were not gods and Jesus is God, the people kept wanting to offer sacrifices to them as gods (Acts 14:8–18).

Jews arrived from Antioch and Iconium to where Paul was preaching about Jesus. They persuaded the crowds against Paul. They stoned Paul and dragged him out of the city, believing that he was dead. The disciples gathered around Paul on the ground, and he rose up and reentered the city. He got Barnabas and went to Derbe. They preached the Gospel in that city and made many disciples and then returned to Lystra, Iconium, and Antioch. There they strengthened the souls of the disciples, encouraged them to continue in the faith, and told them that through many tribulations, they must enter the kingdom of God. They then appointed elders for them in every church (Acts 14:19–23).

Paul and Barnabas decided it would be good to visit the brothers in every city where they formerly preached about Jesus. Barnabas wanted to bring with them the disciple Mark. Paul did not want to bring him because Paul was unhappy with some of his actions in the past. They had a sharp disagreement over this, which led them to separate. Barnabas took Mark with him to Cyprus, and Paul took Silas with him to strengthen the churches in Syria and Cilicia (Acts 15:36–41). While in Lystra, Paul met a disciple named Timothy. Paul was pleased with Timothy and took him with them to strengthen the churches in various cities. However, there were some cities, areas, and nations in which the Holy Spirit forbid them to speak in (Acts 16:1–8).

On one of their travels, Paul and Silas encountered a slave girl who had a spirit of divination. For many days, she followed Paul and Silas, crying out,

> These men are servants of the Most High
> God, who proclaim to you the way of salvation.
> (Acts 16:17)

Paul became annoyed at this and commanded the spirit to come out of her in the name of Jesus Christ. The spirit came out of her, but her owners were enraged because now they could not make money off of her divination. They brought Paul and Silas to the town magistrates. They were sentenced and were beaten badly with rods and put into prison. Around midnight, Paul and Silas were praying and singing hymns to God, and the prisoners were listening to them. There was suddenly a great earthquake that shook the foundations of the prison. All the prison doors opened up, and everyone's chains fell off of them. When the jailer woke and saw that all the prison doors were open, he grabbed his sword and was about to kill himself, thinking that all the prisoners escaped. Paul yelled out for the jailer to not harm himself; everyone was still there. The jailer entered and fell down before Paul and Silas and asked them what he must do to be saved. They told him that he and his household would be saved if they believe in the Lord Jesus. The jailer brought Paul and Silas to his house and cleaned their wounds from the beatings with rods. Paul and Silas spoke the word to him and everyone in his house. He and his family were baptized at once. They all had a meal, and he and his entire house rejoiced that they came to follow God (Acts 16:25–34).

Paul, Silas, and Timothy were teaching in the Jewish synagogue in Berea about Jesus as the Savior. Many Jews received their words eagerly and examined the scriptures daily to see if these things were so. Many of the Greek people there came to believe in Jesus. But Jews came from Thessalonica and stirred up crowds against them. The brothers sent Paul away, but Timothy and Silas stayed there. Paul then went to Athens to teach the people. Paul was upset that the city was full of idols. Some of the people in Athens were for his teaching, and some were against it, but they were interested in hearing it because the people in Athens loved to hear stories and things that were new to them. Paul addressed the people of Athens at the Areopagus, telling them that they should not worship idols and unknown gods. They should worship the one and only true God, who made everything. He told them the story about Jesus and that they need to repent and follow him. When they heard that Jesus was resurrected from the dead, some mocked him, but some men believed him and joined him (Acts chapter 17).

After Paul eventually left Athens, he went to Corinth. He befriended fellow tent makers as himself named Aquila and Pricilla. They had left Italy because Claudius commanded all the Jews to leave Rome. Silas and Timothy met up with him in Corinth. They were testifying to the Jews that the Christ was Jesus. The Jews there opposed and reviled them.

> Paul shook out his garments and said to them, "Your blood be on your own heads! I am innocent. From now on I will go to the Gentiles."
> (Acts 18:6)

After staying and teaching the people of Corinth about Jesus for a year and six months, Paul went with Pricilla and Aquila to Syria. He reasoned with the Jews in the synagogue, and then he went to Caesarea, Antioch, and the region of Galatia and Phrygia, strengthening the disciples everywhere he went. He spent two years in Ephesus teaching the Jews and Greeks in Asia. God was doing extraordinary miracles through Paul. Even handkerchiefs or aprons that touched his skin were brought to people and their diseases and evil spirits left them. Many people came to believe in Jesus because of this. New believers who formerly practiced black magic brought their magic books and burned them in front of everyone. The word of God continued to increase and prevail mightily (Acts 19:1–20).

In Ephesus, the smiths that made idols to worship gathered together. They said, "This Paul is telling the people not to worship idols. We make idols for the people to worship as our living, and he is going to drive us out of business." A riot broke out, and there was much confusion in the city. After the uproar calmed down, Paul left and went to Macedonia and then to Troas. Paul was giving a long speech in an upper room, which lasted until after midnight. A young man fell asleep and fell out of a third-story window that he was sitting in and died. Paul went down and stood over the young man, lifted him up by his hands, and he came back to life. The people there were amazed (Acts 19:21–41, 20:1–12).

Paul spoke to the elders in Ephesus and let them know that he must return to Jerusalem, and God told him that he will suffer while he is there:

> And now, behold, I am going to Jerusalem,
> constrained by the Spirit, not knowing what will
> happen to me there, except that the Holy Spirit
> testifies to me in every city that imprisonment
> and afflictions await me. But I do not account
> my life of any value nor as precious to myself,
> if only I may finish my course and the ministry
> that I received from the Lord Jesus, to testify to
> the gospel of the grace of God. (Acts 20:22–24)

He let them know that once he left Ephesus, they would never see him again. He told them to be strong and remember everything he taught them, because fierce wolves would come into this flock, looking to distort and destroy the Gospel message. The people of Ephesus prayed with Paul, and there was much weeping, because they would never see Paul again after he left.

Paul traveled through many cities on his way to Jerusalem. While in Caesarea, he stayed at the house of Philip the evangelist. While staying in his home, a prophet named Agabus came down from Judea. He took Paul's belt and bound up his own feet and said,

> "Thus says the Holy Spirit, This is how the
> Jews at Jerusalem will bind the man who owns
> this belt and deliver him into the hands of the
> Gentiles." When the people with Paul heard this,
> they and the people there urged him not to go up
> to Jerusalem. Then Paul answered, "What are you
> doing, weeping and breaking my heart? For I am
> ready not only to be imprisoned but even to die in
> Jerusalem for the Lord Jesus." And since he would
> not be persuaded, they ceased and said, "Let the
> will of the Lord be done." (Acts 21:11–14)

Paul entered Jerusalem and was there for a week. Jews from Asia stirred up the crowd, telling them that Paul was teaching the people to not follow the law of God. Paul was seized, but there was great chaos that erupted in the city over this. They were going to kill Paul, but the riot demanded that the soldiers needed to restore peace in the city instead of executing Paul. So they stopped beating Paul to tend to the riot in the city and bound him with two chains and brought him into the barracks. The soldiers actually had to carry Paul into the barracks, because they were surrounded by a crowd that wanted to kill him (Acts 21:27–36).

Paul testified before the council, and there was great division and debate among the council members as to whether Paul was a man sent by God or a heretic. After a day of arguing amongst the council, Paul was brought to the barracks in the evening.

> The following night the Lord stood by him
> and said, "Take courage, for as you have testified
> to the facts about me in Jerusalem, so you must
> also testify in Rome." (Acts 23:11)

When it was day, the Jews made a plot to kill Paul. Over forty of them went to the chief priests and told them to give notice to the tribune to bring Paul to them under the guise that they wanted to question him. While he was being transported, they planned to ambush and kill him. Paul's nephew heard about this and told Paul. Paul alerted a centurion who had Paul's nephew brought to the tribune to inform them of this. He told them that a request would be made to bring Paul to the council for questioning, but there would be an ambush of forty men waiting to kill Paul during the transport. The tribune responded by ordering two hundred soldiers and seventy horsemen to escort Paul to Felix the governor. The tribune, named Claudius Lysias sent a letter to the governor Felix informing him of all the events concerning the apostle Paul. The letter and Paul were delivered to the governor Felix the next day (Acts 23:12–35).

After five days the high priest Ananias arrived to the place of governor Felix and laid out his case against Paul. He accused Paul of stirring up riots among all the Jews of the world and a ringleader of the sect of the Nazarenes. The Jews that were present supported what the high priest said against Paul. Paul was then allowed to speak.

He said that he had been in Jerusalem the past twelve days, and he was not causing problems with anyone, just worshipping the God of their fathers. But Jews from Asia caused all kinds of problems against him because of what he said about the resurrection of the dead.

> It is with respect to the resurrection of the dead that I am on trial before you this day. (Acts 24:21)

Governor Felix decided to keep Paul in custody until his case could be heard with all relevant parties present. Felix kept Paul in prison for two years. He would come and talk with him often, however, hearing Paul's testimony about Jesus Christ. After two years' time, governor Felix was succeeded by Porcius Festivus. Felix left Paul in prison all this time desiring to do the Jews a favor (Acts 24:22–27).

Within three days of Festivus taking over as governor, the chief priests and principal men of the Jews laid out their case against Paul and requested that he be sent to Jerusalem. They planned to ambush and kill Paul along the way. Festivus decided to keep Paul in Caesarea, and he heard the case against him there. Jews came from Jerusalem and brought many serious charges against Paul, but none of them could be proven. Paul said in his defense that he did not commit any offense against the law of the Jews, the temple, or Caesar. Festivus, wishing to do the Jews a favor, asked Paul if he wished to go up to Jerusalem to be tried on these charges. Paul said that he was standing before Caesar's tribunal, where he ought to be tried. He said that he did no wrong to the Jews, as Festivus himself well knew. If he was actually a wrong doer and did anything that deserved death, he would face death. But if there was nothing to their charges against him, no one could give him up to them.

Then Paul said, "I appeal to Caesar."

> Then Festivus, when he had conferred with his council answered, "To Caesar you have appealed; to Caesar you shall go." (Acts 25:12)

After some days passed, King Agrippa and Bernice arrived at Caesarea and greeted Festivus. Festivus told King Agrippa all about Paul's case: the chief priests and elders of Jerusalem laid out their case against Paul asking to condemn him to death. When he heard their charges against Paul, they were not charges deserving of death. Rather, they had certain points of dispute with him about their religion and a man named Jesus, who was dead, but Paul insisted that he was alive. Festivus did not know what to do with the case, so he asked whether he wanted to be tried in Jerusalem, but Paul appealed to Caesar, so Festivus kept him in custody until he could be heard by Caesar. King Agrippa wanted to speak with Paul himself (Acts 25:13–22).

Paul Spoke to King Agrippa before an audience. He told him that he was raised and trained among the strictest party of the Jewish religion, and he became a Pharisee. He said he was being condemned by the Jews for speaking about what all Jews hoped and prayed earnestly for, that God raise the dead. As a Pharisee, he believed he was right in opposing the name of Jesus of Nazareth. In Jerusalem as a Pharisee, he locked up many of the saints in prison under the authority of the chief priest and cast his votes against them to be put to death. He traveled all over persecuting them in a raging fury. On his way to Damascus to persecute followers of Jesus, a light from heaven surrounded him and blinded him. He fell to the ground, and a voice said to him,

> "Saul, Saul, why are you persecuting me? It is hard for you to kick against the goads." And I said, "Who are you, Lord?" And the Lord said, "I am Jesus whom you are persecuting. But rise and stand upon your feet, for I have appeared to you for this purpose, to appoint you as a servant and witness to the things in which you have seen me and to those in which I will appear to you, delivering you from your people and from the Gentiles—to whom I am sending you to open their eyes, so that they may turn from darkness to light and from the power of Satan to God, that they may receive forgiveness of sins and a place

among those who are sanctified by faith in me."
(Acts 26:14–18)

Paul told King Agrippa that he was not disobedient to the heavenly vision, but he declared everywhere, to Jews and Gentiles, that they should repent and turn to God and do deeds in keeping with their repentance. It was for this that the Jews tried to seize and kill him. But God helped him, and he was now standing here testifying to everyone nothing but what the prophets and Moses said would come to pass:

> That the Christ must suffer and that, by being the first to rise from the dead, he would proclaim light both to our people and to the Gentiles. (Acts 26:23)

As Paul said this, King Agrippa rose up and said that Paul was out of his mind due to his great learning. Paul said that he was not out of his mind and that King Agrippa was aware of the prophecies of the prophets and he believed in them. King Agrippa said to Paul,

> "In a short time would you persuade me to be a Christian?" And Paul said, "Whether short or long, I would to God that not only you but also all who hear me this day might become such as I am—except for these chains." (Acts 26:28–29)

King Agrippa rose along with governor Festivus, Bernice, and the people sitting with them. They went away to talk privately and said to each other,

> "This man is doing nothing to deserve death or imprisonment." And Agrippa said to Festivus, "This man could have been set free if he had not appealed to Caesar." (Acts 26:31–32)

It was decided that Paul would go to Rome. A centurion accompanied Paul and other prisoners as they set sail for Rome on a ship. They stopped in many ports along the way, and Paul was treated kindly as a prisoner. At one point, Paul let the centurion and others on the ship know that he perceived that their voyage would result in injury, and loss of cargo, the ship, and their lives. The centurion did not pay attention to what Paul or the captain of the ship told him about these matters. During the winter they reached Crete, and they faced a mighty windstorm. They were violently tossed around and could not navigate the ship. After facing this all night long and unable to get control of the situation, they began to throw the cargo overboard. The storm continued for two more days, and they threw the ship's tackle overboard and lost hope of being able to survive (Acts 27:1–20).

The crew was without food for several days, in hopes this would bring mercy to them from whatever gods they served. Paul stood up and addressed the crew. He told them not to fear. An angel from God appeared to him during the night and informed him of what would happen to them. God had firm plans that Paul would stand before Caesar in Rome. No one on the ship would lose their life because God was with them. However, the ship would in fact be lost. He told them to take heart, because events would come to pass exactly as Paul told them. But they would run aground on some island soon (Acts 27:21–26).

After fourteen days of being at sea without food due to fasting in hopes of having their lives spared, Paul urged them to eat that day. He assured them that not a hair would perish from the head of any of them. He then took bread, gave thanks to God in the presence of everyone, broke the bread, and everyone began to eat. There were 276 people on the ship. On the next morning, the ship ran aground and was partially destroyed. The soldiers wanted to kill all the prisoners so they would not escape. But the centurion wanted to save Paul, so he prevented them from carrying out their plan. They were all shipwrecked on an island called Malta. The native people came out and were kind to the shipwrecked people. While gathered around a fire warming themselves, a snake came out and bit and attached itself to

Paul's hand. The native people were sure that Paul would die from this. The snakebite had no ill effect on Paul, and this caused the native people to think that Paul was a god (Acts 27:27–44 and 28:1–6).

Paul was shipwrecked near the residence of the chief man of the island named Publius. The father of Publius was sick with dysentery and fever. Paul visited him, laid hands on him, and prayed and he was healed. The rest of the people on the island then brought their sick to Paul, and he cured them. The native people honored the men of the ship greatly, and when it was time for them to leave, they put on board a new ship whatever they needed (Acts 28:7–10).

After spending three winter months on the Island of Malta due to the shipwreck, they were able to board a ship from Alexandria that had stayed the winter in a port on the Island. After making several stops along the way, Paul finally reached Rome. Christian brothers there came from far away to happily greet Paul, and he was allowed to stay by himself with a soldier who guarded him. Paul met with the local leaders of the Jews in Rome. He informed them that he did nothing against the Jewish religion. He was found innocent in his trial and would have been released. However, the Jews there objected to this, which forced him to appeal to Caesar in Rome. He told them that the reason why he was wearing these chains was because of the hope had has for Israel. The Jewish people in Rome told him that they had not been informed that he would be coming, and they had not heard anything evil about Paul. But they wished to hear from him, since the Christians had been spoken against by Jews everywhere (Acts 28:11–22).

Paul was appointed a day to be heard.

> From morning till evening he expounded to them, testifying to the kingdom of God and trying to convince them about Jesus both from the Law of Moses and from the Prophets. And some were convinced by what he said, but others disbelieved. And disagreeing among themselves, they departed after Paul made one statement: The Holy Spirit was right in saying to your

fathers through Isaiah the prophet: "Go to this people, and say, 'You will indeed hear but never understand, and you will indeed see but never perceive. For this people's heart has grown dull, and with their ears they can barely hear, and their eyes they have closed; less they should see with their eyes and hear with their ears and understand with their heart and turn, and I would heal them.' Therefore let it be known to you that this salvation of God has been sent to the Gentiles; they will listen." He lived there two whole years at his own expense, and welcomed all who came to him, proclaiming the kingdom of God and teaching about the Lord Jesus Christ with all boldness and without hindrance. (Acts 28:23–31)

CHAPTER 23

LETTERS OF THE APOSTLE PAUL TO THE NEW CHRISTIANS

THE LETTER OF PAUL TO THE ROMANS

I n this chapter, we will look at the letters, or epistles, that the apostles and disciples wrote to various peoples and to each other. It will begin with several of the apostle Paul's letters to the people of the cities that he visited and taught about Jesus Christ. All these letters are richly filled with teachings about Jesus Christ and are essential in learning about him. In each letter, this Bible summary will present some of the important teachings offered by the apostles and disciples. Because this is a summary of the Bible, it is unable to include the entirety of each letter. Please read the letters in the New Testament for yourself. The letters in this Bible summary will be presented in the order that they are written in the Bible. The first one is Paul's letter to the Romans.

Paul started out his letter to the Romans with this introduction:

> Paul, a servant of Jesus, called to be an apostle, set apart for the gospel of God, which he promised beforehand through his prophets in the holy scriptures, concerning his Son, who

was descended from David according to the flesh
and was declared to be the Son of God in power
according to the Spirit of holiness by his resurrection from the dead, Jesus Christ our Lord,
through whom we have received grace and apos-
tleship to bring about the obedience of faith for
the sake of his name among the nations, including you who are called to belong to Jesus Christ,
To all those in Rome who are loved by God
and called to be saints: Grace to you and peace
from God our Father and the Lord Jesus Christ.
(Romans 1:1–7)

Paul then said in the letter to the Romans that he had been
longing for some time to go to Rome to be with the people of there,
but he had been prevented from doing so up to this point.

The following are the teachings Paul provided to the Romans
in his letter to them:

For I am not ashamed of the gospel, for it is
the power of God for salvation to everyone who
believes, to the Jew first and also to the Greek.
For in it the righteousness of God is revealed
from faith for faith, as it is written, "The righteous shall live by faith." (Romans 1:16–17)

For the wrath of God is revealed from heaven
against all ungodliness and unrighteousness of
men, who by their unrighteousness suppress the
truth. For what can be known about God is plain
to them, because God has shown it to them. For
his invisible attributes, namely, his eternal power
and divine nature, have been clearly perceived,
ever since the creation of the world, in the things
that have been made. So they are without excuse.
For although they knew God, they did not honor

him as God or give thanks to him, but they became futile in their thinking, and their foolish hearts were darkened. Claiming to be wise, they became fools, and exchanged the glory of immortal God for images resembling mortal man and birds and animals and creepy things. Therefore God gave them up in the lusts of their hearts to impurity, to the dishonoring of their bodies among themselves, because they exchanged the truth about God for a lie and worshipped and served the creature rather than the Creator, who is blessed forever! Amen. (Romans 1:18–25)

Therefore you have no excuse, O man, every one of you who judges. For in passing judgment on another you condemn yourself, because you, the judge, practice the very same things. We know that the judgment of God rightly falls on those who practice such things. Do you suppose, O man—you who judge those who practice such things and yet do them yourself—that you will escape the judgment of God? (Romans 2:1–3)

There will be trouble and distress for every human being who does evil, but glory and honor and peace for everyone who does good. (Romans 2:9–11)

But now the righteousness of God has been manifested apart from the law, although the Law and the prophets bear witness to it—the righteousness of God through faith in Jesus Christ for all who believe. For there is no distinction: for all have sinned and fall short of the Glory of God, and are justified by his grace as a gift, through the redemption that is in Christ Jesus, whom God put forward as a propitiation by his blood, to be received by faith. This was to show God's righteousness, because in his divine forbearance he had passed over former sins. It was to show his righteousness at the present time, so that he might be just and the justifier of the one who has faith in Jesus. (Romans 3:21–26)

Paul spoke in depth about what truly makes us righteous. We are not saved just by following the Law of the Old Testament (as many people believed) but by having faith in Jesus as our Savior. We cannot earn our salvation just by doing good works. We do good works because of our faith in Jesus.

Therefore, since we have been justified by faith, we have peace with God through our Lord Jesus Christ. (Romans 5:1)

We rejoice in our sufferings, knowing that suffering produces endurance, and endurance produces character, and character produces hope, and hope does not put us to shame, because God's love has been poured into our hearts through the Holy Spirit who has been given to us. (Romans 5:3)

For while we were still weak, at the right time Christ died for the ungodly. For one would scarcely die for a righteous person—though perhaps for a good person one would dare even to die—but God shows his love for us in that while we were still sinners, Christ died for us. Since, therefore, we have now been justified by his blood, much more shall we be saved by him from the wrath of God. For if while we were enemies we were reconciled to God by the death of his

Son, much more, now that we are reconciled, shall we be saved by his life. (Romans 5:6–10)

Sin and death entered the whole world by the sinning of just one man, Adam. Likewise, justification and life for all men entered the whole world by one act of righteousness by Jesus Christ.

Therefore, as one trespass led to condemnation for all men, so one act of righteousness leads to justification and life for all men. For as by the one man's disobedience [Adam's] the many were made sinners, so by the one man's obedience [Jesus's] the many will be made righteous. (Romans 5:18–19)

As sin reigned in death, grace also might reign through righteousness leading to eternal life through Jesus Christ our Lord. (Romans 5:21)

But the free gift is not like the trespass. For if many died through one man's trespass [Adam's], much more have the grace of God and the free gift by the grace of that one man Jesus Christ abounded for many. And the free gift is not like the result of that one man's sin. For the judgment following one trespass brought condemnation, but the free gift following many trespasses brought justification. For if, because of one man's trespass, death reigned through that one man, much more will those who receive the abundance of grace and the free gift of righteousness reign in life through the one man Jesus Christ. (Romans 5:16–17)

Do you not know that all of us who have been baptized into Christ Jesus were baptized into his death? We were buried therefore with

him by baptism into death, in order that, just
as Christ was raised from the dead by the glory
of the Father, we too might walk in newness of
life. For if we have been united with him in a
death like his, we shall certainly be united with
him in a resurrection like this. We know that our
old self was crucified with him in order that the
body of sin might be brought to nothing, so that
we would no longer be enslaved to sin. For one
who has died has been set free from sin. Now
if we died with Christ, we believe that we will
also live with him. We know that Christ, being
raised from the dead, will never die again; death
no longer has dominion over him. For the death
he died he died to sin, once for all, but the life he
lives he lives to God. So you must also consider
yourselves dead to sin and alive to God in Christ
Jesus. (Romans 6:1–11)

Let not sin therefore reign in your mortal body to make you obey its passions. Do not
present your members to sin as instruments for
unrighteousness, but present yourselves to God
as those who have been brought from death to
life, and your members to God as instruments for
righteousness. (Romans 6:12–13)

Do you not know that if you present yourselves to anyone as obedient slaves, you are slaves
to the one whom you obey, either sin, which
leads to death, or of obedience, which leads to
righteousness? (Romans 6:16)

You were once slaves of sin and have become
obedient from the heart to the standard of teaching to which you were committed, and having

been set free from sin, have become slaves to righteousness. (Romans 6:17–18)

For when you were slaves of sin, you were free in regards to righteousness. But what fruit were you getting at that time from the things of which you are now ashamed? For the end of those things is death. But now that you have been set free from sin and have become slaves of God, the fruit you get leads to sanctification and its end, eternal life. For the wages of sin is death, but the free gift of God is eternal life in Christ Jesus our Lord. (Romans 6:20–23)

There is therefore now no condemnation for those who are in Christ Jesus. For the law of the Spirit of life has set you free in Christ Jesus from the law of sin and death. (Romans 8:1–2)

For all who are led by the Spirit of God are sons of God. For you did not receive the spirit of slavery to fall back into fear, but you have received the Spirit of adoption as sons, by whom we cry, "Abba, Father!" The Spirit Himself bears witness to our spirit that we are children of God, and if children, then heirs—heirs of God and fellow heirs with Jesus Christ, provided we suffer with him in order that we may also be glorified with him. (Romans 8:14–17)

Our spirits groan inside us because they cannot wait to be with God in heaven. In heaven, we will be adopted children of God, living in redeemed heavenly bodies. (Summary of Romans 8:18–25)

If we don't know exactly what to pray for, ask God to guide us on what to pray for, and the Holy Spirit will help us. (Summary of Romans 8:26–27)

And we know that for those who love God all things work together for good, for those who are called according to his purpose. For those whom he foreknew he also predestined to be conformed to the image of his Son, in order that he may be the firstborn among many brothers. And those who he predestined he also called, and those whom he called he also justified, and those whom he justified he also glorified. (Romans 8:28–30)

If God is for us, who can be against us? He who did not spare his own Son but gave him up for us all, how will he not also with him graciously give us all things? (Romans 8:31–32)

Who shall bring any charge against God's elect? It is God who justifies. Who is to condemn? Christ Jesus is the one who died—more than that, who was raised—who is at the right hand of God, who is indeed interceding for us. Who shall separate us from the love of Christ? Shall tribulation, or distress, or persecution, or famine, or nakedness, or danger or sword? No, in all these things we are more than conquers through him who loved us. For I am sure that neither death nor life, nor angels nor rulers, nor things present nor things to come, nor powers, nor height nor depth, nor anything else in all creation, will be able to separate us from the love of God in Christ Jesus our Lord. (Romans 8:33–39)

THE APOSTLE PAUL TELLS US HOW TO BE SAVED

If you confess with your mouth that Jesus is Lord and believe in your heart that God raised him from the dead, you will be saved. For the scripture says "Everyone who believes in Jesus will not be put to shame." Jesus gives riches to all who call on him. For everyone who calls on the name of the Lord will be saved. (Romans 10:9–13)

Do not be conformed to this world, but be transformed by the renewal of your mind, that by testing you may discern what is the will of God, what is good and acceptable and perfect. (Romans 12:2)

For as in one body we have many members, and the members do not all have the same function, so we, though many, are one body in Christ, and individually members of one another. Having gifts that differ according to the grace given to us, let us use them. If prophecy, in proportion to our faith; if service, in our serving; the one who teaches, in his teaching; the one who exhorts, in his exhortation; the one who contributes, in generosity; the one who leads, with zeal; the one who does acts of mercy, with cheerfulness. (Romans 12:4–8)

Romans 12:9–21 gives a great summary of how we are supposed to act as followers of Jesus:

Let love be genuine. Abhor what is evil, hold fast to what is good. Love one another in brotherly affection. Outdo one another in showing honor. Do not be slothful in zeal, be fervent in spirit, serve the Lord. Rejoice in hope, be patient in tribulation, be constant in prayer. Contribute to the needs of the saints and seek to show hospitality.

Bless those who persecute you; bless and do not curse them. Rejoice with those who rejoice, weep with those who weep. Live in harmony with one another. Do not be haughty, but associate with the lowly. Never be wise in your own sight. Repay no one evil for evil, but give thought to do what is honorable in the sight of all. If possible, so far as it depends on you, live peaceably with all. Beloved, never avenge yourselves, but leave it to the wrath of God, for it is written, "Vengeance is mine, I will repay, says the Lord." To the contrary, "if your enemy is hungry, feed him; if he is thirsty, give him something to drink; for by doing so you will heap burning coals on his head." Do not be overcome by evil, but overcome evil with good.

Owe no one anything, except to love each other, for the one who loves another has fulfilled the law. For the commandments, "You shall not commit adultery, You shall not murder, You shall not steal, You shall not covet," and any other commandment, are summed up in this word: "You shall love your neighbor as yourself." Love does no wrong to a neighbor; therefore love is the fulfilling of the law. (Romans 13:8–10)

We who are strong have an obligation to bear with the failings of the weak, and not to please ourselves. Let each of us please his neighbor for his good, to build him or her up. For Jesus did not please himself, but as it is written, "The reproaches of those who reproached you fell on me." (Romans 15:1–3)

I appeal to you, brothers, to watch out for those who cause divisions and create obstacles contrary to the doctrine that you have been taught; avoid them. For such persons do not serve our Lord Jesus Christ, but their own appetites, and by smooth talk and flattery they deceive the hearts of the naïve. For your obedience is known to all, so that I rejoice over you, but I want you to be wise as to what is good and innocent to what is evil. The God of peace will soon crush Satan under your feet. The grace of our Lord Jesus Christ be with you. (Romans 16:17–20)

THE FIRST LETTER OF PAUL TO THE CORINTHIANS

Paul's introduction to the people of the church of Corinth in his first letter to them:

Paul, called by the will of God to be an apostle of Christ Jesus, and our brother Sosthenes, To the church of God that is in Corinth, to those sanctified in Christ Jesus, called to be saints together with all those who in every place call upon the name of our Lord Jesus Christ, both their Lord and ours: Grace to you and peace from God our Father and the Lord Jesus Christ. (1 Corinthians 1:1–3)

For the word of the cross is folly to those who are perishing, but to us who are being saved it is the power of God. For it is written, 'I will destroy the wisdom of the wise, and the discernment of the discerning I will thwart.' Where is the one who is wise? Where is the scribe? Where is the debater of this age? Has not God made foolish the wisdom of the world? For since, in the wisdom of God, the world did not know God through wisdom, it pleased God through the folly of what we preach to save those who believe. For Jews demand signs and Greeks seek wisdom, but we preach Christ crucified, a stumbling block to Jews and folly to Gentiles, but to those who are called, both Jews and Greeks, Christ the power of God and the wisdom of God. For the foolishness of God is wiser than men, and the weakness of God is stronger than men. (1 Corinthians 1:18–25)

For consider your calling, brothers: not many of you were wise according to worldly standards, not many were powerful, not many were of noble birth. But God chose what is foolish in the world to shame the wise; God chose what is weak in the world to shame the strong; God chose what is low and despised in the world, even things that are not, to bring to nothing things that are, so that no human being might boast in the presence of God. And because of him you are in Christ Jesus, who became to us wisdom from God, righteousness and sanctification and redemption, so that, as it is written, "Let the one who boasts, boast in the Lord." (1 Corinthians 1:26–31)

What no eyes have seen, nor ear heard, nor the heart of man imagined, what God has prepared for those who love him. (1 Corinthians 2:9)

Do you not know that you are God's temple and God's spirit lives in you? If anyone destroys God's temple, God will destroy him. For God's temple is holy, and you are that temple. (1 Corinthians 3:15–17).

Do you not know that your bodies are members of Christ? Do you not know that your body is a temple of the Holy Spirit within you, whom you have from God? You are not your own, for you were bought with a price. So glorify God in your body. (1 Corinthians 6:15 and 19–20)

For us there is one God, the Father, from whom are all things and for whom we exist, and one Lord, Jesus Christ, through whom are all things and through whom we exist. (1 Corinthians 8:6)

No temptation has overtaken you that is not common to man. God is faithful, and he will not let you be tempted beyond your ability, but with the temptation he will also provide the way of escape, that you may be able to endure it. (1 Corinthians 10:13)

Let no one seek his own good, but the good of his neighbor. (1 Corinthians 10:24)

The apostle Paul said in his letter to the Corinthians:

For I received from the Lord what I also delivered to you, that the Lord Jesus on the night when he was betrayed took bread, and when he had given thanks, he broke it, and said, 'This is my body which is for you. Do this in remembrance of me.' In the same way he also took the cup, after supper, saying, "This cup is the new covenant in my blood. Do this as often as you drink it, in remembrance of me." For as often as you eat this bread and drink this cup, you proclaim the Lord's death until he comes. (1 Corinthians 11:23–26)

When we are judged by the Lord, we are disciplined so that we may not be condemned along with the world. (1 Corinthians 11:32)

Therefore I want you to understand that no one speaking in the Spirit of God ever says "Jesus is accursed!" and no one can say "Jesus is Lord" except in the Holy Spirit. (1 Corinthians 11:3).

Now there are varieties of gifts, but the same Spirit; and there are varieties of service, but the same Lord; and there are varieties of activities, but it is the same God who empowers them all in everyone. To each is given the manifestation of the Spirit of the common good. (1 Corinthians 12:4–7)

We all have jobs to do as members of the family or body of Jesus. Just as each of our body parts are different and have specific jobs to do, and each part is important (1 Corinthians 12:14–31).

On a personal note, the following passage is one of my favorite passages in all the Bible. If we keep what this passage says in mind and implement it every time we interact with others and with God, I believe we will be doing what God wants us to do as his children. Paul wrote this in his first letter to the Corinthians:

If I speak in the tongues of men and of angels, but do not have love, I am a noisy gong or clanging cymbal. And if I have prophetic powers, and understand all mysteries and all knowledge, and if I have all faith, so as to remove mountains, but have not love, I am nothing. If I give away all I have, and if I deliver up my body to be burned, but have not love, I gain nothing. Love is patient and kind; love does not envy or boast; it is not arrogant or rude, it does not insist on its own way; it is not irritable or resentful; it does not rejoice at wrongdoing, but rejoices with the truth. Love bears all things, believes all things, hopes all things, endures all things. Love never ends. As for prophecies, they will pass away; as for tongues, they will cease; as for knowledge, it will pass away. For we know in part and we prophesy in part, but when the perfect comes, the partial will pass away. When I was a child, I thought like a child, I reasoned like a child. When I became a man, I gave up childish ways. For now we see in a mirror dimly, but then face to face. Now I know in part; then I shall know fully, even as I have been fully known. So now faith, hope, and love abide, these three; but the greatest of these is love. (1 Corinthians 13:1–13)

Brothers, do not be children in your thinking. Be infants in evil, but in your thinking be mature. (1 Corinthians 14:20)

The apostle Paul's testimony about Jesus to the Corinthians:

For I delivered to you as of first importance what I also received: that Christ died for our sins in accordance with the scriptures, that he was buried, that he was raised on the third day in accordance with the scriptures, and that he appeared to Cephas, then to the twelve. Then he appeared to more than five hundred brothers at one time, most of whom are still alive, though some have fallen asleep. Then he appeared to James, then to all the apostles. Last of all, as to one untimely born, he appeared also to me. For I am the least of the apostles, unworthy to be called an apostle, because I persecuted the church of God. But by the grace of God I am what I am, and his grace toward me was not in vain. On the contrary, I worked harder than any of them, though it was not I, but the grace of God that is with me. Whether then it was I or they, so we preach and so you believed. (1 Corinthians 15:3–11)

But in fact Christ has been raised from the dead, the firstfruits of those who have fallen asleep. For as by a man came death [Adam], by a man has come also the resurrection of the dead [Jesus]. For as in Adam all die, so also in Christ shall all be made alive. But each in his own order; Christ the firstfruits, then at his coming those who belong to Christ. Then comes the end, when he delivers the kingdom to God the Father after destroying every rule and every authority and every power. For he must reign until he has put all enemies under his feet. The last enemy to be destroyed is death. For "God has put all things in subjection under his feet." When all things are subjected to him, then the Son himself will also be subjected to him who put all things in subjection under him, that God may be all in all. (1 Corinthians 15:20–28)

Paul informs the Corinthians that those who follow Jesus will get a resurrected body.

But someone will ask, "How are the dead raised? With what kind of body do they come?" You foolish person! What you sow does not come to life unless it dies. And what you sow is not the body that is to be, but a bare kernel, perhaps of wheat or of some other grain. But God gives it a body as he has chosen, and to each kind of seed its own body. For not all flesh is the same, but there is one kind for humans, another for animals, another for birds, and another for fish. There are heavenly bodies and earthly bodies, but the glory of the heavenly is of one kind, and the glory of the earthly is of another.

So it is with the resurrection of the dead. What is sown is perishable; what is raised is imperishable. It is sown in dishonor; it is raised in glory. It is sown in weakness; it is raised in power. It is sown a natural body; it is raised a spiritual body. If there is a natural body, there is also a spiritual body. Thus it is written, "The first man Adam became a living being, the last Adam [Jesus] became a life-giving spirit." But it is not the spiritual that is first but the natural, and then the spiritual. The first man was from the earth, a man of dust; the second man is from heaven. As was the man of dust, so also are those who are of the dust, and as is the man of heaven, so also are those who are of heaven. Just as we have born the image of the man of dust, we shall also bear the image of the man of heaven [Jesus]. I tell you this, brothers: flesh and blood cannot inherit the kingdom of God, nor does the perishable inherit the imperishable. Behold! I tell you a mystery. We shall not all sleep, but we shall all be changed, in a moment, in the twinkling of an eye, at the last trumpet. For the trumpet will sound, and the dead will be raised imperishable, and we shall be changed. For this perishable body must put on the imperishable, and this mortal body must put on immortality. When the perishable puts on the imperishable, and the mortal puts on immortality, then shall come to pass the saying that is written: "Death is swallowed up in victory. O death, where is your victory? O death, where is your sting?" (1 Corinthians 15:35–55)

THE SECOND LETTER OF PAUL TO THE CORINTHIANS

Paul wrote a second letter to the people of the Christian churches in Corinth. Here are some of the teachings in that letter:

[Summary] God comforts and helps us so that we are in good shape to comfort and help other people. (2 Corinthians 1:3–7)

For we do not want you to be ignorant, brothers, of the affliction we experienced in Asia. For we were so utterly burdened beyond our strength that we despaired of life itself. Indeed, we felt that we had received the sentence of death. But that was to make us rely not on ourselves but on God who raises the dead. He delivered us from such a deadly peril, and he will deliver us. On him we have set our hope that he will deliver us again. (2 Corinthians 1:8–10)

And even if our gospel is veiled, it is veiled only to those who are perishing. In their case the god of this world has blinded the minds of the unbelievers, to keep them from seeing the light of the gospel of the glory of Christ, who is the image of God. For what we proclaim is not ourselves, but Jesus Christ as Lord, with ourselves as your servants for Jesus's sake. (2 Corinthians 4:3–5)

For God, who said, "Let light shine out of darkness," has shown in our hearts to give the light of the knowledge of the glory of God in the face of Jesus Christ. But we have this treasure in jars of clay, to show that the surpassing power belongs to God and not to us. We are afflicted in every way, but not crushed; perplexed, but not driven to despair; persecuted, but not forsaken; struck down, but not destroyed; always carrying in the body the death of Jesus, so that the life of Jesus may also be manifested in our bodies. For we who live are always being given over to death for Jesus's sake, so that the life of Jesus also may be manifested in our mortal flesh. So death is at work in us, but life in you. (2 Corinthians 4:6–12)

He who raised the Lord Jesus will raise us also with Jesus and bring us with you into his presence. (2 Corinthians 4:14)

We do not lose heart. Though our outer self is wasting away, our inner self is being renewed day by day. For this light momentary affliction is preparing us for an eternal weight of glory beyond all comparison, as we look not to the things that are seen but to the things that are unseen. For the things that are seen are temporary, but the things that are unseen are eternal. (2 Corinthians 4:16–18)

For we know that if the tent that is our earthly home is destroyed [our body], we have a building from God, a house not made by hands, eternal in the heavens. For while we are still in this tent, we groan, being burdened—not that we would be unclothed, but that we would be further clothed, so that what is mortal may be swallowed up by life. He who has prepared us for this very thing is God, who has given us the Spirit as a guarantee. (2 Corinthians 5:1–5)

For we must all appear before the judgment seat of Christ, so that each one may receive what is due for what he has done in the body, whether good or evil. (2 Corinthians 5:10)

Jesus took all of our sins and placed them on himself when he was crucified, so we will be reconciled with God and he will now forgive us of our sins if we come to him. We are ambassadors for Jesus to other people in the world. God sends his messages about himself to the rest of the world through his followers. We are the ones who spread his messages to everyone. (Summary of 2 Corinthians 5:16–20)

We implore you on behalf of Christ, to be reconciled to God. For our sake he made him to be sin who knew no sin, so that in him we might become the righteousness of God. (2 Corinthians 5:21)

God says to his people, "I will make my dwelling among them and walk among them, and I will be their God, and they shall be my people. Therefore, go out from their midst, and separate from them, says the Lord, and touch no unclean thing; then I will welcome you, and I will be a father to you, and you shall be sons and daughters to me, says the Lord Almighty." Since we have these promises, beloved, let us cleanse ourselves from every defilement of body and spirit, bringing holiness to completion in the fear of God. (2 Corinthians 6:16–18)

Whoever sows sparingly will also reap sparingly, and whoever sows bountifully will also reap bountifully. Each one must give as he decided in his heart, not reluctantly or under compulsion, for God loves a cheerful giver. And God is able to make all grace abound to you, so that having sufficiency in all things at all times, you may abound in every good work. As it is written, "He has distributed freely, he has given to the poor; his righteousness endures forever." You will be enriched in every way to be generous in every way, which through us will produce thanksgiving to God. (2 Corinthians 9:6–11)

For although we walk in the flesh, we are not waging war according to the flesh. For the weapons of our warfare are not of the flesh but have divine power to destroy strongholds. We destroy arguments and every lofty opinion raised against the knowledge of God, and take every thought captive to obey Christ, being ready to punish every disobedience, when your obedience is complete. (2 Corinthians 10:3–6)

Let the one wo boasts, boast in the Lord. For it is not the one who commend himself who is approved, but the one whom the Lord commends. (2 Corinthians 10:17)

Paul details the difficulties he has endured as an apostle of Jesus:

But whatever anyone else dares to boast of—I am speaking as a fool—I also dare to boast of that. Are they Hebrews? So am I. Are they Israelites? So am I. Are they offspring of Abraham? So am I. Are they servants of Christ? I am a better one—I am talking like a madman—with far greater labors, far more imprisonments, with countless beatings, and often near death. Five times I received at the hands of the Jews forty lashes less one. Three times I was beaten with rods. Once I was stoned. Three times I was shipwrecked; a night and a day I was adrift at sea; on frequent journeys, in danger from rivers, danger from robbers, danger from my own people, danger from Gentiles, danger in the city, danger in the wilderness, danger at sea, danger from false brothers, in toil and hardship, through many a sleepless night, in hunger and thirst, often without food, in cold and exposure. And, apart from other things, there is the daily pressure on me of my anxiety for all the churches. Who is weak, and I am not weak? Who is made to fall, and I am not indignant? (2 Corinthians 11:21–29)

Fourteen years ago I [Paul] was taken up to heaven, taken to paradise. I heard things which cannot be told, which man may not speak of. To keep me from being conceited because of the surpassing greatness of the revelations, a thorn was given me in the flesh, a messenger of Satan to harass me to keep me from becoming conceited. Three times I pleaded with the Lord about this, that it should leave me. But he said to me "My grace is sufficient for you, for my power is made perfect in weakness." For the sake of Christ, then, I am content with weakness, insults, hardships, persecutions and calamities. For when I am weak, then I am strong. (2 Corinthians 12:2–10)

Examine yourselves, to see whether you are in the faith. Test yourselves. Or do you not realize this about yourselves, that Jesus Christ is in you? (2 Corinthians 13:5)

Finally brothers, rejoice. Aim for restoration, comfort one another, agree with one another, live in peace: and the God of love and peace will be with you. (2 Corinthians 13:11).

THE LETTER OF THE APOSTLE PAUL TO THE GALATIANS

The apostle Paul told the people of Galatia:

For I would have you know brothers, that the gospel that was preached by me is not man's gospel. For I did not receive it from any man, nor was I taught it, but I received it through a revelation of Jesus Christ. (Galatians 1:11)

But when he who had set me apart before I was born, and who called me by his grace, was pleased to reveal his Son to me, in order that I might preach him among the Gentiles, I did not immediately consult with anyone, nor did I go up to Jerusalem to those who were apostles before me, but I went away into Arabia, and returned again to Damascus. Then after three years I went up to Jerusalem to visit Cephas [Peter] and remained with him for fifteen days. And I was still unknown in person to the churches of Judea that are in Christ. They only were hearing it said, "He who used to persecute us is now preaching the faith he once tried to destroy." And they glorified God because of me. (Galatians 1:15–24)

God sent Peter to teach the Jewish people about Jesus, and God sent Paul to teach everyone else about Jesus. (Galatians 2:7)

Yet we know that a person is not justified by works of the law but through faith in Jesus Christ, so we also have believed in Christ Jesus, in order to be justified by faith in Christ and not by works of the law, because by works of the law no one will be justified. (Galatians 2:15–16)

I have been crucified with Christ. It is no longer I who live, but Christ who lives in me. And the life I now live in the flesh I live by faith in the Son of God, who loved me and gave himself for me. (Galatians 2:20)

Christ redeemed us from the curse of the law by becoming a curse for us—for it is written, "Cursed is everyone who is hanged on a tree"—so that in Christ Jesus the blessing of Abraham might come to the gentiles, so that we might receive the promised spirit through faith. (Galatians 3:13)

Why were we given the law? It was added because of transgressions, until the offspring should come to whom the promise had been made, and it was put in place through angels by an intermediary. (Galatians 3:19)

Now before faith came, we were held captive under the law, imprisoned until the coming faith would be revealed. So then the law was our guardian until Christ came, in order that we might be justified by faith. But now that our faith has come, we are no longer under a guardian, for in Christ Jesus you are all sons of God through faith. For as many of you as were baptized into Christ have put on Christ. There is neither Jew nor Greek, slave nor free, there is no male and female, for you are all one in Christ Jesus. And if you are Christ's, then you are Abraham's offspring, heirs to the promise. (Galatians 3:23–29)

I mean that the heir, as long as he is a child, is no different from a slave, though he is the owner of everything, but he is under guardians and managers until the date set by his father. In the same way we also, when we were children, were enslaved by the elementary principles of the world. But when the fullness of time had come, God sent forth his son, born of woman, born under the law, so that we might receive adoptions as sons. And because you are sons, God has sent the Spirit of his Son into your hearts, crying, "Abba, Father!" So you are no longer a slave, but a son, and if a son, then an heir through God. (Galatians 4:1–7)

Formerly, when you did not know God, you were enslaved to those that by nature are not gods. But now that you have come to know God, or rather to be known by God, how can you turn back again to the weak and worthless elementary principles of the world, whose slaves you want to be once more? (Galatians 4:8–9)

For you were called to freedom, brothers. Only do not use your freedom as an opportunity for the flesh, but through love serve one another. For the whole law is fulfilled in one word: "You shall love your neighbor as yourself." But if you bite and devour one another, watch out that you are not consumed by one another. (Galatians 5:13–15)

But I say, walk by the Spirit, and you will not gratify the desires of the flesh. For the desires of the flesh are against the Spirit, and the desires of the Spirit are against the flesh, for these are opposed to each other, to keep you from doing the things you want to do. Now the works of the flesh are evident: sexual immorality, impurity, sensuality, idolatry, sorcery, enmity, strife, jealousy, fits of anger, rivalries, dissensions, divisions, envy, drunkenness, and things like these. I warn you, as I warned you before, that those who do such things will not inherit the kingdom of God. But the fruit of the Spirit is love, joy, peace, patience, kindness, goodness, faithfulness, gentleness, self-control; against such things there is no law. And those who belong to Christ Jesus have crucified the flesh with its passions and its desires. If we live by the Spirit, let us also walk by the Spirit. Let us not become conceited, provoking one another, envying one another. (Galatians 5:16–26)

Brothers, if anyone is caught in any transgression, you who are spiritual should restore him in a spirit of gentleness. Keep watch on yourself, lest you too be tempted. Bear one another's burdens, and so fulfill the law of Christ. (Galatians 6:1–2)

Let us not grow tired of doing good, for in due season we will be rewarded for it, if we do not give up. So then, when we have the opportunity, let us do good to everyone, and especially to those who are of the household of faith. (Galatians 6:9–10)

THE LETTER OF THE APOSTLE PAUL TO THE EPHESIANS

Blessed be the God and Father of our Lord Jesus Christ, who has blessed us in Christ with every spiritual blessing in the heavenly places, even as he chose us in him before the foundation of the world, that we should be holy and blameless before him. In love he predestined us for adoption as sons through Jesus Christ. In him we have redemption through his blood, the forgiveness of our trespasses, according to his purpose, which he set forth in Christ as a plan for the fullness of time, to unite all things in him, things in heaven and things on earth. (Summary of Ephesians 1:3–10)

In him [Jesus] we have obtained an inheritance. In him you also, when you heard the word of truth, the gospel of your salvation, and believed in him, were sealed with the promise of the Holy Spirit, who is the guarantee of our inheritance until we acquire possession of it, to the praise of his glory. (Summary of Ephesians 1:11–14)

God the Father worked his great might in his Son.

Jesus Christ when he raised him from the dead and seated him at his right hand in the heavenly places, far above all rule and authority and power and dominion, and above every name that is named, not only in this age but in the one to come. And he put all things under his feet and gave him as head over all things to the church, which is his body, the fullness of him who fills all in all. (Ephesians 1:20–23)

And you were dead in trespasses and sins in which you once walked, following the course of this world, following the prince of the power of the air, the spirit that is now at work in the sons of disobedience—among whom we all once lived in the passions of our flesh, carrying out the desires of the body and the mind, and were by nature children of wrath, like the rest of mankind. But God, being rich in mercy, because of the great love with which he loved us, even when we were dead in our trespasses, made us alive together with Christ—by grace you have been saved—and raised us up with him and seated us with him in the heavenly places in Christ Jesus, so that in the coming ages he might show the immeasurable riches of his grace in kindness toward us in Christ Jesus. For by grace you have been saved through faith. And this is not your own doing; it is the gift of God, not the result of works, so that no one may boast. For we are his workmanship, created in Christ Jesus for good works, which God prepared beforehand, that we should walk in them. (Ephesians 2:1–10)

But now in Christ Jesus you who were once far off have been brought near by the blood of Christ. For he himself is our peace, who has made us both one and has broken down in his flesh the dividing wall of hostility by abolishing the law of commandments expressed in ordinances, that he might create in himself one new man in place of the two, so making peace, and might reconcile us both to God in one body through the cross, thereby killing the hostility. (Ephesians 2:13–16)

For through Jesus we both have access in one Spirit to the Father. So then you are no longer strangers and aliens, but you are fellow citizens with the saints and members of the household of God, built on the foundation of the apostles and prophets, Christ Jesus himself being the cornerstone, in whom the whole structure, being joined together, grows into a holy temple in the Lord. In him you also are being built together into a dwelling place for God by the Spirit. (Ephesians 2:18–22)

Speaking the truth in love, we are to grow up in every way into him who is the head, into Christ, from whom the whole body, joined and held together by every joint with which it is equipped, when each part is working properly, makes the body grow so that it builds itself up in love. (Ephesians 4:15–16)

Put off your old self, which belongs to your former manner of life and is corrupt through deceitful desires, and be renewed in the spirit of your minds, and put on the new self, created after the likeness of God in true righteousness and holiness. (Ephesians 4:22–24)

Therefore, having put away falsehood, let each one of you speak the truth with his neighbor, for we are members one of another. Be angry and do not sin; do not let the sun go down on your anger, and give no opportunity to the devil. Let the thief no longer steal, but rather let him labor, doing honest work with his own hands, so that he may have something to share with anyone in need. Let no corrupting talk come out of your mouths, but only such as is good for building up, as fits the occasion, that it may give grace to those who hear. And do not grieve the Holy Spirit of God, by whom you were sealed for the day of redemption. Let all bitterness and wrath and anger and clamor and slander be put away from you, along with all malice. Be kind to one another, tenderhearted, forgiving one another, as God in Christ forgave you. (Ephesians 4:25–32)

Therefore be imitators of God, as beloved children. And walk in love, as Christ loves us and gave himself up for us, a fragrant offering and sacrifice to God. (Ephesians 5:1–2)

But sexual immorality and all impurity or covetousness must not even be named among you, as is proper among saints. Let there be no filthiness nor foolish talk nor crude joking, which are out of place, but instead let there be thanksgiving. For you may be sure of this, that everyone who is sexually immoral or impure, or who is covetous [that is, an idolator], has no inheritance in the kingdom of God. (Ephesians 3–5)

At one time you were in darkness, but now you are light in the Lord. Walk as children of light [for the fruit of light is found in all that is good and right and true], and try to discern what is pleasing to the lord. Take no part in the unfruitful works of the darkness, but instead expose them. For it is shameful even to speak of the things they do in secret. But when anything is exposed by the light, it becomes visible, for anything that becomes visible is light. Therefore it says, "Awake, O sleeper, and arise from the dead, and Christ will shine on you." (Ephesians 5:8–14)

Do not get drunk with wine, for that is debauchery, but be filled with the Spirit, addressing one another in psalms and hymns and spiritual songs, singing and making melody to the Lord with your heart, giving thanks always and for everything to God the Father in the name of our Lord Jesus Christ, submitting to one another out of reverence for Christ. (Ephesians 5:18–21)

Wives, submit to your own husbands, as to the Lord. For the husband is the head of the wife even as Christ is the head of the Church, his body, and is himself the savior. Now as the church submits to Christ, so also wives should submit in everything to their husbands. Husbands, love your wives, as Christ loved the church and gave himself up for her, that he might sanctify her, having cleansed her by the washing of water with the word, so that he might present the church to himself in splendor, without spot or wrinkle or any such thing, that she might be holy and without blemish. In the same way husbands should love their wives as their own bodies. He who loves his wife loves himself. For no one ever hated his own flesh, but nourishes and cherishes it, just as Christ does the church, because we are all members of his body. "Therefore a man shall leave his father and mother and hold fast to his wife, and the two shall become one flesh." This mystery is profound, and I am saying that it refers to Christ and the church. However, let each one of you love his wife as himself, and let the wife see that she respects the husband. (Ephesians 5:22–33)

Children, obey your parents in the Lord, for this is right. "Honor your father and mother" [this is the first commandment with a promise], "that it may go well with you and that you may live long in the land." Fathers, do not provoke your children to anger, but bring them up in the discipline and instruction of the Lord. (Ephesians 6:1–4)

Finally, be strong in the Lord and in the strength of his might. Put on the whole armor of God, that you may be able to stand against the schemes of the devil. For we do not wrestle against flesh and blood, but against the rulers, against the authorities, against the cosmic powers over this present darkness, against the spiritual forces of evil in heavenly places. Therefore take up the whole armor of God, that you may be able to withstand in the evil day, and having done all, to stand firm. Stand therefore, having fastened on the belt of truth, and having put on the breastplate of righteousness, and, as shoes for your feet, having put on the readiness given by the gospel of peace. In all circumstances take up the shield of faith, with which you can extinguish all the flaming darts of the evil one; and take the helmet of salvation, and the sword of the Spirit, which is the word of God, praying at all times in the Spirit, with all prayer and supplication. (Ephesians 6:10–18)

THE LETTER OF THE APOSTLE PAUL TO THE PHILIPPIANS

Paul appears to be with Timothy as he wrote this letter as evidenced by his introduction to the people of Philippi:

> Paul and Timothy, servants of Christ Jesus, to all the saints in Christ Jesus who are at Philippi, with the overseers and deacons. Grace to you and peace from God our Father and the Lord Jesus Christ. (Philippians 1:1–2)

Based on what Paul writes next, it appears that he might have written while he was imprisoned somewhere:

> And I am sure of this, that he who began a good work in you will bring it to completion at the day of Jesus Christ. It is right for me to feel this way about you all, because I hold you in my heart, for you are all partakers with me of grace, both in my imprisonment and in the defense and confirmation of the gospel. (Philippians 1:6–7)

Paul used his imprisonment as an opportunity to spread the message about Jesus as Lord and Savior throughout the imperial guard, who were his captors:

> I want you to know, brothers, that what has happened to me has really served to advance the gospel, so that it has become known throughout the whole imperial guard and to the rest that my imprisonment is for Christ. And most of the brothers, having become confident in the Lord by my imprisonment, and much more bold to speak the word without fear. Some indeed preach Christ from envy and rivalry, but others from good will. The latter do it out of love, know-

ing that I am put here for defense of the gospel.
(Philippians 1:12–16)

Paul realizes that he might eventually face death at the hands of one of his captors. (He had been imprisoned numerous times for preaching the Gospel of Jesus Christ.) Yet he also realizes that since he was a follower of Jesus, remaining alive or dying both had tremendous benefits and rewards:

> Yes, and I will rejoice, for I know that through your prayers and the help of the Spirit of Jesus Christ that this will turn out for my deliverance, as it is my eager expectation and hope that I will not be at all ashamed, but that with full courage now as always Christ will be honored in my body, whether by life or death. For me to live is Christ and to die is gain. If I am to live in the flesh, that means fruitful labor for me. Yet which I shall choose I cannot tell. I am hard-pressed between the two. My desire is to depart and be with Christ, for that is far better. But to remain in the flesh is more necessary on your account. Convinced of this, I know that I will remain and continue with you all, for your progress and joy in the faith, so that you may have ample cause to glory in Christ Jesus, because of my coming to you again. (Philippians 1:18–26)

> Only let your manner of life be worthy of the gospel of Christ, so that whether I come and see you or am absent, I may hear of you that you are standing firm in one spirit, with one mind striving side by side for the faith of the gospel, and not frightened in anything by your opponents. This is a clear sign to them of their destruction, but of your salvation, and that from

God. For it has been granted to you that for the sake of Christ you should not only believe in him but also suffer for his sake, engaged in the same conflict that you saw I had and now hear that I still have. (Philippians 1:27–30)

Do nothing from rivalry or conceit, but in humility count others more significant than yourselves. Let each of you look not only to his own interests, but also to the interests of others. Have this mind among yourselves, which is yours in Christ Jesus, who, though he was in the form of God, did not count equality with God a thing to be grasped, but made himself nothing, taking the form of a servant, being born in the likeness of men. And being found in human form, he humbled himself by becoming obedient to the point of death, even death on a cross. Therefore God has highly exalted him and bestowed on him the name that is above every name, so that at the name of Jesus every knee should bow, in heaven and on earth and under the earth, and every tongue confess that Jesus Christ is Lord, to the glory of God the Father. (Philippians 2:1–11)

Therefore, my beloved, as you have always obeyed, so now, not only as in my presence but much more in my absence, work out your own salvation with fear and trembling, for it is God who works in you, both to will and to work for his good pleasure. Do all things without grumbling or questioning, that you may be blameless and innocent, children of God without blemish in the midst of a crooked and twisted generation, among whom you shine as lights in the world, holding fast to the word of life, so that in the day of Christ I may be proud that I did not run in vain or labor in vain. Even if I am to be poured out as a drink offering upon the sacrificial offering of your faith, I am glad and rejoice with you all. Likewise you also should be glad and rejoice with me. (Philippians 2:12–18)

Whatever gain I had in fleshly things, I counted as loss for the sake of Christ. Indeed, I count everything as loss because of the surpassing worth of knowing that Christ Jesus is my Lord. For his sake I have suffered the loss of all things and count them as rubbish, in order that I may gain Christ and be found in him, not having a righteousness of my own that comes from the law, but that which comes through faith in Christ, the righteousness from God that depends on faith—that I may know him and the power of his resurrection, and may share in his sufferings, becoming like him in his death, that by any means possible I may attain the resurrection from the dead. (Philippians 3:7–11)

Not that I have already obtained this or am already perfect, but I press on to make it my own, because Christ Jesus made me his own. Brothers, I do not consider that I have made it my own. But one thing I do: forgetting what lies behind and straining forward to what lies ahead, I press on toward the goal for the prize of the upward call of God in Christ Jesus. (Philippians 3:12–14)

Brothers, join in imitating me, and keep your eyes on those who walk according to the example you have in us. For many, of whom I have often told you and now tell you even with tears, walk as enemies of the cross of Christ. Their end is destruction, their god is their belly, and they glory in their shame, with minds set on earthly things. But our citizenship is in heaven, and from it we await a Savior, the Lord Jesus Christ, who will transform our lowly body to be like his glorious body, by the power that enables him even to subject all things to himself. Therefore, my brothers, whom I love and long for, my joy and crown, stand firm thus in the Lord, my beloved. (Philippians 3:17–21)

Rejoice in the Lord always; again I will say, Rejoice. Let your reasonableness be known to everyone. The Lord is at hand; do not be anxious about anything, but in everything by prayer and supplication with thanksgiving let your requests be made known to God. And let the peace of God, which surpasses all understanding, will guard your hearts and your minds in Christ Jesus.

Finally, brothers, whatever is true, whatever is honorable, whatever is just, whatever is pure, whatever is lovely, whatever is commendable, of there is any excellence, if there is anything worthy of praise, think about these things. What you have learned and received and heard and seen in me—practice these things, and the God of peace be with you. (Philippians 4:4–9)

Not that I am speaking of being in need, for I have learned in whatever situation I am to be content. I know how to be brought low, and I know how to abound. In any and every circumstance, I have learned the secret of facing plenty and hunger, abundance and need. I can do all things through him who strengthens me. (Philippians 4:11–13)

And my God will supply every need of yours according to his riches in glory in Christ Jesus. To our God and Father be glory forever and ever. Amen. (Philippians 4:19–20)

THE LETTER OF THE APOSTLE PAUL TO THE COLOSSIANS

Paul was with Timothy when he wrote this letter to the church of Christ at Colossae.

May you be strengthened with all power, according to God's glorious might, for all endurance and patience with joy, giving thanks to the Father, who has qualified you to share in the inheritance of the saints in light. He has delivered us from the domain of darkness and transferred us to the kingdom of his beloved Son, in whom we have redemption, the forgiveness of sins. (Colossians 1:11–14)

Jesus is the image of the invisible God, the firstborn of all creation. For by him all things were created, in heaven and on earth, visible and invisible, whether thrones or dominions or rulers or authorities—all things were created through him and for him. And he is before all things, and in him all things hold together. And he is the head of the body, the church. He is the beginning, the firstborn from the dead, that in everything he might be preeminent. For in him all the fullness of God was pleased to dwell, and through him to reconcile to himself all things, whether on earth or in heaven, making peace by the blood of his cross. (Colossians 1:15–20)

And you, who once were alienated and hostile in mind, doing evil deeds, Jesus has now reconciled in his body of flesh by his death, in order to present you holy and blameless and above reproach for him, if indeed you continue in the faith, stable and steadfast, not shifting from the hope of the gospel that you heard, which has been proclaimed in all creation under heaven, and of which I, Paul, became a minister. (Colossians 1:21–23)

Now I rejoice in my sufferings for your sake, and in my flesh I am filling up what is lacking in Christ's afflictions for the sake of his body, that is, the church, of which I became a minister according to the stewardship from God that was given to me for you, to make the word of God fully known, the mystery hidden for ages and generations but now revealed to the saints. To them God chose to make known how great among the Gentiles are the riches of the glory of this mystery, which is Christ in you, the hope of glory. (Colossians 1:24–27)

See to it that no one takes you captive by philosophy and empty deceit, according to human tradition, according to the elemental spirits of the world, and not according to Christ. For in him the whole fullness of deity dwells bodily, and you have been filled in him, who is the head of all rule and authority. You have been buried with Christ in baptism, in which you were also raised with him through faith in the powerful working of God, who raised him from the dead.

And you, who were dead in your trespasses, God made alive together with him, having forgiven us all our trespasses, by cancelling the record of debt that stood against us with its legal demands. This he set aside, nailing it to the cross. He disarmed the rulers and authorities and put them to open shame, by triumphing over them in him. (Colossians 2:8–15)

Let no one disqualify you, insisting on asceticism and worship of angels. (Colossians 2:18)

If then you have been raised with Christ, seek the things that are above, where Christ is, seated at the right hand of God. Set your mind on things that are above, not on things that are on earth. For you have died, and your life is hidden with Christ in God. When Christ who is your life appears, then you will also appear with him in glory. (Colossians 3:1–4)

Put to death therefore what is earthly in you: sexual immorality, impurity, passion, evil desire, and covetousness, which is idolatry. On account of these things the wrath of God is coming. In these you too once walked, when you were living in them. But now you must put them all away: anger, wrath, malice, slander, and obscene talk from your mouth. Do not lie to one another, seeing that you have put off the old self with its practices and have put on the new self, which is being renewed in knowledge after the image of its creator. (Colossians 3:5–10)

Colossians 3:12–17 talks about the daily attitude you should have:

Put on then, as God's chosen ones, holy and beloved, compassionate hearts, kindness, humility, meekness, patience, bearing with one another and, if one has a complaint against another, forgiving each other; as the Lord has forgiven you, so you must also forgive. And above all these put on love, which binds everything together in perfect harmony. And let the peace of Christ rule in your hearts, to which indeed you were called in one body. And be thankful. Let the word of Christ dwell in you richly, teaching and admonishing one another in all wisdom, singing psalms and hymns and spiritual songs, with thankfulness in your hearts to God. And whatever you do, in word or deed, do everything in the name of the Lord Jesus, giving thanks to God the Father Through him. (Colossians 3:12–17)

Wives, submit to your husbands, as is fitting to the Lord. Husbands, love your wives, and do not be harsh with them. Children, obey your parents in everything, for this pleases the Lord. Fathers, do not provoke your children, lest they be discouraged. Whatever you do, work heartily, as for the Lord and not for men, knowing that from then Lord you will receive the inheritance as your reward. You are serving the Lord Christ. For the wrongdoer will be paid back for the wrong he has done, and there is no partiality. (Colossians 3:18–25)

The apostle Paul confirms that he was writing this letter to the Colossians from prison:

Continue steadfastly in prayer, being watchful in it with thanksgiving. At the same time, pray also for us, that God may open to us a door for the word, to declare the mystery of Christ, on account of which I am in prison—that I may make it clear, which is how I ought to speak. Walk in wisdom toward outsiders, making the best use of the time. Let your speech always be gracious, seasoned with salt, so that you may know how you ought to answer each person. (Colossians 4:2–6)

I Paul, write this greeting with my own hand. Remember my chains. Grace be with you. (Colossians 4:18)

THE FIRST LETTER OF PAUL TO THE THESSALONIANS

Paul was with Silvanus and Timothy when he wrote his first letter to the Thessalonians:

Paul, Silvanus, and Timothy, To the Church of the Thessalonians in God the Father and the Lord Jesus Christ: Grace to you and peace. (1 Thessalonians 1:1)

And we also thank God constantly for this, that when you received the word of God, which you heard from us, you accepted it not as the word of men but what it really is, the word of God, which is at work in you believers. (1 Thessalonians 2:13)

Paul informs the Thessalonian people that Satan was working to stop his preaching to them face-to-face about Jesus:

But since we were torn away from you, brothers, for a short time, in person not in heart, we endeavored the more eagerly and with great desire to see you face to face, because we wanted to come to you—I, Paul, again and again—but Satan hindered us. (1 Thessalonians 2:17–18)

For you know what instructions we gave you through the Lord Jesus. For this is the will of God, your sanctification: that you abstain from sexual immorality; that each one of you know how to control his own body in holiness and honor, not in the passion of lust like the Gentiles who do not know God; that no one transgresses and wrong his brother in this matter, because the Lord is an avenger in all these things, as we told you beforehand and solemnly warned you. For God has not called us for impurity, but in holiness. Therefore whoever disregards this, disregards not man but God, who gives his holy spirit to you. (1 Thessalonians 4:2–8)

But we do not want you to be uninformed, brothers, about those who are asleep, that you may not grieve as others do who have no hope. For since we believe that Jesus died and rose again, even so, through Jesus, God will bring with him those who have fallen asleep. For this we declare to you by a word from the Lord, that we who are alive, who are left until the coming of the Lord, will not precede those who have fallen asleep. For the Lord himself will descend from heaven with a cry of command, with the voice of an archangel. And with the sound of the trumpet of God. And the dead in Christ will rise first. Then we who are alive, who are left, will be caught up together with them in the clouds to meet the Lord in the air, and so we will always be with the Lord. Therefore encourage one another with these words. (1 Thessalonians 4:13–18)

Paul instructs us to be awake and aware, and we will not be caught off guard by the coming of the Lord:

Now concerning the times and the seasons, brothers, you have no need to have anything written to you. For you are fully aware that the day of the Lord will come like a thief in the night. While people are saying, 'There is peace and security,' then sudden destruction will come upon them as labor pains come upon a pregnant woman, and they will not escape. But you are not in darkness, brothers, for that day to surprise you like a thief. For you are children of light, children of the day. We are not of the night or of the darkness. So then let us not sleep, as others do, but let us keep awake and be sober. (1 Thessalonians 5:1–6)

God has not destined us for wrath, but to obtain salvation through our Lord Jesus Christ, who died for us so that whether we are awake or asleep we might live with him. Therefore, encourage one another and build one another up, just as you are doing. (1 Thessalonians 5:9–11)

We urge you, brothers, admonish the idle, encourage the fainthearted, help the weak, be patient with them all. See that no one repays anyone evil for evil, but always seek to do good to one another and to everyone. Rejoice always, pray without ceasing, give thanks in all circumstances; for this is the will of God in Christ Jesus for you. (1 Thessalonians 5:14–18)

PAUL'S SECOND LETTER TO THE THESSALONIANS

As in the Paul's first letter to the Thessalonians, he was with Silvanus and Timothy when he wrote this letter to the Thessalonians.

This is evidence of the righteous judgment of God, that you may be considered worthy of the kingdom of God, for which you are also suffering—since indeed God considers it just to repay with affliction those who afflict you, and to grant relief to you who are afflicted as well as us, when the Lord Jesus is revealed from heaven with his mighty angels in flaming fire, inflicting vengeance on those who do not know God and on those who do not obey the gospel of our Lord Jesus. They will suffer the punishment of eternal destruction, away from the presence of the Lord and from the glory of his might, when he comes on that day to be glorified in his saints, and to be marveled at among all who have believed, because our testimony to you was believed. (2 Thessalonians 1:5–10)

Now concerning the coming of our Lord Jesus Christ and our being gathered to him, we ask you, brothers, not to be quickly shaken in mind or alarmed, either by a spirit or a spoken word, or a letter seeming to be from us, to the effect that the day of the Lord has come. Let no one deceive you in any way. For that day will not come, unless the rebellion comes first, and the man of lawlessness is revealed, the son of destruction, who oppresses and exalts himself against every so-called god or object of worship, so that he takes his seat in the temple of God, proclaiming himself to be God. Do you not remember that when I was still with you I told you these things? And now you know what is restraining him now so that he may be revealed in his time. For the mystery of lawlessness is already at work. Only he who now restrains it will do so until he is out of the way. And then the lawless one will be revealed, whom the Lord Jesus will kill with the breath of his mouth and bring to nothing by the appearance of his coming. The coming of the lawless one is by the activity of Satan with all power and false signs and wonders, and with all wicked deception for those who are perishing, because they refused to love the truth and so be saved. Therefore God sends them a strong delusion, so that they may believe what is false, in order that all may be condemned who did not believe in truth but had pleasure in unrighteousness. (2 Thessalonians 2:1–12)

But the Lord is faithful. He will establish you and guard you against the evil one. (2 Thessalonians 3:3)

As for you, brothers, do not grow weary in doing good. (2 Thessalonians 3:13)

THE FIRST LETTER OF PAUL TO TIMOTHY

All the other letters that the apostle Paul wrote up to this point that are included in the Bible are letters to newly formed Christian churches in various areas. The following letters to Timothy and Titus are personal letters. Timothy was a close friend of the apostle Paul. He traveled with Paul and helped him to spread the message of the Gospel to others. Timothy and Titus were among the first leaders of the church. Timothy was the bishop of Ephesus. Titus was the bishop of Crete. These letters are called the "Pastoral Letters" because Paul is giving advice to them as church leaders. Below are excerpts of some of the things that Paul wrote to Timothy.

> I thank him who has given me strength, Christ Jesus our Lord, because he judged me faithful, appointing me to his service, though formerly I was a blasphemer, persecutor, and insolent opponent. But I received mercy because I had acted ignorantly in unbelief, and the grace of our Lord overflowed for me with the faith and love that are in Christ Jesus. The saying is trustworthy and deserving of full acceptance, that Christ Jesus came into the world to save sinners, of who I am the foremost. But I received mercy for this reason, that in me, as the foremost, Jesus Christ might display his perfect patience as an example to those who were to believe in him for eternal life. To the King of ages, immortal, invisible, the only God, be honor and glory forever and ever. Amen. (1 Timothy 1:12–17)

> First of all, then, I urge that supplications, prayers, intercessions, and thanksgivings be made for all people, for kings and all who are in high positions, that we may lead a peaceful and quiet life, godly and dignified in every way. This is good, and it is pleasing in the sight of God our Savior, who desires all people to be saved and to come to the knowledge of the truth. For there is one God, and there is one mediator between God and men, the man Christ Jesus, who gave himself as a ransom for all, which is the testimony given at the proper time. For this I was appointed a preacher and an apostle, a teacher of the Gentiles in faith and truth. (1 Timothy 2:1–7)

Great indeed, we confess, is the mystery of godliness: He was manifested in the flesh, vindicated by the Spirit, seen by angels, proclaimed among the nations, believed on in the world, taken up in glory. (1 Timothy 3:16)

Some will depart from the faith in the latter days:

Now the Spirit expressly says that in the later times some will depart from the faith by devoting themselves to deceitful spirits and teachings of demons, through the insincerity of liars whose consciences are seared, who forbid marriage and require abstinence from foods that God created to be received with thanksgiving by those who believe and know the truth. For everything created by God is good, and nothing is to be rejected if it is received with thanksgiving, for it is made holy by the word of God and prayer. (1 Timothy 4:1–5)

Have nothing to do with irreverent, silly myths. Rather train yourself for godliness; for while bodily training is of some value, godliness is of value in every way, as it holds promise for the present life and also for the life to come. For to this end we toil and strive, because we have our hope set on the living God, who is the Savior of all people, especially of those who believe. (1 Timothy 4:7–10)

Do not rebuke an older man but encourage him as you would a father, younger men as brothers, older women as mothers, younger women as sisters, in all purity. (1 Timothy 5:1–2)

If anyone does not provide for his relatives, and especially for members of his household, he has denied the faith and is worse than an unbeliever. (1 Timothy 5:8)

As for those who persist in sin, rebuke them in the presence of all, so that the rest may stand in fear. (1 Timothy 5:20)

If anyone teaches a different doctrine and does not agree with the sound words of our Lord Jesus Christ and the teaching that accords with godliness, he is puffed up with conceit and understands nothing. (1 Timothy 6:3–4)

Now there is great gain in godliness with contentment, for we brought nothing into the world, and we cannot take anything out of the world. But if we have food and clothing, with these we will be content. But those who desire to be rich fall into temptation, into a snare, into many senseless and harmful desires that plunge people into ruin and destruction. For the love of money is a root of all kinds of evils. It is through this craving that some have wandered away from the faith and pierced themselves with many pangs. But as for you, O man of God, flee these things. Pursue righteousness, godliness, faith, love, steadfastness, gentleness. Fight the good fight of faith. Take hold of the eternal life to which you were called and about which you made the good confession in the presence of many witnesses. (1 Timothy 6:6–12)

I charge you in the presence of God, who gives life to all things, and of Christ Jesus, who in his testimony before Pontius Pilate made the good confession, to keep the commandment unstained and free from reproach until the appearing of our Lord Jesus Christ, which he will display at a proper time—he who is the blessed and only Sovereign, the King of kings and Lord of lords, who alone has immortality, who dwells in unapproachable light, whom no one has ever seen or can see. To him be honor and eternal dominion. Amen. (1 Timothy 6:13–16)

As for the rich in this present age, they should not be conceited, and they should not set their hopes on the uncertainty of riches, but on God, who richly provides us with everything to enjoy. They are to do good, do a lot of good works, and be generous and ready to share, thus storing up treasure for themselves as a good foundation for the future, so that they may take hold of what is truly life. (1 Timothy 6:17–19)

THE SECOND LETTER OF THE APOSTLE PAUL TO TIMOTHY

God did not give us a spirit of fear, but of power and love and self-control. (2 Timothy 1:7)

Therefore do not be ashamed of the testimony about our Lord, nor of me his prisoner, but share in suffering for the gospel by the power of God, who saved us and called us to a holy calling, not because of our works but because of his own purpose and grace, which he gave us in Christ Jesus before the ages began, and which now have been manifested through the appearing of our Savior Christ Jesus, who abolished death and brought life and immortality to light through the gospel, for which I was appointed a preacher and apostle and teacher, which is why I suffer as I do. But I am not ashamed, for I know whom I have believed, and I am convinced that he is able to guard until that Day what has been entrusted to me. (2 Timothy 1:8–12)

Share in suffering as a good soldier of Christ Jesus. No soldier gets entangled in civilian pursuits, since his aim is to please the one who enlisted him. An athlete is not crowned unless he competes according to the rules. It is the hard-working farmer who ought to have the first share of the crops. Think over what I say, for the Lord will give you understanding in everything. (2 Timothy 2:3–7)

Remember Jesus Christ, risen from the dead, the offspring of David, as preached in my gospel, for which I am suffering, bound with chains as a criminal. But the word of God is not bound! Therefore I endure everything for the sake of the elect, that they also may obtain salvation that is in Christ Jesus with eternal glory. The saying is trustworthy, for: If we have died with him, we also will live with him; if we endure, we will also reign with him; if we deny him, he will also deny us; if we are faithless, he remains faithful—for he cannot deny himself. (2 Timothy 2:8–13)

God's firm foundation stands, bearing this seal: "The Lord knows who are his," and, "Let everyone who names the name of the Lord depart from iniquity." (2 Timothy 2:19)

> Now in a great house there are not only vessels of gold and silver but also of wood and clay, some for honorable use, some for dishonorable. Therefore, if anyone cleanses himself from what is dishonorable, he will be a vessel for honorable use, set apart as holy, useful to the master of the house, ready for every good work. So flee youthful passions and pursue righteousness, faith, love, and peace, along with those who call on the Lord from a pure heart. Have nothing to do with foolish, ignorant controversies; you know they breed quarrels. And the Lord's servant must not be quarrelsome but kind to everyone, able to teach, patiently enduring evil, correcting his opponents with gentleness. God may perhaps grant them repentance leading to a knowledge of the truth, and they may come to their senses and escape from the snare of the devil, after being captured by him to do his will. (2 Timothy 2:20–26)

Paul informs Timothy what the people will be like on earth in the last days:

> But understand this, that in the last days there will come times of difficulty. For people will be lovers of self, lovers of money, proud, arrogant, abusive, disobedient to their parents, ungrateful, unholy, heartless, unappeasable, slanderous, without self-control, brutal, not loving good, treacherous, reckless, swollen with conceit, lovers of pleasure rather than lovers of God, having the appearance of godliness, but denying its power. Avoid such people. For among them are those who creep into households and capture weak women, burdened with sins and led astray by various passions, always learning and never

able to arrive at a knowledge of the truth. Just as Jannes and Jambres opposed Moses, so these men also oppose the truth, men corrupted in mind and disqualified regarding the faith. But they will not get very far, for their folly will be plain to all, as was that of those two men. (2 Timothy 3:1–9)

Indeed, all who desire to live a godly life in Christ Jesus will be persecuted, while evil people and impostors will go on from bad to worse, deceiving and being deceived. But as for you, continue in what you have learned and have firmly believed, knowing from whom you learned it and how from childhood you have been acquainted with the sacred writings, which are able to make you wise for salvation through faith in Christ Jesus. (2 Timothy 3:12–15)

All scripture is breathed out by God and profitable for teaching, for reproof, for correction, and for training in righteousness, that the man of God may be competent, equipped for every good work. (2 Timothy 3:16–17)

I charge you in the presence of God and of Christ Jesus, who is to judge the living and the dead, and by his appearing and his kingdom; preach the word; be ready in season and out of season; reprove, rebuke, and exhort, with complete patience and teaching. For the time is coming when people will not endure sound teaching, but having itching ears they will accumulate for themselves teachers to suit their own passions, and will turn away from listening to the truth and wander off into myths. As for you, always be sober-minded, endure suffering, do the work of an evangelist, fulfill your ministry. (2 Timothy 4:1–5)

For I am already being poured out as a drink offering, and the time of my departure has come. I have fought the good fight, I have finished the race, I have kept the faith. Henceforth there is laid up for me the crown of righteousness, which the Lord, the righteous judge, will award to me on that Day, and not only to me but also to all who have loved his appearing. (2 Timothy 4:6–8)

Do your best to come to me soon. Luke alone is with me. Get Mark and bring him with you, for he is very useful to me for ministry. At my first defense no one came to stand by me, but all deserted me. May it not be charged against them! But the Lord stood by me and strengthened me, so that through me the message might be fully proclaimed and all the Gentiles might hear it. So I was rescued from the lion's mouth. The Lord will rescue me from every deed and bring me safely into his heavenly kingdom. To him be the glory forever and ever. Amen. (2 Timothy 4:9–18)

THE LETTER OF PAUL TO TITUS

But as for you, teach what accords with sound doctrine. Older men are to be sober-minded, dignified, self-controlled, sound in faith, in love, and in steadfastness. Older women likewise are to be reverent in behavior, not slanderers or slaves to much wine. They are to teach what is good, and so train the young women to love their husbands and children, to be self-controlled, pure, working at home, kind, and submissive to their own husbands, that the word of God may not be reviled. Likewise, urge the younger men to be self-controlled. (Titus 2:1–6)

Show yourself in all respects to be a model of good works, and in your teaching show integrity, dignity, and sound speech that cannot be condemned, so that an opponent may be put to shame, having nothing evil to say about us. (Titus 2:7–8)

For the grace of God has appeared, bringing salvation for all people, training us to renounce ungodliness and worldly passions, and to live self-controlled, upright, and godly lives in the present age, waiting for our blessed hope, the appearing of the glory of our great God and Savior Jesus Christ, who gave himself for us to redeem us from all lawlessness and to purify for himself a people for his own possession who are zealous for good works. (Titus 2:11–14)

Remind them to be submissive to rulers and authorities, to be obedient, to be ready for every good work, to speak evil of no one, to avoid quarreling, to be gentle, and to show perfect courtesy toward all people. For we ourselves were once foolish, disobedient, led astray, slaves to various passions and pleasures, passing our days in malice and envy, hated by others and hating one another. But when the goodness and loving kindness or God our Savior appeared, he saved us, not because of works done by us in righteousness, but according to his own mercy, by the washing of regeneration and renewal of the Holy Spirit, whom he poured out on us richly through Jesus Christ our Savior, so that being justified by his grace we might become heirs according to the hope of eternal life. (Titus 3:1–7)

THE LETTER OF PAUL TO PHILEMON

Paul, a prisoner for Christ Jesus, and Timothy our brother, to Philemon, our beloved fellow worker and Apphia our sister and Archippus our fellow soldier and the church in your house: Grace to you and peace from God our Father and the Lord Jesus Christ.

I thank my God always when I remember you in my prayers, because I hear of your love and of the faith that you have toward the Lord Jesus and for all the saints, and I pray that the sharing of your faith may become effective for the full knowledge of every good thing that is in us for the sake of Christ. For I have derived much joy and comfort from your love, my brother, because the hearts of the saints have been refreshed through you. (Philemon 1:1–7)

Epaphras, my fellow prisoner in Christ Jesus, sends greetings to you, and so do Mark, Aristarchus, Demas, and Luke, my fellow work-ers. The grace of the Lord Jesus Christ be with your spirit. (Philemon 1:23–25)

CHAPTER 24

LETTERS OF OTHER APOSTLES AND DISCIPLES OF JESUS

THE LETTER TO THE HEBREWS

The author of the Letter to the Hebrews is unclear. Some believe Paul or people from Paul's inner circle wrote it to the new Christian churches. Others believe Paul is not the author. The summary of this letter was placed in this section since it is not fully agreed who exactly wrote the Letter to the Hebrews. Regardless of the author, the Letter to the Hebrews contains vital information for Christians.

Long ago, at many times and in many ways, God spoke to our fathers by the prophets, but in these last days he has spoken to us by his Son, whom he appointed the heir of all things, through whom also he created the world. He is the radiance of the glory of God and the exact imprint of his nature, and he upholds the universe by the word of his power. After making purification for sins, he sat down at the right hand of the Majesty on high, having become as much superior to angels as the name he has inherited is more excellent than theirs.

For to which of the angels did God ever say, "You are my Son, today I have begotten you?" Or again, "I will to him be a father, and he shall be to me a son?" And again, when he brings the firstborn in to the world, he says, "Let all God's angels worship him." Of the angels he says, "He makes his angels winds, and his ministers a flame of fire." But of the Son he says. "Your throne, O God, is forever and ever, the scepter of uprightness is the scepter of your kingdom. You have loved righteousness and hated wickedness; therefore God, your God, has anointed you with the oil of gladness beyond your companions." And, "You, Lord, laid the foundation of the earth in the beginning, and the heavens are the work of your hands; they will perish, but you remain; they will all wear out like a garment, like a robe you will roll them up, like a garment they will be changed. But you are the same, and your years will have no end." And to which of the angels has he ever said, "Sit at my right hand until I make your enemies a footstool for your feet?" Are not all ministering spirits sent out to serve for the sake of those who are to inherit salvation? (Hebrews 1:1–14)

Now it was not to angels that God subjected the world to come, of which we are speaking. It has been testified somewhere, "What is man, that you are mindful of him, or the son of man that you care for him? You made him for a little while lower than the angels; you have crowned him with glory and with honor, putting everything in subjection under his feet." Now in putting everything in subjection to him, he left nothing outside his control. At present, we do not yet see everything in subjection to him. But we see him who for a little while was made lower than the angels, namely Jesus, crowned with glory and honor because of the suffering of death, so that by the grace of God he might taste death for everyone.

For it was fitting that he, for whom and by whom all things exist, in bringing many sons to glory, should make the founder of their salvation perfect through suffering. For he who sanctifies and those who are sanctified all have one source. That is why he is not ashamed to call them brothers, saying, "I will tell of your name to my brothers; in the midst of the congregation I will sing your praise." And again, "I will put my trust in him." And again, "Behold, I and the children God has given me."

Since therefore the children share in flesh and blood, he himself likewise partook of the same things, that through death he might destroy the one who has the power of death, that is, the devil, and deliver all those who through fear of death were subject to lifelong slavery. For surely it is not angels that he helps, but he helps the offspring of Abraham. Therefore he had to be made like his brothers in every respect, so that he might become a merciful and faithful high priest in the service of God, to make propitiation for the sins of the people. For because he himself has suffered when tempted, he is able to help those who are being tempted. (Hebrews 2:5–18)

Therefore, holy brothers, you who share in a heavenly calling, consider Jesus, the apostle and high priest of our confession, who was faithful to him who appointed him, just as Moses was also faithful in all of God's house. For Jesus has been counted worthy of more glory than Moses—as much more glory as the builder of a house has more honor than the house itself. [For every house is built by someone, but the builder of all things is God.] Now Moses was faithful in all God's house as a servant, to testify to the things that were to be spoken later, but Christ is faithful over God's house as a son. And we are his house if indeed we hold fast our confidence and our boasting in our hope. (Hebrews 3:1–5)

Take care, brothers, lest there be in any of you an evil, unbelieving heart, leading you to fall away from the living God. But exhort one another every day, as long as it is called 'today', that none of you may be hardened by the deceitfulness of sin. For we have come to share in Christ, if indeed we hold our original confidence form to the end. As it is said, "Today, if you hear his voice, do not harden your hearts as in the rebellion." (Hebrews 3:12–15)

For the word of God is living and active, sharper than any two-edged sword, piercing to the division of soul and spirit, of joints and marrow, and discerning the thoughts and intentions of the heart. And no creature is hidden from his sight, but all are naked and exposed to the eyes of him to whom we must give account. (Hebrews 4:12–13)

Since then we have a great high priest who has passed through the heavens, Jesus, the Son of God, let us hold fast our confession. For we do not have a high priest who is unable to sympathize with our weaknesses, but one who in every respect has been tempted as we are, yet without sin. Let us then with confidence draw near to the throne of grace, that we may receive mercy and find grace to help in time of need. (Hebrews 4:14–16)

So also Christ did not exalt himself to be made a high priest, but was appointed by him who said to him, "You are my Son, today I have begotten you"; as he says in another place, "You are a priest forever, after the order of Melchizedek." In the days of his flesh, Jesus offered up prayers and supplications, with loud cries and tears, to him who was able to save him from death, and he was heard because of his reverence. Although he was a son, he learned obedience through what he suffered. And being made perfect, he became the source of eternal salvation to all who obey him, being designated by God as a high priest after the order of Melchizedek. (Hebrews 5:5–10)

We have this as a sure and steadfast anchor of the soul, a hope that enters into the inner place behind the curtain, where Jesus has gone as a forerunner on our behalf, becoming a high priest forever after the order of Melchizedek. (Hebrews 6:19–20)

For this Melchizedek, king of Salem, priest of the Most High God, met Abraham returning from the slaughter of the kings and blessed him, and to him Abraham apportioned a tenth part of everything. He is first, by translation of his name, king of righteousness, and then he is also king of Salem, that is, king of peace. He is without father or mother or genealogy, having neither beginning of days not end of life, but resembling the Son of God he continues a priest forever. (Hebrews 7:1–3)

The former priests were many in number, because they were prevented by death from continuing in office, but Jesus holds his priesthood permanently, because he continues forever. Consequently, he is able to save to the uttermost those who draw near to God through him, since he always lives to make intercession for them. For it is indeed fitting that we should have such a high priest, holy, innocent, unstained, separated from sinners, and exalted above the heavens. He has no need, like those high priests, to offer sacrifices daily, first for his own sins and then for those of the people, since he did this once for all when he offered up himself. For the law appoints me in their weakness as high priests, but the word of the oath, which came later than the law, appoints a Son who has been made perfect forever. (Hebrews 7:23–28)

Now the point in what we are saying is this: we have such a high priest, one who is seated at the right hand of the throne of Majesty in heaven, a minister in the holy places, in the true tent that the Lord set up, not man. (Hebrews 8:1–2)

But as it is, Christ has obtained a ministry that is much more excellent than the old as the covenant he mediates is better, since it is enacted on better promises. For if that first covenant had been faultless, there would have been no occasion to look for a second.

For he finds fault with them when he says: "Behold, the days are coming, declares the Lord, when I will establish a new covenant with the house of Israel and with the house of Judah, not like the covenant I made with their fathers on the day when I took them by the hand to bring them out of the land of Egypt. For they did not continue in my covenant, and so I showed no concern for them, declares the Lord. For this is the covenant that I will make with the house of Israel after those days, declares the Lord: I will put my laws into their minds, and write them on their hearts, and I will be their God, and they shall be my people. And they shall not teach, each one his neighbor and each one his brother, saying, 'Know the Lord,' for they shall know me, from the least of them to the greatest. For I will be merciful toward their iniquities, and I will remember their sins no more." In speaking of a new covenant, he makes the first one obsolete. And what is becoming obsolete and growing old is ready to vanish away. (Hebrews 8:6–13).

Therefore Jesus is the mediator of a new covenant, so that those who are called may receive the promised eternal inheritance, since a death has occurred that redeems them from the transgressions committed under the first cove-nant. For where a will is involved, the death of the one who made it must be established. For a will takes effect only at death, since it is not in force as long as the one who made it is alive. (Hebrews 9:15–17)

Indeed under the law almost everything is purified with blood, and without the shedding of blood there is no forgiveness of sins. (Hebrews 9:22)

Thus it was necessary for the copies of these heavenly things to be purified with these rites [Old Testament religious sacrifices], but the heavenly things themselves with better sacrifices than these. For Christ has entered, not into holy places made with hands, which are copies of the true things, but into heaven itself, now to appear in the presence of God on our behalf. Nor was it to offer himself repeatedly, as the high priest enters the holy places every year with blood not his own, for then he would have had to suffer repeatedly since the foundation of the world. But as it is, he has appeared once for all at the end of the ages to put away sin by the sacrifice of himself. And just as it is appointed for man to die once, and after that comes judgment, so Christ, having been offered once to bear the sins of many, will appear a second time, not to deal with sin but to save those who are eagerly waiting for him. (Hebrews 9:23–28)

When Christ had offered for all time a single sacrifice for sins, he sat down at the right hand of God, waiting from that time until his enemies should be made a footstool for his feet. For by a single offering he has perfected for all time those who are being sanctified. And the Holy Spirit also bears witness to us; for after saying, "This is the covenant that I will make with them after those days, declares the Lord: I will put my laws on their hearts, and write them on their minds," then he adds, "I will remember their sins and their lawless deeds no more." (Hebrews 10:12–17)

For if we go on sinning deliberately after receiving the knowledge of the truth, there no longer remains a sacrifice for sins, but a fearful expectation of judgment, and a fury of fire that will consume the adversaries. Anyone who has set aside the law of Moses dies without mercy on the evidence of two or three witnesses. How much worse punishment, do you think, will be deserved by the one who has spurned the Son of God, and has profaned the blood of the covenant by which he was sanctified, and has outraged the Spirit of grace? For we know him who said, "Vengeance is mine; I will repay." And again, "The Lord will judge his people." It is a fearful thing to fall into the hands of the living God. (Hebrews 10:26–30)

Now faith is the assurance of things hoped for, the conviction of things not seen. For by it the people of old received their commendation. By faith we understand that the universe was created by the word of God, so that what is seen was not made out of things that are visible. And without faith it is impossible to please God, for whoever would draw near to God must believe that he exists and that he rewards those who seek him. By faith Noah, being warned by God concerning events as yet unseen, in reverent fear constructed an ark for the saving of his household. By this he condemned the world and became an heir of righteousness that comes by faith. By faith Abraham obeyed when he was called to go out to a place that he was to receive as an inheritance. And he went out, not knowing where he was going.

These all died in faith, not having received the things promised, but having seen them and greeted them from afar, and having acknowledged that they were strangers and exiles on the earth. For people who speak thus make it clear that they are seeking a homeland. If they had been thinking of that land from which they had gone out, they would have had opportunity to return. But as it is, they desire a better country, that is, a heavenly one. Therefore God is not ashamed to be called their God, for he has prepared for them a city. (Hebrews 11:1–16)

By faith, Moses, when he was grown up, refused to be called the son of pharaoh's daughter, choosing rather to be mistreated with the people of God than to enjoy the fleeting pleasures of sin. He considered the reproach of Christ greater wealth than the treasures of Egypt, for he was looking to the reward. (Hebrews 11:24–26)

Consider Jesus who endured from sinners such hostility against himself, so that you may not grow weary or fainthearted. In your struggle against sin you have not yet resisted to the point of shedding your blood. And have you forgotten the exhortation that addresses you as sons? "My son, do not regard lightly the discipline of the Lord, nor be weary when reproved by him. For the Lord disciplines the one he loves, and chastises every son whom he receives."

It is for discipline that you have to endure. God is treating you as sons. For what son is there whom his father does not discipline? If you are left without discipline, in which all have participated, then you are illegitimate children and not sons. Besides this, we have had earthly fathers who disciplined us and we respected them. Shall we not much more be subject to the Father of spirits and live? For they disciplined is for a short time as it seemed best to them, but God disciplines us for our good, that we may share his holiness. For the moment all discipline seems painful rather than pleasant, but later it yields the peaceful fruit of righteousness by those who have been trained in it. (Hebrews 12:3–11)

Strive for peace with everyone, and for the holiness without which no one will see the Lord. (Hebrews 12:14)

You have come to Mount Zion and to the city of the living God, the heavenly Jerusalem, and to innumerable angels in festal gathering, and to the assembly of the firstborn who are enrolled in heaven, and to God, the judge of all, and to the spirits of the righteous made perfect, and to Jesus, the mediator of a new covenant, and to the sprinkled blood that speaks a better word than the blood of Abel. (Hebrews 12:22–24)

Let brotherly love continue. Do not neglect to show hospitality to strangers, for thereby some have entertained angels unawares. (Hebrews 13:2)

Keep your life free from the love of money, and be content with what you have, for God has said "I will never leave you nor forsake you." So we can confidently say, 'The Lord is my helper; I will not fear; what can man do to me? (Hebrews 13:5–6)

Do not neglect to do good and share what you have, for such sacrifices are pleasing to God. (Hebrews 13:16)

Obey your leaders and submit to them, for they are keeping watch over your souls, as those who will have to give an account. (Hebrews 13:17)

Now may the God of peace who brought again from the dead our Lord, Jesus, the great shepherd of the sheep, by the blood of the eternal covenant, equip you with everything good that you may do his will, working in us that which is pleasing in his sight, through Jesus Christ, to whom be the glory forever and ever. Amen. (Hebrews 13:20–21)

THE LETTER OF JAMES

Count it all joy, my brothers, when you meet trials of various kinds, for you know that the testing of your faith produces steadfastness. And let steadfastness have its full effect, that you may be perfect and complete, lacking in nothing. (James 1:2–4)

If anyone lacks wisdom, let him ask God who gives generously to all without reproach, and it will be given to him. But let him ask in faith, with no doubting, for the one who doubts is like a wave of the sea that is driven and tossed by the wind. For that person must not suppose that he will receive anything from the Lord; he is a double-minded man, unstable in all his ways. (James 1:5–8)

Blessed is the man who remains steadfast under trial, for when he has stood the test he will receive the crown of life, which God has promised to those who love him. (James 1:12)

Let no one say when he is tempted, "I am being tempted by God," for God cannot be tempted with evil, and he himself tempts no one. But each person is tempted when he is lured and enticed by his own desire. Then desire when it has conceived gives birth to sin, and sin when it is fully grown brings forth death. (James 1:13–15)

Do not be deceived, my beloved brothers. Every good gift and every perfect gift is from above, coming down from the Father of lights with whom there is no variation or shadow due to change. Of his own will he brought us forth by the word of truth, that we should be a kind of firstfruits of his creatures. (James 1:16–18)

Let every person be quick to hear, slow to speak, slow to anger; for the anger of man does not produce the righteousness of God. Therefore put away all filthiness and rampant wickedness and receive with meekness the implanted word, which is able to save your souls. (James 1:19–21)

Be doers of the Word of God, and not hearers only, deceiving yourselves. Religion that is pure and undefiled before God, the Father, is this: to visit orphans and widows in their affliction, and to keep oneself unstained form the world. (James 1:22 and 27)

Do not treat people differently if they are rich or poor, popular or unpopular. Treat everyone well. (Summary of James 2–7)

For judgment is without mercy to one who has shown no mercy. Mercy triumphs over judgment. (James 2:13)

What good is it, my brothers, if someone says he has faith but does not have works? Can that faith save him? If a brother or a sister is poorly clothed and lacking in daily food, and one of you says to them, "Go in peace, be warm and filled," without giving them the things needed for the body, what good is that? So also faith by itself, if it does not have works, is dead. (James 2:14–17)

But someone will say, "You have faith and I have works." Show me your faith apart from your works, and I will show you my faith by my works. Do you want to be shown, you foolish person, that faith apart from works is useless? Was not Abraham our father justified by works when he offered up his son Isaac on the altar? You see that faith was active along with his works, and faith was completed by his works; and the scripture was fulfilled that says, "Abraham believed God, and it was counted to him as righteousness"—and he was called a friend of God. You see that a person is justified by works and not by faith alone. For as the body apart from the spirit is dead, so also faith apart from works is dead. (James 2:18–26)

A harvest of righteousness is sown in peace by those who make peace. (James 3:18)

What causes quarrels and what causes fights among you? Is it not this, that your passions are at war within you? You desire and do not have, so you murder. You covet and cannot obtain, so you fight and quarrel. You do not have, because you do not ask. You ask and do not receive, because you ask wrongly, to spend it on your passions. You adulterous people! Do you not know that friendship with the world is enmity with God? Therefore whoever wishes to be a friend of the world makes himself an enemy of God. Or do you suppose it is to no purpose that the scripture says, "He yearns jealously over the spirit that he has made to dwell in us?" But he gives more grace. Therefore it says, "God opposes the proud, but gives grace to the humble." Submit yourselves therefore to God. Resist the devil and he will flee from you. Draw near to God and he will draw near to you. Cleanse your hands, you sinners, and purify your hearts, you double-minded. Humble yourselves before the Lord and he will exalt you. (James 4:1–10)

Do not speak evil against one another, brothers. The one who speaks against a brother or judges his brother, speaks evil against the law and judges the law. There is only one lawgiver and judge, he who is able to save and destroy. But who are you to judge your neighbor? (James 4:11–12)

Whoever knows the right thing to do and fails to do it, for him it is sin. (James 4:17)

But above all, my brothers, do not swear, either by heaven or by earth or by any other oath, but let your "yes" be yes and your "no" ne no, so that you may not fall under condemnation. (James 5:12)

Is anyone among you suffering? Let him pray. Is anyone cheerful? Let him sing praise. Is anyone among your sick? Let him call for the elders of the church, and let them pray over him, anointing him with oil in the name of the Lord. And the prayer of faith will save the one who is sick and the Lord will raise him up. And if he has committed sins, he will be forgiven. Therefore, confess your sins to one another and pray for one another, that you may be healed. The prayer of a righteous person has great power as it is working. Elijah was a man with a nature like ours, and he prayed fervently that it might not rain, and for three years and six months it did not rain on earth. Then he prayed again, and heaven gave rain and the earth bore fruit. (James 5:13–18)

If anyone among you wanders from the truth and someone brings him back, let him know that whoever brings back a sinner from his wandering will save his soul from death and will cover a multitude of sins. (James 5:19–20)

THE FIRST LETTER OF PETER

Peter, an apostle of Jesus Christ, to those who are elect exiles of the dispersion in Pontus, Galatia, Cappadocia, Asia, and Bithynia, according to the foreknowledge of God the Father, in the sanctification of the Spirit, for obedience to Jesus Christ and for sprinkling with his blood: May grace and peace be multiplied to you. (1 Peter 1:1–2)

Blessed be the God and Father of our Lord Jesus Christ! According to his great mercy, he has caused us to be born again to a living hope through the resurrection of Jesus Christ from the dead, to an inheritance that is imperishable, undefiled, and unfading, kept in heaven for you, who by God's power are being guarded through faith for a salvation ready to be revealed in the last time. In this you rejoice, though now for a little while, if necessary, you have been grieved by various trials, so that the tested genuineness of your faith—more precious than gold that perishes though it is tested by fire—may be found to result in praise and glory and honor at the revelation of Jesus Christ. Though you have not seen him, you love him. Though you do not now see him, you believe in him and rejoice with joy that is inexpressible and filled with glory, obtaining the outcome of your faith, the salvation of your souls. (1 Peter 1:3–9)

Therefore, preparing your minds for action, and being sober-minded, set your hope fully on the grace that will be brought to you at the revelation of Jesus Christ. As obedient children, do not be conformed to the passions of your former ignorance, but as he who called you is holy, you also be holy in all your conduct, since it is written, "You shall be holy as I am holy." (1 Peter 1:13–16)

And if you call on him as Father who judges impartially according to each one's deeds, conduct yourselves with fear throughout the time of your exile, knowing that you were ransomed from the futile ways inherited from your forefathers, not with perishable things such as silver or gold, but with the precious blood of Christ, like that of a lamb without blemish or spot. He was foreknown before the foundation of the world but was made manifest in the last times for the sake of you who through him are believers in God, who raised him from the dead and gave him glory, so that your faith and hope are in God. (1 Peter 1:17–21)

As you come to Jesus, a living stone rejected by men but in the sight of God chosen and precious, you yourselves like living stones are being built up as a spiritual house, to be a holy priesthood, to offer spiritual sacrifices acceptable to God through Jesus Christ. (1 Peter 2:4–5)

But you are a chosen race, a royal priesthood, a holy nation, a people for his own possession, that you may proclaim the excellencies of him who called you out of darkness into his marvelous light. Once you were not a people, but now you are God's people; once you had not received mercy, but now you have received mercy. (1 Peter 2:9–10)

Beloved, I urge you as sojourners and exiles to abstain from the passions of the flesh, which wage war against your soul. Keep your conduct among the Gentiles honorable, so that when they speak against you as evildoers, they may see your good deeds and glorify God on the day of visitation. (1 Peter 2:11–12)

Servants, be subject to your masters with all respect, not only to the good and gentle but also the unjust. For this is a gracious thing, when, mindful of God, one endures sorrow while suffering unjustly. For what credit is it if, when you sin and are beaten for it, you endure? But if when you do good and suffer for it you endure, this is a gracious thing in the sight of God. For to this you have been called, because Christ also suffered for you, leaving you an example, so that you might follow in his steps. He committed no sin, neither was deceit found in his mouth. When he was reviled, he did not revile in return; when he suffered, he did not threaten, but continued entrusting himself to him who judges justly. Jesus bore our sins in his body on the tree that we might die to sin and live to righteousness. By his wounds you have been healed. For you were straying like sheep, but now have returned to the Shepherd and Overseer of your souls. (1 Peter 2:18–25)

Finally, all of you, have unity of mind, sympathy, brotherly love, a tender heart, and a humble mind. Do not repay evil for evil or reviling for reviling, but on the contrary, bless, for to this you were called, that you may obtain a blessing. For "Whoever desires to love life and see good days, let him keep his tongue from evil and his lips from speaking deceit; let him turn away from evil and do good; let him seek peace and pursue it. For the eyes of the Lord are on the righteous, and his ears are open to their prayer. But the face of the Lord is against those who do evil." (1 Peter 3:8–12)

Now who is there to harm you if you are zealous for what is good? But even if you should suffer for righteousness sake, you will be blessed. Have no fear of them, nor be troubled, but in your hearts honor Christ the Lord as holy, always being prepared to make a defense to anyone who asks you for a reason for the hope that is in you; yet do it with gentleness and respect, having a good conscience, so that, when you are slandered, those who revile your good behavior in Christ may be put to shame. (1 Peter 3:13–16)

Baptism now saves you, not as a removal of dirt from the body but as an appeal to God for a good conscience, through the resurrection of Jesus Christ, who has gone into heaven and is at the right hand of God, with angels, authorities, and powers having been subjected to him. (1 Peter 3:21–22)

For this is why the gospel was preached even to the dead, that though condemned in the flesh in human estimation, they might live in the spirit in the estimation of God. (1 Peter 4:6)

Above all, keep loving one another earnestly, since love covers a multitude of sins. Show hospitality to one another without grumbling. As each has received a gift, use it to serve one another, as good stewards of God's varied grace. (1 Peter 4:8–10)

Beloved, do not be surprised at the fiery trial when it comes upon you to test you, as though something strange were happening to you. But rejoice insofar as you share Christ's sufferings, that you may also rejoice and be glad when his glory is revealed. If you are insulted for the name of Christ, you are blessed, because the Spirit of glory and of God rests upon you. (1 Peter 4:12–14)

Yet if anyone suffers as a Christian, let him not be ashamed, but let him glorify God in that name. Therefore let those who suffer according to God's will entrust their souls to a faithful Creator while doing good. (1 Peter 4:16 and 19)

Humble yourselves, therefore, under the mighty hand of God so that at the proper time he may exalt you, casting all your anxieties on him, because he cares for you. Be sober minded; be watchful. Your adversary the devil prowls around like a roaring lion, seeking someone to devour. Resist him, firm in your faith, knowing that the same kinds of suffering are being experienced by your brotherhood throughout the world. And after you have suffered a little while, the God of all grace, who has called you to his eternal glory in Christ, will himself restore, confirm, strengthen, and establish you. To him be the dominion forever and ever. Amen. (1 Peter 5:6–11)

THE SECOND LETTER OF PETER

Jesus's divine power has granted to us all things that pertain to life and godliness, through the knowledge of him who called us to his own glory and excellence, by which he has granted to us his precious and very great promises, so that through them you may become partakers of the divine nature, having escaped from the corruption that is in the world because of sinful desire. For this very reason, make every effort to supplement your faith with virtue, and virtue with knowledge, and knowledge with self-control, and self-control with steadfastness, and steadfastness with godliness, and godliness with brotherly affection, and brotherly affection with love. For if these qualities are yours and are increasing, they keep you from being ineffective or unfruitful in the knowledge of our Lord Jesus Christ. For whoever lacks these qualities is so nearsighted that he is blind, having forgotten that he was cleansed from his former sins. Therefore, brothers, be all the more diligent to make your calling and election sure, for if you practice these qualities you will never fall. For in this way there will be richly provided for you an entrance into the eternal kingdom of our Lord and Savior Jesus Christ. (2 Peter 1:3–11)

Jesus let Peter know that he would be martyred soon:

Therefore I intend always to remind you of these qualities, though you know them and are established in the truth that you have. I think it right, as long as I am in this body, to stir you up by way of reminder, since I know that the putting off of my body will be soon, as our Lord Jesus Christ made clear to me. And I will make every effort so that after my departure you may be able at any time to recall these things. (2 Peter 1:12–15)

For we did not follow cleverly devised myths when we made known to you the power and coming of our Lord Jesus Christ, but we were eyewitnesses of his majesty. For when he had received honor and glory from God the Father, and the voice was borne to him by the Majestic Glory, "This is my beloved son, with whom I am well pleased," we ourselves heard this very voice borne from heaven, for we were with him on the holy mountain. And we have something more sure, the prophetic word, to which you will do well to pay attention to as a lamp shining in a dark place, until the day dawns and the morning star rises in your hearts, knowing first of all, that no prophecy of scripture comes from someone's own interpretation. For no prophecy was ever produced by the will of man, but men spoke form God as they were carried along by the Holy Spirit. (2 Peter 1:20–21)

For if God did not spare angels when they sinned, but cast them into hell and committed them to chains of gloomy darkness to be kept until the judgement; if he did not spare the ancient world, but preserved Noah, an herald of righteousness, with seven others, when he brought a flood upon the world of the ungodly; if by turning the cities of Sodom and Gomorrah to ashes as he condemned them to extinction, making them an example of what is going to happen to the ungodly; and if he rescued righteous Lot, greatly distressed by the sensual conduct of the wicked [for as that righteous man lived among them day after day, he was tormenting his righteous soul over their lawless deeds that he saw and heard]; then the Lord knows how to rescue the godly from trials, and to keep the unrighteous under punishment until the day of judgment, especially those who indulge in the lust of defiling passions and despise authority. (2 Peter 2:4–10)

Scoffers will come in the last days with scoffing, following their own sinful desires. They will say, "Where is the promise of his coming?" For ever since the fathers fell asleep, all things are continuing as they were since the beginning of creation. For they deliberately overlook this fact, that the heavens existed long ago, and the earth was formed out of water and through water by the word of God, and that by means of these the world that then existed was deluged with water and perished. But by the same word the heavens and the earth that now exist are stored up for fire, being kept until the day of judgment and destruction of the ungodly.

But do not overlook this one fact, beloved, that with the Lord one day is a thousand years, and a thousand years as one day. The Lord is not slow to fulfill his promise as some count slowness, but is patient towards you, not wishing that any should perish, but that all should reach repentance. But the day of the Lord will come like a thief, and then the heavens will pass away with a roar, and the heavenly bodies will be burned up and dissolved, and the earth and the works that are done on it will be exposed. Since all these things are thus to be dissolved, what sort of people ought you to be in lives of holiness and godliness, waiting for the hastening of the coming of the day of God, because of which the heavens will be set on fire and dissolved, and the heavenly bodies will melt as they burn! But according to his promise we are waiting for a new heavens and a new earth in which righteousness dwells. (2 Peter 3:3–13)

THE FIRST LETTER OF JOHN

This is the message we have heard from God and proclaim to you, that God is light, and in him is no darkness at all. If we say we have fellowship with him while we walk in darkness, we lie and do not practice the truth. But if we walk in the light, as he is in the light, we have fellowship with one another, and the blood of Jesus his Son cleanses us from all sin. If we say we have no sin, we deceive ourselves, and the truth is not in us. If we confess our sins, he is faithful and just to forgive our sins and to cleanse us from all unrighteousness. If we say we have not sinned, we make him a liar, and his word is not in us. (1 John 1:5–10)

My little children, I am writing these things to you so that you may not sin. But if anyone does sin, we have an advocate with the Father, Jesus Christ the righteous. He is the propitiation for our sins, and not for ours only but also for the sins of the whole world. And by this we know that we have come to know him, if we keep his commandments. Whoever says "I know him" but does not keep his commandments is a liar, and the truth is not in him, but whoever keeps his word, in him truly the love of God is perfected. By this we may know that we are in him: whoever says he abides in him ought to walk in the same way in which he walked. (1 John 2:1–6)

Whoever says he is in the light and hates his brother is still in darkness. Whoever loves his brother abides in the light, and in him there is no cause for stumbling. But whoever hates his brother is in the darkness and walks in the darkness, and does not know where he is going, because the darkness has blinded his eyes. (1 John 2:9–11)

Do not love the world or the things in the world. If anyone loves the world, the love of the Father is not in him. For all that is in the world— the desires of the flesh and the desires of the eyes and pride in possessions—is not from the Father but is from the world. And the world is passing away along with its desires, but whoever does the will of God abides forever. (1 John 2:15–17)

Children, it is the last hour; and just as you heard that the antichrist was coming, so now many antichrists have appeared. Thus we know this is the last hour. They went out from us, but they were not really of our number; if they had been, they would have remained with us. Their desertion shows that none of them was of our number. But you have the anointing that comes from the holy one, and you all have knowledge. I write to you not because you do not know the truth but because you do, and because every lie is alien to the truth. Who is the liar? Whoever denies that Jesus is the Christ. Whoever denies the Father and the Son, this is the antichrist. No one who denies the Son has the Father, but whoever confesses the Son has the Father as well. Let what you heard from the beginning abide in you. If what you heard from the beginning abides in you, then you too will abide in the Son and in the Father. And this is the promise that he made to us—eternal life. (1 John 2:18–23)

See what kind of love the Father has given to us, that we should be called children of God;

and so we are. The reason why the world does not know us is that it did not know him. Beloved, we are God's children now, and what we will be has not yet appeared; but we know that when he appears we shall be like him, because we shall see him as he is. And everyone who thus hopes in him purifies himself as he is pure. (1 John 3:1–3)

For this is the message that you have heard from the beginning, that we should love one another. Do not be surprised, brothers, that the world hates you. We know that we have passed out of death into life, because we love the brothers. Whoever does not love abides in death. Everyone who hates his brother is a murderer, and you know that no murderer has eternal life abiding in him. (1 John 3:11–15)

By this we know love, that he [Jesus] laid down his life for us, and we ought to lay down our lives for the brothers. But if anyone has the world's goods and sees his brother in need, yet closes his heart against him, how does God's love abide in him? Little children, let us not love in word or talk but in deed and truth. (1 John 3:16–19)

Whatever we ask we receive from God, because we keep his commandments and do what pleases him. And this is his commandment, that we believe in the name of his Son Jesus Christ and love one another, just as he commanded us. Whoever keeps his commandments abides in God, and God in him. And by this we know that he abides in us, by the Spirit whom he has given us. (1 John 3:22–24)

Beloved, do not believe every spirit, but test the spirit to see whether they are from God, for many false prophets have gone out into the world. By this you will know the Spirit of God: every spirit that confesses that Jesus Christ has come in the flesh is from God, and every spirit that does not confess Jesus is not from God. This is the spirit of the antichrist, which you heard was coming and now is in the world already. Little children, you are from God and have overcome them, for he who is in you is greater than he who is in the world. (1 John 4:1–4)

Beloved, let us love one another, for love is from God, and whoever loves has been born of God and knows God. Anyone who does not love does not know God, because God is love. In this the love of God was made manifest among us, that God sent his only Son into the world, so that we might live through him. In this is love, not that we have loved God but that he loved us and sent his Son to be the propitiation for our sins. Beloved, if God so loved us, we also ought to love one another. No one has ever seen God; if we love one another, God abides in us and his love is perfected in us. (1 John 4:7–12)

By this we know that we abide in him and he in us, because he has given us of his spirit. And we have seen and testify that the Father has sent his Son to be the Savior of the world. Whoever confesses that Jesus is the Son of God, God abides in him, and he in God. So we have come to know and to believe the love that God has for us. God is love, and whoever abides in love abides in God, and God abides in him. By this is love perfected with us, so that we may have confidence for the day of judgment, because as he is so also are we in this world. There is no fear in love, but perfect love casts out fear. For fear has to do with punishment, and whoever fears has not been perfected in love. We love because he first loved us. (1 John 4:13–19)

If anyone says "I love God," and hates his brother, he is a liar; for he who does not love his brother who he has seen cannot love God whom he has not seen. And this commandment we have from him: whoever loves God must also love his brother. (1 John 4:20–21)

Everyone who believes that Jesus is the Christ has been born of God, and everyone who loves the Father loves whoever has been born of him. By this we know that we love the children of God, when we love God and obey his commandments. For this is the love of God, that we keep his commandments. And his commandments are not burdensome. For everyone who has been born of God overcomes the world. And this is the victory that has overcome the world—our faith. Who is it that overcomes the world except the one who believes that Jesus is the Son of God? (1 John 5:1–5)

God gave us eternal life, and this life is in his Son. Whoever has the Son has life; whoever does not have the Son of God does not have life. (1 John 5:11–12)

I write these things to you who believe in the name of the Son of God that you may know that you have eternal life. This is the confidence that we have toward God, that if we ask anything according to his will he hears us. And if we know that he hears us in whatever we ask, we know that we have the requests that we have asked of him. (1 John 5:13–15)

We know that everyone who has been born of God does not keep on sinning, but he who was born of God protects him, and the evil one does not touch him. We know that we are from God, and the whole world lies in the power of the evil one. And we know that the Son of God has come and has given us understanding, so that we may know him who is true, and we are in him who is true, in his Son Jesus Christ. He is the true God and eternal life. Little children, keep yourselves from idols. (1 John 8:18–21)

THE SECOND LETTER OF JOHN

And now I ask you, dear lady—not as though I was writing you a new commandment, but the one we have had from the beginning—that we love one another. And this is love, that we walk according to his commandments; this is the commandment, just as you have heard from the beginning, so that you should walk in it. For many deceivers have gone out into the world, those who do not confess the coming of Jesus Christ in the flesh. Such a one is the deceiver and the antichrist. Watch yourselves, so that you may not lose what we have worked for, but may win a full reward. Everyone who goes ahead and does not abide in the teaching of Christ, does not have God. Whoever abides in the teaching has both the Father and the Son. If anyone comes to you and does not bring this teaching, do not receive him into your house or give him any greeting, for whoever greets him takes part in his wicked works. (2 John 1:5–11)

THE THIRD LETTER OF JOHN

Beloved, do not imitate evil but imitate good. Whoever does good is from God; whoever does evil has not seen God. (3 John 1:11)

THE LETTER OF JUDE

Jude, a servant of Jesus Christ and brother of James, To those who are called, beloved in God the Father and kept for Jesus Christ: May mercy, peace, and love be multiplied to you. (Jude 1:2)

In the Letter of Jude, Jude informs his audience that certain ungodly people crept into the followers of Jesus who pervert the grace of God into sensuality and deny Jesus Christ as God and Master. It claims that Jesus is the one who saved the people out of the land of Egypt, and then later destroyed those who did not believe (Jude 1:5). Jesus is the one who put the angels who left their own proper dwelling and position of authority into chains of gloomy darkness until the great day of judgment (Jude 1:6).

Jude reveals that certain people blaspheme all that they do not understand. They are destroyed by following their instincts as understanding like unreasoning animals (Jude 1:10).

It was also about these that Enoch, the seventh from Adam, prophesied, saying, "Behold, the Lord comes with ten thousands of his holy ones, to execute judgment on all and to convict the ungodly of all their deeds of ungodliness that they have committed in such an ungodly way, and all the harsh things that ungodly sinners have spoken against him." These are grumblers, malcontents, following their own sinful desires; they are loud-mouthed boasters, showing favoritism to gain advantage. (Jude 1:14–16)

But you must remember, beloved, the predictions of the apostles of our Lord Jesus Christ. They said to you, "In the last time there will be scoffers, following their own ungodly passions." It is these who cause divisions, worldly people, devoid of the Spirit. But you, beloved, building yourselves up in your most holy faith and praying in the Holy Spirit, keep yourselves in the love of God, waiting for the mercy of our Lord Jesus Christ that leads to eternal life. And have mercy on those who doubt; save others by snatching them out of the fire; to others show mercy with fear, hating even the garment stained by the flesh. (Jude 1:17–23)

Now to him who is able to keep you from stumbling and to present you blameless before the presence of his glory with great joy, to the only God, our Savior, through Jesus Christ our Lord, be glory, majesty, dominion, and authority, before all time and now and forever. Amen. (Jude 1:24–25)

CHAPTER 25

THE BOOK OF REVELATION (TEEN/STUDENT VERSION)

have included two versions of the book of Revelation in this *Bible Summary for Adults and Students*. Some of the events which will take place in the book of Revelation did not occur yet and are, therefore, future events. During these events, God will pour out his undiluted wrath on areas of this future world which have rejected God and are unrepentant before he returns for good and makes everything perfect, unblemished, and new. The depiction of God's wrath on some of the unrepentant future world may be unsettling and confusing to younger readers. Therefore, I have included two versions of the summary of the book of Revelation. In this first "Teen/Student Version," the middle part of the book of Revelation, which details God's wrath on portions of a future sinful world, is summarized and easier for young readers to process. In the "Adult Version," God's wrath in the middle part of the summary of the book of Revelation is presented in full detail. It is up to the reader or teacher to decide which version is most appropriate for your use.

Before we enter the summary of the book of Revelation, I would like to explain that based on my understanding of the full Bible, there may be a rapture of God's people just prior to the Great Tribulation events depicted in the book of Revelation. Many other people also believe this to be true, while some do not. Additionally, there is disagreement among those who believe in the rapture about when it will happen: just before the Great Tribulation events, in the middle of the Great Tribulation events, or just after the Great Tribulation events.

After studying the Bible intensively for over twenty years, and learning from numerous respected Bible teachers, I believe the following is a summary of the future events that will take place in the book of Revelation, which could be immediately preceded by a rapture of those who already believe in and follow Jesus Christ:

> God decides this present era of mankind is near the end, and God's next era with man must begin. Everyone who is alive at this time who has not yet made a choice about following God are forced to make a choice: Choose to follow God, or choose to not follow him.

1. Those that already follow God who are alive on earth at that time do not need to go through the Great Tribulation. They have already made a choice to follow him.

2. The rapture happens. Those who already follow God are taken up instantly to be with Jesus in the air and will be with him in heaven forever. Jesus comes in the air just for this. He gathers believers that are alive, takes them with him to avoid the Great Tribulation, and they leave.

3. For the remainder of the people on earth who have either rejected following Jesus, or who have not yet chosen to follow him, there will be approximately a seven-year period in which both the devil (Antichrist) and supernatural messengers of God (two supernatural witnesses of God, angels, 144,000 God-anointed servants) will be out in the open, for *everyone* to see and hear. This will be the most chaotic, devastating, and supernatural series of events in the history of the world. Both a direct messenger from Satan (Antichrist) and messengers from God will each tell the world to "Follow me" (the devil), and "Follow me" (God). Everyone alive who has not yet made a choice to follow

Jesus (those that had already followed Jesus were raptured) *must* make a choice to follow either God or Satan.

4. This will be a seven-year period of chaos (half of the world's population will die through wars, natural disasters, plagues, and famines—God's wrath along with the wrath of the Antichrist are both poured out on a sinful, unbelieving world). Many people will come to believe in God and follow him during this time. Although some of them will lose their life in this period (some will survive it), all will be eternally saved. Many, however, will choose to follow the Antichrist during this period and will be condemned.

5. At the end of the seven-year period of the Antichrist terrorizing the world, Jesus returns. He defeats the Antichrist and all his followers with just words that come from his mouth. The Antichrist along with his companion the false prophet are thrown into hell alive. Satan is then chained up for a thousand years so he will no longer tempt and torment the world. During this thousand years, Jesus will perfectly rule the world in person from Jerusalem.

6. After one thousand years, God lets Satan loose to give the world one last free choice of whom to follow: God or Satan. Satan causes one last rebellion against God, in which he convinces many to turn against God. God defeats Satan permanently, and Satan and his followers are condemned to hell.

7. God makes a new heaven and a new earth, and the sin of mankind which began with Adam and Eve is finally over and everything is perfected with mankind.

All the events in the above brief summary of the book of Revelation can be found in the book of Revelation in the Bible except for the rapture. However, there are several passages in the Bible that appear to explain that a rapture will happen, which will now be presented. The section of each passage that discusses what appears to be the rapture will be in italics.

Throughout the Bible, God refers to those who have died as having gone to sleep. In many passages that appear to discuss the rapture, it talks about those who have gone to sleep meeting Jesus (those who believed in God who have died). However, in the rapture passages, it talks about those who follow God that are still awake (alive) meeting Jesus.

The following passage confirms that God will not pour out his wrath on those who believe in God. In the Great Tribulation, God pours out his wrath on a world who rejected him. What about those who follow him and are alive (awake) at this time? God takes them out of the world before his wrath is poured out on it. Wrath is not appointed for them, because they already believe in and follow God:

> *For God has not destined us for wrath,* but to obtain salvation through our Lord Jesus Christ, who died for us *so that whether we are awake or asleep we might live with him (italics added).* (1 Thessalonians 5:9–10)

In the next passage, it states that those who follow God (brothers) who are alive when Jesus returns will be caught up along with those who are raised from the dead who believed in God and will meet Jesus in the air, who has come in the air to gather them to be with him:

> We do not want you to be unaware, brothers, about those who have fallen asleep, so that you may not grieve like the rest, who have no hope. For if we believe that Jesus died and rose, so too will God, through Jesus, bring with him those who have fallen asleep. Indeed, we tell you this, on the word of the lord, that *we who are alive, who are left until the coming of the Lord, will surely not precede those who have fallen asleep (italics added).* For the Lord himself, with a word of command, with the voice of an archangel and

with the trumpet of God, will come down from heaven, and the dead in Christ shall rise first. *Then we who are alive, who are left, will be caught up together with them in the clouds to meet the Lord in the air. Thus we shall always be with the Lord. Therefore, console another with these words (italics added).* (1 Thessalonians 4:13–18)

The following passage explains that not every believer will die. Some, while alive, will be changed in a moment, and they will meet the dead who had faith in God who were resurrected, and both will instantly change from mortal to immortal:

> I tell you this, brothers: flesh and blood cannot inherit the kingdom of God, nor does the perishable inherit the imperishable. *Behold! I tell you a mystery. We shall not all sleep, but we shall be changed, in a moment, in the twinkling of an eye, at the last trumpet (itlalics added).* For the trumpet will sound, and the dead will be raised imperishable, *and we shall be changed (italics added).* For this perishable body must put on the imperishable, and the mortal body must put on immortality. (1 Corinthians 15:50–53)

This paragraph details how at an ordinary time in which no one expects, Jesus (Son of Man) will return to snatch people away:

> For as were the days of Noah, so will be the coming of the Son of Man. For as in those days before the flood they were eating and drinking, marrying and giving in marriage, until the day when Noah entered the ark, and they were unaware until the flood came and swept them all away, so will the coming of the Son of Man. *Then two men will be in the field; one will be taken and*

one left. Two women will be grinding at the mill; one will be taken and one left (italics added). Therefore, stay awake, for you do not know on what day your Lord is coming. (Matthew 24:37–42)

The following passage states how God's people will be delivered out of the Great Tribulation:

At that time shall arise Michael, the great prince who has charge of our people. And there shall be a time of trouble, such as never has been since there was a nation till that time. *But at that time your people shall be delivered, everyone whose name shall be found written in the book (italics added).* (Daniel 12:1)

This final passage details a group of people in heaven who have come out of the Great Tribulation. In Revelation 20:4, it discusses a group of people in heaven who were there because they became martyrs for God rather than follow the Antichrist during the Great Tribulation. This following group is a group in heaven that came out of the Great tribulation, but were not martyrs like the first group. They came out of the Great Tribulation another way:

After this I had a vision of a great multitude, which no one could count, from every nation, race, people, and tongue. They stood before the throne and before the Lamb, wearing white robes and holding palm branches in their hands. Then one of the elders spoke up and said to me, "Who are these wearing white robes, and where did they come from?" I said to him, "My lord, you are the one who knows." He said to me, *"These are the ones coming out of the great tribulation; (italics added)* they have washed their robes and made them white in the blood of the Lamb. For this reason they stand before God's throne and worship him day and night in his temple. The one who sits on the throne will shelter them. They will not hunger or thirst anymore, nor will the sun or any heat strike them. For the Lamb who is in the center of the throne will shepherd them and lead them to springs of life-giving water, and God will wipe away every tear from their eyes." (Revelation 7:9–17)

The following is the summary of the book of Revelation. I tried to directly quote from the Bible as much as I could so that the summary would not be distorted in any way.

The revelation of Jesus Christ, which God gave to him, to show his servants what must happen soon. He made it known by sending his angel to his servant John, who gives witness to the word of God and the testimony of Jesus Christ by reporting what he saw. Blessed is the one who reads aloud and blessed are those who listen to this prophetic message and heed what is written in it, for the appointed time is near. (Revelation 1:1–3)

John, to the seven churches in Asia: grace to you and peace from him who is and who was and who is to come, and from the seven spirits before his throne, and from Jesus Christ, the faithful witness, the firstborn of the dead and ruler of the kings of the earth. To him who loves us and has freed us from our sins by his blood, who has made us into a kingdom, priests for his God and Father, to him be the glory and power forever [and ever]. Amen. Behold, he is coming amid the clouds, and every eye will see him, even those who pierced him. And the peoples of the earth will lament him. Yes. Amen. "I am the Alpha and the Omega," says the Lord God, "the one who is and who was and who is to come, the almighty." (Revelation 1:4–8)

I, John, your brother, who share with you the distress, the kingdom, and the endurance we have in Jesus, found myself on the island called Patmos because I proclaimed God's word and gave testimony to Jesus. I was caught up in spirit on the Lord's day and heard behind me a voice as loud as a trumpet, which said, "Write on a scroll what you see and send it to the seven churches: to Ephesus, Smyrna, Pergamum, Thyatira Sardis, Philadelphia, and Laodicea." Then I turned to see whose voice it was that spoke to me, and when I turned, I saw seven gold lampstands and in the midst of the lampstands one like a son of man, wearing an ankle-length robe, with a gold sash around his chest. The hair on his head was as white as wool or as snow, and his eyes were like a fiery flame. His feet were like polished brass refined in a furnace, and his voice was like the sound of rushing water. In his right hand he held seven stars. A sharp two-edged sword came out of his mouth, and his face shone like the sun at its brightest.

When I caught sight of him, I fell down at his feet as though dead. He touched me with his right hand and said, "Do not be afraid. I am the first and the last, the one who lives. Once I was dead, but now I am alive forever and ever. I hold the keys to death and the netherworld. Write down, therefore, what you have seen, and what is happening, and what will happen afterwards.

This is the secret meaning of the seven stars you saw in my right hand, and of the seven lampstands: the seven stars are the angels of the seven churches, and the seven lampstands are the seven churches." (Revelation 1:9–20)

To the angel of the church in Ephesus, write this: "The one who holds the seven stars in his right hand and walks in the midst of the seven gold lampstands says this: 'I know your works, your labor, and your endurance, and that you cannot tolerate the wicked; you have tested those who call themselves apostles but are not, and discovered that they are impostors. Moreover, you have endurance and have suffered for my name, and you have not grown weary. Yet I hold this against you: you have lost the love you had at first. Realize how far you have fallen. Repent, and do the works you did at first. Otherwise, I will come to you and remove your lampstand from its place, unless you repent. Whoever has ears ought to hear what the Spirit says to the churches. To the victor I will give the right to eat from the tree of life that is in the garden of God.'" (Revelation 2:1–7)

To the angel of the church of Smyrna, write this: "The first and last, who once died but came to life says this: 'I know your Tribulation and poverty, but you are rich. I know the slander of those who claim to be Jews and are not, but rather are members of the assembly of Satan. Do not be afraid of anything that you are going to suffer. Indeed, the devil will throw some of you into prison, that you may be tested, and you will face an ordeal for ten days. Remain faithful until death, and I will give you the crown of life. Whoever has ears ought to hear what the Spirit says to the churches. The victor shall not be harmed by the second death.'" (Revelation 2:8–11)

To the angel of the church in Pergamum, write this: "The one with the sharp two-edged sword says this: 'I know that you live where Satan's throne is, and yet you hold fast to my name and have not denied your faith in me, not even in the days of Antipas, my faithful witness, who was martyred among you, where Satan lives. Yet I have a few things against you. You have some people there who hold to the teaching of Balaam, who instructed Balak to put a stumbling block before the Israelites: to eat food sacrificed to idols and to play the harlot. Likewise, you also have some people who hold to the teaching of the Nicolaitans. Therefore, repent. Otherwise, I will come to you quickly and wage war against them with the sword of my mouth. Whoever has ears ought to hear what the Spirit says to the churches. To the victor I shall give some of the hidden manna; I shall also give a white amulet upon which is inscribed a new name, which no one knows except the one who receives it.'" (Revelation 2:12–17)

To the angel of the church in Thyatira, write this: "The Son of God, whose eyes are like a fiery flame and whose feet are like polished brass, says this: 'I know your works, your love, faith service, and endurance, and that your last works are greater than the first. Yet I hold this against you, that you tolerate the woman Jezebel, who calls herself a prophetess, who teaches and misleads my servants to play the harlot and to eat food sacrificed to idols. I have given her time to repent, but she refuses to repent of her harlotry. So I will cast her on a sickbed and plunge those who commit adultery with her into intense suffering unless they repent of her works. I will also put her children to death. Thus shall all the churches come to know that I am the searcher of hearts and minds and that I will give each of you what your works deserve. But I say to the rest of you in Thyatira, who do not uphold this teaching and know nothing of the so-called deep secrets of Satan: on you I will place no further burden, except that you must hold fast to what you have until I Come. To the victor, who keeps my ways until the end, I will give authority over the nations. He will rule them with an iron rod. Like clay vessels they will be smashed, just as I received authority from my Father. And to him I will give the morning star. Whoever has ears ought to hear what the Spirit says to the churches.'"

To the angel of the church in Sardis, write this: "The one who has the seven spirits of God and the seven stars says this: 'I know your works, that you have the reputation of being alive, but you are dead. Be watchful and strengthen what is left, which is going to die, for I have not found your works complete in the sight of my God. Remember then how you accepted and heard; keep it, and repent. If you are not watchful, I will come like a thief, and you will never know at what hour I will come upon you. However, you have a few people in Sardis who have not soiled their garments; they will walk with me dressed in white, because they are worthy. The victor will thus be dressed in white, and I will never erase his name from the book of life but will acknowledge his name in the presence of my Father and his angels. Whoever has ears ought to hear what the Spirit says to the churches.'" (Revelation 3:1–6)

To the angel of the church in Philadelphia, write this: "The holy one, the true, who holds the key of David, who opens and no one shall close, who closes and no one shall open, says this: 'I know your works [behold, I have left an open door before you, which no one can close]. You have limited strength, and yet you have kept my word and have not denied my name. Behold, I will make those of the assembly of Satan who claim to be Jews and are not, but are lying, behold, I will make them come and fall prostrate at your feet, and they will realize that I love you. Because you have kept my message of endurance, I will keep you safe in the time of trial that is going to come to the whole world to test the inhabitants of the earth. I am coming quickly. Hold fast to what you have, so that no one may take your crown. The victor I will make into a pillar in the temple of my God, and he will never leave it again. On him I will inscribe the name of my God and the name of the city of my God, the new Jerusalem, which comes down out of heaven from my God, as well as my new name. Whoever has ears ought to hear what the Spirit says to the churches.'" (Revelation 3:7–13)

To the angel of the church in Laodicea, write this: "The Amen, the faithful and true witness, the source of God's creation, says this: 'I know your works; I know you are neither cold nor hot. So, because you are lukewarm, neither hot nor cold, I will spit you out of my mouth. For you say, "I am rich and affluent and have no need of anything," and yet do not realize that you are wretched, pitiable, poor, blind, and naked. I advise you to buy from me gold refined by fire so that you may be rich, and white garments to put on so that your shameful nakedness may not be exposed, and buy ointment to smear on your eyes so that you may see. Those whom I love, I reprove and chastise. Be earnest, therefore, and repent. Behold, I stand at the door and knock. If anyone hears my voice and opens the door, [then] I will enter his house and dine with him and he with me. I will give the victor the right to sit with me on my throne, as I myself first won the victory and sit with my Father on his throne. Whoever has ears ought to hear what the Spirit says to the churches.'" (Revelation 3:14–22)

After this, the apostle John had a vision of an open door to heaven. He heard a voice that sounded like a trumpet that spoke to him before. It said,

Come up here and I will show you what must happen afterwards. (Revelation 4:1)

John's spirit was then immediately caught up to heaven. He was before a throne in heaven, and the one who sat on it had an appearance that sparkled like jasper and carnelian. There was a halo surrounding the throne that was a brilliant as an emerald. Also surrounding the throne were twenty-four other thrones. Sitting in them were twenty-four elders who were dressed in white garments and had gold crowns on their heads. From the main throne came flashes of lightning, peals of thunder, and rumblings. There were seven flaming torches which burned in front of the throne, which are the seven spirits of God. In front of the throne was something that looked like a sea of glasslike crystal (Revelation 4:1–6).

There were four living creatures covered with eyes in front and in back. They were around the throne and in the center. The first creature looked like a lion, the second resembled a calf, the third had a face like a human, and the fourth resembled an eagle in flight. Each creature had six wings. Day and night they exclaimed without ceasing:

> Holy, holy, is the Lord God almighty, who was, and who is, and who is to come. (Revelation 4:8)

Whenever the four creatures gave glory to God, the twenty-four elders fell down before God, threw their crowns before his throne, and said,

> Worthy are you, Lord our God, to receive glory and honor and power, for you created all things; because of your will they came to be and were created. (Revelation 4:11)

> I saw a scroll in the right hand of the one who sat on the throne. It had writing on both sides and was sealed with seven seals. Then I saw a mighty angel who proclaimed in a loud voice, "Who is worthy to open the scroll and break tis seven seals?" But no on in heaven or on earth or under the earth was able to open the scroll or examine it. I shed many tears because no one was found worthy to open the scroll or to examine it. One of the elders said to me, "Do not weep. The lion of the tribe of Judah, the root of David, had triumphed, enabling him to open the scroll with its seven seals." (Revelation 5:1–5)

John then saw in the midst of the throne, the elders, and the four living creatures a Lamb that appeared to have been slain. The Lamb took the scroll from the right hand of the one who sat upon the throne. When he took the scroll, the four living creatures, the twenty-four elders, numerous angels, and every creature in heaven and on the earth and under the earth gave great praise and worship to the Lamb who was slain and now sat on the throne; he alone was worthy to open the scroll (Revelation 5:6–14). The events will all take place in the future. None of what is stated has taken place on earth yet.

What is revealed to the apostle John is that God will send his judgment upon the people of the earth in the future, the ones who will reject God. Many supernatural events will take place during this brief period of God's judgment on the sinful people of the world. The people who believe in and follow God during this time will survive this great time of distress and will be sheltered by God from his judgment on the earth (Revelation 7:9–17).

However, for those who will continue to reject God, God's wrath will be poured out on those sinful people who are not sheltered from his wrath. God's wrath will take the form of huge natural disasters; supernatural disasters which have never take place before on the earth; signs and wonders in the sun, moon, and stars; plagues, famines, and great wars involving many troops. These judgments will be sent by God to the people to repent of their evil ways and to turn to God and follow him. Some will repent, and they will be saved. Others will not repent due to their stubborn, evil hearts (Revelation chapters 8 and 9).

During this time of unprecedented tribulation in the world, God will cause great miracles to happen to tell the world to repent of their sinful ways, to follow him, and they will be saved. God will send two witness from heaven to preach to the world about God night and day for 1,260 days in the city of Jerusalem, and they will be protected by God so nothing can stop them from preaching to the people (Revelation chapter 11).

During this time, John witnessed that war broke out in heaven. The angel Michael was leading an army of God which defeated the devil (Satan) and threw him down to the earth for a very short time.

The devil sent out two figures working together on his behalf, called "the beast" and "the false prophet." They will try to deceive the world into following them instead of following God. However, God will send three angels flying around the world, continually proclaiming to the people of the world,

> Do not follow the Beast and the False Prophet; repent and follow God and you will be saved!" (Revelation chapter 13 and 14)

At one point, a huge army will gather on a vast plain in Israel called Megiddo for what is known as the Battle of Armageddon. The beast and the false prophet will be there as leaders of much of this fighting force. When this takes place, Jesus returns to earth to confront the beast and the false prophet and their evil followers (Revelation 19:11–21).

> Then I heard something like the sound of a great multitude or the sound of rushing water or mighty peals of thunder, as they said: "Alleluia! The Lord has established his reign, our God, the almighty. Let us rejoice and be glad and give him glory. For the wedding day of the Lamb has come, his bride has made herself ready. She was allowed to wear a bright, clean linen garment." [The linen represents the righteous deeds of the holy ones.] Then the angel said to me, "Write this: Blessed are those who have been called to the wedding feast of the Lamb." And he said to me, "These words are true; they come from God." I fell at his feet to worship him. But he said to me, "Don't! I am a fellow servant of yours and of your brothers who bear witness to Jesus. Worship God. Witness to Jesus is the spirit of prophecy." (Revelation 19:6–10)

Then I saw the heavens opened, and there was a white horse; its rider was called "Faithful and True." He judges and wages war in righteousness. His eyes were like a fiery flame, and on his head were many diadems. He had a name inscribed that no one knows except himself. He wore a cloak that had been dipped in blood, and his name was called the Word of God. The armies of heaven followed him, mounted on white horses and wearing clean white linen. Out of his mouth came a sharp sword to strike the nations. He will rule them with an iron rod, and he himself will tread out in the wine press the wine of the fury and wrath of God the almighty. He has a name written on his cloak and on his thigh, "King of kings and Lord of Lords."

Then I saw an angel standing on the sun. He cried out in a loud voice to all the birds flying high overhead, "Come here. Gather for God's great feast, to eat the flesh of kings, the flesh of military officers, and the flesh of warriors, the flesh of horses and of their riders, and the flesh of all, free and slave, small and great." Then I saw the beast and the kings of the earth and their armies gathered to fight against the one riding the horse and against his army. The beast was caught and with it the false prophet who had performed in its sight the signs by which he led astray those who had accepted the mark of the beast and those who had worshipped its image. The two were thrown alive into the fiery pool burning with sulfur. The rest were killed by the sword that came out of the mouth of the one riding the horse, and all the birds gorged themselves on their flesh. (Revelation 19:11–21)

Then I saw an angel come down from heaven, holding in his hand the key to the abyss and a heavy chain. He seized the dragon, the ancient serpent, which is the Devil or Satan, and tied it up for a thousand years and threw it into the abyss, which he locked over it and sealed, so that it could no longer lead the nations astray until the thousand years are completed. After this, it is to be released for a short time.

Then I saw thrones; those who sat on them were entrusted with judgment. I also saw the souls of those who had been beheaded for their witness to Jesus and for the word of God, and who had not worshipped the beast or its image nor had accepted the mark on their foreheads or hands. They came to life and reigned with Christ for a thousand years. The rest of the dead did not come to life until the thousand years were over. This is the first resurrection. Blessed and holy is the one who shares in the first resurrection. The second death has no power over these; they will be priests of God and of Christ, and they will reign with him for the thousand years.

When the thousand years are completed, Satan will be released from his prison. He will go out to deceive the nations at the four corners of the earth, Gog and Magog, to gather them for battle; their number is like the sand of the sea. They invaded the breadth of the earth and surrounded the camp of the holy ones and the beloved city. But fire came down from heaven and consumed them. The Devil who had led them astray was thrown into the pool of fire and sulfur, where the beast and the false prophet were. There they will be tormented day and night forever and ever. (Revelation 20:1–10)

Next I saw a large white throne and the one who was sitting on it. The earth and the sky fled from his presence and there was no place for them. I saw the dead, the great and the lowly, standing before the throne, and the scrolls were opened. Then another scroll was opened, the book of life. The dead were judged according to their deeds, by what was written in the scrolls. The sea gave up its dead; then Death and Hades gave up their dead. All the dead were judged according to their deeds. Then Death and Hades were thrown into the pool of fire. This pool of fire is the second death. Anyone whose name was not found written in the book of life was thrown into the pool of fire. (Revelation 20:11–15)

Then I saw a new heaven and a new earth. The former heaven and the former earth had passed away, and the sea was no more. I also saw the holy city, a new Jerusalem, coming down out of heaven from God, prepared as a bride adorned for her husband. I heard a loud voice from the throne saying, "Behold, God's dwelling is with the human race. He will dwell with them and they will be his people and God himself will always be with them as their God. He will wipe every tear from their eyes, and there shall be no more death or mourning, wailing or pain, for the old order has passed away." (Revelation 21:1–4)

The one who sat on the throne said, "Behold, I make all things new." Then he said, "Write these words down, for they are trustworthy and true." He said to me, "They are accomplished. I am the Alpha and the Omega, the beginning and the end. To the thirsty I will give a gift from the spring of life-giving water. The victor will inherit these gifts, and I shall be his God, and he will be my son. (Revelation 21:5–7)

Then John saw the New Jerusalem coming down out of heaven. It was radiant like jasper and clear as crystal. It had a giant high wall with twelve gates. Angels were stationed on the twelve gates. Also, on the gates were the inscribed names of the twelve tribes of Israel. Three gates faced north, three faced south, three faced east, and three faced west. The wall had twelve stones as its foundations. On each stone was the name of one of the twelve apostles. New Jerusalem was a square city; its length was equal to its width. The city was 1,500 miles in length, width, and height. The wall of the city was made of jasper, while the city was made of pure gold, which was clear as glass. The foundations of the city wall were made of twelve precious stones. Each of its gates were made of a huge single pearl. The streets of New Jerusalem were made of pure gold, which was as transparent as glass (Revelation 21:9–21).

I saw no temple in the city, for its temple is the Lord God almighty and the Lamb. The city had no need of sun or moon to shine on it, for the glory of God gave it light, and its lamp was the Lamb. The nations will walk by its light, and to it the kings of the earth will bring their treasure. During the day its gates will never be shut, and there will be no night there. The treasure and wealth of the nations will be brought there, but nothing unclean will enter it, nor anyone who does abominable things or tells lies. Only those will enter whose names are written in the Lamb's book of life. (Revelation 21:22–27)

Then the angel showed me the river of life-giving water, sparkling like crystal, flowing from the throne of God and of the Lamb down the middle of the street. On either side of the river grew the tree of life that produces fruit twelve times a year, once each month; the leaves of the trees serve as medicine for the nations. Nothing accursed will be found there anymore. The throne of God and of the Lamb will be in it, and his servants will worship him. They will look upon his face, and his name will be on their foreheads. Night will be no more, nor will they need light from lamp or sun, for the Lord God shall give them light, and they shall reign forever and ever. (22:1–5)

God then said,

Behold, I am coming soon.

Blessed is he who keeps the prophetic message of this book (Revelation 22:7).

I bring with me the recompense I will give each according to his deeds. I am the Alpha and the Omega, the first and the last, the beginning and the end. (Revelation 22:12–13)

Blessed are they who wash their robes so they have the right to the tree of life and enter the city through its gates. Outside are the dogs, the sorcerers, the unchaste, the murderers, the idol-worshipers, and all who love and practice deceit. (Revelation 22:14–15)

I, Jesus, sent my angel to give you this testimony for the churches. I am the root and offspring of David, the bright morning star. The Spirit and the bride say, "Come." Let the hearer say, "Come." Let the one who thirsts come forward, and the one who wants it receive the give of life-giving water. (Revelation 22:16–17)

The one who gives this testimony says, "Yes, I am coming soon." Amen! Come, Lord Jesus! The grace of the Lord Jesus be with you all. (Revelation 22:21)

THE BOOK OF REVELATION
ADULT VERSION

I have included two versions of the book of Revelation in this *Bible Summary for Adults and Students*. Some of the events which will take place in the book of Revelation did not occur yet and are, therefore, future events. During these events, God will pour out his undiluted wrath on areas of this future world which have rejected God and are unrepentant before he returns for good and makes everything perfect, unblemished, and new. The depiction of God's wrath on some of the unrepentant future world may be unsettling and confusing to younger readers. Therefore, I have included two versions of the summary of the book of Revelation. In this first "Teen/Student Version," the middle part of the book of Revelation, which details God's wrath on portions of a future sinful world, is summarized and easier for young readers to process. In the "Adult Version," God's wrath in the middle part of the summary of the book of Revelation is presented in full detail. It is up to the reader or teacher to decide which version is most appropriate for your use.

Before we enter the summary of the book of Revelation, I would like to explain that based on my understanding of the full Bible, there may be a rapture of God's people just prior to the Great Tribulation events depicted in the book of Revelation. Many other people also believe this to be true, while some do not. Additionally, there is disagreement among those who believe in the rapture about when it will happen: just before the Great Tribulation events, in the middle of the Great Tribulation events, or just after the Great Tribulation events.

After studying the Bible intensively for over twenty years, and learning from numerous respected Bible teachers, I believe the following is a summary of the future events that will take place in the book of Revelation, which could be immediately preceded by a rapture of those who already believe in and follow Jesus Christ:

God decides this present era of mankind is near the end, and God's next era with man must begin. Everyone who is alive at this time who has not yet made a choice about following God are forced to make a choice: Choose to follow God, or choose to not follow him.

1. Those that already follow God who are alive on earth at that time do not need to go through the Great Tribulation. They have already made a choice to follow him.

2. The rapture happens. Those who already follow God are taken up instantly to be with Jesus in the air and will be with him in heaven forever. Jesus comes in the air just for this. He gathers believers that are alive, takes them with him to avoid the Great Tribulation, and they leave.

3. For the remainder of the people on earth who have either rejected following Jesus, or who have not yet chosen to follow him, there will be approximately a seven-year period in which both the devil (Antichrist) and supernatural messengers of God (two supernatural witnesses of God, angels, 144,000 God-anointed servants) will be out in the open, for *everyone* to see and hear. This will be the most chaotic, devastating, and supernatural series of events in the history of the world. Both a direct messenger from Satan (Antichrist) and messengers from God will each tell the world to "Follow me" (the devil), and "Follow me" (God). Everyone alive who has not yet made a choice to follow Jesus (those that had already followed Jesus were raptured) *must* make a choice to follow either God or Satan.

4. This will be a seven-year period of chaos (half of the world's population will die through wars, natural disasters, plagues, and famines—God's wrath along with the wrath of the Antichrist are both poured out on a sinful, unbelieving world). Many people will come to believe in God and follow him during this time. Although some of them will lose their life in this period (some will survive it), all will be eternally saved. Many, however, will choose to follow the Antichrist during this period and will be condemned.

5. At the end of the seven-year period of the Antichrist terrorizing the world, Jesus returns. He defeats the Antichrist and all his followers with just words that come from his mouth. The Antichrist, along with his companion the false prophet are thrown into hell alive. Satan is then chained up for a thousand years so he will no longer tempt and torment the world. During this thousand years, Jesus will perfectly rule the world in person from Jerusalem.

6. After a thousand years, God lets Satan loose to give the world one last free choice of who to follow: God or Satan. Satan causes one last rebellion against God in which he convinces many to turn against God. God defeats Satan permanently, and Satan and his followers are condemned to hell.

7. God makes a new heaven and a new earth, and the sin of mankind which began with Adam and Eve is finally over, and everything is perfected with mankind.

All the events in the above brief summary of the book of Revelation can be found in the book of Revelation in the Bible except for the rapture. However, there are several passages in the Bible that appear to explain that a rapture will happen, which will now be presented. The section of each passage that discusses what appears to be the rapture will be in italics.

Throughout the Bible, God refers to those who have died as having gone to sleep. In many passages that appear to discuss the rapture, it talks about those who have gone to sleep meeting Jesus (those who believed in God who have died). However, in the rapture passages, it talks about those who follow God that are still awake (alive) meeting Jesus.

The following passage confirms that God will not pour out his wrath on those who believe in God. In the Great Tribulation, God pours out his wrath on a world who rejected him. What about those who follow him and are alive (awake) at this time? God takes them out of the world before his wrath is poured out on it. Wrath is not appointed for them, because they already believe in and follow God:

> *For God has not destined us for wrath,* but to obtain salvation through our Lord Jesus Christ, who died for us *so that whether we are awake or asleep we might live with him (italics added).* (1 Thessalonians 5:9–10)

In the next passage, it states that those who follow God (brothers) who are alive when Jesus returns will be caught up along with those who are raised from the dead who believed in God and will meet Jesus in the air, who has come in the air to gather them to be with him:

> We do not want you to be unaware, brothers, about those who have fallen asleep, so that you may not grieve like the rest, who have no hope. For if we believe that Jesus died and rose, so too will God, through Jesus, bring with him those who have fallen asleep. Indeed, we tell you this, on the word of the lord, that *we who are alive, who are left until the coming of the Lord, will surely not precede those who have fallen asleep (italics added).* For the Lord himself, with a word of command, with the voice of an archangel and with the trumpet of God, will come down from heaven, and the dead in Christ shall rise first. *Then we who are alive, who are left, will be caught*

up together with them in the clouds to meet the Lord in the air. Thus we shall always be with the Lord. Therefore, console another with these words (italics added). (1 Thessalonians 4:13–18)

The following passage explains that not every believer will die. Some, while alive, will be changed in a moment, and they will meet the dead who had faith in God who were resurrected, and both will instantly change from mortal to immortal:

> I tell you this, brothers: flesh and blood cannot inherit the kingdom of God, nor does the perishable inherit the imperishable. *Behold! I tell you a mystery. We shall not all sleep, but we shall be changed, in a moment, in the twinkling of an eye, at the last trumpet (italics added).* For the trumpet will sound, and the dead will be raised imperishable, *and we shall be changed.* For this perishable body must put on the imperishable, and the mortal body must put on immortality. (1 Corinthians 15:50–53)

This paragraph details how at an ordinary time in which no one expects, Jesus (Son of Man) will return to snatch people away:

> For as were the days of Noah, so will be the coming of the Son of Man. For as in those days before the flood they were eating and drink-ing, marrying and giving in marriage, until the day when Noah entered the ark, and they were unaware until the flood came and swept them all away, so will the coming of the Son of Man. *Then two men will be in the field; one will be taken and one left. Two women will be grinding at the mill; one will be taken and one left (italics added).* Therefore, stay awake, for you do not know

on what day your Lord is coming. (Matthew
24:37–42)

The following passage states how God's people will be delivered
out of the Great Tribulation:

At that time shall arise Michael, the great
prince who has charge of our people. And there
shall be a time of trouble, such as never has been
since there was a nation till that time. *But at that
time your people shall be delivered, everyone whose
name shall be found written in the book (italics
added).* (Daniel 12:1)

This final passage details a group of people in heaven who have
come out of the Great Tribulation. In Revelation 20:4, it discusses
a group of people in heaven who were there because they became
martyrs for God rather than follow the Antichrist during the Great
Tribulation. This following group is a group in heaven that came out
of the Great tribulation but were not martyrs like the first group.
They came out of the Great Tribulation another way:

After this I had a vision of a great multitude,
which no one could count, from every nation,
race, people, and tongue. They stood before the
throne and before the Lamb, wearing white robes
and holding palm branches in their hands. Then
one of the elders spoke up and said to me, "Who
are these wearing white robes, and where did they
come from?" I said to him, "My lord, you are
the one who knows." He said to me, *"These are
the ones coming out of the great tribulation; (italics
added)* they have washed their robes and made
them white in the blood of the Lamb. For this
reason they stand before God's throne and worship him day and night in his temple. The one

who sits on the throne will shelter them. They will not hunger or thirst anymore, nor will the sun or any heat strike them. For the Lamb who is in the center of the throne will shepherd them and lead them to springs of life-giving water, and God will wipe away every tear from their eyes." (Revelation 7:9–17)

The following is the summary of the book of Revelation. I tried to directly quote from the Bible as much as I could so that the summary would not be distorted in any way.

The revelation of Jesus Christ, which God gave to him, to show his servants what must happen soon. He made it known by sending his angel to his servant John, who gives witness to the word of God and the testimony of Jesus Christ by reporting what he saw. Blessed is the one who reads aloud and blessed are those who listen to this prophetic message and heed what is written in it, for the appointed time is near. (Revelation 1:1–3).

John, to the seven churches in Asia: grace to you and peace from him who is and who was and who is to come, and from the seven spirits before his throne, and from Jesus Christ, the faithful witness, the firstborn of the dead and ruler of the kings of the earth. To him who loves us and has freed us from our sins by his blood, who has made us into a kingdom, priests for his God and Father, to him be the glory and power forever [and ever]. Amen. Behold, his is coming amid the clouds, and every eye will see him, even those who pierced him. And the peoples of the earth will lament him. Yes. Amen. "I am the Alpha and the Omega," says the Lord God, "the one who is and who was and who is to come, the almighty." (Revelation 1:4–8)

I, John, your brother, who share with you the distress, the kingdom, and the endurance we have in Jesus, found myself on the island called Patmos because I proclaimed God's word and gave testimony to Jesus. I was caught up in spirit on the Lord's day and heard behind me a voice as loud as a trumpet, which said, "Write on a scroll what you see and send it to the seven churches: to Ephesus, Smyrna, Pergamum, Thyatira Sardis, Philadelphia, and Laodicea." Then I turned to see whose voice it was that spoke to me, and when I turned, I saw seven gold lampstands and in the midst of the lampstands one like a son of man, wearing an ankle-length robe, with a gold sash around his chest. The hair on his head was as white as wool or as snow, and his eyes were like a fiery flame. His feet were like polished brass refined in a furnace, and his voice was like the sound of rushing water. In his right hand he held seven stars. A sharp two-edged sword came out of his mouth, and his face shone like the sun at its brightest.

When I caught sight of him, I fell down at his feet as though dead. He touched me with his right hand and said, "Do not be afraid. I am the first and the last, the one who lives. Once I was dead, but now I am alive forever and ever. I hold the keys to death and the netherworld. Write down, therefore, what you have seen, and what is happening, and what will happen afterwards. This is the secret meaning of the seven stars you saw in my right hand, and of the seven lampstands: the seven stars are the angels of the seven churches, and the seven lampstands are the seven churches." (Revelation 1:9–20)

To the angel of the church in Ephesus, write this: "The one who holds the seven stars in his right hand and walks in the midst of the seven gold lampstands says this: 'I know your works, your labor, and your endurance, and that you cannot tolerate the wicked; you have tested those who call themselves apostles but are not, and discovered that they are impostors. Moreover, you have endurance and have suffered for my name, and you have not grown weary. Yet I hold this against you: you have lost the love you had at first. Realize how far you have fallen. Repent, and do the works you did at first. Otherwise, I will come to you and remove your lampstand from its place, unless you repent. Whoever has ears ought to hear what the Spirit says to the churches. To the victor I will give the right to eat from the tree of life that is in the garden of God.'" (Revelation 2:1–7)

To the angel of the church of Smyrna, write this: "The first and last, who once died but came to life says this: 'I know your Tribulation and poverty, but you are rich. I know the slander of those who claim to be Jews and are not, but rather are members of the assembly of Satan. Do not be afraid of anything that you are going to suffer. Indeed, the devil will throw some of you into prison, that you may be tested, and you will face an ordeal for ten days. Remain faithful until death, and I will give you the crown of life. Whoever has ears ought to hear what the Spirit says to the churches. The vic-

tor shall not be harmed by the second death.'"
(Revelation 2:8–11)

To the angel of the church in Pergamum,
write this: "The one with the sharp two-edged
sword says this: 'I know that you live where
Satan's throne is, and yet you hold fast to my
name and have not denied your faith in me, not
even in the days of Antipas, my faithful witness,
who was martyred among you, where Satan lives.
Yet I have a few things against you. You have
some people there who hold to the teaching of
Balaam, who instructed Balak to put a stumbling
block before the Israelites: to eat food sacrificed
to idols and to play the harlot. Likewise, you also
have some people who hold to the teaching of
the Nicolaitans. Therefore, repent. Otherwise, I
will come to you quickly and wage war against
them with the sword of my mouth. Whoever
has ears ought to hear what the Spirit says to
the churches. To the victor I shall give some of
the hidden manna; I shall also give a white amulet upon which is inscribed a new name, which
no one knows except the one who receives it.'"
(Revelation 2:12–17)

To the angel of the church in Thyatira,
write this: "The Son of God, whose eyes are like
a fiery flame and whose feet are like polished
brass, says this: 'I know your works, your love,
faith service, and endurance, and that your last
works are greater than the first. Yet I hold this
against you, that you tolerate the woman Jezebel,
who calls herself a prophetess, who teaches and
misleads my servants to play the harlot and to
eat food sacrificed to idols. I have given her time

to repent, but she refuses to repent of her harlotry. So I will cast her on a sickbed and plunge
those who commit adultery with her into intense
suffering unless they repent of her works. I will
also put her children to death. Thus shall all the
churches come to know that I am the searcher of
hearts and minds and that I will give each of you
what your works deserve. But I say to the rest of
you in Thyatira, who do not uphold this teaching
and know nothing of the so-called deep secrets
of Satan: on you I will place no further burden, except that you must hold fast to what you
have until I come. To the victor, who keeps my
ways until the end, I will give authority over the
nations. He will rule them with an iron rod. Like
clay vessels they will be smashed, just as I received
authority from my Father. And to him I will give
the morning star. Whoever has ears ought to hear
what the Spirit says to the churches.'"

To the angel of the church in Sardis, write
this: "The one who has the seven spirits of God
and the seven stars says this: 'I know your works,
that you have the reputation of being alive, but
you are dead. Be watchful and strengthen what is
left, which is going to die, for I have not found
your works complete in the sight of my God.
Remember then how you accepted and heard;
keep it, and repent. If you are not watchful, I
will come like a thief, and you will never know at
what hour I will come upon you. However, you
have a few people in Sardis who have not soiled
their garments; they will walk with me dressed in
white, because they are worthy. The victor will
thus be dressed in white, and I will never erase his
name from the book of life but will acknowledge
his name in the presence of my Father and his

angels. Whoever has ears ought to hear what the Spirit says to the churches.'" (Revelation 3:1–6)

To the angel of the church in Philadelphia, write this: "The holy one, the true, who holds the key of David, who opens and no one shall close, who closes and no one shall open, says this: 'I know your works [behold, I have left an open door before you, which no one can close]. You have limited strength, and yet you have kept my word and have not denied my name. Behold, I will make those of the assembly of Satan who claim to be Jews and are not, but are lying, behold, I will make them come and fall prostrate at your feet, and they will realize that I love you. Because you have kept my message of endurance, I will keep you safe in the time of trial that is going to come to the whole world to test the inhabitants of the earth. I am coming quickly. Hold fast to what you have, so that no one may take your crown. The victor I will make into a pillar in the temple of my God, and he will never leave it again. On him I will inscribe the name of my God and the name of the city of my God, the new Jerusalem, which comes down out of heaven from my God, as well as my new name. Whoever has ears ought to hear what the Spirit says to the churches.'" (Revelation 3:7–13)

To the angel of the church in Laodicea, write this: "The Amen, the faithful and true wit-ness, the source of God's creation, says this: 'I know your works; I know you are neither cold nor hot. So, because you are lukewarm, neither hot nor cold, I will spit you out of my mouth. For you say, "I am rich and affluent and have no need of anything," and yet do not realize that you are wretched, pitiable, poor, blind, and naked. I advise you to buy from me gold refined by fire so that you may be rich, and white garments to put on so that your shameful nakedness may not be exposed, and buy ointment to smear on your eyes so that you may see. Those whom I love, I reprove and chastise. Be earnest, therefore, and repent. Behold, I stand at the door and knock. If anyone hears my voice and opens the door, [then] I will enter his house and dine with him and he with me. I will give the victor the right to sit with me on my throne, as I myself first won the victory and sit with my Father on his throne. Whoever has ears ought to hear what the Spirit says to the churches.'" (Revelation 3:14–22)

After this, the apostle John had a vision of an open door to heaven. He heard a voice that sounded like a trumpet that spoke to him before. It said,

> Come up here and I will show you what must happen afterwards. (Revelation 4:1)

John's spirit was them immediately caught up to heaven. He was before a throne in heaven, and the one who sat on it had an appearance that sparkled like jasper and carnelian. There was a halo surrounding the throne that was a brilliant as an emerald. Also surrounding the throne were twenty-four other thrones. Sitting in them were twenty-four elders who were dressed in white garments and had gold crowns on their heads. From the main throne came flashes of lightning, peals of thunder, and rumblings. There were seven flaming torches which burned in front of the throne, which are the seven spirits of God. In front of the throne was something that looked like a sea of glasslike crystal (Revelation 4:1–6).

There were four living creatures covered with eyes in front and in back. They were around the throne and in the center. The first creature looked like a lion, the second resembled a calf, the third had a face like a human, and the fourth resembled an eagle in flight. Each creature had six wings. Day and night they exclaimed without ceasing:

> Holy, holy, is the Lord God almighty, who was, and who is, and who is to come. (Revelation 4:8)

Whenever the four creatures gave glory to God, the twenty-four elders fell down before God, threw their crowns before his throne and said,

> Worthy are you, Lord our God, to receive glory and honor and power, for you created all things; because of your will they came to be and were created. (Revelation 4:11)

> I saw a scroll in the right hand of the one who sat on the throne. It had writing on both sides and was sealed with seven seals. Then I saw a mighty angel who proclaimed in a loud voice, "Who is worthy to open the scroll and break its seven seals?" But no on in heaven or on earth or under the earth was able to open the scroll or examine it. I shed many tears because no one was found worthy to open the scroll or to examine it. One of the elders said to me, "Do not weep. The lion of the tribe of Judah, the root of David, had triumphed, enabling him to open the scroll with its seven seals." (Revelation 5:1–5)

John then saw in the midst of the throne, the elders, and the four living creatures a Lamb that appeared to have been slain. The Lamb took the scroll from the right hand of the one who sat upon the throne. When he took the scroll, the four living creatures, the twenty-four elders, numerous angels, and every creature in heaven and on the earth and under the earth gave great praise and worship to the Lamb who was slain and now sat on the throne; he alone was worthy to open the scroll (Revelation 5:6–14).John watched as the Lamb broke open the first of the seven seals. One of the four living creatures cried out in a voice like thunder, "Come forward." John came forward and looked. He saw a white horse. Its rider had a bow. The rider was given a crown, and he rode forth "victorious to further his victories" (Revelation 6:1–2).

The second seal was then opened by the Lamb. A red horse came out.

> Its rider was given power to take peace away from the earth, so that people would slaughter one another. And he was given a huge sword. (Revelation 6:3–4)

The Lamb opened the third seal. John saw a black horse, and its rider had a scale in his hand. A voice came out of the midst of the four living creatures that said,

> A ration of wheat cost a day's pay, and three rations of barley cost a day's pay. But do not damage the olive oil or the wine. (Revelation 6:6)

The fourth seal was opened by the Lamb. John saw a pale green horse. Its rider was named Death, and he was accompanied by Hades.

> They were given authority over a quarter of the earth, to kill with sword, famine, and plague, and by means of the beasts of the earth. (Revelation 6:8)

The Lamb broke open the fifth seal.

[John saw] underneath the altar the souls of those who had been slaughtered because of the witness they bore to the word of God. They cried out in a loud voice, "How long will it be, holy and true master, before you sit in judgment and avenge our blood on the inhabitants of the earth?" Each of them was given a white robe, and they were told to be patient a little while longer until the number was filled with their fellow servants and brothers who were going to be killed as they had been. (Revelation 6:9–11)

John watched as the Lamb opened the sixth seal. When he did,

There was a great earthquake; the sun turned as black and as dark as sackcloth and the whole moon became like blood. The stars in the sky fell to the earth like unripe figs shaken loose from the tree in a strong wind. Then the sky was divided like a torn scroll curling up, and every mountain and island was moved from its place. The kings of the earth, the nobles, the military officers, the rich, the powerful, and every slave and free person hid themselves in the caves and among mountain crags. They cried out to the mountains and the rocks, "Fall on us and hide us from the face of the one who sits on the throne and from the wrath of the Lamb, because the great day of their wrath has come and who can withstand it?" (Revelation 6:12–17)

John then saw the seal of God will be put on the foreheads of 144,000 of his servants. These 144,000 servants will comprise 12,000 servants from each of the twelve tribes of Israel: the tribes of Judah, Reuben, Gad, Asher, Naphtali, Manasseh, Simeon, Levi, Issachar, Zebulun, Joseph, and Benjamin (Revelation 7:1–8).

After this I had a vision of a great multitude, which no one could count, from every nation, race, people, and tongue. They stood before the throne and before the Lamb, wearing white robes and holding palm branches in their hands. Then one of the elders spoke up and said to me, "Who are these wearing white robes, and where did they come from?" I said to him, "My lord, you are the one who knows." He said to me, *"These are the ones coming out of the great tribulation*; they have washed their robes and made them white in the blood of the Lamb. For this reason they stand before God's throne and worship him day and night in his temple. The one who sits on the throne will shelter them. They will not hunger or thirst anymore, nor will the sun or any heat strike them. For the Lamb who is in the center of the throne will shepherd them and lead them to springs of life-giving water, and God will wipe away every tear from their eyes." (Revelation 7:9–17)

When he broke open the seventh seal, there was silence in heaven for about a half an hour. And I saw that the seven angels who stood before God were given seven trumpets. (Revelation 8:1–2)

Then another angel held a gold censer. It was full of smoke from burning incense and the prayers of the holy ones. The angel then took the censer, filled it with burning coals from the altar, and threw it down to the earth. There was an earthquake along with peals of thunder, flashes of lightning, and rumblings (Revelation 8:3–5).

Seven angels were holding seven trumpets, preparing to blow them.

When the first one blew his trumpet, there came hail and fire mixed with blood, which was hurled down to the earth. A third of the land was burned up, along with a third of the trees and all green grass.

When the second angel blew his trumpet, something like a large burning mountain was hurled into the sea. A third of the creatures living in the sea died, and a third of the ships were wrecked.

When the third angel blew his trumpet, a large star burning like a torch fell from the sky. It fell on a third of the rivers and on the springs of water. The star was called "Wormwood," and a third of all the water turned to wormwood. Many people died from this water, because it was made bitter.

When the fourth angel blew his trumpet, a third of the sun, a third of the moon, and a third of the stars were struck, so that a third of them became dark. The day lost its light for a third of the time, as did the night. Then I liked again and heard an eagle flying high overhead cry out in a loud voice, "Woe! Woe! Woe! To the inhabitants of the earth from the rest of the trumpet blasts that the three angels are about to blow!" (Revelation 8:6–13)

Then the fifth angel blew his trumpet, and I saw a star that had fallen from the sky to the earth. It was given the key for the passage to the abyss. It opened the passage to the abyss, and smoke came up out of the passage like smoke from a huge furnace. The sun and the air were darkened by the smoke from the passage. Locusts came out of the smoke onto the land, and they were given the same power as scorpions of the earth. They were told not to harm the grass of the earth or any plant or any tree, but only those people who did not have the seal of God on their foreheads. They were not allowed to kill them but only to torment them for five months; the torment they inflicted was like that of a scorpion when it stings a person. During that time these people will seek death but will not find it, and they will long to die but death will escape them. (Revelation 9:1–6)

Then the sixth angel blew his trumpet, and I heard a voice coming from the [four] horns of the gold altar before God, telling the sixth angel who held the trumpet, "Release the four angels who are bound at the banks of the great river Euphrates." So the four angels were released, who were prepared for this hour, day, month, and year to kill a third of the human race. The number of cavalry troops was too hundred million; I heard their number. Now in my vision this is how I saw the horses and their riders. They wore red, blue, and yellow breastplates, and their horses' heads were like heads of lions, and out of their mouths came fire, smoke, and sulfur. By these three plagues of fire, smoke, and sulfur that came out of their mouths a third of the human race was killed. For the power of the horses is in their mouths and in their tails; for their tails are like snakes, with heads that inflict harm.

The rest of the human race, who were not killed by these plagues, did not repent of the works of their hands, to give up the worship of demons and idols made from gold, silver, bronze, stone, and wood, which cannot see or hear or walk. Nor did they repent of their murders, their

magic potions, their unchastity, or their robber-
ies. (Revelation 9:13–21)

A mighty gleaming angel then appeared, saying,

> There shall be no more delay. At the time
> when you hear the seventh angel blow his trum-
> pet, the mysterious plan of God shall be fulfilled,
> as he promised to his servants the prophets.
> (Revelation 10:6–7)

> Then I was given a measuring rod like a staff
> and I was told, "Come and measure the temple of
> God and the altar, and count those who are wor-
> shipping in it. But exclude the outer court of the
> temple; do not measure it, for it has been handed
> over to the Gentiles, who will trample the holy
> city for forty-two months. I will commission my
> two witnesses to prophesy for those twelve hun-
> dred and sixty days, wearing sackcloth." These
> are the two olive trees and the two lampstands
> that stand before the Lord of the earth. In any-
> one wants to harm them, fire comes out of their
> mouths and devours their enemies. In this way,
> anyone wanting to harm them is sure to be slain.
> They have the power to close up the sky so that
> no rain can fall during the time of their prophesy-
> ing. They also have the power to turn water into
> blood and to afflict the earth with any plague as
> often as they wish.
>
> When they have finished their testimony,
> the beast that comes up from the abyss will wage
> war against them and conquer them and kill
> them. Their corpses will lie in the main street of
> the great city, which has the symbolic names of

"Sodom" and "Egypt," where indeed their Lord was crucified.

Those from every people, tribe, tongue, and nation will gaze on their corpses for three and a half days, and they will not allow their corpses to be buried. The inhabitants of the earth will gloat over them and be glad and exchange gifts because these two prophets tormented the inhabitants of the earth. But after three and a half days, a breath of life from God entered them. When they stood on their feet, great fear fell on those who saw them. They heard a loud voice from heaven say to them, "Come up here." So they went up to heaven in a cloud as their enemies looked on. At that moment there was a great earthquake, and a tenth of the city fell in ruins. Seven thousand people were killed during the earthquake; the rest were terrified and gave Glory to the God of heaven. (Revelation 11:1–13)

John then saw the seventh angel blow his trumpet. There were loud voices in heaven that said,

The kingdom of the world now belongs to our Lord and to his Anointed, and he will reign forever and ever. (Revelation 11:15)

The twenty-four elders fell down and gave praise, saying,

You have assumed your great power and established your reign. The nations raged, but your wrath has come, and the time for the dead to be judged, and to recompense your servants, the prophets, and the holy ones and those who fear your name, the small and the great alike, and to destroy those who destroy the earth.' Then

God's temple in heaven was opened, and the arc of his covenant could be seen in the temple. There were flashes of lightning, rumblings, and peals of thunder, and earthquake, and a violent hailstorm. (Revelation 11:15–19)

A great sign appeared in the sky, a woman clothed with the sun, with the moon under her feet, and on her head a crown of twelve stars. She was with child and wailed aloud in pain as she labored to give birth. Then another sign appeared in the sky; it was a huge red dragon, with seven heads and ten horns, and on its seven heads were seven diadems. Its tail swept away a third of the stars in the sky and hurled them down to earth. Then the dragon stood before the woman about to give birth, to devour her child when she gave birth. She gave birth to a son, a male child, destined to rule all the nations with an iron rod. Her child was caught up to God and his throne. The woman herself fled into the desert where she had a place prepared by God, that she might be taken care of for twelve hundred and sixty days. (Revelation 12:1–6)

Then war broke out in heaven; Michael and his angels battled against the dragon. The dragon and his angels fought back, but they did not prevail and there was no longer any place for them in heaven. The huge dragon, the ancient serpent, who is called the Devil and Satan, who deceived the whole world, was thrown down to the earth and its angels were thrown down with it. (Revelation 12:7–9)

Then I heard a loud voice in heaven say: "Now have salvation and power come, and the kingdom of our God and the authority of his Anointed. But woe to you, earth and sea, for the Devil has come down to you in great fury, for he knows he has but a short time." (Revelation 12:10–12)

Then I saw a beast come out of the sea with ten horns and seven heads; on its horns were ten diadems, and on its heads blasphemous names. The beast I saw was like a leopard, but it had feet like a bear's, and its mouth was like the mouth of a lion. To it the dragon gave its own power and throne, along with great authority. I saw one of its heads seemed to be mortally wounded, but the mortal wound was healed. Fascinated, the whole world followed after the beast. They worshipped the dragon because it gave its authority to the beast; they also worshipped the beast and said, "Who can compare with the beast or who can fight against it?"

The beast was given a mouth uttering proud boasts and blasphemies, and it was given authority to act for forty-two months. It opened its mouth to utter blasphemies against God, blaspheming his name and his dwelling and those who dwell in heaven. It was also allowed to wage war against the holy ones and to conquer them, and it was granted authority over every tribe, people, tongue, and nation. All the inhabitants of the earth will worship it, all whose names were not written from the foundation of the world in the book of life, which belongs to the Lamb who was slain. (Revelation 13:1–8).

Then I saw another beast come up out of the earth; it had two horns like a lamb's but spoke like a dragon. It wielded all the authority of the first beast in its sight and made the earth and its inhabitants worship the first beast, whose mortal wound had been healed. It performed great signs, even making fire come down from heaven to earth in the sight of everyone. It deceived the inhabitants of the earth with the signs it was allowed to perform in the sight of the first beast, telling them to make an image for the beast who had been wounded by the sword and revived. It was then permitted to breathe life into the beast's image, so that the beast's image could speak and [could] have anyone who did not worship it put to death. It forced all the people, small and great, rich and poor, free and slave, to be given a stamped image on their right hands or their foreheads, so that no one could buy or sell except one who had the stamped image of the beast's name or the number that stood for its name.

Wisdom is needed here; one who understands can calculate the number of the beast, for it is a number that stands for a person. His number is six hundred and sixty-six. (Revelation 13:11–18)

John then saw the Lamb standing on mount Zion. With him stood the one hundred and forty-four thousand who had the Lamb's name and the Father's name written on their foreheads. They have been ransomed from the earth and follow the Lamb wherever he goes. They have been ransomed as the fristfruits of the human race for the Lamb and God, and they are unblemished. (Revelation 14:1–5)

Then I saw another angel flying high over-head, with everlasting good news to announce to those who dwell on earth, to every nation, tribe, tongue, and people. He said in a loud voice, "Fear God and give him glory, for his time has come to sit in judgment. Worship him who made heaven and earth and sea and springs of water." A second angel followed, saying: "Fallen, fallen is Babylon the great, that made all the nations drink the wine of her licentious passion." A third angel followed them and said in a loud voice, "Anyone who worships the beast or its image, or accepts its mark on forehead or hand, will also drink the wine of God's fury, poured full strength into the cup of his wrath, and will be tormented in burning sulfur before the holy angels and before the Lamb. The smoke of the fire that torments them will rise forever and ever, and there will be no relief day or night for those who worship the beast or its image or accept the mark of its name." (Revelation 14:6–12)

I heard a voice from heaven say, "Write this: Blessed are the dead who die in the Lord from now on." "Yes," said the Spirit, "let them find rest from their labors, for their works accompany them." (Revelation 14:13)

Then I looked and there was a white cloud, and sitting on the cloud one who looked like a son of man, with a gold crown on his head and a sharp sickle in his hand. Another angel came out of the temple, crying out in a loud voice to the one sitting on the cloud, "Use your sickle and reap the harvest, for the time to reap has come, because the earth's harvest is fully ripe." So the one who was sitting on the cloud swung his sickle over the earth, and the earth was harvested.

Then another angel came out of the temple in heaven who also had a sharp sickle. Then another angel [came] from the altar, [who] was in charge of the fire, and cried out in a loud voice to the one who had the sharp sickle, "Use your sharp sickle and cut the clusters from the earth's vines, for its grapes are ripe." So the angel swung his sickle over the earth and cut the earth's vintage. He threw it into the great winepress of God's fury. The winepress was trodden outside the city and blood poured out of the winepress to the height of a horse's bridle for two hundred miles. (Revelation 14:14–20)

Then I saw in heaven another sign, great and awe-inspiring; seven angels with the seven last plagues, for through them God's fury is accomplished. One of the four living creatures gave the seven angels seven gold bowls filled with the fury of God, who lives for ever and ever. (Revelation 15:1–7)

I heard a loud voice speaking from the temple to the seven angels, "Go and pour out the seven bowls of God's fury upon the earth." The first angel went and poured out his bowl upon the earth. Festering and ugly sores broke out on those who had the mark of the beast or worshipped his image.

The second angel poured out his bowl upon the sea. The sea turned to blood like that from a corpse; every creature living in the sea died.

The third angel poured out his bowl on the rivers and springs of water. They also turned to blood. Then I heard the angel in charge of the waters say: "You are just, O Holy One, who are and who were, in passing this sentence. For they have shed the blood of the holy ones and the prophets, and you [have] given them blood to drink; it is what they deserve." Then I heard the altar cry out, "Yes, Lord God almighty, your judgments are true and just."

The fourth angel poured out his bowl on the sun. It was given the power to burn people with fire. People were burned by the scorching heat and blasphemed the name of God who had power over these plagues, but they did not repent or give him glory.

The fifth angel poured out his bowl on the throne of the beast. Its kingdom was plunged into darkness, and people bit their tongues in pain and blasphemed the God of heaven because of their pains and sores. But they did not repent of their works.

The sixth angel emptied his bowl on the great river Euphrates. The water was dried up to prepare the way for the kings of the East. I saw three unclean spirits like frogs come from the mouth of the dragon, from the mouth of the beast, and from the mouth of the false prophet. These were demonic spirits who performed signs. They went out to the kings of the whole world to assemble them for the battle on the great day of God the almighty. ["Behold, I am coming like a thief." Blessed is the one who watches and keeps his clothes ready, so that he may not go naked and people see him exposed.] They then assembled the kings in the place that is named Armageddon in Hebrew.

The seventh angel poured out his bowl into the air. A loud voice came out of the temple from the throne, saying, "It is done." Then there were lightning flashes, rumblings, and peals of thunder, and a great earthquake. It was such a violent earthquake that there has never been one like it since the human race began on earth. The great city was split into three parts, and the gentile cities fell. But God remembered great Babylon, giving it the cup filled with the wine of his fury and wrath. Every island fled, and mountains disappeared. Large hailstones like huge weights came down from the sky on people, and they blasphemed God for the plague of hail because the plague was so severe. (Revelation 16:1–21)

Then one of the seven angels who were holding the seven bowls came and said to me, "Come here. I will show you the judgment on the great harlot who lives near the many waters. The kings of the earth have had sexual relations with her, and the inhabitants of the earth became drunk on the wine of her harlotry. Then he carried me away in spirit to a deserted place where I saw a woman seated on a scarlet beast that was covered with blasphemous names, with seven heads and ten horns. The woman was wearing purple and scarlet and adorned with gold, precious stones, and pearls. She had in her hand a gold cup that was filled with the abominable and sordid deeds of her harlotry. On her forehead was written aname, which is a mystery, "Babylon the great, the mother of harlots and of abominations of the earth." I saw that the woman was drunk on the blood of the holy ones and on the blood of the witnesses to Jesus.

When I saw her I was greatly amazed. The angel said to me, "Why are you amazed? I will explain to you the mystery of the woman and of the beast that carries her, the beast with the seven heads and the ten horns. The beast that you saw existed once but now exists no longer. It will come up from the abyss and is headed for destruction. The inhabitants of the earth whose names have not been written in the book of life from the foundation of the world shall be amazed when they see the beast, because it existed once but exists no longer, and yet it will come again. Here is a clue for one who has wisdom. The seven heads represent seven hills upon which the woman sits. They also represent seven kings: five have already fallen, one still lives, and the last has not yet come, and when he comes he must remain only for a short while. The beast that existed once but exists no longer is an eighth king, but really belongs to the seven and is headed for destruction. The ten horns that you saw represent ten kings who have not yet been crowned; they will receive royal authority along with the beast for one hour. They are of one mind and will give their power and authority to the beast. They will fight with the Lamb, but the Lamb will conquer them, for he is Lord of lords and king of kings, and those with him are called, chosen and faithful."

Then he said to me, "The waters that you saw where the harlot lives represent large numbers of peoples, nations, and tongues. The ten horns that you saw and the beast will hate the harlot; they will leave her desolate and naked; they will eat her flesh and consume her with fire. For God

has put it into their minds to carry out his purpose and to make them come to an agreement to
give their kingdom to the beast until the words of
God are accomplished. The woman whom you
saw represents the great city that has sovereignty
over the kings of the earth." (Revelation 17:1–18)

John then saw an angel with great authority come down from
heaven.

The earth was illuminated by his splendor.
He said, "Fallen, fallen is Babylon the great. She
has become a haunt for demons, she is a cage for
every unclean spirit, a cage for every unclean bird,
a cage for every unclean and disgusting beast. For
all the nations have drunk the wine of her licentious passion. The kings of the earth had sexual
relations with her, and the merchants of the earth
grew rich from her drive for luxury." (Revelation
18:1–3).

The angel then gave a command to the people to depart from
her as to not take part in her sins. Her sins pile up to heaven, and she
will now be paid back double for her deeds.

To the measure of her boasting and wan-
tonness repay her in her torment and grief; for
she said to herself, "I sit enthroned as queen;
I am no widow, and I will never know grief."
Therefore, her plagues will come in one day, pestilence, grief, and famine; she will be consumed
by fire. For mighty is the Lord God who judges
her. (Revelation 18:7–8)

The kings of the earth who had sexual relations with her will
weep when they see the smoke of her burning.

They will keep their distance for fear of the torment inflicted on her, and they will say: "Alas, alas, great city, Babylon, mighty city. In one hour your judgment has come." (Revelation 18:10)

John said that the merchants of the earth will weep and mourn over the destruction of Babylon, because now no one will buy their goods.

The merchants who deal in these goods, who grew rich from Babylon, will keep their distance for fear of the torment inflicted on her. Weeping and mourning, they cry out: "Alas, alas, great city, wearing fine linen, purple and scarlet, adorned in gold, precious stones, and pearls. In one hour this great wealth has been ruined." (Revelation 18:15–17)

John then states that a mighty angel made a declaration that Babylon is destroyed, and it will never return again. One of the reasons for her destruction was this:

In her was found the blood of prophets and holy ones, and all who have been slain on the earth. (Revelation 18:24)

Then there was a great celebration in heaven over the destruction of the great harlot (Revelation 19:1–5).

Then I heard something like the sound of a great multitude or the sound of rushing water or mighty peals of thunder, as they said: "Alleluia! The Lord has established his reign, our God, the almighty. Let us rejoice and be glad and give him glory. For the wedding day of the Lamb has come, his bride has made herself ready. She was

allowed to wear a bright, clean linen garment."
[The linen represents the righteous deeds of the
holy ones.] Then the angel said to me, "Write
this: 'Blessed are those who have been called to
the wedding feast of the Lamb.'" And he said
to me, "These words are true; they come from
God." I fell at his feet to worship him. But he
said to me, "Don't! I am a fellow servant of yours
and of your brothers who bear witness to Jesus.
Worship God. Witness to Jesus is the spirit of
prophecy." (Revelation 19:6–10)

Then I saw the heavens opened, and there
was a white horse; its rider was called "Faithful
and True." He judges and wages war in righteousness. His eyes were like a fiery flame, and
on his head were many diadems. He had a name
inscribed that no one knows except himself. He
wore a cloak that had been dipped in blood,
and his name was called the Word of God. The
armies of heaven followed him, mounted on
white horses and wearing clean white linen. Out
of his mouth came a sharp sword to strike the
nations. He will rule them with an iron rod, and
he himself will tread out in the wine press the
wine of the fury and wrath of God the almighty.
He has a name written on his cloak and on his
thigh, "King of kings and Lord of Lords."

Then I saw an angel standing on the sun.
He cried out in a loud voice to all the birds flying high overhead, "Come here. Gather for God's
great feast, to eat the flesh of kings, the flesh of
military officers, and the flesh of warriors, the
flesh of horses and of their riders, and the flesh
of all, free and slave, small and great." Then I
saw the beast and the kings of the earth and their

armies gathered to fight against the one riding the horse and against his army. The beast was caught and with it the false prophet who had performed in its sight the signs by which he led astray those who had accepted the mark of the beast and those who had worshipped its image. The two were thrown alive into the fiery pool burning with sulfur. The rest were killed by the sword that came out of the mouth of the one riding the horse, and all the birds gorged themselves on their flesh. (Revelation 19:11–21)

Then I saw an angel come down from heaven, holding in his hand the key to the abyss and a heavy chain. He seized the dragon, the ancient serpent, which is the Devil or Satan, and tied it up for a thousand years and threw it into the abyss, which he locked over it and sealed, so that it could no longer lead the nations astray until the thousand years are completed. After this, it is to be released for a short time.

Then I saw thrones; those who sat on them were entrusted with judgment. I also saw the souls of those who had been beheaded for their witness to Jesus and for the word of God, and who had not worshipped the beast or its image nor had accepted the mark on their foreheads or hands. They came to life and reigned with Christ for a thousand years. The rest of the dead did not come to life until the thousand years were over. This is the first resurrection. Blessed and holy is the one who shares in the first resurrection. The second death has no power over these; they will be priests of God and of Christ, and they will reign with him for the thousand years.

When the thousand years are completed, Satan will be released from his prison. He will go out to deceive the nations at the four corners of the earth, Gog and Magog, to gather them for battle; their number is like the sand of the sea. They invaded the breadth of the earth and surrounded the camp of the holy ones and the beloved city. But fire came down from heaven and consumed them. The Devil who had led them astray was thrown into the pool of fire and sulfur, where the beast and the false prophet were. There they will be tormented day and night forever and ever. (Revelation 20:1–10)

Next I saw a large white throne and the one who was sitting on it. The earth and the sky fled from his presence and there was no place for them. I saw the dead, the great and the lowly, standing before the throne, and the scrolls were opened. Then another scroll was opened, the book of life. The dead were judged according to their deeds, by what was written in the scrolls. The sea gave up its dead; then Death and Hades gave up their dead. All the dead were judged according to their deeds. Then Death and Hades were thrown into the pool of fire. This pool of fire is the second death. Anyone whose name was not found written in the book of life was thrown into the pool of fire. (Revelation 20:11–15)

Then I saw a new heaven and a new earth. The former heaven and the former earth had passed away, and the sea was no more. I also saw the holy city, a new Jerusalem, coming down out of heaven from God, prepared as a bride adorned for her husband. I heard a loud voice from the throne saying, "Behold, God's dwelling is with the human race. He will dwell with them and they will be his people and God himself will always be with them as their God. He will wipe every tear from their eyes, and there shall be no more death or mourning, wailing or pain, for the old order has passed away." (Revelation 21:1–4)

The one who sat on the throne said, "Behold, I make all things new." Then he said, "Write these words down, for they are trustworthy and true." He said to me, "They are accomplished. I am the Alpha and the Omega, the beginning and the end. To the thirsty I will give a gift from the spring of life-giving water. The victor will inherit these gifts, and I shall be his God, and he will be my so." (Revelation 21:5–7)

Then John saw the New Jerusalem coming down out of heaven. It was radiant like jasper and clear as crystal. It had a huge high wall with twelve gates. Angels were stationed on the twelve gates. Also, on the gates were the inscribed names of the twelve tribes of Israel. Three gates faced north, three faced south, three faced east, and three faced west. The wall had twelve stones as its foundations. On each stone was the name of one of the twelve apostles. New Jerusalem was a square city; its length was equal to its width. The city was 1,500 miles in length, width, and height. The wall of the city was made of jasper, while the city was made of pure gold which was clear as glass. The foundations of the city wall were made of twelve precious stones. Each of its gates were made of a huge, single pearl. The streets of New

Jerusalem were made of pure gold, which was as transparent as glass (Revelation 21:9–21).

> I saw no temple in the city, for its temple is the Lord God almighty and the Lamb. The city had no need of sun or moon to shine on it, for the glory of God gave it light, and its lamp was the Lamb. The nations will walk by its light, and to it the kings of the earth will bring their treasure. During the day its gates will never be shut, and there will be no night there. The treasure and wealth of the nations will be brought there, but nothing unclean will enter it, nor anyone who does abominable things or tells lies. Only those will enter whose names are written in the Lamb's book of life. (Revelation 21:22–27)

> Then the angel showed me the river of life-giving water, sparkling like crystal, flowing from the throne of God and of the Lamb down the middle of the street. On either side of the river grew the tree of life that produces fruit twelve times a year, once each month; the leaves of the trees serve as medicine for the nations. Nothing accursed will be found there anymore. The throne of God and of the Lamb will be in it, and his servants will worship him. They will look upon his face, and his name will be on their foreheads. Night will be no more, nor will they need light from lamp or sun, for the Lord God shall give them light, and they shall reign forever and ever. (22:1–5)

God then said,

> Behold, I am coming soon.

Blessed is he who keeps the prophetic message of this book (Revelation 22:7).

> I bring with me the recompense I will give each according to his deeds. I am the Alpha and the Omega, the first and the last, the beginning and the end. (Revelation 22:12–13)
>
> Blessed are they who wash their robes so they have the right to the tree of life and enter the city through its gates. Outside are the dogs, the sorcerers, the unchaste, the murderers, the idol-worshipers, and all who love and practice deceit. (Revelation 22:14–15)
>
> I, Jesus, sent my angel to give you this testimony for the churches. I am the root and offspring of David, the bright morning star. The Spirit and the bride say, "Come." Let the hearer say, "Come." Let the one who thirsts come forward, and the one who wants it receive the give of life-giving water. (Revelation 22:16–17)
>
> The one who gives this testimony says, "Yes, I am coming soon." Amen! Come, Lord Jesus! The grace of the Lord Jesus be with you all. (Revelation 22:21)

ABOUT THE AUTHOR

Michael Kotch is a licensed psychologist in the state of Pennsylvania, working at a Christian-counseling outpatient private practice since 2006. He attained his doctorate degree in clinical psychology from Widener University in 2003. Michael is the teacher of a weekly Bible study program at his church for adults. He is also the fifth-grade religious instruction teacher at his church. Michael has a video series on YouTube called "Teaching the Bible with Michael Kotch." It is an overview of the entire Bible, which is taught in approximately thirty one-hour video presentations. Michael is the author of seven Bible-based books, which are the following:

> *Bible Summary for Catholics*
> *The Benefits of Trials for Christians*
> *Easy-to-Read Bible Summary for Teens and Adults*
> *Temptations and Trials Faced by Bible Legends*
> *The Good Things Jesus Does for Us, to Us, and through Us When We Follow Him*
> *Lessons for Christians from the Trials of Job*
> *Faith through Your Hardships Draws Others to Christ*

Michael lives in a small town in Southeast Pennsylvania with his wife, Mary, and his children, Jacob and Johanna.

CPSIA information can be obtained
at www.ICGtesting.com
Printed in the USA
BVHW031919021020
590215BV00001B/2